The Means to Kill

The Means to Kill

*Essays on the Interdependence
of War and Technology from
Ancient Rome to the Age of Drones*

Edited by
GERRIT DWOROK *and*
FRANK JACOB

McFarland & Company, Inc., Publishers
Jefferson, North Carolina

LIBRARY OF CONGRESS CATALOGUING-IN-PUBLICATION DATA

The means to kill : essays on the interdependence of war and technology from ancient Rome to the age of drones / edited by Gerrit Dworok and Frank Jacob.
 p. cm.
Includes bibliographical references and index.

ISBN 978-0-7864-9717-1 (softcover : acid free paper) ∞
ISBN 978-1-4766-2280-4 (ebook)

1. Military art and science—Technological innovations—History. 2. Military weapons—Technological innovations. 3. Military history. I. Dworok, Gerrit, 1983– editor of compilation. II. Jacob, Frank, 1984– editor of compilation. III. Title: Essays on the interdependence of war and technology from ancient Rome to the age of drones.

U27.M39 2016
355'.0709—dc23   2015036161

BRITISH LIBRARY CATALOGUING DATA ARE AVAILABLE

© 2016 Gerrit Dworok and Frank Jacob. All rights reserved

No part of this book may be reproduced or transmitted in any form or by any means, electronic or mechanical, including photocopying or recording, or by any information storage and retrieval system, without permission in writing from the publisher.

Front cover: General Atomics MQ-1 Predator drone schematic and explosion (Department of Defense); medieval crossbow and background © 2016 Thinkstock

Printed in the United States of America

McFarland & Company, Inc., Publishers
 Box 611, Jefferson, North Carolina 28640
 www.mcfarlandpub.com

Table of Contents

Preface
    FRANK JACOB *and* GERRIT DWOROK   1

Introduction
    FRANK JACOB, GERRIT DWOROK *and* JEFFREY M. SHAW   3

Part I: Ancient Rome and the Medieval Ages

Ancient Naval Artillery Support
    JORIT WINTJES   17

Stirrup, Composite Bow and Traction Trebuchet: Some Remarks on the Interdependence of War and Technology in the Early Middle Ages
    CHRISTIAN SCHOLL   30

The Medieval Arms Race: The Confrontation of Orient and Occident in the Crusades and the Reconquista
    THOMAS SCHUETZ   45

Gunpowder and Cannons: Gunnery in the Late Middle Ages
    MARC-ANDRÉ KARPIENSKI   57

Mining and Warfare: An Overview of Centuries of Interdependence
    OLAF WAGENER   71

Part II: The Age of the World Wars

The German Navy League, Navalism and the Perception of the Imperial German Navy as a Technological Masterpiece, 1898–1914
    SEBASTIAN DIZIOL   85

The Soviet Propaganda Film as an Instrument of Warfare:
Sergey Eisenstein's Montage Technique and the "Global
Civil War of Ideologies"
  GERRIT DWOROK 98
Four Technical Artifacts of the Great War
  KURT MÖSER 111
The Special Operations Executive (SOE) and the Use and
Abuse of Peacetime Technology, 1940–45: A Case Study
of Unconventional Warfare
  RODERICK BAILEY 126
The Liberal Attraction to Technological Progress and the RAF
  TOMÁŠ KUČERA 137
Resource Policy and Technical Understanding: Aspects of
Hitler's Wartime Economy
  ECKEHARD DWOROK 153

Part III: The Cold War

A Weapon Changed the World: The AK-47 and the
Consequences for Asymmetric Warfare
  FRANK JACOB 169
Tous Azimuts: Yugoslavia's Defense Policy in the Cold War
  JAMES HORNCASTLE 182
Technology, Warfare and Intra-Alliance Rivalry:
The U.S.–West German Main Battle Tank Harmonization
in the 1970s
  BENEDICT VON BREMEN 197
Equipping the Marine Corps for the 21st Century, 1975–1990
  NATHAN R. PACKARD 210
From AirLand Battle to Effects-Based Operations: United
States Air Force and Army Doctrine Development from
1980 to 2001
  DANIEL FUHRER 228

Part IV: The Age of "New Wars"

Technology and War: Nanotechnology, Precision and
Globalization
  JEFFREY M. SHAW 245

The Fallacy of Humane Killing: Interwar Debates About
  Air Power and Twenty-First Century "Killer Robots"
    ADAM PAGE   260
Death from the Skies: A Just-War Perspective on the Rise of
  Unmanned Weapons Systems and the Reduction of
  Combatant and Noncombatant Casualties
    TIMOTHY J. DEMY   277

About the Contributors   293

Index   297

Preface

FRANK JACOB *and* GERRIT DWOROK

The subject of war plays a decisive role for the work of historians and the commemorative cultures of societies. Recent controversies on World War I have set an illustrative example for this fact. Even after a hundred years of historical research and public commemoration, there are still questions that remain unanswered. On the occasion of the centenary of the outbreak of the Great War, for instance, experts and the media have passionately debated the issue of war guilt.

The *interdependence of warfare and technology*, which is discussed in the present volume, also refers to this historical subject. Despite the fact that it has never attracted as much publicity as the emotional question of guilt, it is no less important since it puts a focus on a striking factor of global history. Frank Jacob, intending to analyze this structural interrelation, came up with the idea of an international conference in 2013. Only a few months later, fifteen specialists from around the world met in Würzburg, Bavaria, where the Department of Modern History I (chaired by Prof. Wolfgang Altgeld) hosted the conference "On the Interdependence of War and Technology." The lectures given at this conference as well as some additional essays are presented here. We are happy to present essays that deal with the topic from different and rewarding points of view and provide a broad chronological as well as regional perspective.

The realization of this project would not have been possible if the editors had not been actively supported. A number of people and institutions contributed substantially to this volume, and we take the opportunity to thank them:

First of all, we thank Wolfgang Altgeld, who has campaigned for a "young researchers'" project once again, for providing us with support in all possible ways. His support was especially crucial given the fact that, in German academic circles, the importance of the humanities in general, and history in particular, is often neglected. In this context, we also thank the members of his staff (especially Dr. Petra Ney-Hellmuth and Martin Süß) who helped to organize and execute the conference. Without their assistance, the quality of research presented at the during the conference would not have been as strong as it was, and the editing process would not have been possible at all. Moreover, we thank Riccardo Altieri for his help with this work, as well as Ghotel Würzburg for hosting our guests throughout the conference. Finally, we thank the historians and political scientists who contributed to the collection and thereby made the whole project possible.

Introduction

FRANK JACOB, GERRIT DWOROK
and JEFFREY M. SHAW

Trutz von Trotha (1946–2013), the German sociologist of violence and war, believed that cruelty was an inherent element of society, and an important tool employed for political domination:

> Cruelty is a mirror of the living conditions and achievements of a society. It appears to be as old as humanity itself and crosses societal and cultural boundaries. No society can say that it does not allow cruelty to exist, even if societies differ to an extreme in the amount of space they give to cruelty and which forms are practiced in these particular spaces.[1]

Cruelty and violence are often manifest through technology. Since time immemorial, advances in various fields of technology have allowed groups to dominate their neighbors. While historians studying war and technology usually focus on the events of the Great War,[2] the interrelationship between war itself and the technology used in warfare is evident throughout the ages. The industrialization of violence and warfare during the First World War most often provides the base of studying war and technology, although the relationship between war, technology, and violence is evident in other eras as well.

During the Russo-Japanese War (1904–1905), a war that John W. Steinberg[3] dubbed "World War Zero," Japanese soldier Tadayoshi Sakurai (1879–1965) experienced the decisive impact of the new weapons of war employed with great effect at the siege of Port Arthur. He wrote:

> After this battle we captured some machine-guns; this was the firearm most dreaded by us. A large iron plate serves the purpose of a shield, through which aim is taken, and the trigger can be pulled while the gun is moving upward, downward, to the left, or to the right. More than six hundred bullets are pushed out automatically in one minute, as if a long, continuous rod of balls was being thrown out of the gun. It can also be made to sprinkle its shot as roads are

watered with a hose. It can cover a larger or smaller space, or fire to a greater or less distance as the gunner wills.[4]

Sakurai revealed that the enemies were already using the new technology in this most destructive war. He explained that the enemy soldiers "were wonderfully clever in the use of this machine. They would wait till our men came very near them, four or five *ken* only, and just at the moment when we proposed to shout a triumphant Banzai, this dreadful machine would begin to sweep over us as if with the besom of destruction, the result being hills and mounds of dead."[5] After the battle, one could find corpses on the "fields of honor" that had been hit by 47 or even 70 bullets at a time.[6] The destructive potential of modern technologies used in the first major war of the 20th century was thus revealed to the world.

It is impossible to write a history of war without considering political, economic, social or technological aspects[7] since all of them have become part of warfare itself. Despite historians like Anselm Doering-Manteuffel often limiting the specific research field dealing with the correlation of war, technology and science to the Industrial Age,[8] the modern age should be seen as only one field of study when examining the relationship between war and technology. Certainly the First World War represents the apogee of war's relationship to technology. However, this war was only a catalyst[9] for an ongoing process that in former centuries would have required much more time to come to fruition.

Technological advances in weaponry and warfare during the first decades of the twentieth century occurred in weeks or months instead of decades or centuries, especially with regard to the development of new weaponry like tanks, warplanes and submarines.[10] The scale of the First World War demanded that industry improve daily production and that scientists speed up the process of invention. New weapons and new technologies were needed to decide the outcome of this large-scale industrial war. Although the French produced 13,600 grenades per year in 1914, just one year later they were able to produce 100,000 per day. In 1916, the British fired 1.2 million grenades against their enemies in the Battle of the Somme[11] and reached 4.3 million during the Third Battle of Ypres.[12]

Warfare at this time was no longer just a military issue. The arms industry and scientists who developed new technologies like the Haber-Bosch method or chemical weapons like gas in due course established the modern trifecta of war: science, technology and mass destruction.[13] Because new technological options were being used in the course of a modern war, in 1899 Ivan Bloch (1872–1922) predicted a war without any infantry battles; as such a scenario would no longer be possible due to the paralysis resulting from the presence of modern weapons on the battlefield.[14] However, infantry attacks and mass assaults remained an integral part of the First World War, and even today, it is not only superiority with regard to the technological progress of an army that is able to decide the outcome of a war or conflict.[15]

Despite the essential interrelationship between war and technology, only a few historians have tried to situate this phenomenon in a broader historical narrative.[16] While the connections between warfare and economics prior to the First World War have been studied in some detail,[17] technology's role in the increase in lethality on the battlefield has received less attention.

Technology may facilitate grater levels of violence and lethality on the battlefield, but it is also essential for human progress, especially when combined with science.[18] Without technology, there is also no culture,[19] as technology provides a bulwark between human beings and nature, freeing humankind to pursue those things not immediately necessary for survival. Employing tools and other devices made available through early technologies, better-equipped peoples were able to survive and prosper in an antagonistic environment, or in a state of nature which technology helped alleviate. Among these early tools were various types of weapons, which were employed either for hunting or for subjugating and eliminating hostile competitors' tribes.

In 1941, U.S. science writer Waldemar Kaempffert (1877–1956) explained that weapons were developed in a fashion similar to other technological inventions and tools used throughout the course of human history: "The musket, the cannon, the machine gun are labor-saving devices in precisely the same sense that a steam shovel is a labor-saving device."[20] When one adds the observations of German historian Karl Heinz Metz that human needs could only reach as far as his technological possibilities,[21] military inventions must be seen as the attempt to overcome existing borders of defensive or offensive actions against other human beings. Therefore, a close look at the interrelationship between war and technology will provide insight into a tremendously important factor of the history of warfare itself and the record of human progress particularly regarding its violent expression.

War and Technology

Technology has always been a part of humanity's vision of the future.[22] These utopian visions have not always portended violence and danger; many futuristic images were based on the idea of a peaceful society living harmoniously with a type of technology that could be employed for humankind's benefit.[23] However, the reality has often been otherwise, especially as regards the relationship between new technologies and increased lethality in warfare. When the British killed close to 10,000 Sudanese fighters during the Battle of Omdurman (1898), while losing just 482 soldiers of their own, many spectators thought it was the beginning of a new world order that would symbolize Western supremacy based on modern technology.[24] Developing technology could always be used as a destructive element as well, and the military use of scientific inventions became an essential part of this process.[25] To fulfill the Clausewitzian doctrine of the "overthrowing of the enemy,"[26] technological advances were sought which had dual roles—a military application as well as applications in other segments of society.[27] This process continues, especially within the leading states of the 21st century, as these states represent the leading example of integrating non-military technologies into a military role, often times even when unintended.[28]

Although the interrelationship between war and technology may appear to be an obvious one, the process of integrating technologies into the military sphere may not always be so easy to discern.[29] To return to the example of the First World War, massed infantry engagements still remained part of the military planning because the planners in the general staffs always tended to have the last major war in mind.[30] Because the military has not often been interested in the adoption of new technologies into their arsenals, outdated paradigms such as infantry assaults or cavalry warfare remained part of modern wars in the 20th century. In many cases, desperation and the need to counter an opponent's strength opens the door for further innovative integrations of new technologies into the military sphere.[31]

Many contemporary scholars have identified what they claim to be a Revolution in Military Affairs (RMA) resulting from the application of new technologies to the battlefield in ways so innovative that the fundamental nature of warfare has been irrevocably changed. However, this process of adaptation to new technologies has always been a part of warfare, whether in ancient times or even during the more recent Napoleonic Wars. It is perhaps only the speed with which new innovations are integrated into existing military frameworks and doctrines that is different today—not the fact that technology itself has continued to influence the outcome of conflicts between nations that wield new technologies, however advanced, successfully, and those that do not.[32]

Of course, weapons became obsolete quickly in the decades of the second half of the 19th and early 20th centuries, so new improvements were introduced. Those who did not utilize these improvements could lose the next decisive battle.[33] Consequently, new technologies changed warfare *per se*; one just has to think of the machine gun, shrapnel grenades, or the use of heavy artillery.[34] However, these new weapons not only provided greater firepower but also increased an army's level of speed and mobility.[35] The railways also became a decisive military factor, and from the start, they were built with military assumptions and tactical planning in mind.[36] Kaempffert had also shown that more than one technology was needed to manage the much larger armies of the late 19th century with regard to their coordination and control: "Moltke needed nine railways to deploy an army of 400,000 and to control a reserve of 100,000, and even with this aid his rapid maneuvers—far more rapid than were Napoleon's—would have been impossible without the telegraph."[37]

Rapid industrialization and the accompanying increase in technological advancements in numerous fields has facilitated the infusion of advanced products into the military realm. Some scholars propose that warfare might be humanized, and advanced technologies might hold the promise of reducing violence in contemporary warfare. Nevertheless, the opposite seems to be the norm, especially as one witnesses the suffering of the civilian and noncombatant populations in this age of total warfare.[38] Has not technology's integration into the military resulted in greater lethality? This holds true even when examining apparently innocuous developments such as the telephone.[39] Facing the high level of violence that was, for example, experienced by the soldiers in the "blood mill" of Verdun, those who believed in peaceful technological utopias began to doubt that technological advancements might make warfare less costly.[40]

A cyclical process ensued as nations sought to employ advanced technologies to counter their adversaries on the battlefield. Developments such as aircraft and tanks[41] required constant updating and refinement in order to keep them more powerful and effective than those of the enemy.[42] However it is not only in the development and employment of individual weapons and systems that this trend is clearly manifest, since human history consists of every possible form of violence.[43] Warfare is fundamentally nothing more than the organized application of violence, and in order to overcome natural human processes like group dynamics,[44] technology provides society with the means to achieve objectives at the expense of an adversary, either internal or external.[45] While the ideology which provides the foundation for resorting to war might be based on revolutionary ideas or might have emerged as a result of propaganda, physical violence itself is definitely a consequence of industrialized production of weapons, greater mobility, increasing numbers of inventions and the adoption of technologies from the civil sector.[46]

Regardless of these developments, warfare is not influenced by technology alone. There are several factors that decide victory or defeat. While the decisive factors were increasingly transferred from the battlefield to the laboratories and research institutes preparing chemical or, today, perhaps cyber warfare,[47] a new enemy to technological supremacy appeared: asymmetric warfare.[48] The so-called "new wars"[49] indicate that the age of mass armies might be over. While specially trained soldiers are fighting in professional armies that are equipped with the highest form of technology, the "disappearance of the enemy"[50] has made modern warfare rather complex. Technology by itself is not enough to ensure victory on the battlefield, and the fight against guerrilla troops engaged in international terrorism seems to demonstrate this idea.[51] "The utopia of technologized warfare fails, when the enemy is not accepting it at all,"[52] and Martin van Creveld's so-called "low-intensity wars"[53] may be the trend of the future—a trend because of which continued technological advances may have a difficult time rolling back.

The military itself has attempted to find a solution to low-intensity conflicts, creating a degree of angst among officers accustomed to operating against an enemy that looks much like themselves.[54] Even the technological superiority of the U.S. military may not appear to be much more than a "paper tiger"[55] when deployed against an unconventional adversary. There is a perception that warfare in the classical sense, meaning a war between two or more nation-states, is no longer likely, but has been replaced by these low-intensity conflicts, which manifest in "new wars."[56] Military planners are, therefore, forced to react to this issue and are trying to find an adequate solution. Next to technology, there are factors like geography,[57] religion, ideology,[58] and nationalism that determine the outcome of wars and must be taken into account when considering the means available for compelling an enemy to do your will. However, no matter the kind of war waged in the future, whether it is a civil war[59] or a war of civilizations,[60] technology will continue to be a key factor in determining the outcome.

The Essays

As the history of war is not restricted to the history of events but is highly influenced by technological progress in particular,[61] the present volume aims to give a diachronic insight into the interrelationship between war and technology from the Ancient Roman Empire to the twenty-first century. This book traces some previously examined historical eras, but also provides a broader perspective of the history of warfare.[62] Various scholars and authors have been assembled to examine some of the more salient examples of the interrelationship of war and technology.

The first essay focuses on the adaptation process itself; when and how technological novelties are adapted for military purposes and for what reason. What historical reasons are there that might explain the differences in the amount of time required to bring various technologies that may not have been developed for military purposes into the military domain? Is there a "helix of death" created by the interrelationship of war and technology? In other words, have technological advances over time contributed to greater battlefield lethality? Also examined in this volume are some of the developments in irregular warfare that have taken place since the end of the Cold War. However, in addition to the theoretical issues which this volume examines, we also want to provide the reader with an interesting and engaging look at specific time periods and the relationship between war and technology within those eras, asking whether or not advances in various technological fields have in fact led to an increase in warfare's lethality during those times.

The first part of the book provides an insight into the use of technology during the Roman Empire and the Medieval Ages. Jorit Wintjes deals with the impact of the use of ancient artillery in naval operations, which provided opportunities at that time for amphibious landing operations. Through his analysis of the use of "naval artillery" in Roman military history, he highlights the already existing interrelationship of technology and warfare during the period of Roman antiquity. Christian Scholl then takes us to the Medieval era by dealing with the introduction of "key technologies" into European warfare: the stirrup, the composite bow, and the traction trebuchet. He tries to answer the question of how far warfare in Early-Medieval Europe was influenced by the adoption of these new technologies. The idea that this process might lead to an early arms race is examined in the essay by Thomas Schuetz, who deals with the Crusades and the Spanish Reconquista to show that technological superiority on the part of one belligerent could lead to an attempt by the other parties to develop technological innovations designed to provide a counter weight, thus creating a cyclical process. The religiously-motivated war between the Christian and Islamic worlds provides a backdrop for this idea.

It is widely accepted that the invention of gunpowder fundamentally changed warfare's nature and lethality. However, it was an evolutionary rather than a revolutionary process, as Marc-André Karpienski explains in his essay on the development of cannons in the Late Middle Ages. Gunpowder provided both military and non-military advantages, for example, in the field of mining gunpowder facilitated advances in efficiency. Olaf Wagener's essay provides a detailed description of mining as an element of siege warfare. Not only could defensive walls be destroyed or overcome by infantry, now the option to burrow beneath the walls existed as a result of employing mining technologies of the civil sector towards military ends.

Despite an already existing interrelationship between war and technology in antiquity and the medieval age, the modern era witnessed an increase in the speed of this symbiotic relationship between warfare and technology, especially in the twentieth century. This is examined further in the second part of the volume. Technology became a part of everyday life, and society was often patterned around the advancements that the technological sector provided. The establishment of naval power in Germany was part of a large propaganda campaign by the German Navy League. Sebastian Diziol explains how a "notion of modernity" was inextricably linked to the introduction of new technologies of naval warfare.

The First World War, the seminal catastrophe of the 20th century, is the

10 Introduction

supreme example of the increased lethality inherent in the interrelationship between war and technology, but not just with regard to the actual weapons employed by the belligerents such as tanks and artillery. Kurt Möser depicts this specific interrelationship by focusing on four technical artifacts: the army spade, the sea mine, the aerial camera, and the optical signaling apparatus. He argues that the adoption of technologies during the course of this war must be seen from a symbolic perspective and not only from a strictly functional perspective. He explains that there was also a "material turn" that was directly connected to the new dimension of warfare in the beginning of the 20th century.

What may appear to be relatively benign technologies such as the camera and increases in the speed of communications are also part of the examination of technologies that impact the lethality of warfare. For example, still photography made it possible to provide a better understanding of the events for non-combatants and those behind the lines supporting the war efforts of the various nations involved in the First World War.[63] Movies were also used as a source to understand how the war was seen by a wider public audience, and what we would consider today to be a simple communication device—i.e., the telephone—was also used to influence the outcome of war.[64] Gerrit Dworok provides an essay on the use of the Soviet propaganda film as a specific and important instrument of Soviet warfare. He focuses on two movies of Sergey Eisenstein: *Battleship Potemkin* and *October*. However, films were not the only example of integrating technology and military concerns. During the Second World War, the British used the Special Operations Executive (SOE) to develop methods for sabotaging the enemy. Roderick Bailey deals with the development and the actions of the SOE and shows how "sleeve-guns" and "rat-grenades" came into existence as technology-based weapons for sabotaging and spying. Bailey examines the impact of more modest technologies into the military panoply, which Tomáš Kučera further explains in his essay on the RAF—why and how civilian authorities in Britain sought to provide an ethical framework for attacking enemy population centers during wartime. Eckehard Dworok describes Hitler's position on modern warfare, which was based on technological supremacy, and explains why he misread the outcome of the First World War and failed to understand the impact that technology could have on warfare in the twentieth century.

Because the outcomes of neither the "War to end all Wars" nor the Second World War was a lasting peace, the third part of the present volume deals with the interrelationship of war and technology during the Cold War. A weapon that was intended to end the Second World War by helping Red Army soldiers overcome the Wehrmacht, the AK-47, changed the course of warfare throughout the whole Cold War period and even beyond. Frank Jacob describes this specific impact with regard to international weapons trade. The AK-47 has been a symbol of resistance movements for over five decades, and it has been the chosen instrument of rebellion around the world. The AK-47 is an example of a relatively unsophisticated and easy-to-produce weapon having an impact on warfare similar to the most advanced and lethal weapons ever produced. James Horncastle continues the Cold War discussion with an examination of smaller states like Yugoslavia which were also influenced by the technological developments that were part of the larger scale of this transnational conflict. Benedict von Bremen goes even further by describing technology's role as a catalyst for the internal struggles inside the power blocs of the Cold War. He also analyzes the public discussion between the United States and Germany during the 1970s that led to the Main Battle Tank (MBT) concept.

During the last decades of the Cold War, changes in the nature of warfare forced military staffs to begin to consider the interrelationship between technology and war. Nathan R. Packard describes the changes with regard to the Marine Corps and its attitude to technology. Maritime pre-positioning and the "over-the-horizon-assault" are examined to show the factors responsible for the development of U.S. Marine Corps doctrine between 1975 and 1990. Daniel Fuhrer, on the other hand, analyzes the operational changes from AirLand Battle to Effects-Based Operations. He shows how far the doctrines of the U.S. Army and Air Force changed from 1980 until 2000 by taking a detailed look at military manuals and several research journals that influenced tactics as well as strategies. He describes a switch to technologically oriented war solutions within the U.S. Army and Air Force. Such changes have helped the United States and other emerging powers to adapt to the evolution of "New Wars" or "Low-Intensity Conflicts."

Thereafter, in the last part of the book Jeffrey M. Shaw, Adam Page, and Timothy J. Demy provide different approaches to discussions about the interrelationship of war and technology in the 21st century. While Shaw provides a counter-argument to the idea that technological advances will most likely always lead to increased battlefield lethality, Page analyzes the debates about "Killer Robots" by providing a flashback to the inter-war discussion on the use of air power. Demy concludes the volume by examining the increasingly important questions such as the extent to which modern unmanned weapons systems are adaptable to the just war theory and tradition.

All of the essays in this volume give detailed insight into specific cases of the interrelationship of war and technology throughout the ages. The volume is designed to not only illuminate various examples of the interrelationship of war and technology in past ages, but to allow the reader to think about the broader implications of the continued integration of advanced technologies into the military sphere, either by nation states themselves or increasingly by non-state actors. The consequences of this trend may have important repercussions for all of us.

NOTES

1. Trutz von Trotha, "*On Cruelty: Conceptual Considerations and the Summary of an Interdisciplinary Debate*" in *On cruelty, Sur la cruauté, Über Grausamkeit*, ed. Jakob Rösel and Trutz von Trotha (Cologne: Rüdiger Köppe Verlag, 2011), 4–5.
2. Due to the centennial, a lot of books dealing with the Great War were published. To name just a few: Christopher Clark, *The Sleepwalkers: How Europe Went to War in 1914* (New York: Harper & Collins, 2012); Peter Hart, *The Great War: A Combat History of the First World War* (Oxford/New York: Oxford University Press, 2013); Herfried Münkler, *Der Große Krieg: Die Welt 1914 bis 1918* (Berlin: Rowohlt, 2013).
3. *The Russo-Japanese War in Global Perspective: World War Zero*, 2 vols., ed. John W. Steinberg, Bruce W. Menning, and David Schimmelpenninck van Der Oye (Leiden/Boston: Brill, 2005).
4. Sakurai Tadayoshi, *Human Bullets: A Soldier's Story of Port Arthur* (Boston/New York: Houghton, Mifflin and Company, 1907), 152.
5. Ibid., 153.
6. Ibid.
7. Martin van Creveld, *Die Gesichter des Krieges: Der Wandel bewaffneter Konflikte von 1900 bis heute* (Munich: Siedler Verlag, 2009), 8.
8. Anselm Doering-Manteuffel, "Kriegserfahrungen, Wissenschaft und Technik," in *Kriegserfahrungen—Krieg und Gesellschaft in der Neuzeit: Neue Horizonte der Forschung*, ed. Georg Schild and Anton Schindling (Paderborn: Ferdinand Schöningh, 2009), 197.
9. Karl Heinz Metz, *Ursprünge der Zukunft: Die Geschichte der Technik in der westlichen Zivilisation* (Paderborn: Ferdinand Schöningh, 2006), 420.
10. Ibid., 421–427.
11. Peter Hart, *The Somme. The Darkest Hour on the Western Front* (New York: Pegasus, 2008).
12. Creveld, *Gesichter*, 84.
13. Karl Heinz Metz, *Geschichte der Gewalt* (Darmstadt: Wissenschaftliche Buchgesellschaft, 2010), 123–125.
14. Ivan Bloch, *Is War Now Impossible? Being an Abridgment of the War of the Future in Its Technical, Economic, and Political Relations* (Whitefish, MT: Kessinger, 2008 [originally published 1899]).
15. Manuel Köppen, *Das Entsetzen des Beobachters: Krieg und Medien im 19. und 20. Jahrhundert* (Heidelberg: Universitätsverlag Winter, 2005), 201.
16. Martin van Crefeld, *Technology and War: From 2000 B.C. to the Present* (New York: Free Press, 1991).
17. Werner Sombart, *Krieg und Kapitalismus* (München: Duncker & Humblot, 1913).
18. Metz, *Ursprünge*, 450.
19. Ibid., 556.
20. Waldemar Kaempffert, "War and Technology," *American Journal of Sociology* 46:4 (1941), 443.
21. Metz, *Ursprünge*, 12.
22. Many utopian or future imaginations were based on technological progress. A good example would be the literary work of Jules Verne (1828–1905).
23. Köppen, *Entsetzen*, 196.
24. Ibid., 199.
25. Kaempffert, "War and Technology," 432.

26. Carl von Clausewitz, *Vom Kriege* (Neuenkirchen: RaBaKa Publishing, 2010), S.179.

27. Herfried Münkler, *Über den Krieg: Stationen der Kriegsgeschichte im Spiegel ihrer theoretischen Reflexion* (Weilerswist: Velbrück Wissenschaft, 2002), 200.

28. Hwang Byong-Moo, "Changing Military Doctrines of the PRC: The Interaction Between the People's War and Technology," *Journal of East Asian Affairs* 11:1 (1997), 222–224.

29. Kurt Möser, *Fahren und Fliegen in Krieg und Frieden. Kulturen individueller Mobilitätsmaschinen 1880–1930* (Heidelberg et al.: Verlag Regionalkultur, 2009), 12.

30. Metz, *Geschichte der Gewalt*, 116; Möser, *Fahren und Fliegen*, 482; Münkler, *Über den Krieg*, 253.

31. Möser, *Fahren und Fliegen*, 497.

32. Geoffrey Parker, *The Military Revolution: Military Innovation and the Rise of the West, 1500–1800* (Cambridge: Cambridge University Press, 1996).

33. Creveld, *Die Gesichter*, 93.

34. Metz, *Geschichte der Gewalt*, 117.

35. Möser, *Fahren und Fliegen*, 481.

36. Kaempffert, "War and Technology," 436; Metz, *Geschichte der Gewalt*, 119.

37. Kaempffert, "War and Technology," 437.

38. Metz, *Geschichte der Gewalt*, 120.

39. Dierk Spreen, *Tausch, Technik, Krieg: Die Geburt der Gesellschaft im technisch-medialen Apriori* (Berlin et al.: Argument Verlag, 1998), 11.

40. Ibid., 187

41. Creveld, *Gesichter*, 93–97.

42. The tank was invented to deal with machine gun posts on the battlefield. Metz, *Ursprünge*, 419.

43. Metz, *Geschichte der Gewalt*, 7.

44. Niels Bierbaumer, "Neurogeschichte von Gewalt und Kriegserfahrung," in *Kriegserfahrungen—Krieg und Gesellschaft in der Neuzeit: Neue Horizonte der Forschung*, ed. Georg Schild and Anton Schindling (Paderborn: Ferdinand Schöningh, 2009), 90.

45. There are many examples for the use of specific technologies that were developed to reach a higher grade of enemy destruction. Eric Katz, *Death by Design: Science, Technology, and Engineering in Nazi Germany* (New York: Pearson, 2006).

46. Metz, *Geschichte der Gewalt*, 118.

47. Ibid., 129–138.

48. Beatrice Heuser, *Rebellen. Partisanen. Guerilleros: Asymmetrische Kriege von der Antike bis heute* (Paderborn: Ferdinand Schöningh, 2013); Klaus-Peter Lohmann, "Zur Entwicklung der modernen Kriegführung. Grundlegende Asymmetrien und eine mögliche Strategie," in *Asymmetrische Kriegführung—ein neues Phänomen der Internationalen Politik*, ed. Josef Schlröfl and Thomas Pankratz (Baden-Baden: Nomos, 2004).

49. The term was introduced by Mary Kaldor, *New and Old Wars: Organized Violence in a Global Era* (Cambridge, Polity Press, 2012) and further developed by Herfried Münkler, *Die neuen Kriege* (Hamburg: Rowohlt, 2002). For a critical evaluation of that term see Dieter Langewiesche, "Wie neu sind die 'Neuen Kriege'? Eine erfahrungsgeschichtliche Analyse," in *Kriegserfahrungen—Krieg und Gesellschaft in der Neuzeit: Neue Horizonte der Forschung*, ed. Georg Schild and Anton Schindling (Paderborn: Ferdinand Schöningh, 2009), 289–302.

50. Metz, *Geschichte der Gewalt*, 116.

51. Creveld, *Gesichter*, 7, 316, and 324.

52. Metz, *Geschichte der Gewalt*, 302.

14 Introduction

53. Martin van Creveld, *Die Zukunft des Krieges* (Hamburg: Murmann, 2004), 45–55.
54. Ibid., 21.
55. Ibid., 22.
56. Münkler, *Über den Krieg*, 220, and 253.
57. Prof. Sarah Danielsson (CUNY) and Prof. Frank Jacob (CUNY) are actually preparing a subsequent conference that will deal with this specific interrelationship.
58. Merle L. Pribbenow II, "The -Ology War: Technology and Ideology in the Vietnamese Defense of Hanoi, 1967," *The Journal of Military History* 67:1 (2003), 200.
59. Hans Magnus Enzensberger, *Aussichten auf den Bürgerkrieg* (Frankfurt: Suhrkamp, 1996).
60. Samuel P. Huntington, *The Clash of Civilizations and the Remaking of World Order* (New York: Simon & Schuster, 2011).
61. Volker Schmidtchen, *Kriegswesen im späten Mittelalter* (Weinheim: VCH Verlagsgesellschaft, 1990), 8.
62. Hans Delbrück, *Geschichte der Kriegskunst im Rahmen der politischen Geschichte*, 4 Vols. (Berlin: Stilke, 1920–1923) and Max Jähns, *Handbuch einer Geschichte des Kriegswesens: Von der Uhrzeit bis zur Renaissance*, 2 Vols. (Leipzig: Verlag von Fr. Wilh. Grunow, 1878–1880) already made attempts to take a broader look to the development of warfare and to determine factors of the process. While Delbrück was mainly focusing on the political aspects of warfare, Jähn tried to line out the interdependence between warfare and weaponry, tactics, and fortification.
63. Horst Tonn, "Medialisierung von Kriegserfahrungen," in *Kriegserfahrungen—Krieg und Gesellschaft in der Neuzeit: Neue Horizonte der Forschung*, ed. Georg Schild and Anton Schindling (Paderborn: Ferdinand Schöningh, 2009), 110.
64. Köppen, *Entsetzen*, 1.

Works Cited

Bierbaumer, Niels. "Neurogeschichte von Gewalt und Kriegserfahrung," in *Kriegserfahrungen—Krieg und Gesellschaft in der Neuzeit: Neue Horizonte der Forschung*, ed. Georg Schild and Anton Schindling. Paderborn: Ferdinand Schöningh, 2009, 83–107.

Bloch, Ivan. *Is War Now Impossible? Being an Abridgment of the War of the Future in Its Technical, Economic, and Political Relations*. Whitefish, MT: Kessinger, 2008 (originally published 1899).

Hwang, Byong-Moo. "Changing Military Doctrines of the PRC: The Interaction Between the People's War and Technology." *Journal of East Asian Affairs* 11:1 (1997): 221–266.

Christopher, Clark. *The Sleepwalkers: How Europe Went to War in 1914*. New York: Harper & Collins, 2012.

Clausewitz, Carl von. *Vom Kriege*. Neuenkirchen: RaBaKa Publishing, 2010.

Creveld, Martin van. *Die Gesichter des Krieges: Der Wandel bewaffneter Konflikte von 1900 bis heute*. Munich: Siedler Verlag, 2009.

Creveld, Martin van. *Die Zukunft des Krieges*. Hamburg: Murmann, 2004.

Crefeld, Martin van. *Technology and War: From 2000 B.C. to the Present*. New York: Free Press, 1991.

Delbrück, Hans. *Geschichte der Kriegskunst im Rahmen der politischen Geschichte*, 4 Vols. Berlin: Stilke, 1920–1923.

Doering-Manteuffel, Anselm. "Kriegserfahrungen, Wissenschaft und Technik," in

Kriegserfahrungen—Krieg und Gesellschaft in der Neuzeit: Neue Horizonte der Forschung, ed. Georg Schild and Anton Schindling. Paderborn: Ferdinand Schöningh, 2009, 197–211.
Dworok, Gerrit. "Die totalitäre Versuchung," in *MUT. Forum für Kultur, Politik und Geschichte* 559 (2014): 32–39.
Enzensberger, Hans Magnus. *Aussichten auf den Bürgerkrieg*. Frankfurt: Suhrkamp, 1996.
Hart, Peter. *The Great War: A Combat History of the First World War*. Oxford/New York: Oxford University Press, 2013.
Hart, Peter. *The Somme: The Darkest Hour on the Western Front*. New York: Pegasus, 2008.
Heuser, Beatrice. *Rebellen. Partisanen. Guerilleros: Asymmetrische Kriege von der Antike bis heute*. Paderborn: Ferdinand Schöningh, 2013.
Huntington, Samuel P. *The Clash of Civilizations and the Remaking of World Order*. New York: Simon & Schuster, 2011.
Jähns, Max. *Handbuch einer Geschichte des Kriegswesens. Von der Urzeit bis zur Renaissance*, 2 Vols. Leipzig: Verlag von Fr. Wilh. Grunow, 1878–1880.
Kaempffert, Waldemar. "War and Technology." *American Journal of Sociology* 46:4 (1941): 431–444.
Kaldor, Mary. *New and Old Wars: Organized Violence in a Global Era*. Cambridge, Polity Press, 2012.
Katz, Eric. *Death by Design: Science, Technology, and Engineering in Nazi Germany*. New York: Pearson, 2006.
Köppen, Manuel. *Das Entsetzen des Beobachter: Krieg und Medien im 19. und 20. Jahrhundert*. Heidelberg: Universitätsverlag Winter, 2005.
Langewiesche, Dieter. "Wie neu sind die 'Neuen Kriege'? Eine erfahrungsgeschichtliche Analyse," in *Kriegserfahrungen—Krieg und Gesellschaft in der Neuzeit: Neue Horizonte der Forschung*, ed. Georg Schild and Anton Schindling. Paderborn: Ferdinand Schöningh, 2009, 289–302.
Lohmann, Klaus-Peter. "Zur Entwicklung der modernen Kriegführung. Grundlegende Asymmetrien und eine mögliche Strategie," in *Asymmetrische Kriegführung—ein neues Phänomen der Internationalen Politik*, ed. Josef Schlröfl and Thomas Pankratz. Baden-Baden: Nomos, 2004.
Metz, Karl Heinz. *Geschichte der Gewalt*. Darmstadt: Wissenschaftliche Buchgesellschaft, 2010.
Metz, Karl Heinz. *Ursprünge der Zukunft: Die Geschichte der Technik in der westlichen Zivilisation*. Paderborn: Ferdinand Schöningh, 2006.
Möser, Kurt. *Fahren und Fliegen in Krieg und Frieden: Kulturen individueller Mobilitätsmaschinen 1880–1930*. Heidelberg: Verlag Regionalkultur, 2009.
Münkler, Herfried. *Der Große Krieg: Die Welt 1914 bis 1918*. Berlin: Rowohlt, 2013.
Münkler, Herfried. *Die neuen Kriege*. Hamburg: Rowohlt, 2002.
Münkler, Herfried. *Über den Krieg: Stationen der Kriegsgeschichte im Spiegel ihrer theoretischen Reflexion*. Weilerswist: Velbrück Wissenschaft, 2002.
Oman, Charles. *A History of the Art of War: The Middle Ages from the Fourth to the Fourteenth Century*. London: Methuen & Co., 1898.
Parker, Geoffrey. *The Military Revolution: Military Innovation and the Rise of the West, 1500–1800*. Cambridge: Cambridge University Press, 1996.
Pribbenow, Merle L., II. "The -Ology War: Technology and Ideology in the Vietnamese Defense of Hanoi, 1967." *The Journal of Military History* 67:1 (2003), 175–200.
Sakurai, Tadayoshi. *Human Bullets: A Soldier's Story of Port Arthur*. Boston/New York: Houghton, Mifflin and Company, 1907.

Schmidtchen, Volker. *Kriegswesen im späten Mittelalter.* Weinheim: VCH Verlagsgesellschaft, 1990.
Spreen, Dierk. *Tausch, Technik, Krieg: Die Geburt der Gesellschaft im technisch-medialen Apriori.* Berlin: Argument Verlag, 1998.
Tonn, Horst. "Medialisierung von Kriegserfahrungen," in *Kriegserfahrungen—Krieg und Gesellschaft in der Neuzeit: Neue Horizonte der Forschung,* ed. Georg Schild and Anton Schindling. Paderborn: Ferdinand Schöningh, 2009, 109–133.
Trotha, Trutz von. "On Cruelty: Conceptual Considerations and the Summary of an Interdisciplinary Debate," in *On cruelty, Sur la cruauté, Über Grausamkeit,* ed. Jakob Rösel and Trutz von Trotha. Cologne: Rüdiger Köppe Verlag, 2011, 1–67.

PART I.
ANCIENT ROME AND THE MEDIEVAL AGES

Ancient Naval Artillery Support

JORIT WINTJES

Introduction

Amphibious landings are among the most complex military operations to pull off, not the least so because a multitude of things can go wrong very quickly once the first soldier has hit the ground and especially if the enemy is well-prepared. The first wave of the attacking infantry might, in trying to get ashore, encounter heavy resistance already on the beach. The landing ground could, moreover, be covered by further enemy forces positioned on higher ground immediately beyond the beach, laying into the attacking infantry with abandon. As a result, the invading forces could get into disarray rather quickly and—at least initially—fail to gain a firm foothold. Instead, what had begun as a fairly organized attempt at an amphibious landing could turn into confused, disorganized and pretty unhealthy fighting in the surf. At that point, the whole situation would be in danger of getting out of control, necessitating some emergency measures like sending warships really closely inshore to hammer away at the enemy.

What sounds like a scene taken directly out of D-Day—the close support given by RN and USN destroyers on Omaha Beach comes to mind, for example[1]—in reality happened around two millennia earlier when Julius Caesar crossed over to Britain in 55 BC. Although according to Caesar's own account, it was not the naval artillery support alone that eventually turned the tide,[2] naval fire support obviously was a very effective instrument he could rely on, and it was far from unique to Caesar's campaign. This is shown for example by the campaigns of Germanicus in Germany, who in the winter of AD 15/16 had 1,000 ships built to bolster his already existing transport fleet. Some of these ships were equipped with platforms to allow the use of artillery.[3] As

Germanicus' Germanic opponents were not known for assembling large fleets of warships, the only reason for equipping ships in this way must obviously have been naval artillery support for troops disembarking from the ships.

The discussion on ancient artillery usually focuses on the technology itself and not so much on its impact on operations.[4] In fact, most of the available sources about the interrelationship of technology and warfare yield information about the technology. Nevertheless, for the end user, it was operations that mattered—the proof of the pudding is in the eating, as they say. The main focus of this paper, therefore, is on the operational use of artillery, specifically on naval artillery used in the fire support role within the context of the professional Roman army. This paper concentrates on Roman military history, as most of the extremely limited evidence covers Roman operations. Due to the lack of available evidence, the primary aim of a paper like this cannot be to *answer* all or even many of the questions regarding naval fire support in the ancient world. Instead, this paper aims at getting an idea of what these questions might be in the first place.

Layers of Complexity—Operating Ancient Artillery

When dealing with the actual use of ancient artillery, it is necessary to look at it from an operator's perspective. By doing so, it is fairly easy to identify four key issues. The first one is the technical capability of the piece, i.e., its range, penetrative capability and—related to that—the type and size of ammunition required for maximum effect. As the surviving literary evidence almost exclusively focuses on the construction of artillery pieces, there is fairly little information on range or penetrative capabilities. However, a considerable amount of experimental data is available. Ever since Erwin Schramm made his groundbreaking experiments,[5] archaeologists, re-enactors and other enthusiasts have shot all sorts of different projectiles at anything from ballistic gelatin and replicas of ancient armor to pigs' heads.[6] As a result, both the range bands that could be covered by ancient artillery pieces and the actual destructive capabilities of the ammunition are fairly well understood.[7] One has to bear in mind, though, that given the lack of professional experience in constructing artillery pieces, differences of material and modern health and safety concerns probably result in lower maximum ranges than could be achieved in antiquity.[8]

The second issue is the actual handling of the piece. Two aspects stand out as being of particular importance: the crew requirement (in other words, how many crewmen a particular piece needed, and what level of specialist training was required of them) and the handling procedures, i.e., did each crewman have a specific role, were they "cross-trained" to operate any part of the piece, was there a rank issue involved, etc. Regarding these two important aspects, very little information is available. While reconstructions are routinely put to the test by firing different types of ammunition at different targets, no systematic experimental research has been made so far into how, for example, the setup of the crew may have influenced the rate of fire. Also, modern testing is usually done only for a comparatively short period—a couple of times during an hour-long display, perhaps, or even less. There is no experimental data available on the effect of sustained fire on ancient artillery pieces and how a crew might be able to counter these effects and how effects like crew fatigue influenced the effectiveness of the artillery piece as a weapon system. Likewise, nearly nothing is known about fire drills. While a two-man crew for a light piece might have organized how they operated in an individual way, a larger crew must invariably have had some sort of training in working together. Regarding the latter in the context of an army as professional as the Roman imperial, one has to raise a couple of questions—did the Romans have gun captains? Did the crews train together regularly? Did larger crews work on a crew-only principle, or did they have a core crew of "gunners," so to speak, which would in the field be augmented by ammunition carriers as the need arose? With the evidence currently available, it is impossible to answer these questions; they are, however, useful for illustrating the complexity of operating ancient artillery.

Having looked at some of the technicalities of an ancient artillery piece and the questions that arise once one wants to put this artillery piece into action, the third important issue that must be addressed is target identification and fire control. Target shooting is quite often done in modern experiments and has shown that ancient artillery pieces were indeed capable of considerable precision.[9] This, however, has little to do with firing for effect in an actual combat situation, where the whole process of firing can be broken down into three key steps: identifying the potential target, firing the artillery piece at that target and observing the effect of the firing. Once these steps are completed, the whole procedure starts again. While this appears to be fairly obvious, how this all actually worked out in reality is quite unclear. Identifying targets sounds like a simple enough step, and in the case of field artillery, it was presumably fairly easy to coordinate the firing of several pieces in order to prevent some targets from being engaged by several pieces and others not at all. Nonetheless, how did this work with ship-borne artillery? Coordination between individual ships required working means of ship-to-ship communication, about which, unfortunately, very little is known. With the target identified and neutralized, the next question arises—was there a procedure for shifting fire? Did the crews act in local control with the firing being effectively planned by the gun captain—if such a function existed in the first place? Again, no evidence survives offering answers to these questions. Moreover, most of what is actually known about operational details is related to the use of bolt-throwers. However, in the case of stone throwers, who were often positioned behind the troops firing in a ballistic arc overhead at an enemy unseen by the crew, some sort of indirect fire control or spotting procedures must have existed.[10] Unfortunately, experimental data on this is lacking, and ancient sources are silent.

Finally, when talking about the employment of artillery in the context of the Roman military, it is necessary to look at matters of general organization even though again, dauntingly few sources survive. In fact, the organizational setup of artillery within the Roman military is almost entirely in the dark. While the command structure of infantry units is fairly well known, we simply do not know with any precision what the command structure of artillery elements actually looked like, how they integrated into larger units, and how their command structure then related to that of the infantry's. At the root of this quite serious issue—after all, it is unknown *who* gave *whom* the order to fire, which is actually a pretty important element in the overall process of employing artillery—lies the already mentioned problem that far too little is known about who operated the pieces. It can be stated, with some confidence, that hardly every single soldier had the necessary skills to do so, which means that on the lowest level, the crews were specialists. This seems to be vindicated by looking at sources like Tarrutienus Paternus' list of *immunes* in the Roman army and inscriptional material testifying to the existence of *ballistarii*, which may be translated as "artillerists."[11] As *immunes*, the soldiers were exempt from certain everyday chores, thus indicating a higher status and—possibly—a higher pay grade; this indicates that the *ballistarii* were indeed specialists, presumably charged not only with crewing the artillery pieces but also with doing maintenance and repair work. Still, who gave the orders? There are scraps of evidence for *magistri*,[12] yet it is not clear how these positions related to the one best understood in the Roman army—the centurion. Did these *magistri* serve under centurions as something like gun captains or section leaders, or does the term denote someone of higher rank? Is this term a term of *function* and not of *rank* (which centurion is)? Did centurions then command artillery detachments, and if so, were these artillery specialists as well, or was it part of the ordinary centurion's job to be able to command artillery? There are a lot more questions than answers. In fact, pretty much the only thing that can be stated with any certainty is that the Romans managed to do quite difficult things with their artillery on a regular basis.

Artillery on the Boat

Turning from these general issues to ship-borne artillery and how it could be employed in the fire support role, it is now necessary to put these four main problems of technical capability, management of the piece, target identification and fire control as well as general organization into a naval context.

Looking first at the issue of technical capability, naval artillery support differs from the use of artillery as field artillery in several important ways; one is that the ship firing at an enemy ashore is likely to do so at a considerably greater distance than would be the case with field artillery. Although little is known with any precision about the actual combat ranges of amphibious assaults, one can, nevertheless, assume that on the battlefield, artillery was used in a broad range band from perhaps 50 to 75 meters, or close range, to up to 400 meters or even beyond, or long range.[13] As ships employed in the naval artillery support role had—quite logically—to stay where they still had some water under their keel-plank, naval artillery could hardly fire at close range. The nature of many beaches in certain coastal areas in North-Western Europe, with comparatively large areas of very shallow water beyond the swash zone, only aggravates the problem; to take but one example, the beach that Caesar assaulted in 55 BC, a strip of shingle between Deal and Walmer, even today is roughly 100 meters from the top of the beach to the edge of the water, with another 100–150 meters of extremely shallow water (1–2 meters) beyond that.[14] As a warship firing at targets on the beach would need at least some space for maneuvering, Caesar's naval fire support could well have engaged targets at 300 meters or more.

Relying mainly on long-range fire, which forms another important difference in the use of artillery as field artillery, has one of two "side-effects." The first one is about weapons effects. Stone throwers lend themselves more to firing effectively at longer ranges, as the weapons effect does not diminish as significantly with increasing range as it does in the case of bolt-throwers; to put it bluntly, a stone ball falling from the sky is likely to ruin one's day at long ranges as well as at short ranges.[15] With bolt-throwers, however, things are quite different, as the bolt loses penetrative power at long ranges.

Stone-throwers, therefore, appear to be better suited to the naval fire support role.[16] The second "side effect" concerns the construction of the artillery pieces. The easiest way to counter the negative influence of range on the penetrative power and general effectiveness of bolt throwers and further improve the effectiveness of stone throwers is by employing bigger machines. This is easy to do on land, and there is literary evidence of the employment of artillery pieces of considerable size extant.[17] However, as the weight and size of the stone ball increases, so do that of the artillery piece, and quite dramatically so: a modern reconstruction of a piece capable of firing a one-talent-ball (roughly 26 kg) can easily get as big as a house.[18] Obviously, putting something like this onto a ship creates considerable problems.

Turning from purely technical issues to the problem of handling the pieces, more questions arise. As stated above, any ancient artillery piece needed a crew. In order to operate the piece properly, this crew then required a certain amount of space in which to work. As the crew increases, so does—rather logically—the space taken up by it. On the battlefield, this is not really a problem unless there are serious issues with the topography, but on an ancient ship, even on its upper deck, the space was cramped. To illustrate, a rather smallish bolt-thrower might have a crew of two or three men, and together with all these men, the artillery piece may have occupied a circle with a diameter of at least 2 meters. Thus, accommodating already a small bolt-thrower on a ship where the upper deck may only be 6 meters wide is certainly not an easy proposition.[19] As a result, there are limits to both the size and number of the artillery pieces employed.[20] Herein lies a key difference in modern naval artillery, which usually is—or was—capable of fielding far bigger guns than field artillery ever could. Whereas modern naval artillery easily outguns field artillery—at least until the advent of self-propelled guns with C4ISTR and shoot-and-scoot capabilities—ancient naval artillery was easily outgunned by field artillery.

The size of the piece and the limited space available on the upper deck of an ancient warship also raise the issue of firing arcs; while stone throwers might, with the mast and rigging put down when the ship was cleared for action, have enjoyed unlimited firing arcs, firing directly at a target dead ahead, or dead astern, for that matter, with a bolt-thrower probably was impossible, requiring the ship to be positioned in a way allowing the artillery pieces to actually bear onto the target.

Little information is available on how long an artillery barrage lasted, but the general idea one gets from accounts both of artillery fire on land and in the naval support role is that artillery could be employed over a prolonged period of time. After all, certainly, Caesar's naval artillery support during the landing in Britain must have taken more than only a few minutes to turn the tide.[21] However, firing artillery pieces over a longer period of time invariably raises the issue of ammunition supply that gains complexity as the rate of fire and the length of the engagement increases. While ammunition for a few pot shots at the enemy commander may well find its place in the gear of the crewmen—in some sort of "ready ammunition" way—firing over a longer period of time creates the need for both getting sufficient ammunition to the artillery pieces and having them in the first place. Already not the easiest thing to do on land, firing over a longer time period raises potentially very interesting problems aboard a ship: How much ammunition is stored aboard? Does an ancient warship, capable of operating closely inshore, have sufficient storage available for potentially hundreds of ballista bolts or stone balls in the first place? Although a single stone ball may have weighed as little as 1 kg, one shot per piece was hardly a sufficient ammunition load. Assuming a rate of fire of three or four shots per minute,[22] a barrage of only 15 minutes' duration would already equate to around 50 to 60 shots, or 50 to 60 kg of ammunition load per artillery piece. Three artillery pieces aboard one ship would, therefore, already require 150 to 180 kg for a 15-minute barrage. As any Roman warship employed in the fire support role is unlikely to have run out of ammunition after a quarter of an hour, the real numbers will have been substantially higher, resulting in considerable weight numbers. Suitable ammunition for an hour-long engagement, for example, would have meant finding space for 600 to 900 pieces of ammunition weighing anything between 600 and 900 kg aboard the ship.

And where *was* this amount of ammunition in the first place? Were there any procedures in place for manhandling the ammunition to the artillery pieces? One would assume that the ammunition was stored fairly close to the artillery pieces, but would that be all of it? Would that be possible? Were there any special requirements with ship construction? Tacitus mentions the construction of ships with special modifications for the use of artillery, but this seems to relate mainly to the need for having sufficient platform space for handling the piece.[23] Did the need for carrying ammunition have an effect on the design of warships that after all were hulls crammed to the gunwale with rowers and not known for having large or any spaces below deck? On all these questions the literary sources are silent, and experimental data currently does not exist.

Another very obvious and problematic difference between handling artillery on the battlefield and on ship is that on the battlefield, the ground on which the artillery piece is placed does not require any "handling," leaving aside the issue of preparing fixed fortifications. On a ship, however, placing the artillery down does require special handling. All the experimental data on firing ancient artillery pieces and on the effectiveness of ancient artillery fire rests on firm ground, so to speak. The effects of being positioned on a moving platform are unknown, but one would assume that the skills required for hitting a target were considerable and had to be present both with the crew manning the weapon and with those commanding and manning the ship. One wonders, for example, whether there were any special drills to keep a ship in the same position for a longer period of time, or, if not, whether crews were trained in keeping their aim on a target even if the ship changed its position.

This leads directly to the problem of target identification and fire control. In the case of naval artillery support, the artillery piece was aboard a moving platform, a situation that already complicated matters considerably.[24] Moreover, naval artillery was prevented from firing at close ranges by the simple fact that between the ship and the enemy lay both the beach and a shallow water zone; the targets thus were a considerable distance away. As a result, they were more difficult to identify, and the falling of the shots were harder to spot. Also, coordinating fire must have been much more difficult to achieve as it required effective means of ship-to-ship communication. Coupled with the need for an overall commander to give orders, as Caesar did during the landing in Britain, command and control must have posed a daunting challenge and come with a large number of detail problems: how was the target selection done, and how, if at all, were the targets prioritized, how was the neutralization of a target communicated, did fire plans exist, etc.? While there is no evidence whatsoever allowing us to answer these questions, the information available on actual operations allows us at least to state that naval fire support must have been a quite complicated affair.

Caesar's invasion of Britain in 55 BC is a case in point here. Superficially, it looks like a fairly simple affair—the enemy contests the beach and occupies higher ground that is then hammered until the enemy decides to call it a day. In contrast, a closer look at it reveals an operation of considerable complexity. First of all, Caesar did not have an endless supply of warship mounting artillery.[25] Therefore, he would logically have tried to employ them where the need was greatest, achieving concentration of fire at places where the enemy not only resisted successfully but also tried to counterattack. Accordingly, either Caesar himself or the commanders aboard the ships must have had some sort of situational awareness of what happened on the beach no matter how they managed to achieve that. Also, they must have been able to determine when to engage a target and when to switch to another. Moreover, with much of the fighting on the beach being rather disorganized and hand-to-hand,[26] one wonders how Caesar prevented his naval artillery from laying into his own men. Whether there were any procedures to prevent blue-on-blue incidents is an interesting question in itself; hitting friendly infantry artillery certainly did not carry the same political implications as in the 21st century, and ancient commanders probably had a somewhat different attitude towards the value of the life of the individual soldier. Nevertheless, blue-on-blue incidents must have been highly detrimental to any unit's morale, and for that reason if not for any other, they were to be avoided. In all, any use of naval artillery in the way Caesar used it in 55 BC required considerable fire control skills. Unfortunately, no evidence whatsoever survives about how the Romans managed to acquire them.

Closely connected to the fire control problem are general organization issues. Achieving concentration of fire was much more difficult with naval artillery support than with field artillery. Due to the space limitations on all but really big warships—which were probably excluded from operating close to the beach—a similar degree of physical concentration is impossible. On the battlefield, it is possible to pack artillery much closer together than could ever be achieved on ships unless one would want to tie them together. Concentration of fire could, therefore, only be achieved by coordinating the fire of several ships on one and the same target, which required not only proper target identification procedures ensuring everybody involved actually fired at the same target, but also sufficient communications among the individual ships employed in the artillery support role. Communications is also a key issue when it comes to controlling an artillery effort of a group of ships as a whole. Even though this is much more preferable to individual ships acquiring targets on their own, it requires working lines of communications among all the ships taking part in the bombardment effort ensuring that no intended target is missed and between the ships and the commander with whom the fire plan originated. Unfortunately, as has already been mentioned, there is very little surviving evidence about ship-to-ship communications. It is particularly unclear how in the context of a landing operation involving 100 or more ships and soon turning into a pretty chaotic affair, communications survived to such a degree that a coordinated naval artillery effort was possible.

Conclusion

Reviewing the evidence and a couple of key issues of operating ancient artillery in general and ancient ship-borne artillery in the fire support role in particular has produced two results: The first one is fairly simple, but the second one is slightly disappointing. First, what can be stated with some confidence is that operating ancient artillery, particularly ship-borne artillery, happened, and apparently quite frequently. Caesar used naval artillery support in 55 BC, and although the beach was not contested during his second foray to Britain in 54 BC, he certainly was prepared to use artillery. During Germanicus' campaigns in Germany in AD 15 and AD 16, Tacitus explicitly mentions preparations for providing naval artillery support,[27] and during amphibious operations in both the Claudian invasion of Britain and the ensuing operations along the Southern and Eastern coasts of Britain, ships equipped with artillery would have been in use. Also, during the Flavian push to the "end of the world" in Scotland between AD 78 and 83, Tacitus again testifies to the use of naval forces to harass the enemy,[28] and one would assume that naval artillery played some role in that as well.

Second, though we can get some idea about the challenges Roman gunners faced when trying to support their comrades on the beach, we simply do not have enough data at the moment to understand how they overcame these challenges. Herein lies an opportunity for future research: If experimentation with ancient artillery pieces moved on from merely *testing* pieces to actually *operating* them, then we might get a clearer idea about possible solutions for the large number of issues a Roman artilleryman had on hand.

NOTES

1. Gordon A. Harrison, *United States Army in World War II—The European Theater of Operations: Cross-Channel Attack* (Washington: U.S. Government Printing Office, 1951), 321–322.

2. According to Caesar's account (for which see Caes. BG 4.24.2–26.5), three factors were responsible for his eventual success—the naval fire support, an exemplum of outstanding bravery by the eagle bearer of his legio X, who, seeing his comrades hesitating to join the fight, jumped into the surf basically shouting "follow me!," and Caesar's tactic to send pennypackets of reinforcements in boats to those places on the beach where the need was the greatest.

3. Tac. Ann. 2.6.1.

4. For general overviews see Eric W. Marsden, *Greek and Roman Artillery: Historical Development* (Oxford: Clarendon Press, 1969); Eric W. Marsden, *Greek and Roman Artillery: Technical Treatises* (Oxford: Clarendon Press, 1971); Dietwulf Baatz, *Bauten und Katapulte des römischen Heeres* (Stuttgart: Steiner, 1994); Alan Wilkins, *Roman Artillery* (Princes Risborough: Shire Publications, 2003); Flavio Russo, *L'artiglieria delle legion: Le macchine da guerra che resero invincibile l'escrito romano* (Rome: Istituto Poligrafico e Zecca dello Stato, 2004). Tracey Rihll, *The Catapult: A History* (Yardley: Westholme Publishing, 2007), offering a comprehensive bibliography (Rihl 2007, 345–365).

5. Major-General Erwin Schramm commanded the 3rd kgl. sächs. Feldartillerie-Brigade and fired reconstructions of both bolt- and stone-throwers at various targets including iron-plated shields, see Erwin Schramm, *Die antiken Geschütze der Saalburg: Bemerkungen zu ihrer Rekonstruktion.* (Berlin: Weidmann, 1918); see also Marsden, *Historical Development*, 86–87.

6. For the effect a ballista bolt hit has on a reconstructed lorica segmentata see Wilkins, *Roman Artillery*, 52.

7. For a general overview see Marsden, *Historical Development*, 86–98.

8. Ancient artillerists apparently preferred animal sinews to hair for manufacturing springs, see Heron Bel. W 110 and Veg. Mil. 4.9; for a fuller discussion of the issue see Marsden, *Historical Development*, 86–89; Wilkens, *Roman Artillery*, 36–37; Rihll, *Catapult*, 228–231. Marsden's own reconstruction was "powered by springs of weak rubber, much inferior to hair" (Marsden, Historical Development, 86 n. 3); even so, he managed to fire at ranges over 300 yards.

9. The accuracy of Greek and Roman artillery pieces is well-attested in the surviving sources; for modern experiments see e.g., Wilkins, *Roman Artillery*, 22–23.

10. On the employment of stone throwers behind the infantry see Arr. Alan. 19, a key text for the use of field artillery; see Albert B. Bosworth, "Arrian and the Alani," *Harvard Studies in Classical Philology* 81 (1977): 217–255; James G. Devoto, ed., trans., Flavius Arrianus ΤΕΧΝΗ ΤΑΚΤΙΚΑ and ἘΚΤΑΞΙΣ ΚΑΤΑ ἈΛΑΝΩΝ (Chicago: Ares, 1998), with a modern translation; see also Rihll, *Catapult*, 190.

11. Dig. 50.6.7; for a full discussion of the evidence see Marsden, *Historical Development*, 191–196. The only ballistarius actually attested may be a certain Priscinus

who served with legio I Italica; the inscription has been dated to around AD 300; see Wilhelm Kubitschek, "Aus Sammlung Trau in Wien: ein Vexillum-Aufsatz," *Jahreshefte des Österreichischen Archäologischen Instituts in Wien* 29 (1934): 44-48; the reading of the inscription, however, is not undisputed, cf. Lemke 2013, 360 n. 18. The ballistarii appear again in the context of the late Roman army, where they form specialist units, though it is unclear, whether they were really artillerymen, as suggested by Marsden, *Historical Development*, 196-197 and Hoffmann 1970, 181-182; they have also been identified as the late Roman equivalent to crossbowmen, see Campbell 1986, 131-132, Chevedden 1995, 144-145; see also Dietwulf Baatz, "Katapulte und mechanische Handwaffen des spätrömischen Heeres," *Journal of Roman Military Equipment Studies* 10 (1999): 5-20. The ballistarii have often been associated with a remark by Vegetius, who noted that one contubernium from each century was tasked with operating artillery (Veg. Mil. 2.8), though whether Vegetius really knew what he was writing about is not beyond doubt.

12. CIL V 6632 attests a certain Aelius Optatus as magister ballistariorum of legio XX.

13. In a series of famous experiments, the German Major General Erwin Schramm, at the time commanding the 3. kgl. sächs. Feldartillerie-Brigade Nr. 32 in Bautzen, tested reconstructions of ancient bolt- and stone throwers at the artillery depot in Metz and at a range near Dresden; with one of his bolt-throwers he achieved both a range of 370 m and a considerable penetration against an iron-plated shield (Schramm, *Antike Geschütze*, 27-36); in 1904, Schramm demonstrated one of his reconstructions to emperor Wilhelm II, who was almost injured when Schramm's ballista misfired (Wilkins, *Roman Artillery*, 24-25); while it was probably not an exceedingly pleasant experience for the emperor, it certainly served nicely to illustrate the potential dangers in operating complex machines incorporating high-powered springs. For a general discussion of artillery ranges including the relevant ancient sources see Marsden, *Historical Development*, 88-90, Wilkins, *Roman Artillery*, 61-65.

14. This calculation is admittedly rather imprecise, as the coastline underwent considerable changes, though at least during the last two centuries there was no constant process of erosion (see Walmer Environment Study Group, *Think Globally*, 3).

15. The effect of hits by stone throwers is mentioned several times in the surviving sources; one of the more graphic examples is Flavius Josephus' account of the siege of the Jotapata in AD 67—here one of the defenders meets his end at the hands of Roman artillerists: τις ... ἀπαράσσεται τὴν κεφαλὴν ὑπὸ τῆς πέτρας (J. BJ. 3.245).

16. Larger bolt throwers could fire bolts with considerable penetrative power though the most famous example is the wound Alexander the Great took during the Battle of Gaza, when a bolt went straight through his shield and his breastplate into his shoulder (Arrian Anab. 2.27.2).

17. Vitr. 10.12.3 lists 18 different sizes of ballistae ranging from smallish pieces throwing stones of 2 librae (around 650 gr) to what must have been—if it really existed—a monstrous piece hurtling a ball of 360 librae (118 kg); on Vitruvius' list in general see Rihll, *Catapult*, 177-180, for size estimations 290-294. It is usually assumed that the largest ballista in regular use with the Roman army was one capable of throwing a ball of 27 kg (Wilkins, *Roman Artillery*, 14-15), but larger pieces may have been used even as field artillery—Tac. Hist. 3.23.2 mentions a particularly large piece hurling ingentibus saxis at the enemy during the Second Battle of Bedriacum. While he does not give the weight of the saxa, they do not seem to have been of any "regular" proportions.

28   I. Ancient Rome and the Medieval Ages

18. For a reconstruction attempt of a one-talent ball-thrower as described by Vitruvius see Wilkins, *Roman Artillery*, 55–60.

19. The exact dimensions of the ships employed by the Caesar or Germanicus in North-Western Europe are unknown. Modern reconstructions give at least a general idea—thus, the well-known trireme reconstruction Olympias has a width of less than 5m (see John S. Morrison and John F. Coates, *The Athenian Trireme: The History and Reconstruction of an Ancient Greek Warship* (Cambridge: Cambridge University Press, 1995), 199), while Roman quinqueremes from the late republic and early empire are supposed to have been around 6–7m at most (see John F. Coates, "The Naval Architecture and Oar Systems of Ancient Galleys," in *The Age of the Galley*, ed. Robert Gardiner (London: Conway Maritime, 1995), 138–139).

20. The issue of space requirements for operating artillery pieces aboard ships has almost totally escaped scholarly attention; interestingly, this has not been the case with artillery towers, where issues of space and handling have been discussed, see e.g. Marsden, *Historical Development*, 126–163.

21. Caesar does not report the length of the engagement although he states that as a result of the artillery fire, the Britons pulled back a bit after a short while (paulum modo pedem rettulerunt, Caes. BG 4.25.2). The general impression Caesar's account leaves is not one of a few quick salvoes (Caes. BG 4.25.1-2).

22. Modern reconstructions can achieve higher rates of fire over short periods of time. For the sake of the calculation, a constant rate of fire has been assumed; the rate of fire has been deliberately set fairly low, as the rate of fire will have decreased the longer the engagement went.

23. Tac. Ann. 2.6.1: multae pontibus stratae, super quas tormenta veherentur.

24. The accuracy issue with ship-borne artillery does not get a lot of attention, but see, Coates, *Naval Architecture*, 135: "Judging ranges, however, must have been a matter of great skill."

25. Caesar does not state the exact number of warships he had in 55 BC; however, for the landing in 54 BC, he reports 28 warships as having been available (Caes. Gall. 5.2.2). As he lost 12 ships in 55 BC (Caes. Gall. 4.31.3), he can have employed 40 warships at most; the actual number, however, probably was much lower, as the ships lost in 54 BC will have been mostly transports.

26. Caes. Gall. 4.24.2-3.

27. Tac. Ann. 2.6.1.

28. Tac. Agr. 25.1: simul terra, simul mari bellum impelleretur.

Works Cited

Baatz, Dietwulf. *Bauten und Katapulte des römischen Heeres* (Stuttgart: Steiner, 1994).

Baatz, Dietwulf. "Katapulte und mechanische Handwaffen des spätrömischen Heeres," *Journal of Roman Military Equipment Studies* 10 (1999): 5–20.

Bosworth, Albert B. "Arrian and the Alani," *Harvard Studies in Classical Philology* 81 (1977): 217–255.

Coates, John F. "The Naval Architecture and Oar Systems of Ancient Galleys," in *the Age of the Galley*, ed. Robert Gardiner. London: Conway Maritime, 1995. 127–141.

Devoto, James G. ed., trans., *Flavius Arrianus ΤΕΧΝΗ ΤΑΚΤΙΚΑ and ἘΚΤΑΞΙΣ ΚΑΤΑ ἈΛΑΝΩΝ*. Chicago: Ares, 1998.

Harrison, Gordon A. *United States Army in World War II—The European Theater of Operations: Cross-Channel Attack*. Washington: U.S. Government Printing Office, 1951.

Kubitschek, Wilhelm. "Aus Sammlung Trau in Wien: ein Vexillum-Aufsatz," *Jahreshefte des Österreichischen Archäologischen Instituts in Wien* 29 (1934): 44–48.
Marsden, Eric W. *Greek and Roman Artillery: Historical Development.* Oxford: Clarendon Press, 1969.
Marsden, Eric W. *Greek and Roman Artillery: Technical Treatises.* Oxford: Clarendon Press, 1971.
Morrison, John S., and John F. Coates. *The Athenian Trireme: The History and Reconstruction of an Ancient Greek Warship.* Cambridge: Cambridge University Press, 1995.
Rihll, Tracey. *The Catapult: A History.* Yardley: Westholme Publishing, 2007.
Russo, Flavio. *L'artiglieria delle legion: Le macchine da guerra che resero invincibile l'escrito romano.* Rome: Istituto Poligrafico e Zecca dello Stato, 2004.
Schramm, Erwin. *Die antiken Geschütze der Saalburg: Bemerkungen zu ihrer Rekonstruktion.* Berlin: Weidmann, 1918.
Walmer Environment Study Group, *Think Globally, Act Locally.* Sandwich: Walmer Environment Study Group, 2014.
Wilkins, Alan. *Roman Artillery.* Princes Risborough: Shire publications, 2003.

Stirrup, Composite Bow and Traction Trebuchet
Some Remarks on the Interdependence of War and Technology in the Early Middle Ages

Christian Scholl

In Late Antiquity and the Early Middle Ages, a number of technological innovations such as the stirrup, the composite bow and the traction trebuchet were introduced into Europe by Nomadic peoples from East Asia. Modern research has been dealing with these devices for decades, with the stirrup having caused the most heated debates. The so-called "stirrup controversy" was triggered in 1962 by the American historian Lynn White, who saw both the military and the social foundations of Early Medieval Europe shaken by the stirrup.[1]

Taking White's view on the military implications of the stirrup as a starting point, this essay deals with the question as to what extent warfare in Early-Medieval Europe was affected by the technological innovations mentioned above. In addition, it examines the way modern research has interpreted the impact of these devices. The central thesis of this work is that the immediate effects of these innovations were often overestimated because none of them brought about a radical change in the conduct of war in the Early Middle Ages.

As already stated, the most widely discussed of the aforementioned devices is the stirrup.[2] The Byzantines had adopted this tool from the Avars around the year 600[3] before it spread to Longobard Italy in the course of the 7th century and to the Frankish kingdom in the early 8th century.[4] There, according to Lynn White, the stirrup induced a military revolution, changing the way of fighting overnight:

> The stirrup made possible [...] a vastly more effective mode of attack: Now the rider could lay his lance at rest, held between the upper arm and the body, and

make at his foe, delivering the blow not with his muscles but with the combined weight of himself and his charging stallion. The stirrup [...] effectively welded horse and rider into a single fighting unit capable of a violence without precedent. The fighter's hand no longer delivered the blow: it merely guided it. The stirrup thus replaced human energy with animal power, and immensely increased the warrior's ability to damage his enemy. Immediately [...] it made possible mounted shock combat, a revolutionary new way of doing battle.[5]

Hence, White is of the opinion that frontal attacks carried out by mounted soldiers in full gallop ("mounted shock combat") were impossible before the arrival of the stirrup. He fails to see, however, that this way of fighting had already been practiced by the heavily armored riders of Antiquity, the *clibanarii* and *cataphractarii*, who fought with long lances, but without stirrups.[6] Nevertheless, although White overestimates the importance of the stirrup, there is no doubt that it facilitated the attack with the couched lance because this device made it easier for the rider to keep his position on the horse when he hit his enemy.[7]

As Bernard Bachrach has pointed out, however, there was a device more essential for this kind of fighting: a new saddle whose front and back areas were high enough to prevent the rider from falling off his horse when colliding with the enemy. This saddle with a higher pommel and cantle was developed around 1100.[8] Consequently, it was not before this time—and thus about 400 years after the introduction of the stirrup—that fighting with the couched lance was commonly practiced by Western European knights.

This is shown by numerous pictorial sources that depict cavalrymen fighting with the couched lance from the 12th century onwards. In all pictorial sources drawn between the 8th and the 11th centuries, the cavalrymen do not fight with a long lance held in the couched position under their arms, but with a shorter spear held with one hand only (Figure 1).

Until around 1100, cavalrymen used this weapon to thrust "downwards in a stabbing motion, or upwards [...] to strike an opponent under his armor or to lift him from his horse."[9]

The pictorial sources of the 8th and early 9th centuries showing cavalrymen in combat reveal something else that contradicts White's thesis: Although these codices were created at least 100 years after the alleged "military revolution" induced by the stirrup, the riders portrayed in them do not make use of this device. It is not before the late 9th and early 10th centuries that we come across the first representations of stirrups in Western iconography (Figure 2).

As there are still several pictures from that period which show riders without stirrups, one can conclude "[f]rom manuscript illumination [...] that stirrups did not impress the Carolingian world as an important technical innovation."[10] Apart from that, even in the pictures with representations of

Figure 1. Two riders, one fighting with a spear above his head, the other with a composite bow (~ 820) (Württembergische Landesbibliothek Stuttgart, Cod. Bibl. 23, fol. 32v).

stirrups, the riders continue fighting with a spear held above their heads, which underlines the fact that the use of the stirrup by no means led to fighting with the couched lance immediately.[11]

It was not before the 11th century that stirrups had spread all over Latin Europe. This can be deduced from the most famous pictorial source of the Middle Ages, the Bayeux Tapestry, depicting scenes of the Battle of Hastings in 1066. According to this source, both Normans and even some of the Anglo-Saxons who are fleeing the battlefield in the last scene of the tapestry made use of stirrups. Thus, the pictorial sources suggest that there was a time span of more than 300 years between the first appearance of this device and its overall use in Western Europe.

This suggestion is confirmed by the written sources of the Early Middle Ages that do not mention the stirrup at all. No annals, chronicles, vitae or deeds from the 8th or 9th centuries allude to this device.[12] It is not before the end of the 10th century that the stirrup is mentioned for the first time in a Western source, namely in the histories of the monk Richer of Reims (ca. 940–998).[13] If the stirrup had been as extraordinary an innovation as Lynn White claimed, it would certainly not have taken hundreds of years before its first mentioning in the written documentation.

Concerning the stirrup, one has to conclude that both the written and the pictorial sources imply that this tool was "little used by the Carolingians during the 8th and 9th centuries."[14] As a result, the military revolution caused

Figure 2. Riders with stirrups, archers with composite bows (~ 925) (Universitätsbibliothek Leiden, Ms. PER F 17, fol. 9r).

by the stirrup in the 8th century is nothing but an invention by Lynn White; neither was this device generally used immediately after its introduction into Western Europe, nor did it exert an influence on the fighting style at once. As will be shown below, the military impact of the second weapon this article deals with, the composite bow was overestimated by a number of historians as well.

The composite bow was the characteristic weapon of Eastern nomadic tribes. This weapon is not made from only one material like the ordinary self-bow but is "a bow whose stave embodies a laminated construction involving more than one type of material, such as wood, sinew, and horn."[15] The most important advantage of the composite bow was the combination of power and shortness: the traditional "Skythian bow" used in Antiquity, for example, was between 75 and 100 cm long.[16] In order to be nearly as effective, a self-bow had to be at least twice as large.[17] The consequence of this difference in length was the fact that composite bows could be used on horseback without difficulties,[18] whereas powerful self-bows such as the English longbows of the Late Middle Ages could only be used by infantry soldiers. Shorter self-bows suitable for mounted bowmen were not powerful enough to pose a threat to an enemy.

Although composite bows were already known in Europe before the 5th century BC[19] and used by both Greeks and Romans, it was not before the invasion of the Huns in Late Antiquity that historians paid particular attention to bows and archery. Afterwards, nearly all authors who wrote about the Huns, among them Ammianus Marcellinus (ca. 330–395), Olympiodorus of Thebes (ca. 365–after 425) and Zosimus (late 5th, early 6th century), praised the Huns' capabilities in fighting with bow and arrow from a great distance.[20] Due to accounts like these, a number of modern historians named the composite bow, which was brought to Europe by the Huns from the 4th century onwards, a radically new "wonder weapon"[21]; others speak about "a military revolution" triggered by the Huns.[22]

Historians praising the "Hunnic bow" are right insofar as the bow used by the Huns was indeed more powerful than the traditional "Skythian bow" because it was larger. The "Skythian bow" generally was not longer than one meter, whereas the "Hunnic bow" had a length of 130 to 160 cm.[23] Despite its considerable size, this bow could be used on horseback because it was asymmetric; the upper part of the handle was larger than the lower.[24] However, even though the bow used by the Huns differed from and was more powerful than older models of composite bows, neither was it a "wonder weapon," nor did it cause any "revolution." After all, similar kinds of bows had already been used by the Sarmatians in the 1st century and the Sassanids in the 3rd century. Such bows had even been known to the Romans long before the "Hunnic invasion" because Sarmatian and Persian mercenaries in the Roman legions had brought these bows with them. For these reasons, the alleged "wonder weapon" of the Huns is "just a myth."[25]

Nevertheless, the Huns' way of fighting left significant traces in the Mediterranean. After their contact with Hunnic troops, both the Roman and the Byzantine armies increased their units of mounted archers equipped with composite bows significantly, for example by recruiting Hunnic mercenaries.[26] The new importance of archery warfare becomes even more evident in the fact that by the 6th century, historians started to praise this kind of fighting, whereas military theorists of the past, such as Vegetius (late 4th century), had a low opinion of them.[27]

The Byzantine historiographer Procopius of Caesarea (ca. 500–562), who gives accounts of the wars the Byzantines fought against the Persians, Vandals and Ostrogoths in the 6th century, is the first author who portrays the archers of his time—both the Roman and Persian ones—in the best light, thus renouncing the view that the soldiers of the present are less brave than those of the past:

> [T]he bowmen of the present are expert horsemen, and are able without difficulty to direct their bows to either side while riding at full speed, and to shoot an opponent whether in pursuit or in flight. They [...] charge the arrow with such an impetus as to kill whoever stands in the way, shield and corselet alike having no power to check its force. Still there are those who take into consideration none of these things, who reverence and worship the ancient times [...]. But no such consideration will prevent the conclusion that most great and noble deeds have been performed in these wars.[28]

In his book about the Gothic War, Procopius not only repeats that "all the Romans and their allies, the Huns, are excellent mounted bowmen" but also goes on to claim that the military supremacy of the Byzantines over the Goths solely went back to the fact that "not a single man among the Goths has had practice in this branch, for their horsemen are accustomed to use only spears and swords, while their bowmen enter battle on foot."[29] Even if this statement is exaggerated—the Goths did not fight as statically as described by Procopius, and they lost the war primarily because of the economic superiority of the Byzantine Empire and not due to the lack of mounted bowmen—it gives evidence of the great influence mounted archers armed with composite bows exerted on warfare in the Early Middle Ages.

Considering the importance of composite bows, it is not surprising that the Romans and Byzantines were not the only ones adopting this weapon. Nearly all "Germanic" tribes who came in contact with the Huns or Avars, among them the Langobards, Alemanni and Franks, adopted composite bows. As the scarce archaeological evidence of bow and arrow between the 5th and the 7th centuries suggests, they did so, however, for prestige only.[30] However, the mere fact that the composite bow became an important symbol of power in the Early Middle Ages hints at its military significance.

It was not before the Carolingian era that composite bows became widely used in Central Europe not only for symbolic but also for military reasons.[31] In particular, the significance of mounted archers fighting with composite bows increased considerably at that time. This is far from surprising, as the Carolingian armies fought against two enemies who were well versed in this kind of warfare: the Muslims in the Southwest and after the incorporation of Bavaria into the Frankish kingdom in the 780s, the Avars in the Southeast.

The growing importance of archery in Carolingian times can be deduced from a significant increase of sources mentioning bows and arrows.[32] Although most of these sources do not provide further information on the bows, there is one poem from the 9th century that mentions a Frankish warrior holding a bow composed of several materials, among them horn, which

36   I. Ancient Rome and the Medieval Ages

clearly hints at a composite bow.[33] Further evidence for the use of composite bows in Carolingian times is given by a number of pictorial sources. Composite bows are shown, for example, in both the psalter of Stuttgart, dating from around 820, and the Leiden Maccabee manuscript from the early 10th century (Figures 1 and 2).[34]

In the late Carolingian era, a new distance weapon came into use: the crossbow. Crossbows had been already used in Ancient Greece and Rome,[35] but they were not known in Early Medieval Latin Europe. As was the case with the stirrup, the first Medieval author to mention "arcubalistae" was Richer of Reims.[36] The first visual representation of a crossbow was already found about a century before in a commentary on the Book Ezekiel written by Haimo of Auxerre (9th century). The illustration (Figure 3) shows the siege of Jerusalem, and the crossbows used by two of the besiegers have arms with recurved ends, a fact that provides the possibility that this new powerful weapon evolved from the composite bow.[37] The assumption that Haimo just copied representations of ancient crossbows can be excluded because his crossbow representations differ from ancient ones. For example, as far as the locking mechanism is concerned, the crossbows depicted by Haimo prove superior to ancient models.[38]

Figure 3. First representation of crossbows (9th century) (Bibliothèque Nationale de France, Paris, Ms. Lat. 12302, fol. 1r).

Thus, concerning the composite bow, one can conclude that the Franks not only adopted this weapon from Eastern Nomadic tribes but also developed it further into the crossbow. The last innovation this article deals with is also a distance weapon: the trebuchet. This weapon was brought to Europe by the Avars when they invaded the Balkan Peninsula in the 6th century.

The first source mentioning a new kind of siege weapon was the *Miracula Sancti Demetrii*, composed around 610 by John, bishop of Thessaloniki (late 6th, early 7th century). In this source, the bishop describes the siege of his town by the Avars in the late 6th century. According to this account, the Avars used more than 50 siege engines, which John calls *petroboloi* ("rock-throwers"), and describes them as follows:

> These *petroboloi* had quadrilateral [trusses] that were wider at the base and became progressively narrower toward the top. Attached to these machines were thick axles plated with iron at the ends, and there were nailed to them pieces of timber like beams of a large house. Hanging from the back side of these pieces of timber were slings and from the front strong ropes, by which, pulling down and releasing the sling, they propel the stones up high and with a loud noise. And on being discharged they sent up many great stones so that neither earth nor human constructions could withstand the impacts.[39]

As this description demonstrates, the machines employed by the Avars during the siege of Thessaloniki differed fundamentally from the siege engines of Antiquity.[40] Whereas the latter were torsion catapults which discharged missiles by releasing twisted ropes, the trebuchets used by the Avars were based on the lever principle. These machines consisted of a beam attached to an axle and at the end of the shorter arm of the beam, pulling ropes were attached. When the ropes were pulled down, the longer arm swung upward and released the projectile. This kind of artillery was unknown in ancient Europe but had already been used in China between the 5th and 3rd centuries BC.[41] Thus, it is probable that the Avars had become acquainted with this technology in Asia and exported it from there to Europe.

The sources imply that the trebuchets used by the Avars were much more powerful than any kind of artillery used before. In the aforementioned *Miracula Sancti Demetrii*, for example, the author speaks about "mountains and hills" that were hurled against the city of Thessaloniki.[42] Although the sources tend to exaggerate or highlight special engines of an extraordinary size—an Arab source of the 13th century mentions a gigantic trebuchet with a crew of 1200 men, which is far from realistic[43]—the power of traction trebuchets has been confirmed by a number of reconstructions.[44] Apart from its firepower, traction artillery had the advantage of simplicity, which made it possible to quickly erect and dismantle these machines during a siege. Torsion catapults, on the other hand, were quite sophisticated and much more difficult to construct and handle—complexity combined with high costs and even little firepower was one of the main reasons why the Roman army abandoned the two-armed torsion catapult in Late Antiquity.[45]

An army equipped with traction trebuchets doubtlessly had an advantage in siege warfare, and it is not surprising that the Avars succeeded in conquering a number of Byzantine castles in the late 6th and early 7th centuries, and the Byzantines as well as the Arabs adopted the traction trebuchet quite rapidly.[46] However, even though the traction trebuchet was a weapon more powerful than ancient torsion catapults, it was not powerful enough to cause a "revolution" in siege warfare. After all, a large pulling crew was needed to throw heavy stones suitable for destroying enemy fortifications, but both for reasons of coordination and mechanics, the crews could hardly consist of more than 50 men.[47] Consequently, it was nearly impossible to destroy a strong fortification by traction trebuchets. This could not be achieved before a new kind of trebuchet using a counterweight instead of a pulling crew was invented in the High Middle Ages.[48]

Thus, altogether one can say that the technological innovations brought to Europe in the Early Middle Ages exerted a significant influence on warfare. The stirrup, for example, at least alleviated fighting with the couched lance even though it was not vital for this kind of combat. Without the composite bow, there would have been hardly any mounted archers in the Middle Ages because the ordinary self-bow made from wood was not an effective weapon when used on horseback. The traction trebuchet, finally, superseded the torsion catapults of Antiquity both in range and power, so it was far more effective in siege warfare than its ancient predecessor.

None of these innovations, however, brought about a "military revolution," changing the way of fighting overnight, as argued by researchers of the past and present. The stirrup was known in Central Europe from 700 AD onwards, but it took at least 200 years until it was commonly used and another 200 years until it played a role in "shock combat" with the couched lance. The composite bow had been known to the Romans all through Antiquity, but it did not play a major part in their armies before the 4th/5th centuries. In Central Europe, it even took until the 8th century before archers fighting with composite bows became an integral part of the army and another 200 years until the more powerful crossbow arose out of the composite bow. Even the traction trebuchet was not powerful enough to revolutionize siege warfare; profound changes in this kind of war did not occur before the development of the counterweight trebuchet in the High Middle Ages.

Therefore, one can finally conclude that in the Early Middle Ages, it was a matter of centuries—and not just decades or years as in the modern period—until a new technology or technical device resulted in a new form of fighting or a "revolutionary" new kind of weapon.

Notes

1. Lynn T. White, *Medieval Technology and Social Change* (Oxford: Oxford University Press, 1962), 38. In his monograph, White goes so far as to maintain that the social system of the Middle Ages, commonly called feudalism, was solely based on the stirrup. Thus, his thesis, which draws on the German historian Heinrich Brunner, is a classic example of a technical determinism that attributes the radical change of society to one single technological device. It is hardly surprising that White's thesis about feudalism arising from the stirrup has provoked harsh criticism, with the first critical review having appeared just one year after the publication of his monograph, cf. P.H. Sawyer and R.H. Hilton, "Technical Determinism: The Stirrup and the Plough," *Past & Present* 24 (1963): 90–100. Meanwhile, modern research has completely refuted White's claim about the origins of feudalism, cf. Herwig Wolfram, "Karl Martell und das fränkische Lehnswesen: Aufnahme eines Nichtbestandes," in *Karl Martell in seiner Zeit*, ed. Jörg Jarnut, Ulrich Nonn and Michael Richter (Sigmaringen: Jan Thorbecke, 1994), 64. If modern researchers nowadays refer to White in writing about the beginnings of feudalism, they do so "rather for the sake of curiosity" ("mehr kuriositätshalber"), cf. Reinhard Schneider, *Das Frankenreich*, 4th edition (München: Oldenbourg, 2001), 124.
2. A summary of the debate about the military implications of the stirrup is given by Kelly DeVries and Robert D. Smith, *Medieval Military Technology*, 2nd edition (Toronto: University of Toronto Press, 2012), 100–114.
3. The stirrup is first mentioned in a military treatise written between 570 and 630 and generally attributed to the Byzantine Emperor Mauricios (539–602), cf. George T. Dennis, trans., *Maurice's Strategikon: Handbook of Byzantine Military Strategy* (Philadelphia: University of Pennsylvania Press, 1984), 30.
4. Cf. for the spread of the stirrup to the Longobards Dieter Hägermann and Helmuth Schneider, Propyläen Technikgeschichte, vol. 1: Landbau und Handwerk. 750 v. Chr. bis 1000 n. Chr. (Berlin: Propyläen Verlag, 1997); 439, for the spread to the Frankish kingdom Florin Curta, "The earliest Avar-Age Stirrups, or the 'Stirrup Controversy' Revisited," in *The Other Europe in the Middle Ages*, ed. Florin Curta (Leiden, Boston: Brill, 2008), 297.
5. White, *Medieval Technology*, 2.
6. Karen R. Dixon and Pat Southern, *The Roman Cavalry* (London: B.T. Batsford, 1992), 141; Marcus Junkelmann, *Die Reiter Roms*, vol. 3: *Zubehör, Reitweise, Bewaffnung* (Mainz: Philipp von Zabern, 1992), 100–120.
7. The importance of the stirrup for the attack with the couched lance is mentioned by Malte Prietzel, *Krieg im Mittelalter* (Darmstadt: Wissenschaftliche Buchgesellschaft, 2006), 25.
8. Bernard S. Bachrach, "Animals and Warfare in Early Medieval Europe," *Settimane di Studio del Centro Italiano di sull'alto Medioevo* 31 (1985): 746–747.
9. DeVries and Smith, *Medieval Military Technology*, 11.
10. Bernard S. Bachrach, "Charles Martel, Mounted Shock Combat, the Stirrup, and Feudalism," *Studies in Medieval and Renaissance History* 7 (1970): 60.
11. Dieter Hägermann, "Das Karolingische Imperium: Ein Resultat kriegstechnischer Innovationen?" *Technikgeschichte* 59 (1992): 309.
12. Hägermann, *Das Karolingische Imperium*, 308; Bachrach, *Charles Martel*, 57.
13. Hartmut Hoffmann, ed., *Richer von Saint-Remi: Historiae* (Hannover: Hahnsche Buchhandlung, 2000), 100.
14. Bachrach, *Charles Martel*, 65.

40   I. Ancient Rome and the Medieval Ages

15. Otto Maenchen-Helfen, *The World of the Huns: Studies in their History and Culture* (Berkeley, Los Angeles, London: University of California Press, 1973), 223. For different types of composite bows cf. Charles Grayson, "Composite Bows," in *The Traditional Bowyer's Bible*, vol. 2, ed. Jim Hamm (New York: Lyons Press, 1993), 113–154.
    16. John C. Coulston, "Roman Archery Equipment," in *The Production and Distribution of Roman Military Equipment: Proceedings of the Second Roman Military Equipment Research Seminar*, ed. Christopher M. Bishop (Oxford: BAR 1985), 241.
    17. Holger Riesch, "Quod nullus in hostem habeat baculum sed arcum: Pfeil und Bogen als Beispiel für technologische Innovationen der Karolingerzeit," *Technikgeschichte* 61 (1994): 210.
    18. Walter Pohl, *Die Awaren: Ein Steppenvolk in Mitteleuropa, 567–822 n. Chr.*, 2nd edition (München: C.H. Beck, 2002), 170; Riesch, Pfeil und Bogen, 211.
    19. Erhard Godehardt, "Der skythische Bogen," in *Reflexbogen: Geschichte und Herstellung*, ed. Volker Alles (Ludwigshafen: Hörning, 2009), 30.
    20. John C. Rolfe, trans. and ed., *Ammianus Marcellinus*, vol. 3 (London and Cambridge, Mass.: William Heinemann and Harvard University Press, 1939), 385: "And on this account, you would not hesitate to call them [= the Huns] the most terrible of all warriors, because they fight from a distance with missiles having sharp bone [...] joined to the shafts with wonderful skill"; Roger C. Blockley, *The Fragmentary Classicising Historians of the Later Roman Empire: Eunapius, Olympiodorus, Priscus and Malchus*, vol. 2 (Liverpool: Francis Cairns, 1983), 183: "[Olympiodorus] discusses Donatus and the Huns and the natural talent of their kings for archery"; Ronald T. Ridley, trans., *Zosimus: A New History* (Canberra: Central Printing Australian National University, 1982), 79: "They [= the Huns] were totally incapable and ignorant of conducting a battle on foot, but by [...] shooting from their horses, they wrought immense slaughter."
    21. The term "wonder weapon" ("Wunderwaffe") is used, for example, by István Bóna, *Das Hunnenreich* (Stuttgart: Theis, 1971), 167.
    22. Peter Heather, *The Fall of the Roman Empire: A New History of Rome and the Barbarians* (Oxford: Oxford University Press, 2007), 158.
    23. Coulston, *Roman Archery Equipment*, 243; Heather, *Fall of the Roman Empire*, 156.
    24. Holger Riesch, "Reflexbogen, Reiterköcher und Steppenpfeile: Elemente des asiatischen Bogenschießens in Europa von der Spätantike bis zur Zeit der Renaissance," in *Reflexbogen: Geschichte und Herstellung*, ed. Volker Alles (Ludwigshafen: Hörning, 2009), 73.
    25. Riesch, *Reflexbogen, Reiterköcher und Steppenpfeile*, 74.
    26. Ridley, *Zosimus*, 125: "This done, the emperor [Honorius] summoned ten thousand Huns as allies."
    27. N.P. Milner, trans., *Vegetius: Epitome of Military Science* (Liverpool: Liverpool University Press, 1993), 20: "The result is that those who in battle are exposed unprotected to wounds, think not about fighting but fleeing. For what is a foot-archer to do, without a cataphract or a helmet, when he cannot hold a shield along with a bow?" According to Volker Schmidtchen, distance weapons were generally disregarded in the Western World from Antiquity onwards, cf. Volker Schmidtchen, "Sieg der Technik? Anmerkungen zur Rolle und Bedeutung von Waffen und Gerät für Streitkräfte in Krieg und Frieden," in *Sozialgeschichte der Technik: Ulrich Troitzsch zum 60. Geburtstag*, ed. Günter Bayerl and Wolfhard Weber (Münster et al.: Waxmann, 1998), 169.
    28. H.B. Dewing, ed., trans., *Procopius*, vol. 1 (London and Cambridge, Mass.: William Heinemann and Harvard University Press, 1971), 7–9.

29. H.B. Dewing, trans. and ed., *Procopius*, vol. 3 (London and Cambridge, Mass.: William Heinemann and Harvard University Press, 1968), 261.
30. Andreas Bracher, "Der Reflexbogen als Beispiel gentiler Bewaffnung," in *Typen der Ethnogenese unter besonderer Berücksichtigung der Bayern*, vol. 1, ed. Herwig Wolfram and Walter Pohl (Wien: Verlag der Österreichischen Akademie der Wissenschaften, 1990), 145.
31. DeVries and Smith, *Medieval Military Technology*, 37.
32. Examples are given by Riesch, *Pfeil und Bogen*, 219–221.
33. Ernst Dümmler, ed., "Ermoldus Nigellus: Carmen in Honorem Hludovivi," in *MGH Poetae Latini Aevi Carolini*, vol. 2, ed. Ernst Dümmler (Berlin: Weidmann, 1884), 16.
34. Bracher, *Reflexbogen*, 145, and others have argued that the pictorial sources of the Carolingian era do not give any insights into the "reality" of that time because they followed ancient examples. However, as the depiction of stirrups in the Leiden codex shows, artists of the Early Middle Ages did include innovations unknown to Antiquity in their works. Apart from that, research in art history has shown that Carolingian iconography by no means confined itself to copying ancient motifs, but rather referred to the recent past or contemporary "reality" to create its pictures, cf. Riesch, "Pfeil und Bogen," 213.
35. DeVries and Smith, *Medieval Military Technology*, 42.
36. Hoffmann, *Richer von Saint-Remi*, 227.
37. Riesch, *Pfeil und Bogen*, 222.
38. Egon Harmuth, "Die Armbrustbilder des Haimo von Auxerre," *Waffen- und Kostümkunde: Zeitschrift der Gesellschaft für historische Waffen- und Kostümkunde* 12 (1970): 130.
39. Paul Lemerle, trans. and ed., *Les plus anciens recueils des miracles de Saint Démétrius et la pénétration des Slaves dans les Balkans*, vol.1 (Paris: Éditions du centre national de la recherche scientifique, 1979), 143, 154. English translation in Paul Cheveddon, "The Invention of the Counterweight Trebuchet: A Study in Cultural Diffusion," *Dumbarton Oaks Papers* 54 (2000): 74.
40. For the difference between traction and torsion artillery cf. Carroll M. Gillmor, "The Introduction of the Traction Trebuchet into the Latin West," *Viator: Medieval and Renaissance Studies* 12 (1981): 2.
41. Liang Jieming, *Chinese Siege Warfare: Mechanical Artillery & Siege Weapons of Antiquity. An illustrated History* (Singapore: Leong Kit Meng, 2006), 19.
42. Cheveddon, *Invention of the Counterweight Trebuchet*, 74.
43. Mark Feuerle, "Das Hebelwurfgeschütz: Eine technische Innovation des Mittelalters," *Technikgeschichte* 69 (2002): 10–11.
44. W.T.S. Tarver, for example, had two traction trebuchets reconstructed in 1989 and 1991. The machine of 1991 could discharge a 4.7 kg ball a distance of about 100 m with a crew of sixteen pullers. A ball of 3.1 kg could even be thrown 145 m by fourteen pullers, cf. W.T.S. Tarver, "The Traction Trebuchet: A Reconstruction of an Early Medieval Siege Engine," *Technology and Culture* 36 (1995): 162.
45. Paul E. Cheveddon, "Artillery in Late Antiquity: Prelude to the Middle Ages," in *The Medieval City under Siege*, ed. Ivy A. Corfis and Michael Wolfe (Woodbridge: The Boydell Press, 1995), 163.
46. Although the first unequivocal evidence for the traction trebuchet in Byzantium is not found before 1071 (cf. Gillmor, "Introduction of the Traction Trebuchet," 1–2), a passage in the chronicle of the Byzantine historian Theophylact Simocatta (ca. 580–640) about the siege of a Persian castle by Emperor Heraclius (ca. 575–641) hints

at the use of trebuchets, cf. Michael and Mary Whitby, trans. *The History of Theophylact Simocatta: An English Translation with Introduction and Notes* (Oxford: Oxford University Press, 1986), 68. According to this passage, the Byzantines bombarded the castle itself, which they hardly would have done with ancient torsion artillery because this was basically an anti-personnel weapon. Besides, Simocatta mentions the labors of the people operating the machine, which probably alludes to the hard work of the pulling crews. The Arabs used traction trebuchets probably by the late 7th and doubtlessly in the 9th century, cf. Donald R. Hill, "Trebuchets," *Viator: Medieval and Renaissance Studies* 4 (1974): 100–102.

47. For the difficulties arising from large crews operating traction trebuchets cf. Feuerle, *Hebelwurfgeschütz*, 11.

48. For the debate about the origin of the counterweight trebuchet cf. Feuerle, *Hebelwurfgeschütz*, 36.

Works Cited

Primary Sources

Blockley, Roger C. *The Fragmentary Classicising Historians of the Later Roman Empire: Eunapius, Olympiodorus, Priscus and Malchus*, vol. 2. Liverpool: Francis Cairns, 1983.

Dennis, George T. trans. *Maurice's Strategikon: Handbook of Byzantine Military Strategy*. Philadelphia: University of Pennsylvania Press, 1984.

Dewing, H.B. ed., trans. *Procopius*, vol. 1. London and Cambridge, Mass.: William Heinemann and Harvard University Press, 1971.

Dewing, H.B. ed., trans. *Procopius*, vol. 3. London and Cambridge, Mass.: William Heinemann and Harvard University Press, 1968.

Dümmler, Ernst ed. "Ermoldus Nigellus: Carmen in Honorem Hludovivi Imperatoris," in *MGH Poetae Latini Aevi Carolini*, vol. 2, ed. Ernst Dümmler. Berlin: Weidmann, 1884, 5–79.

Hoffmann, Hartmut ed. *Richer von Saint-Remi: Historiae*. Hannover: Hahnsche Buchhandlung, 2000.

Lemerle, Paul ed., trans. *Les plus anciens recueils des miracles de Saint Démétrius et la pénétration des Slaves dans les Balkans*, vol.1. Paris: Éditions du centre national de la recherche scientifique, 1979.

Milner, N.P. trans. *Vegetius: Epitome of Military Science*. Liverpool: Liverpool University Press, 1993.

Rolfe, John C. ed., trans. *Ammianus Marcellinus*, vol. 3. London and Cambridge, Mass.: William Heinemann and Harvard University Press, 1939.

Ridley, Ronald T. trans. *Zosimus: A New History*. Canberra: Central Printing Australian National University, 1982.

Whitby, Michael, and Mary Whitby trans. *The History of Theophylact Simocatta: An English Translation with Introduction and Notes*. Oxford: Oxford University Press, 1986.

Secondary Sources

Bachrach, Bernhard S. "Charles Martel, Mounted Shock Combat, the Stirrup, and Feudalism," *Studies in Medieval and Renaissance History* 7 (1970): 35–75.

Bachrach, Bernhard S. "Animals and Warfare in Early Medieval Europe," *Settimane di Studio del Centro Italiano di sull'alto Medioevo* 31 (1985): 707–751.

Bóna, István. *Das Hunnenreich*. Stuttgart: Theis, 1971.

Bracher, Andreas. "Der Reflexbogen als Beispiel gentiler Bewaffnung," in *Typen der Ethnogenese unter besonderer Berücksichtigung der Bayern*, vol. 1, ed. Wolfram Herwig and Walter Pohl. Wien: Verlag der Österreichischen Akademie der Wissenschaften, 1990, 137-146.

Cheveddon, Paul E. "Artillery in Late Antiquity: Prelude to the Middle Ages," in *The Medieval City under Siege*, ed. Ivy A. Corfis and Michael Wolfe. Woodbridge: The Boydell Press, 1995, 131-173.

Cheveddon, Paul E. "The Invention of the Counterweight Trebuchet: A Study in Cultural Diffusion," *Dumbarton Oaks Papers* 54 (2000): 71-116.

Coulston, John C. "Roman Archery Equipment," in *The Production and Distribution of Roman Military Equipment: Proceedings of the Second Roman Military Equipment Research Seminar*, ed. Christopher M. Bishop. Oxford: BAR, 1985, 220-366.

Curta, Florin. "The earliest Avar-Age Stirrups, or the 'Stirrup Controversy' Revisited," in *The Other Europe in the Middle Ages*, ed. Florin Curta. Leiden and Boston: Brill, 2008, 297-326.

DeVries, Kelly, and Robert D. Smith. *Medieval Military Technology*, 2nd edition. Toronto: University of Toronto Press, 2012.

Dixon, Karen R., and Pat Southern. *The Roman Cavalry*. London: B.T. Batsford, 1992.

Feuerle, Mark. "Das Hebelwurfgeschütz: Eine technische Innovation des Mittelalters," *Technikgeschichte* 69 (2002): 1-39.

Gillmor, Carroll M. "The Introduction of the Traction Trebuchet into the Latin West," *Viator: Medieval and Renaissance Studies* 12 (1981): 1-8.

Godehardt, Erhard "Der skythische Bogen," in *Reflexbogen: Geschichte und Herstellung*, ed. Volker Alles. Ludwigshafen: Hörning, 2009, 27-59.

Grayson, Charles. "Composite Bows," in *The Traditional Bowyer's Bible*, vol. 2, ed. Jim Hamm. New York: Lyons Press, 1993, 113-154.

Hägermann, Dieter. "Das Karolingische Imperium: Ein Resultat kriegstechnischer Innovationen?" *Technikgeschichte* 59 (1992): 305-317.

Hägermann, Dieter, and Helmuth Schneider. *Propyläen Technikgeschichte, vol. 1: Landbau und Handwerk. 750 v. Chr. bis 1000 n. Chr.* Berlin: Propyläen Verlag, 1997.

Harmuth, Egon. "Die Armbrustbilder des Haimo von Auxerre," *Waffen- und Kostümkunde: Zeitschrift der Gesellschaft für historische Waffen- und Kostümkunde* 12 (1970): 127-130.

Heather, Peter. *The Fall of the Roman Empire: A New History of Rome and the Barbarians.* Oxford: Oxford University Press, 2007.

Hill, Donald R. "Trebuchets," *Viator: Medieval and Renaissance Studies* 4 (1973): 99-116.

Liang, Jieming. *Chinese Siege Warfare: Mechanical Artillery & Siege Weapons of Antiquity. An Illustrated History.* Singapore: Leong Kit Meng, 2006.

Junkelmann, Marcus. *Die Reiter Roms, vol. 3: Zubehör, Reitweise, Bewaffnung.* Mainz: Verlag Philipp von Zabern, 1992.

Maenchen-Helfen, Otto. *The World of the Huns. Studies in their History and Culture.* Berkeley, Los Angeles, London: University of California Press, 1973.

Pohl, Walter. *Die Awaren: Ein Steppenvolk in Mitteleuropa, 567-822 n. Chr.*, 2nd Edition. München: C.H. Beck, 2002.

Prietzel, Malte. *Krieg im Mittelalter.* Darmstadt: Wissenschaftliche Buchgesellschaft, 2006.

Riesch, Holger. "Quod nullus in hostem habeat baculum sed arcum: Pfeil und Bogen als Beispiel für technologische Innovationen der Karolingerzeit," *Technikgeschichte* 61 (1994): 209-226.

Riesch, Holger. "Reflexbogen, Reiterköcher und Steppenpfeile: Elemente des asiatischen Bogenschießens in Europa von der Spätantike bis zur Zeit der Renaissance," in *Reflexbogen: Geschichte und Herstellung*, ed. Volker Alles. Ludwigshafen: Hörning, 2009, 71–113.

Sawyer, P.H., and R.H. Hilton. "Technical Determinism: The Stirrup and the Plough," *Past & Present* 24 (1963): 90–100.

Schmidtchen, Volker. "Sieg der Technik? Anmerkungen zur Rolle und Bedeutung von Waffen und Gerät für Streitkräfte in Krieg und Frieden," in *Sozialgeschichte der Technik. Ulrich Troitzsch zum 60. Geburtstag*, ed. Günter Bayerl and Wolfhard Weber. Münster, New York, München and Berlin: Waxmann, 1998, 163–170.

Schneider, Reinhard. *Das Frankenreich*, 4th Edition. München: Oldenbourg, 2001.

Tarver, W.T.S. "The Traction Trebuchet: A Reconstruction of an Early Medieval Siege Engine," *Technology and Culture* 36 (1995): 136–167.

White, Lynn T. *Medieval Technology and Social Change*. Oxford: Oxford University Press, 1962.

Wolfram, Herwig. "Karl Martell und das fränkische Lehnswesen: Aufnahme eines Nichtbestandes," in *Karl Martell in seiner Zeit*, ed. Jörg Jarnut, Ulrich Nonn and Michael Richter. Sigmaringen: Jan Thorbecke Verlag, 1994, 61–78.

The Medieval Arms Race
The Confrontation of Orient and Occident in the Crusades and the Reconquista

THOMAS SCHUETZ

This essay takes a closer look at the relationship between technological innovations and warfare from the 11th to the 13th centuries, with a special focus on the impact of the confessional conflict between Latin Christendom and Western Islam.

The expansion of Islam as a system of governance and ideology from the middle of the 8th century and the subsequent recapturing of large parts of some of these territories by their Christian opponents from the 11th century onward created areas of intercultural exchange in Sicily, on the Iberian Peninsula and in Palestine,[1] where the possibility for a creative exchange between both cultures enriched the Latin world with the antique heritage preserved in Arabic translations as well as independent achievements of Islamic scientists.[2] These are well-established facts because we have a wide-ranging written tradition concerning medicine, philosophy or astrology; the stimulation of European developments through the reception of Islamic wisdom in the medieval times has been a historiographical subject ever since.[3]

However, in this context, the history of medieval technology has been neglected. Apart from very few exceptions,[4] medieval technological experts have remained silent, and we have to work with sometimes ambivalent and always scarce information from second-hand written and material sources. Certain ongoing popular debates concerning questions like when the first cannons were used or what the exact design of a weapon at a definite time looked like cannot be answered; the material sources are much too scarce and the literary tradition is by far not exact enough to go into such details.[5] Nevertheless, the assumption of Azar Gat that the armament of pre-modern times remained pretty much unchanged over centuries seems to be exaggerated as well.[6]

The thesis of this paper is that the confrontation of Orient and Occident in the Crusades and the Reconquista created an environment for the development of innovative technological solutions in warfare. I would like to define this position in the following three steps: First, we need to take a look at the relevant socio-economic frame in both cultural spheres to understand the contemporary meaning of technology and warfare; second, we need to describe how the long-lasting confessional conflict altered these settings; and finally, we need to show how the resulting technological innovations can be traced in the sources and where the inspiration for these innovations originated.

Social hindrances for innovative technologies can be traced in both cultural spheres. Among Latin Christendom, the phenomenon of craft guilds created production conditions that limited the creativity and flexibility of the individual technician in a significant matter; nevertheless, certain innovative technologies, preeminently printing, flourished under these exact conditions. It had been assumed in the older historiography, namely the Historical Materialism, that the Islamic institution of *futuūah* had a comparable influence to the European craft guilds.[7] Both were essentially religious confraternities of craftsmen of the same occupation, and they often lived in the same quarters. However, while the European craft guilds often controlled the economic and legal conditions of their crafts—at least on a local level—the Islamic *futuūah* had never been in such a strong position. The administration, taxation and quality control were either under the control of the educated Islamic elites, the 'ulamā, or in the hands of the sovereign. The structure of the patrilineal-craftsman families among Muslims and among the Muslims' Christian or Jewish subjects created relations of production that bore certain hindrances towards innovations. Because comparably large families had to be fed and employed, methods of mechanization and rationalization[8] were of no concern, and because one patrilineal-craftsman family had the exclusive privilege for one field of production in a certain community,[9] neither stimulation through competition nor through the exchange of technology was a common phenomenon.

Before the age of the Crusades, cultural practices that aimed to limit the consequences of warfare can be traced in both cultural spheres.[10] In the 10th century, the Latin-Christian world saw the *Pax Dei* and *Treuga Dei* movement, which focused on limiting the feuds by putting certain days, social groups and buildings under sacrosanct protection and binding the nobility through vows to accept these boundaries.[11] The Augustinian theory of just war[12] played a crucial part in the legitimation of warfare, and knightly rules of engagement developed alongside with the establishment of models for aristocratic behavior.[13]

Meanwhile, on the other side of the Mediterranean, the commitment of every Muslim to fight as ġāzī until the final victory of Islam was predominantly neglected, and warfare was the responsibility of a relatively small group of mercenaries and slaves. The later slave soldiers who were mainly of Turkic origin—known as mamlūk or ghulam—were established in the aftermath of the Abbasid revolution. In inner cultural conflicts, like in the case of the frequently-fought wars of succession, the loss in combat was seen as divine intervention—an interpretation that showed a remarkable resemblance to the Christian practice of ordeal.

Technological innovative weaponry—or weapons that seemed to be new to the contemporary—appeared to endanger this equilibrium. As the reception of the crossbow in the West shows, it is not a new weapon for the historian; there are proofs of Hellenistic Gastraphetes and Roman Ballistae. However, when the medieval European crossbow appeared, the connotation was that of an unknightly and unchristian weapon.[14] Such a perception was reflected by the churchly ban of the weapon pronounced in 1139 at the Second Council of the Lateran when the use of bows was banned as well. This ban wasn't enough to let the crossbow disappear; we have numerous proofs of castles and towns equipped with crossbows and victims of bolts from crossbows. Nevertheless, the actual utilization of this weapon doesn't mean that its use was accepted. Archaeological finds of bolts at the scene of Hastings document the use of crossbows during this battle of 1066, but on the Bayeux Tapestry, there are no crossbows displayed.

This example shows that it would be an exaggeration to claim that medieval inner cultural conflicts have been ritualized comparable to Lorenz's theory of ritualization concerning tribal warfare.[15] Combatants and civilians still got wounded, disabled and killed, and resources were destroyed.[16] Nonetheless, it can be summarized that in both cultural spheres, the inner cultural warfare was limited to military experts and aimed at subjugating the enemy and integrating the enemies' resources into one's own wealth. The complete annihilation of the enemy, his followers, his resources and infrastructure could not be the desired aim.

In the confrontation of the Latin-Christian cultural sphere and the Arabic-Islamic cultural sphere, these inner cultural rules of engagement and social hindrances for technological experts lost all significance.[17] Irrespective of whether the concept of Holy War and militis christiani has been influenced by the ideas of jihad and ġāzī or not,[18] the Catholic Christians were as determined in their absolute claim as the Sunni Muslims were. While acts of mercy have been common practice in inner cultural conflicts—whether as a result of true religious devotion or political strategy—numerous massacres of civilians or prisoners appeared during the Age of Crusades.[19]

For the question we are concerned with, the interdependence of technology and warfare, these conditions opened new fields of practice to technical experts. As we have seen, both cultures knew military experts—knights and *mamlūks*—but the responsibility for the development of siege engines and fortifications was in the hands of the master-builder or his Arabic equivalent, the *muhandis*. Master-builder and *muhandis* needed to be versed in the practices of military and civilian engineering, architecture, sculpture and structural design. These occupational areas had not yet been differentiated.[20] In addition, they both stood in the Greco-Roman tradition of architect-engineers and were both still very closely linked to the social frame of craftsmanship. They passed their knowledge through verbal and practical education from master to apprentice, often within families, and their literate education seemed to be marginal. Even though there are indications of an interaction between *muhandis* and scientists in the Islamic world in the late 10th century, the practical works of the mathematician Abū al-Wafā' al-Būzjānī (940–998)[21] and the Portfolio of Villard de Honnecourt from the 13th century include more Euclidian geometry than was used by Roman architects.[22] Still, apart from the reception of mathematics, new technologies from China were of central importance.

During the phase of expansion, the Islamic Empire came in contact with the Chinese cultural area and adopted a number of established Chinese technologies that had been unknown in Central Asia. Among them were paper, gunpowder and printing. Paper and gunpowder were transferred first in the Arabic speaking world[23] and later in the West, while printing—as Mitterauer has shown—soon sank into oblivion.[24]

In this context, two innovative technologies that originated in China were of central importance in the Near East when Orient and Occident fought for dominance: gunpowder[25] and the trebuchet—a catapult that used the energy from of a raised counterweight to throw a projectile. Because of the rather fragmented sources, it is impossible to describe the following trends in the uses and developments of these innovative weapons in detail, but a certain evolution can be traced.

The Chinese invention of black powder was used not as a propellant, but rather as a fire accelerant. Ceramic pots, filled with black powder and other inflammables, were hurled over the walls, aiming to harm defenders with fire and smoke.[26] With the innovative siege engine of the trebuchet— also of Chinese origin—the range of the projectiles increased considerably.

Ever since the reception of the portfolio of Villard de Honnecourt from the 13th century inspired Eugène Viollet-le-Duc (1814–1879) to reconstruct a trebuchet in the midst of the 19th century, uncountable trebuchets have been built over Europe and North America. The numerous experiments with these reconstructions have shown that the trebuchet was at least equal or superior in range to all older types of war engines and personal ranged weapons. Modern tests with reconstructed Trebuchets reached ranges of 150 to 200 meters, and it has be estimated that elaborate trebuchets had a range from up to 550 meters while the Welsh longbow only reached up to 300 meters at best.[27] Even though these numbers are profoundly speculative, it can be noted that before the advent of the cannon, the only defensive weapon against a trebuchet was another trebuchet.[28]

The projectiles from a trebuchet had a comparably flat ballistic trajectory; the angle at the start was normally much smaller than 45 degrees. That meant that the height of the trebuchet's emplacement was decisive for the range for this type of weapon. Because trebuchets were used for defensive as well as offensive purposes, the extensive use in siege warfare initiated certain developments in the construction of fortifications.

At first, the construction materials changed. Wood was a common material in the early middle ages, and in the form of motte-and-bailey castles, picket fences and wooden towers, were the usual features of rural feudal settlements across Northern Europe.[29] Freshly cut wood shows excellent properties related to strength and flexibility. However, without proper preservation, these qualities disappeared after a few years, and the only known wood preservations of the time—like linseed oil or wax—would have increased the combustibility and were, therefore, not used.

Of course, the availability of certain construction materials was in this context a *conditio sine qua non*. Also, a lack of wooden castles in arid regions of the Iberian Peninsula can simply be explained by the local availability of construction materials. Nevertheless, the development of siege engines led to the substitution of masonry for wood whenever possible. The advantage of the trebuchet was range, not penetrating power. Even though we have some written records of breaches in defensive walls caused by the bombardment from trebuchets, these have been the exception rather than the rule. The siege of Jerusalem in 1187 might illustrate this. Even though Saladin had a large number of siege engines—trebuchets, catapults, mangonels and petraries—at his disposal, the breach in the wall was created by miners who were covered by the projectiles from the siege engines.

In order to protect the interior of fortified places from projectiles, especially fire-pots, masonry vaults were built instead of wooden-beamed ceilings.[30] The Crac de Chevaliers can illustrate these developments. It was a fortress that had been initially fortified by the noble family of St. Gilles, but in the year of 1142, the family could no longer sustain the costs and transferred the fortress to the Knights Hospitallers, who had to reconstruct the whole site after earthquakes from 1170 onward. The Egyptian Mamluks under Sultan Baibar took the fortress in the year 1271—after extensive utilization of trebuchets—and reconstructed it as well. As a result, we have an example where master-builders have worked as well as *muhandis*. This fortress was furnished with elaborate masonry vaults to protect the interior of the site from enemy fire—in the primary meaning of "fire." On the top of the walls, large, wide platforms provided the space to deploy and operate trebuchets for defensive purposes. These preserved platforms were higher than the rest of the walls to gain advantage in range. In front of these towers stood two lower broad semicircular salients of the front wall, which were designed for archers and the protection of the base of the main towers. These so-called barbicans were from Persian origins, as the nomenclature indicates.

There are more than Persian and Chinese influences carved in stone at this site. Even though Lawrence's thesis[31] that the Crusader Castles have been dominated by Western influences does not reflect the current status of research, it is highly likely that that practice of multiple rings of fortifications—at least in the case of castles, not towns—has been inspired by Western models, namely the motte-and-bailey castle.[32] On the other hand, the technology needed to realize a magnificent site like the Crac de Chevaliers was of Islamic origin. The pointed arch and the ripped vault have slowly and gradually been developed in the time since the 8th century, and these two technologies have been the basis for the great Gothic churches and the vaulted embattlements of the crusading era.[33]

These developments were not limited to the zones of conflict between Orient and Occident. Through the persistent exchange of technical and military experts—as well as the role of crusaders as pilgrims—the innovative fighting methods and tools found their way into the centers of the respective cultural spheres. European castles and cities followed these new constructive methods, and the innovative weaponry was used in inner European conflicts.[34]

The creative encounter with these features also created new innovative solutions as the example of the Albarrana shows. An Albarrana is a separate tower in front of the wall of a castle or town. This tower is connected by a bridge at the height of the wall's battlements. This type of defensive tower can only be found on the Iberian Peninsula.

One remarkable result of the confrontation of Latin-Christendom and Sunni-Islam was that the cost of conflicts rose. Siege engines and fortifications grew in size and price, and as a result, larger garrisons to defend and larger armies to besiege them were needed. These developments functioned in a mutually stimulating manner. Accordingly, noble families of minor importance couldn't compete any longer with wealthier and more powerful political entities like wealthy noble families, rich cities or religious orders—a development that foreshadowed the later development activated by the cannon in Eurasia and India in the Late Middle Ages and Early Modern Era.

The aforesaid development might imply that an evolutionary development of weapons and fortifications could be traced or reconstructed. Even on a very basic level, such a conclusion might not be feasible, as Koselleck's concept of the sources' veto suggests.[35] The earliest image of a basic trebuchet outside China dates from the first half of the 12th century. This means we have a gap of 500 years between the earliest use outside China and the earliest picture. This picture is proof of the continuous use of simple forms of the trebuchet along with more elaborate constructions, and not an illustration of an early form. The written sources are even more ambiguous and unclear as the example of *um schara* shows. In Arabic sources, siege engines are generally called *makina*, a Greek loanword. In very few cases, these machines have proper names like in the case of *um schara*. The name means "Mother of Hair,"[36] and the leading expert on trebuchets, Mark Feuerle, believed that this name makes it plausible that this siege engine was a traction-trebuchet because the ropes on the counterweight side might have evoked the conception of female hair.[37] If Feuerle had been right, this would have been the proof that the traction-trebuchet was used by the Arabs in the 7th century, but Vitruv wrote that the best strings for traction-catapults came from female hair, which could lead the argumentation in a different direction. The source doesn't help to solve this problem because it is not a description of *um schara*, but rather the account of the fight between the Caliph Abd al-Malik against the pretender, Abdallah ibn az-Zubairs, who found his last refuge in the holy city of Mecca, where it came to the showdown between them in 692. We only know of *um schara* because the use of a siege engine against the holy city seemed to be potentially sinful, if not dangerous to his pious followers. Abd al-Malik fired the weapon and, in retrospect, his behavior was justified by winning the war.

Even though it is not feasible to reconstruct the exact evolution of weapons and fortifications, based on the methods and theories of the history of technology, it is possible to describe the relevant contexts and dependencies. The demand for more effective weapons and stronger defensive fortifications created the Reverse Salient Situation as described by Thomas P. Hughes.[38] When the demand to solve a problem—in our case, to defeat the enemy in a longlasting and brutal conflict—led to an agreement among the knights, *mamlūks* and noblemen—the relevant groups—technological inventions could show the desired results. The participation in the search for innovative solutions was especially attractive for the highly qualified master-builders and muhandis because the mutual demand for their capabilities created potentially increased revenues or enhancement of status for them.

I would like to illustrate this with just one example. The names of two master-builders—John and Alexander—are known to us from the close rolls of the royal chancery of the English King Henry III (1216–1272). In the year 1257, the King granted the master-builders robes—fur-lined with the furs of squirrels. That was a privilege of the royal entourage and can be seen as proof for the foresaid enhancement of status. Again it shows how marginal the

52   I. Ancient Rome and the Medieval Ages

information in medieval sources is because we don't know anything else from the master-builders John and Alexander.

Confronted with the demand for innovations, *muhandis* and master-builders had the possibility either to copy technologies that had already been established among their adversaries or search for new solutions—or in modern terms: "to make or buy." As the transfer of the trebuchet and black powder shows, the reception of alien technologies often occurred and, of course, this transfer of technologies was always an eclectic reception that only considered those technologies whose usefulness was apparent to the receiving side.[39] Thus, the example of the Albarrana has shown that new creative solutions sometimes were of only local significance.

In summary, it can be said that the confrontation between Orient and Occident created conditions for the reception of innovative foreign technologies and the development of new creative solutions that led to notable social changes concerning the social status of technological experts and the accumulation of power for certain political entities. This also foreshadowed later developments in the late medieval and early modern times such as the impacts of granulated gunpowder, wheeled gun carriage, leaden projectiles and cannons made of bronze at the end of the Hundred Years' War,[40] the growth of armies, the implementation of the musket and the development of the trace italienne in Early Modern Times.[41]

Notes

1. Tillmann Nagel, *Die islamische Welt bis 1500* (München: Oldenburg, 1998), 1–24; Michael Terrasse, *Islam et Occident méditerranéen de la conquête aux Ottomane* (Paris: Comité des travaux historiques et scientifiques 2001), 11; Roger Collins, *The Arab Conquest of Spain 710-797* (Oxford: John Wiley & Sons, 1989), 3.

2. John Freely, *Platon in Bagdad: Wie das Antike Wissen zurück nach Europa kam* (Stuttgart: Klett-Cotta, 2012), 183–218.

3. Fuat Sezgin, *Einführung in die Geschichte der Arabisch-Islamischen Wissenschaften* (Frankfurt am Main: Inst. für Gesch. der Arabisch-Islamischen Wiss., 2003), 85–168.

4. Marcus Popplow, *Technik im Mittelalter* (München: Beck, 2010), 7–18.

5. Elisabeth Vaupel, "Schießpulver und Pyrotechnik," in *Europäische Technik im Mittelalter*, ed. Uta Lindgren (Berlin: Gebr. Mann Verlag, 1997), 301.

6. Azar Gat, *War in Human Civilization* (Oxford: Oxford University Press, 2008), 147–443.

7. Johannes Grabmayer, *Europa im späten Mittelalter 1250–1500* (Darmstadt: Wiss. Buchges., 2004), 16; Hagen Hof, *Wettbewerb im Zunftrecht* (Graz: Böhlau, 1983), 58.

8. Richard Hodges, *Dark Age Economics* (London: Gerald Duckworth, 1989), 164.

9. Maya Shatzmiller, *Labour in the Medieval Islamic World* (Leiden: Brill Academic Pub, 1994), 101–168.

10. Frank Neiske, *Europa im frühen Mittelalter* (Darmstadt: Primus, 2007), 140; Hans Eberhard Mayer, *Geschichte der Kreuzzüge* (Stuttgart: Urban, 2005), 28.

11. Thomas Gergen, *Pratique juridique de la Paix et Trêve de Dieu* (Frankfurt a.M.: Lang, 2004),127–216.
   12. Augustine of Hippo, "Contra Faustum Manichaeum" in *Sancti Aurelii Augustini, Hipponensis episcopi, opera omnia*, ed. Jacques P. Migne vol. 42 of Patrologia Latina (Paris: Migne, 1886), 22,74f.
   13. Norbert Elias, *Über den Prozeß der Zivilisation* (Berlin: Suhrkamp, 1969), 80.
   14. Volker Schmidtchen, "Mittelalterliche Kriegstechnik zwischen Tradition und Innovation," in *Europäische Technik im Mittelalter*, ed. Uta Lindgren (Berlin: Gebr. Mann Verlag, 1997), 309.
   15. Konrad Lorenz, *Das sogenannte Böse* (München: Deutscher Taschenbuch-Verlag, 1974), 162–207.
   16. Peter Reid, *A Brief History of Medieval Warfare* (London: Robinson, 2007), 28–30.
   17. Thomas Schuetz, "Castra—ribat— Kastellburg," in *Der umkämpfte Ort—von der Antike zum Mittelalter*, ed. Olaf Wagener (Frankfurt a.M.: Peter Lang, 2009), 68–70.
   18. Alain Demurger, *Die Ritter des Herrn* (München: C.H. Beck, 2003), 326–330.
   19. Steven Ranchman, *A History of the Crusades* Vol. I (Cambridge: Cambridge University Press, 1951), 179–288; Rainer Christoph Schwinges, *Kreuzzugsideologie und Toleranz* (Stuttgart: Hiersemann, 1977), 261; Amin Maalouf, *The Crusades Through Arab Eyes* (London: Ali Saqi Book, 1984), 37–56.
   20. Martin Warnke, *Bau und Überbau: Soziologie der mittelalterlichen Architektur nach den Schriftquellen* (Frankfurt a.M.: Syndikat, 1976).
   21. Adolph P. Youschkevitch, "Abu'l Wafa Al-Buzjani, Muhammad Ibn Muhammad Ibn Yahya Ibn Ismail Ibn Al-Abbas," in *Dictionary of scientific biography* Vol. I. ed. Charles C. Gillispie (New York: Scribner, 1970), 41.
   22. Hans R. Hahnloser, ed. *Villard de Honnecourt. Kritische Gesamtausgabe des Bauhüttenbuches ms. Fr. 19093 der Pariser Nationalbibliothek* (Graz: Akademische Druck.- u. Verlagsanst. 1972), plate 39–41.
   23. David Nicolle, *Arms and Armour of the Crusading Era* (London: Greenhill Books, 1999), 146–148, 704–706.
   24. Michael Mitterauer, *Warum Europa* (München: Beck, 2004), 235–273.
   25. Vaupel, *Schießpulver und Pyrotechnik*, 303.
   26. Ibid., 302.
   27. Reid, *A Brief History*, 73.
   28. Schmidtchen, *Mittelalterliche Kriegstechnik zwischen Tradition und Innovation*, 312.
   29. Helen Nicholson, *Medieval Warfare* (Houndsmill: Palgrave Macmillan, 2003), 77; Uta Freeden and Siegmar Schnurbein, *Spuren der Jahrtausende: Archäologie und Geschichte in Deutschland* (Stuttgart: Konrad Theiss, 2002), 430.
   30. Robert B.C. Huygens, *De constructione castri Saphet: construction es fonctions d'un château fort franc en Terre Sainte* (Amsterdam: North-Holland, 1981), 41–42: Keppel A.C. Cresswell, *Fortification in Islam Before AD 1250* (London: Cumberlege, 1952), 119.
   31. Thomas E. Lawrence, *The Influence of the Crusades on European Military Architecture to the End of the Twelfth Century* (London: Immel, 1981).
   32. Ronnie Ellenblum, "Frankish and Muslim Siege Warfare and the Construction of Concentric Castles" in *Dei gesta per Francos*, ed. Michael Balard et al. (Aldershot: Ashgate, 2001), 190.

33. Kenneth J. Conant, and Henry M. Willard, "Early Examples of Pointed Arch and Vault in Romanesque Architecture," *Viator* 2 (1978): 211.
34. Thomas Schuetz, *Baumeister und Muhandis* (Hildesheim: Olms, 2011), 391–419.
35. Reinhart Koselleck, "Standortbindung und Zeitlichkeit" in *Objektivität und Parteilichkeit*, ed. Reinhart Koselleck et al. (München: DTV, 1977), 45.
36. Kalervo Huuri, *Zur Geschichte des mittelalterlichen Geschützwesens aus orientalischen Quellen* (Helsinki: Druckerei A.G. der Finnischen Literaturgesellschaft, 1941), 142.
37. Mark Feuerle, "Das Hebelwurfgeschütz. Eine technische Innovation des Mittelalters," *Technikgeschichte* 69 (2002), 1–41.
38. Thomas P. Hughes, *Networks of Power: Electrification in Western Society; 1880–1930* (Baltimore, Md.: Johns Hopkins University Press, 1988), 79–81.
39. Schuetz, *Muhandis und Baumeister*, 202.
40. Clifford J. Rogers, "The Military Revolutions of the Hundred Years' War," *The Journal of Military History*, 57/2 (1993): 244.
41. Michael Roberts, "The Military Revolution 1560–1660," in *The Military Revolution Debate*, ed. by. Clifford J. Rogers (Boulder: Westview Press, 1995): 13–35; Geoffrey Parker, "'The Military Revolution' a Myth?" *Journal of Modern History* 48 (June 1976): 197–201.

Works Cited

Collins, Roger. *The Arab Conquest of Spain 710–797*. Oxford: John Wiley & Sons, 1989.
Conant, Kenneth J., and Willard, Henry M. "Early Examples of Pointed Arch and Vault in Romanesque Architecture," *Viator* 2 (1978): 203–214.
Cresswell, Keppel A.C. *Fortifications in Islam Before AD 1250*. London: Cumberlege, 1952.
Demurger, Alain. *Die Ritter des Herrn. Die Geschichte der geistlichen Ritterorden*. München: C.H. Beck, 2003.
Elias, Norbert. *Über den Prozeß der Zivilisation: Wandlungen des Verhaltens in den weltlichen Oberschichten des Abendlandes*. Berlin: Suhrkamp, 1969.
Ellenblum, Ronnie. "Frankish and Muslim Siege Warfare and the Construction of Concentric Castles," in *Dei gesta per Francos: Etudes sur les croisades dédiées à Jean Richard—Crusade Studies in Honour of Jean Richard* ed. Michael Balard, Benjamin Z. Kedar and Jonathan Riley-Smith. Aldershot: Ashgate, 2001, 187–198.
Freeden, Uta, and Siegmar Schnurbein. *Spuren der Jahrtausende: Archäologie und Geschichte in Deutschland*. Stuttgart: Konrad Theiss, 2002.
Freely, John. *Platon in Bagdad: Wie das Antike Wissen zurück nach Europa kam*. Stuttgart : Klett-Cotta, 2012.
Feuerle, Mark. "Das Hebelwurfgeschütz. Eine technische Innovation des Mittelalters," *Technikgeschichte* 69 (2002): 1–41.
Gat, Azr. *War in human civilization*. Oxford: Oxford University Press, 2008.
Gergen, Thomas. *Pratique juridique de la Paix et Trêve de Dieu à partir du concile de Charroux (989–1250)*. Frankfurt a.M.: Lang, 2004.
Grabmayer, Johannes. *Europa im späten Mittelalter 1250–1500*. Darmstadt: Wiss. Buchges., 2004.
Hahnloser, Hans R. ed. *Villard de Honnecourt: Kritische Gesamtausgabe des Bauhüttenbuches ms. Fr. 19093 der Pariser Nationalbibliothek*. Graz: Akademische Druck.- u. Verlagsanst, 1972.

Hippo, Augustine of. "Contra Faustum Manichaeum," in *Sancti Aurelii Augustini, Hipponensis episcopi, opera omnia*, ed. Jacques P. Migne vol. 42 of *Patrologia Latina*. Paris: Migne, 1886.
Hodges, Richard. *Dark Age Economics: Origins of Towns and Trade*, AD 600–1000. London: Gerald Duckworth, 1989.
Hof, Hagen. *Wettbewerb im Zunftrecht: Zur Verhaltensgeschichte der Wettbewerbsregelung durch Zunft und Stadt, Reich und Landesherr bis zu den Stein-Hardenbergschen Reformen*. Graz: Böhlau, 1983.
Hughes, Thomas P. *Networks of Power: Electrification in Western Society; 1880–1930*. Baltimore, Md.: Johns Hopkins University Press, 1988.
Huuri, Kalervo. *Zur Geschichte des mittelalterlichen Geschützwesens aus orientalischen Quellen*. Helsinki: Druckerei A.G. der Finnischen Literaturgesellschaft, 1941.
Huygens, Robert B.C. *De constructione castri Saphet: construction es fonctions d'un château fort franc en Terre Sainte*. Amsterdam: North-Holland, 1981.
Koselleck, Reinhart. "Standortbindung und Zeitlichkeit. Ein Beitrag zur historiographischen Erschließung der geschichtlichen Welt," in *Objektivität und Parteilichkeit*, ed. Reinhart Wolfgang Koselleck, Wolfgang J. Mommsen and Jörn Rüsen. München: DTV, 1977, 17–46.
Lawrence, Thomas E. *The Influence of the Crusades and European Military Architecture to the End of the Twelfth Century*. London: Immel, 1988.
Lorenz, Konrad. *Das sogenannte Böse—Zur Naturgeschichte der Aggression*. München: Deutscher Taschenbuch-Verlag, 1974.
Ludwig, Karl-Heinz. "Technik im Hohen Mittelalter zwischen 1000 und 1350/1400," in *Propyläen Technikgeschichte Vol. 2: Metalle und Macht*, ed. Wolfgang König. Berlin: Ullstein 1997, 11–208.
Maalouf, Amin. *The Crusades Through Arab Eyes*. London: Ali Saqi Book, 1984.
Mayer, Hans Eberhard. *Geschichte der Kreuzzüge*. Stuttgart: Urban, 2005.
Mitterauer, Michael. *Warum Europa. Mittelalterliche Grundlagen eines Sonderwegs*. München: Beck, 2004.
Nagel, Tilman. *Die islamische Welt bis 1500: Oldenburger Grundriss der Geschichte Bd. 24*. München: Oldenburg, 1998.
Neiske, Frank. *Europa im frühen Mittelalter 500–1050: Eine Kultur- und Mentalitätsgeschichte*. Darmstadt: Primus, 2007.
Nicholson, Helen. *Medieval Warfare: Theory and Practice of War in Europe, 300–1500*. Houndsmill: Palgrave Macmillan, 2003.
Nicolle, David. *Arms and Armour of the Crusading era 1050–1350 / Islam, Eastern Europa and Asia*. London: Greenhill Books, 1999.
Parker, Geoffrey. "'The Military Revolution' a Myth?," *Journal of Modern History* 48 (June 1976): 197–201.
Popplow, Marcus. *Technik im Mittelalter*. München: Beck, 2010.
Roberts, Michael. "The Military Revolution 1560–1660," in *The Military Revolution Debate. Readings on the Military Transformation of Early Modern Europe*, ed. Clifford J. Rogers. Boulder: Westview Press, 1995, 13–35.
Rogers, Clifford J. "The Military Revolutions of the Hundred Years' War," *The Journal of Military History*, 57/2 (1993): 241–278.
Runciman, Sevn. *A History of the Crusades Vol. I. The First Crusade and the Foundation of Jerusalem*. Cambridge: Cambridge University Press, 1951.
Schuetz, Thomas. *Baumeister und Muhandis: Technologietransfer zwischen Orient und Okzident*. Hildesheim: Olms, 2011.
Schuetz, Thomas. "Castra—ribat—Kastellburg. Gab es eine Vermittlung antiken Wissens

über den islamischen Kulturraum," in *Der umkämpfte Ort—von der Antike zum Mittelalter*, ed. Olaf Wagener. Frankfurt a.M.: Peter Lang, 2009, 61–74.

Shatzmiller, Maya. *Labour in the Medieval Islamic World*. Leiden: Brill Academic Pub, 1994.

Schmidtchen, Volker. "Mittelalterliche Kriegstechnik zwischen Tradition und Innovation," in *Europäische Technik im Mittelalter*, ed. Uta Lindgren. Berlin: Gebr. Mann Verlag, 1997, 305–316.

Schwinges, Rainer Christoph. *Kreuzzugsideologie und Toleranz. Studien zu Wilhem von Tyrus* (Stuttgart: Hiersemann, 1977).

Sezgin, Fuat. *Einführung in die Geschichte der Arabisch-Islamischen Wissenschaften*. Frankfurt a.M.: Inst. für Gesch. der Arabisch-Islamischen Wiss., 2003.

Terrasse, Michael. *Islam et Occident méditerranéen de la conquête aux Ottomane*. Paris: Comité des travaux historiques et scientifiques, 2001.

Vaupel, Elisabeth. "Schießpulver und Pyrotechnik," in *Europäische Technik im Mittelalter*, ed. Uta Lindgren. Berlin: Gebr. Mann Verlag, 1997, 301–304.

Warnke, Martin. *Bau und Überbau. Soziologie der mittelalterlichen Architektur nach den Schriftquellen*. Frankfurt a.M.: Syndikat, 1976.

Youschkevitch, Adolph P. "Abu'l Wafa Al-Buzjani, Muhammad Ibn Muhammad Ibn Yahya Ibn Ismail Ibn Al-Abbas," in *Dictionary of scientific biography Vol. I*. ed. Charles C. Gillispie. New York: Scribner, 1970, 39–43.

Gunpowder and Cannons
Gunnery in the Late Middle Ages

MARC-ANDRÉ KARPIENSKI

The story of the cannon is a story of success. During the two centuries of the Late Middle Ages, cannons and other guns replaced all other means for throwing and hurling stones or bolts, and the new era of gunpowder was heralded. This development was more an evolutionary than revolutionary change but still fundamental.

This essay shows the interaction between technical progress and the warlike use of cannons in the Late Middle Ages. Any improvement in efficiency and effectiveness resulted in an increasing use of cannons. This changed the way in which wars were fought, and, therefore, the way in which wars and the actions conducted in them were perceived.

I am going to focus firstly on the expansion of gun use in the Late Middle Ages. Secondly, I am going to explicate the progress of cannon technology during the 14th and 15th centuries. Finally, I am going to embed these changes into the context of the perception of violence.[1]

Artillery on the Rise

From the 11th century onwards, fortifications of castles or towns were built all over Europe. These allowed a literally outgunned combatant to compensate for his disadvantage on the field. Influenced by these domestic developments and the encounters of the Crusades, European rulers and their soldiers devised different ways to overcome fortifications in battle. From surrounding and starving out the enemy, to digging mines, and to attacking him with hurled stones and shot bolts, medieval creativity knew only technical limits.[2]

The first European recipes for gunpowder date from the mid–13th century, and the first pictorial representation of a cannon can be found in the Milemete manuscript from the year 1326.[3] How these technologies of making gunpowder and cannons diffused from China to Europe is still unclear and so far of minor importance for this article.

The amount of evidence for firearms increased during the first half of the 14th century throughout Europe. Account books of cities make reference to cannons, and the use of these weapons in sieges and battles are mentioned in chronicles.[4] Sometimes, it is possible to more accurately determine from procurement and inventory lists the type of guns, and it is remarkable that the guns of the 14th century were rather small. In battles, their task was primarily to frighten the enemy, especially the horses. Thus, a cavalry charge would collapse while the horses were not under control of their riders. In sieges, the fire of the cannons was directed to the defenders and the buildings in the cities. On the other side, guns were used by the besieged to bombard the siege towers and other wooden structures of the besiegers.[5]

In the second half of the 14th century, wall-breaking artillery appeared slowly in reports, for example, from the Hundred Years' War.[6] This also began the time of the giant cannons, whose military usefulness is in question, if one considers, for example, production costs and transportation difficulties.[7] In contrast, as a representation of power, these pieces of ordnance were indispensable in a hierarchical society.[8]

We can find many accounts on the use of cannons in sieges in the 15th century. Relatively well known is the Siege of Harfleur 1415 by King Henry V of England (1386–1422).[9] After the failure in undermining the walls, the English began to use their 12 heavy guns, which accompanied the main army, to batter the walls. In addition, "really fine buildings, almost as far as the middle of the town, were totally demolished or threatened with inevitable collapse or, at least, their framework falling apart, had suffered excessive damage."[10] The siege lasted a month, and the cannons destroyed a good part of the outer fortifications, which allowed assaults on the town. We can see in this example that cannons were quite useful in bringing down the walls.

Not always did walls have to be shot ripe for an attack; sometimes, the show of force was the only thing needed to make the besieged surrender. For example, from 1449–1450, French armies conducted 60 sieges in Normandy, and all of them were short and successful. Many smaller garrisons thought twice about their chances against a winning attacker with its massive artillery. Bayonne surrendered before the first shot was fired, and other sieges were terminated after a few days.[11] By that time, around 1450, cannons had became a necessary part of every army that wanted to besiege an enemy.

That is why the king of France had a redoubtable artillery train at the end of the 15th century, which was one of the biggest and most modern in

Europe. Michael Mallett, in his book about the Italian Wars, puts it this way: "Charles VIII [1470–1498] had at his disposal the largest, best-equipped and best-manned artillery train in Europe."[12] On his march to Naples 1494/5 his army bombarded and sacked small towns and castles very efficiently and massacred the people there. This tactic opened up many others' gates and let the defenders negotiate and surrender.[13]

Cannons were also used in battles, but keep in mind that they were not a mobile arm in the Late Middle Ages.[14] When cannons were used in battle, they stayed in their first position and could normally not move in the course of the fighting. The heavy siege cannons had also a low rate of fire, so lighter cannons could probably shoot more than heavier ones. Their overwhelming use in sieges is reflected in books on warfare from the Late Middle Ages. These books set priorities on the use of guns in siege warfare, and merely mention the use of cannons in battles.[15]

Progress of the Art

In order to gain superiority over others, better technology always plays an important role in warfare. That does not mean that the technical superior always wins the battles, nor does it mean that all wars are affected by this run to a better technology. Still, better weapons can help to win. The Late Middle Ages were a time of constant improvements of the cannons, and there were different adjustable points to improve this weapon.

Different ways to make a barrel of a gun were known. The small cannons and handguns[16] were firstly made of wrought iron, which was drilled out till the sufficient bore was reached.[17] Heavier guns were welded together with staves and rings of iron.[18] For smaller cannons in particular, bronze-cast was used from the second half of the 14th century.[19] It was the expertise of bell founders that was transferred into this military sphere.[20] Later on, the bronze-cast increased even for heavier pieces and became the normal method of gun-making in the early modern period as well.[21] We have a lot of evidence for this kind of technique, for example, for the casting of cannons at the Marienburg by the Teutonic Order. The Order billed, in its accounting books, how much copper and tin they bought and how much was used for the cast.[22] It even mentioned when old cannons were melted,[23] or when a cast was not satisfactory.[24] The iron-cast also gained importance in the 15th century. One development that was very useful was a technique called decarburizing, in German, *frischen*. The iron was melted more than once so that the carbon would be reduced by this and the iron could be treated more easily. This indirect melting was a prerequisite for this kind of iron casting.[25]

In respect of gunpowder production, we find a decisive improvement a little before 1420. Before that time, the powder was milled, so it was pulverized or fine-grained at the end. A better powder is achieved by increasing the grain size of the powder. This corned gunpowder allowed a slower and constant rate of burning and was, therefore, more efficient and gentle to the barrels.[26] The gunpowder also became cheaper in the course of the 15th century. It is always difficult to compare medieval prices, but we can still assume that the price of gunpowder fell from the 1380s to the 1430s to less than half, and probably only one-fifth of its original price.[27]

Progress was achieved even with bullets. First, mostly stone balls for the heavier wall breaching cannons were used, but they crashed when the impact velocity was too high. Iron balls with a high specific gravity and sufficient hardness and toughness appeared around 1450 and ousted the stone balls till the end of the century.[28] By this change, the bore of the guns could be made smaller, so the guns got lighter and more mobile. Cannonballs made of iron had an equal weight in comparison to cannonballs made of stone, so aiming at and hitting a target with different shots became easier. The smaller cannonballs could be shot wider, and they hit with more accuracy because of their lower air resistance, which depends mostly on the diameter of the cannonball.

The gun-carriage was also improved so that the cannons could more easily be set up and transported.[29] Perhaps the most important invention was the trunnion in the last third of the 15th century. Before that, all the cannons were fixed in a kind of frame, which was part of the gun-carriage, but with the trunnion, the gun could be mounted directly on a two-wheeled carriage.

Around 1450, guns had reached a degree of development that made them the ultimate weapon in sieges, but we should keep in mind that there were boundaries too. Smaller fortifications and less well-equipped and manned fortresses could be reduced in a short period of time with this new artillery, but still many walled towns and fortresses could hold out as long as two hundred years. I mentioned Harfleur above, which had to capitulate after a massive bombardment. One could see it as a success for the artillery and the army of King Henry V. On the other hand, one could say that even by using a great number of cannons, the whole English invasion army became stuck in front of one city for several weeks,[30] and although the campaigning season was short, they lost many dead, wounded and sick.[31] Charles VIII conquered Naples in 1494 as intended, but the cannons were not the decisive factor there, nor were they in the battle of Fornovo the next year, which was lost by the French. We can also find enough examples where sieges had to be lifted, and the besieged were, in the end, the superior ones. Even great princes with well-organized troops and a great amount of artillery could lose. The sieges of Soest 1447 and Neuss 1474/5 are only two examples.[32] The Ottomans were successful in Constantinople but failed to conquer Belgrade in 1456 although they had a massive artillery train at hand.[33] The artillery of the Late Middle Ages was not a "silver bullet" or "Wunderwaffe."

Besides these difficulties, there were further problems with cannons, like accidents. King James II of Scotland died in 1460 when an artillery piece exploded next to him.[34] Henry V of England besieged the Welsh fortress of Aberystwyth in 1408/09, and two of his cannons exploded.[35] At the Siege of Cherbourg in 1450, the French had some of their artillery pieces in an area that was flooded. During low tide, they shot, and before high tide came, they abandoned the cannons. Overall, four guns exploded. One can only presume that the water was not helpful in this case.[36]

Other examples of casualties with guns can be found in the book *Die Abenteuer des Ritters Theuerdank*.[37] It is a fictional work from 1517, but it has a non-fictional background. Originally, it was dedicated to and modeled after Maximilian (1459–1519), the Emperor of the Holy Roman Empire. The hero of the story, the gallant knight Theuerdank, underwent a lot of adventures and also accidents with guns. In Chapter 39, he looks into the barrel of a gun at the moment of shooting (and survives it by luck and skill). In Chapter 50, three cannons are shot, and one of them bursts because of too much gunpowder. These are only two examples. There are three more accidents with guns and powder and six attempts to kill Theuerdank by shooting at him with cannons and handguns.[38] Consequently, we can see that gunpowder weapons were an important part of warfare in this story, and this reflects experiences the writers and the sponsor of this book did undergo. They also experienced failures in this weapon system. Material defects and faulty workmanship were known and dreaded.

Violence and War

Cannons played a major role in the development of states with their fiscal and organizational structures. There was a tendency toward bigger armies of mercenaries and standing armies in the Late Middle Ages. A sufficient artillery train for demolishing fortifications was also necessary for the princes of that time. In order to pay for and organize this, the princes had to establish tax systems, a bureaucracy to extract the money and distribute it, and had to give the local elites the ability to invest their social capital in the state system.[39] It is fair to say that cannons were not the all-determining flash point for this. Many other developments helped to establish the modern European state and changed the way in which wars were fought.[40]

Even so, how did this affect the violence that was conducted in wars? I think there is no way of measuring a descending or ascending quantity of violence. The only way to find out something about this is to take a look into the sources and see how violence is judged there. Did the authors notice a new quality of violence because of the use of guns? Is there a kind of cruelty that surmounted the normal violence of war?[41]

If the authors of chronicles see one party in a conflict as an enemy, the actions of this enemy are often judged as excessive. The violent acts became cruel acts,[42] with or without the use of cannons in this conflict. Because of the limitations of this article and to get another perspective on the question of violence in war, I will concentrate mainly on examples from treatises on guns and gunpowder from the 15th century by master gunsmiths[43] and two other short extracts from the 16th century. I will begin with these.

We can find skeptical voices on the use of guns, but they are not in the majority. Well known are these words of Martin Luther (1483–1546): "Guns and cannons are a cruel and harmful instrument, blast walls and rocks and carry people up into the air. I think that it was the devil's own invention, because he cannot fight with embodied weapons and fists. Against guns neither strength nor virtue helps. He is dead even before you can see it."[44]

In a similar way Georg Agricola (1494–1555) reproduced these worries of others:

> But a missile can be shot into the body of one person, an arrow too, may it fired by a bow, a scorpion or a catapult; in contrast an iron bullet of a gun can be shot through many people's bodies. And no marble or rock, which stands out against it, is so solid that the bullet cannot penetrate it with its blow and force [...].
>
> [You can say] that this plague was sent from hell to the earth, so that the Orcus snaps up with one shot several tumbling people.[45]

Two things you can see here: First, the smoke as well as the noise of guns evoked associations with hell as it was imagined. Second, the penetrating force of cannonballs was so great that it could break walls and kill several people at once. Both were quite new for the medieval world and probably fearsome. We should address the second point a bit further.

The use of force and the violence connected with it is an essential part of war.[46] Whatever kind and level of violence was accepted by the medieval society was deeply related to the social status of the perpetrator and the victim. A knight was probably not killed by another knight; instead, he was made prisoner. On the other hand, a knight could not expect to be spared after he lost against socially inferior enemies when he would not spare them either. This is the reason why conflicts between groups of different social statuses were very violent. Social superiority (to be noble) is grounded in a belief of one's military superiority.[47] Now, we have the emergence of a new class of soldiers, the gunsmiths and the artillerymen, who kill with their nondiscriminatory weapons and from a distance. In a society that upheld certain warrior virtues of honor and personal courage, this could arouse displeasure.

How did the artillerymen react to this? Konrad Kyeser (1366–after

1405),[48] who probably wrote the most well-known treatise on gunnery, the Bellifortis,[49] praised the use of guns as appropriate for the noble man and wrote that even Alexander the Great, the hero of the court culture, was proud to use mechanical and chemical knowledge.[50]

Violence he did not pick as a central theme. The effects of his proposed weapons were not really highlighted. On many occasions, he told the reader that his weapons work or that they would bring success,[51] yet the text does not get specific in the case of killing, destroying, mutilating etc. As a work for the court, the well-written and often nicely illustrated Bellifortis should bring pleasure and advertise the skills of the writer.[52]

A real instruction manual, the Feuerwerksbuch, was written in 1420 by an anonymous author.[53] Perhaps this author wrote about the violence his weapons brought? This is not the case. In fact, one can rarely find any hints of the violent consequences of the use of cannons and combustibles. Perhaps one cannot expect that this text would emphasize the consequences of gun use like a package insert.

My last examples are from Johannes Bengedans (born ca. 1400), a master gunsmith who served the king of Denmark and Sweden and afterwards hoped for a position at the Teutonic Order. He left us a treatise on gunpowder and guns. His book is full of useful information on producing gunpowder and on the operation of the described weapons. He wrote of the destruction of towers, belfries and cats and that it is possible to defeat the enemy.[54] The shooting of an incendiary composition on the enemies is then commented in this way:

> [...] and [you should] shoot it against the army.
> Look, what they do then. [...]
> And you can count on it
> that you undo their hostile scheme and win.[55]

On a few occasions he became more explicit:

> The shot should be targeted on an army,
> and it is a dreadful and horrible incendiary composition.
> Where it hits, there it burns enormously.[56]

A specially prepared trunk, which could be shot, is presented as well. It worked like a canister shot:

> If it is thrown or shot at an army,
> it clears the space and rankles,
> and makes so much room in the crowd,
> that hardly every fourth man get off lightly,
> and penetrates armour and man.[57]

Not every bloody detail is mentioned here, and there is no sense of regret in doing "the job" from the author; however, the killing on the battlefield is at least sometimes mentioned.

A similar outcome can be found by taking a look at the illustrations. Many treatises on guns and powder-making were illustrated. Even in these illustrations, one can rarely see the dying on the battlefield. The pictures look more like instructional drawings as one might expect. The potential of the weapons for violence is only seldom apparent.[58]

Conclusion

During the Late Middle Ages, a new weapon appeared in wars that replaced many other ways to conquer towns and castles. The success of this weapon may be due to its potential for further development. Engineers, craftsmen and gunsmiths worked on this technological advance, which directly influenced the increased use of cannons in sieges and on battlefields. This transformation had, of course, effects on the way in which wars were fought. The armored elite became more vulnerable through this process, which was recognized, but still, the military professionals adopted this weapon and used it for their purpose. In the same way, the authors of the instruction manuals saw cannons as tools for successful warfare and did not express moral problems. We probably find here a way of professionalism that helped the experts to write in a manner that was unemotional and unaffected by the horrors of war and the violent outcomes of their weapons.

Notes

1. For further information on wars in general and especially medieval types of war, see: Hans-Henning Kortüm, *Kriege und Krieger. 500–1500* (Stuttgart: Kohlhammer Verlag, 2010), 41–44; Hans-Henning Kortüm, "Kriegstypus und Kriegstypologie. Über Möglichkeiten und Grenzen einer Typusbildung von 'Krieg' im Allgemeinen und von 'mittelalterlichem Krieg' im Besonderen," in *Formen des Krieges: Von der Antike bis zur Gegenwart, Krieg in der Geschichte* 37, ed. Dietrich Beyrau, Michael Hochgeschwender and Dieter Langewiesche (Paderborn: Verlag Ferdinand Schöningh, 2007), 71–98. For basic information and a modern view on technology, see: Armin Grunwald, ed., *Handbuch Technikethik* (Stuttgart: Verlag J.B. Metzler, 2013). Heßler focuses on the cultural approach on technology: Martina Heßler, *Kulturgeschichte der Technik, Historische Einführungen* 13 (Frankfurt/New York: Campus Verlag, 2012). A wider focus on the changes of warfare in the Late Middle Ages und Early Modern Times is given by: John R. Hale, *War and Society in Renaissance Europe 1450–1620: Fontana History of European War and Society* (London: Fontana Press, 1985); Bert S. Hall, *Weapons and Warfare in Renaissance Europe: Gunpowder, Technology, and Tactics* (Baltimore/London: Johns Hopkins University Press, 1997). A comprehensive overview in German is available in Malte Prietzel, *Kriegführung im Mittelalter. Handlungen, Erinnerungen, Bedeutungen, Krieg in der Geschichte* 32 (Paderborn: Verlag Ferdinand Schöningh, 2006), 243–244.

2. Purton gives an overview on the medieval sieges up to the 13th century: Peter Purton, *A History of the Early Medieval Siege, c. 450–1220* (Woodbridge: Boydell Press, 2009). For the different technical means see: Jim Bradbury, *The Medieval Siege* (Wood-

bridge: Boydell Press, 2002), 241–280; Volker Schmidtchen, *Kriegswesen im späten Mittelalter. Technik, Taktik, Theorie* (Weinheim: VCH Verlagsgesellschaft, 1990), 151–165.
    3. Hall, *Weapons*, 44.
    4. There are great difficulties in identifying different types of cannons because of the various names given to them: Hall, *Weapons*, 43–45; James Riddick Partington, *A History of Greek Fire and Gunpowder* (Baltimore: Johns Hopkins University Press, 1999), 116–118. For the Early Modern Age, see: Anna Just, *Die Entwicklung des deutschen Militärwortschatzes in der späten frühneuhochdeutschen Zeit (1500–1648): Schriften zur diachronen und synchronen Linguistik* 3 (Frankfurt: Peter Lang Verlag, 2012), 259–292.
    5. At the end of the 14th century, the first fortifications were built with the purpose of placing guns on and in it: Philippe Contamine, *War in the Middle Ages* (Oxford/Malden: Blackwell Publishing, 2002), 202–205.
    6. Partington, *History*, 104–105. Bradbury has a different opinion and sees the beginning of an efficient use of wall-breaking cannons a bit later: Bradbury, *Siege*, 288. For a quantitative view on early guns, see, Contamine, *War*, 146–150.
    7. Peter Purton, *A History of the Late Medieval Siege, 1200–1500* (Woodbridge: Boydell Press, 2010), 275–276; Volker Schmidtchen, *Bombarden, Befestigungen, Büchsenmeister: Von den ersten Mauerbrechern des Spätmittelalters zur Belagerungsartillerie der Renaissance. Eine Studie zur Entwicklung der Militärtechnik* (Düsseldorf: Droste Verlag, 1977), 32–42.
    8. Volker Schmidtchen, "Mehr als nur functional.... Reflexionen zur Meta-Ebene militärischer Technik," in *Technik zwischen artes und arts: Cottbuser Studien zur Geschichte von Technik, Arbeit und Umwelt* 31, ed. Reinhold Bauer, James Williams and Wolfhard Weber (Münster et al.: Waxmann Verlag, 2008), 159–166, 159–162.
    9. Desmond Seward, *Henry V as Warlord* (London: Penguin, 2001), 64–69.
    10. Frank Taylor and John S. Roskell, trans., *Gesta Henrici Quinti: The Deeds of Henry the Fifth* (Oxford: Clarendon Press, 1975), 39. For the Latin text see page 38: "[...] et perpulcra edificia fere usque medium ville vel totaliter corruerunt, vel inevitabilem minabantur ruinam, vel saltem dissolutis compagibus enormiter ledebantur."
    11. Bradbury, *Siege*, 292.
    12. Michael Mallett and Christine Shaw, *The Italian Wars, 1494–1559: War, State and Society in Early Modern Europe* (Harlow: Pearson, 2012), 182.
    13. Mallett, *Italian*, 20–27.
    14. Contamine, *War*, 198–200.
    15. See for example the book on war by Philip of Cleve. 27 chapters are on sieges, but only 5 on battles: Peter Renner, "Das Kriegsbuch Herzog Philipps von Cleve. Untersuchungen mit besonderer Berücksichtigung und kritischer Ausgabe des Buchs von Krieg zu Wasser nach den Handschriften" (Ph.D. diss., Ruprecht-Karls-Universität Heidelberg, 1960), 122, 124–125.
    16. The first hints for the use of handguns you can find for the city of Perugia in 1364, when 500 of these weapons were used. For further information, see: Schmidtchen, *Kriegswesen*, 206.
    17. Schmidtchen, *Kriegswesen*, 194.
    18. Schmidtchen, *Bombarden*, 18–25.
    19. Schmidtchen, *Kriegswesen*, 197.
    20. Georg Ortenburg, *Waffe und Waffengebrauch im Zeitalter der Landsknechte: Heerwesen der Neuzeit Abt I Das Zeitalter der Landsknechte* 1 (Koblenz: Bernard & Graefe Verlag, 1984), 64.

66   I. Ancient Rome and the Medieval Ages

21. Schmidtchen, *Bombarden*, 27, 51.

22. For research on the gun use of the Teutonic Order as apparent in the accounting books, see: Volker Schmidtchen, *Die Feuerwaffen des Deutschen Ritterordens bis zur Schlacht bei Tannenberg 1410: Bestände, Funktion und Kosten, dargestellt anhand der Wirtschaftsbücher des Ordens von 1374-1410*. Nordost-Archiv 10 (Lüneburg: Nordostdt. Kulturwerk, 1977).

23. Erich Joachim, edit., *Das Marienburger Tresslerbuch der Jahre 1399-1409* (Königsberg: Thomas & Oppermann Verlag, 1896), 201: "…item 3m[ark]. an 1 firdung [1/114tel Mark] vor zwu buchsen an nuwes wider zu gyssen und vor koppir zeen und vor ander arbeyt zu den buchsen;."

24. Joachim, *Tresslerbuch*, 506-507: "grose bochse: item 105m. an 8 den. vor 38 zentener und 22 pfunt kopper, den zentener vor 11 fird., als man das vorder ende anderweyt gos."

25. For an overview on the medieval methods of iron work, see: Günter Bayerl, *Technik in Mittelalter und Früher Neuzeit* (Stuttgart: Theiss Verlag, 2013), 150-151.

26. Ortenburg, *Waffe*, 50-51; Hall, *Weapons*, 69-74, 79-87.

27. Contamine, *War*, 197-198; Hall, *Weapons*, 58.

28. Schmidtchen, *Bombarden*, 102-109.

29. Ortenburg, *Waffe*, 65-69, 70; Schmidtchen, *Bombarden*, 63-83.

30. But not all the English sieges were so short. The siege of Meaux for example lasted from October 1421 to May 1422: Seward, *Henry*, 186-192.

31. Purton, *Late medieval siege*, 250.

32. Purton, *Late medieval siege*, 316-322.

33. Purton, *Late medieval siege*, 324-332. Further failed sieges can be found in Kelly DeVries, "The Walls come tumbling down. The Campaigns of Philip the Good and the Myth of Fortification Vulnerability to early gunpowder Weapons," in *The Hundred Years War: A wider Focus. History of Warfare* 25, ed. L.J. Andrew Villalon, Donald J. Kagay (Leiden/Boston: Brill Academic Publication, 2005), 429-446.

34. Robert Lindsay of Pitscottie, *The Chronicles of Scotland*, Vol. 1, ed. John Graham Dalyell (Edinburgh: George Ramsay and Company, 1814), 159.

35. Seward, *Henry*, 23.

36. Hall, *Weapons*, 116.

37. For a facsimile, see: *Die Abenteuer des Ritters Theuerdank: Kolorierter Nachdruck der Gesamtausgabe Nürnberg 1517* (Köln: Taschenverlag, 2003); For further information on Emperor Maximilian, see: *Manfred Hollegger, Maximilian I (1459-1519). Herrscher und Mensch einer Zeitenwende* (Stuttgart: Kohlhammer Verlag, 2005).

38. The accidents happen in chapters 57, 58 and 60. Guns are shot at Theuerdank in chapters 76, 78, 79, 80, 84 and 91.

39. Jan Glete, *War and State in Early Modern Europe: Spain, the Dutch Republic and Sweden as Fiscal-Military States, 1500-1660* (London: Routledge, 2002), 121.

40. And even the costly siege warfare before the gunpowder age played its part in this story: Purton, *Late medieval siege*, 111; Hale, *War*, 232-252. For an overview on the political developments of the late Middle Ages, see: John Watts, *The Making of Polities. Europe, 1300-1500* (Cambridge: Cambridge University Press, 2009). On new forms of warfare, its complexity and the use of written communication, see: Rainer Leng, "Ars Belli. Deutsche taktische und kriegstechnische Bilderhandschriften und Traktate im 15. und 16. Jahrhundert. Vol. 1.," in *Imagines Medii Aevi: Interdisziplinäre Beiträge zur Mittelalterforschung* 12 (Wiesbaden: Reichert Verlag, 2002), 97-99, 102-105.

41. For further information on cruelness, see: Bernd Hüppauf, *Was ist Krieg?*

Zur Grundlegung einer Kulturgeschichte des Krieges. Histoire 37 (Bielefeld: Transcript Verlag, 2013), 424–453; Trutz von Trotha, "Grausamkeit," in *Gewalt. Ein interdisziplinäres Handbuch*, ed. Christian Gudehus and Michaela Christ (Stuttgart/Weimar: Verlag J.B. Metzler, 2013), 221–226.
    42. Gerrit Himmelsbach, *Die Renaissance des Krieges. Kriegsmonographien und das Bild des Krieges in der spätmittelalterlichen Chronistik am Beispiel der Burgunderkriege* (Zürich: Chronos Verlag, 1999), 140–149.
    43. For more information on master gunsmiths, see: Schmidtchen, *Bombarden*, 176–196; Rainer Leng, "getruwelich dienen mit Buchsenwerk. Ein neuer Beruf im Spätmittelalter: Die Büchsenmeister," in *Strukturen der Gesellschaft im Mittelalter: Interdisziplinäre Mediävistik in Würzburg*, ed. Dieter Rödel, Joachim Schneider (Wiesbaden: Reichert Verlag, 1996), 302–322. On the obligation of the master gunsmiths to write treatises, see: Marcus Popplow, *Technik im Mittelalter* (München: C.H. Beck Verlag, 2010), 24: Leng, *Ars*, 101. For the new writing culture at the courts, see: Leng, *Ars*, 94–95.
    44. Translation by the author: *D. Martin Luthers Werke: Kritische Gesamtausgabe. Tischreden*. 3. Band. Sammlungen Lauterbachs, Wellers u.a. (30er Jahre) (Weimar: Verlag H. Böhlau, 1912), 403: "Postea dixit de machinis bellicis et de bombardis, crudelissimis instrumentis, quae muros et petras perrumpunt, homines in acie dissipant: Ego arbitror, quod ist ipsius Sathanae proprium inventu. Nam hic non potest armis ugnari et brachis; hic perit omnis virtus viri. Er ist todt, ee man in sihet. Si Adam talia instrumenta vidisset, quae liberi sui adversus se invicem struxissent, maerore consumptus fuisset."
    45. Translation by the author: Georg Agricola, *Zwölf Bücher vom Berg- und Hüttenwesen*, ed. Agricola-Gesellschaft (Berlin: VDI-Verlag, 1928), 8.
    46. Jan Philipp Reemtsma, *Vertrauen und Gewalt. Versuch über eine besondere Konstellation der Moderne* (Hamburg: Hamburger Edition, 2008), 104–124.
    47. Kortüm, *Kriege*, 210–211. On medieval wars, see: Kortüm, *Kriegstypus*.
    48. Leng, *Ars*, 111–112.
    49. There are more than 50 manuscripts still in existence.
    50. Rainer Leng, "Zum Verhältnis von Kunst und Krieg in den illustrierten Kriegslehren des 15. und 16. Jahrhunderts," in *"Mars und die Musen"- Das Wechselspiel von Militär, Krieg und Kunst in der Frühen Neuzeit: Herrschaft und soziale Systeme in der Frühen Neuzeit 5*, ed. Jutta Nowosadtko and Matthias Rogg (Münster: LIT-Verlag, 2008), 33–57, 45; Rainer Leng, "Selektion und Missverständnisse. Rezeption antiker Kriegstechnik im späten Mittelalter," in *War in Words. Transformations of War from Antiquity to Clausewitz: Transformationen der Antike* 19, ed. Marco Formisano and Hartmut Böhme (Berlin/New York: De Gruyter, 2011), 340.
    51. *Conrad Kyeser aus Eichstädt, Bellifortis*, ed. Götz Quarg (Düsseldorf: VDI-Verlag, 1967), 3v: "Carpe quod quod debes, sic prevalebis adversis." (Translations by the author: "Use what you have to use, thus you will outmatch your enemies."); 105v: "Nimirum devinces inimicos quoscumque rebelles." ("Without fail, you will completely defeat the enemies and all possible insurgents."); 107v: "Nocet elementum summum cuimque putabis." ("The fire damages everyone, who you are going to provide with it."); 108v: "Turcis vel Tartaris poteris per illos nocere." ("The Turks and Tatars you can harm with it."); 109v: "Atque frustrum quidquid suo nocebit retento." ("And everything will be in vain, what is being done to its defense.") The edition and its German translation are criticized by: Leng, *Ars*, 37–38.
    52. Regina Cermann, *Der 'Bellifortis' des Konrad Kyeser. Codices. Manuscripti & Impressi. Supplementum* 8 (Purkersdorf: Hollinek Verlag, 2013), 87.

68   I. Ancient Rome and the Medieval Ages

53. An old edition of the first printed version from 1529 you can find here: Wilhelm Hassenstein, ed., *Das Feuerwerkbuch von 1420: 600 Jahre Deutsche Pulverwaffen und Büchsenmeisterei* (München: Verlag der deutschen Technik, 1941). A newer version is available here: Manuel Baetz, ed., *Das Feuerwerksbuch von 1420: Faksimile und übertragen in modernes Deutsch* (Obermarchtal: Survival-Press, 2001); For further information on the Feuerwerkbuch von 1420, see: Leng, *Ars*, 198–221.

54. Hans Blosen and Rikke Agnete Olsen, ed., *Das Büchsenmeister- und Kriegsbuch des Johannes Bengedans: Kriegskunst und Kanonen*. 2 Vols. (Arhus: Aarhus Universitetsforlag, 2006), 16r, 18r, 21r, 26v, 33v, 43r, 44v.

55. Translation by the author: Blosen and Olsen, *Büchsenmeister- und Kriegsbuch*, 19r: "Unde scheten to deme volke dar/Wat se danne bedriven des nym war [...]/Unde kanst dan darup synnen/Dat du ere upsate konst breken unde ghewynnen."

56. Translation by the author: Blosen and Olsen, *Büchsenmeister- und Kriegsbuch*, 23v, 45v and 25r (here cited): "Der schote sal nach eynem here werden ghedan/Und eis eyn greselik unde eyn gruelich fur/Wo et komet dar bernet it gar ungehur."

57. Translation by the author: Blosen and Olsen, *Büchsenmeister- und Kriegsbuch*, 28r: "Wert se in eyn her geworpen adder geschoten/Se maket eyn rum unde is sere verdroten/Unde maket in deme drange sodan rum/Dat de verde geneset kum/Unde dorchslet harnasch unde man."

58. Rainer Leng, "Gründe für berufliches Töten. Büchsenmeister und Kriegshauptleute zwischen Berufsethos und Gewissensnot," in *Der Krieg im Mittelalter und in der Frühen Neuzeit: Gründe, Begründungen, Bilder, Bräuche, Recht*, ed. Horst Brunner (Wiesbaden: Reichert Verlag, 1999), 310.

Works Cited

Agricola, Georg. *Zwölf Bücher vom Berg- und Hüttenwesen*, ed. Agricola-Gesellschaft. Berlin: VDI-Verlag, 1928.
Baetz, Manuel, ed. *Das Feuerwerksbuch von 1420. Faksimile und übertragen in modernes Deutsch*. Obermarchtal: Survival-Press, 2001.
Günter Bayerl, *Technik in Mittelalter und Früher Neuzeit*. Stuttgart: Theiss Verlag, 2013.
Blosen, Hans, and Rikke Agnete Olsen, ed. *Das Büchsenmeister- und Kriegsbuch des Johannes Bengedans: Kriegskunst und Kanonen*. 2 Vols. Arhus: Aarhus Universitetsforlag, 2006.
Bradbury, Jim. *The Medieval Siege*. Woodbridge: Boydell Press, 2002, 241–280.
Cermann, Regina. *Der 'Bellifortis' des Konrad Kyeser*. Codices. Manuscripti & Impressi. Supplementum 8. Purkersdorf: Hollinek Verlag, 2013.
Contamine, Philippe. *War in the Middle Ages*. Oxford/Malden: Blackwell Publishing, 2002, 202–205.
DeVries, Kelly. "The Walls come tumbling down. The Campaigns of Philip the Good and the Myth of Fortification Vulnerability to early gunpowder Weapons," in *The Hundred Years War: A Wider Focus. History of Warfare* 25, ed. L.J. Andrew Villalon, Donald J. Kagay. Leiden, Boston: Brill Academic Publication, 2005, 429–446.
Die Abenteuer des Ritters Theuerdank. Kolorierter Nachdruck der Gesamtausgabe Nürnberg 1517. Köln: Taschenverlag, 2003.
Glete, Jan. *War and State in Early Modern Europe: Spain, the Dutch Republic and Sweden as Fiscal-Military States, 1500–1660*. London: Routledge, 2002.
Grunwald, Armin, ed. *Handbuch Technikethik*. Stuttgart: Verlag J.B. Metzler, 2013.

Hale, John R. *War and Society in Renaissance Europe 1450–1620*, Fontana History of European War and Society. London: Fontana Press, 1985.
Hall, Bert S. *Weapons and Warfare in Renaissance Europe: Gunpowder, Technology, and Tactics*. Baltimore/London: Johns Hopkins University Press, 1997.
Hassenstein, Wilhelm, ed. *Das Feuerwerkbuch von 1420: 600 Jahre Deutsche Pulverwaffen und Büchsenmeisterei*. München: Verlag der deutschen Technik, 1941.
Kortüm, Hans-Henning. *Kriege und Krieger: 500–1500*. Stuttgart: Kohlhammer Verlag, 2010, 41–44.
Kortüm, Hans-Henning. "Kriegstypus und Kriegstypologie. Über Möglichkeiten und Grenzen einer Typusbildung von 'Krieg' im Allgemeinen und von 'mittelalterlichem Krieg' im Besonderen," in *Formen des Krieges. Von der Antike bis zur Gegenwart*, Krieg in der Geschichte 37, ed. Dietrich Beyrau, Michael Hochgeschwender and Dieter Langewiesche. Paderborn: Verlag Ferdinand Schöningh, 2007, 71–98.
Heßler, Martina. *Kulturgeschichte der Technik*, Historische Einführungen 13. Frankfurt/New York: Campus Verlag, 2012.
Himmelsbach, Gerrit. *Die Renaissance des Krieges. Kriegsmonographien und das Bild des Krieges in der spätmittelalterlichen Chronistik am Beispiel der Burgunderkriege*. Zürich: Chronos Verlag, 1999, 140–149.
Hollegger, Manfred. *Maximilian I (1459–1519). Herrscher und Mensch einer Zeitenwende*. Stuttgart: Kohlhammer Verlag, 2005.
Hüppauf, Bernd. *Was ist Krieg? Zur Grundlegung einer Kulturgeschichte des Krieges*. Histoire 37. Bielefeld: Transcript Verlag, 2013, 424–453.
Joachim, Erich, ed. *Das Marienburger Tresslerbuch der Jahre 1399–1409*. Königsberg: Thomas & Oppermann Verlag, 1896.
Just, Anna. *Die Entwicklung des deutschen Militärwortschatzes in der späten frühneuhochdeutschen Zeit (1500–1648)*: Schriften zur diachronen und synchronen Linguistik 3. Frankfurt: Peter Lang Verlag, 2012, 259–292.
Kyeser aus Eichstädt, Conrad. *Bellifortis*, ed. Götz Quarg. Düsseldorf: VDI-Verlag, 1967.
Leng, Rainer. "Ars Belli. Deutsche taktische und kriegstechnische Bilderhandschriften und Traktate im 15. und 16. Jahrhundert. Vol. 1.," in *Imagines Medii Aevi. Interdisziplinäre Beiträge zur Mittelalterforschung* 12. Wiesbaden: Reichert Verlag, 2002.
Leng, Rainer. "getruwelich dienen mit Buchsenwerk. Ein neuer Beruf im Spätmittelalter: Die Büchsenmeister," in *Strukturen der Gesellschaft im Mittelalter. Interdisziplinäre Mediävistik in Würzburg*, ed. Dieter Rödel, Joachim Schneider. Wiesbaden: Reichert Verlag, 1996, 302–322.
Leng, Rainer. "Gründe für berufliches Töten. Büchsenmeister und Kriegshauptleute zwischen Berufsethos und Gewissensnot," in *Der Krieg im Mittelalter und in der Frühen Neuzeit. Gründe, Begründungen, Bilder, Bräuche, Recht*, ed. Horst Brunner. Wiesbaden: Reichert Verlag, 1999, 307–348.
Leng, Rainer. "Selektion und Missverständnisse. Rezeption antiker Kriegstechnik im späten Mittelalter," in *War in Words. Transformations of War from Antiquity to Clausewitz*. Transformationen der Antike 19, ed. Marco Formisano and Hartmut Böhme. Berlin/New York: De Gruyter, 2011, 333–374.
Leng, Rainer. "Zum Verhältnis von Kunst und Krieg in den illustrierten Kriegslehren des 15. und 16. Jahrhunderts," in *"Mars und die Musen." Das Wechselspiel von Militär, Krieg und Kunst in der Frühen Neuzeit*. Herrschaft und soziale Systeme in der Frühen Neuzeit 5, ed. Jutta Nowosadtko and Matthias Rogg. Münster: LIT-Verlag, 2008, 33–57.

Lindsay of Pitscottie, Robert. *The Chronicles of Scotland,* Vol. 1, ed. John Graham Dalyell. Edinburgh: George Ramsay and Company, 1814.
Mallett, Michael, and Christine Shaw. *The Italian Wars, 1494–1559: War, State and Society in Early Modern Europe.* Harlow: Pearson, 2012.
Partington, James Riddick. *A History of Greek Fire and Gunpowder.* Baltimore: Johns Hopkins University Press, 1999, 116–118.
Popplow, Marcus. *Technik im Mittelalter.* München: C.H. Beck Verlag, 2010.
Prietzel, Malte. *Kriegführung im Mittelalter. Handlungen, Erinnerungen, Bedeutungen,* Krieg in der Geschichte 32. Paderborn: Verlag Ferdinand Schöningh, 2006, 243–244.
Purton, Peter. *A History of the Early Medieval Siege, c. 450–1220.* Woodbridge: Boydell Press, 2009.
Purton, Peter. *A History of the Late Medieval Siege, 1200–1500.* Woodbridge: Boydell Press, 2010, 275–276.
Reemtsma, Jan Philipp. *Vertrauen und Gewalt: Versuch über eine besondere Konstellation der Moderne.* Hamburg: Hamburger Edition, 2008.
Renner, Peter. "Das Kriegsbuch Herzog Philipps von Cleve. Untersuchungen mit besonderer Berücksichtigung und kritischer Ausgabe des Buchs von Krieg zu Wasser nach den Handschriften." Ph.D. diss., Ruprecht-Karls-Universität Heidelberg, 1960.
Schmidtchen, Volker. *Bombarden, Befestigungen, Büchsenmeister: Von den ersten Mauerbrechern des Spätmittelalters zur Belagerungsartillerie der Renaissance. Eine Studie zur Entwicklung der Militärtechnik.* Düsseldorf: Droste Verlag, 1977, 32–42.
Schmidtchen, Volker. *Die Feuerwaffen des Deutschen Ritterordens bis zur Schlacht bei Tannenberg 1410: Bestände, Funktion und Kosten, dargestellt anhand der Wirtschaftsbücher des Ordens von 1374–1410.* Nordost-Archiv 10. Lüneburg: Nordostdt. Kulturwerk, 1977.
Schmidtchen, Volker. *Kriegswesen im späten Mittelalter: Technik, Taktik, Theorie.* Weinheim: VCH Verlagsgesellschaft, 1990, 151–165.
Seward, Desmond. *Henry V as Warlord.* London: Penguin, 2001, 64–69.
Taylor, Frank, and John S. Roskell, trans. *Gesta Henrici Quinti. The deeds of Henry the Fifth.* Oxford: Clarendon Press, 1975.
Trotha, Trutz von. "Grausamkeit," in *Gewalt. Ein interdisziplinäres Handbuch,* ed. Christian Gudehus and Michaela Christ. Stuttgart/Weimar: Verlag J.B. Metzler, 2013, 221–226.
Watts, John. *The Making of Polities: Europe, 1300–1500.* Cambridge: Cambridge University Press, 2009.

Mining and Warfare
An Overview of Centuries of Interdependence

OLAF WAGENER

Mining has been part of siege warfare since antiquity. Whenever a fortified place was attacked, the besieger had three options to enter: to get through the walls by destroying them; to get over the walls by scaling; or to find a way underneath the walls by mining.

There are two different kinds of mining, or sapping, between which a distinction must be made: The first is the so-called "covered mining." That means that the attackers try to get at the base of the wall under the protection of some kind of cover, often called a "mantlet." When they reached the wall, they tried to make their way through the wall with the help of axes or similar tools. This work could be done by any kind of soldier; there was no need for specialized miners for the digging. In this case, the defenders would know where the besieger was trying to get through and would try to disturb them by throwing stones and other objects from the top of the wall. The method of the so-called gallery mining, on the other hand, meant "real mining." The attackers built a tunnel beneath the earth and tried to hide their efforts from the besieged. The aim was either to destroy the foundations of the wall, making them collapse, or to get into the castle and thus force the defenders to surrender. In this event, it was often necessary to enlist the help of specialized workers who knew how to build a tunnel in the rocks.

In this essay, I will mainly focus on the second method, gallery mining, because in this case, it becomes very clear how knowledge and techniques from civilian specialists were used for military purposes.

Some famous sieges in antiquity also saw mining in the course of action, but in most cases, we do not have sufficient information about the degree to which miners were used for military purposes. The Assyrians, for example, who often attacked towns like Lachish by means of sapping the base of the wall, had no obviously specialized corps of engineers for that task.[1] In the Roman Army, there may have been a generalized knowledge of mining techniques, at least in the corps of engineers that was created early on, maybe even in the fifth century BC.[2] Even Julius Caesar (100–44 BC) mentioned two times that mining was undertaken most effectively when the workers were miners in their civilian lives as well.[3]

The example of Dura Europos shall also be mentioned here, the siege of a Roman town in modern Syria in 256/57 by the Sassanids. Although no written sources have survived, archaeological research discovered Persian siege mines and Roman countermines, and it is possible that even some kind of chemical warfare took place in the mines.[4]

Castle Desenberg near Höxter, North Rhine-Westphalia, Germany, is first mentioned in the course of a siege in 1070.[5] The castle is situated on the top of a volcanic hill that arises above the surrounding plains. In 1168, Widukind von Schwalenberg, owner of the castle, took part in a rebellion against Duke Heinrich der Löwe (1130–1195), who began to besiege the castle. The chronicler Helmold von Bosau (1120–1177), a contemporary of the events, tells what happened at Castle Desenberg: Because it was impossible to conquer the castle in its high position by means of a normal siege or with the help of machines, Heinrich der Löwe sent word and called for workers from the Rammelsberg. These workers started the difficult task of digging a mine in the foot of the hill. They also searched for the castle well. After they had found the well, they blocked it so that the defenders of the castle ran out of water. After that, Widukind surrendered the castle to Heinrich.[6]

This episode is very important because the so-called Rammelsberg near Goslar was a very important mining area—mentioned as such as early as 968, with mining ending there in 1988.[7] Thus, Heinrich der Löwe, who was enfeoffed with the "Goslarer Reichsvogtei" in 1152, knew very well whom to ask for—the best specialists in mining affairs in the whole area. Unfortunately, no traces of the siege mine are known, so no definite answer can be given to the question of whether this report is true or not—can miners really find a well within a hill, was it pure luck, or was it just a nice story?

Four examples of besieged castles in Palatinate and Alsace shall be mentioned here because of the written sources and especially the archaeological remains:

The castle "Guirsberg-Schänzel" is situated in the south of Alsace, France, near Colmar. It was built by a noble family, which took its name from the castle. Because of a murder committed by one of the Guirsberg, King Rudolf von Habsburg (1218–1291) in April 1289, decided to besiege the castle. One chronicler tells that the siege began on August 29, 1289, but other sources tell us that the King acted in the course of the siege on June 30, 1289. The siege lasted for 23 or even 31 weeks until the defenders gave up, on February 6, 1290. It was a very expensive affair: 1400 breads, two cattle, two pigs and two tons of wine per week were not sufficient, and more than 1900 livres had to be paid as wages for the miners.[8]

Today, the castle is totally destroyed, but there are still traces of the mines that were dug in the southeast corner of the castle hill and perhaps also in the northwest. At 330 meters' distance from the castle, the camp of the besiegers can be found, from where they most probably shot at the castle with the help of a trebuchet.[9]

Castle Berwartstein is situated on a steep rock of red sandstone near Wissembourg. It was first mentioned in 1152 and consists of an outer bailey at the foot of the rock and the main castle on its top. In 1314, the castle was besieged by the towns of Strasbourg and Hagenau, and after five weeks, the 25 defenders surrendered. In the middle of the eastern side of the castle rock, a steep mine shaft leads upwards through the rock but does not reach the upper platform. This shaft is thought to be the rest of a siege mine from 1314. The attackers tried to reach the level of the main castle, but at some meters before they reached it, the defenders gave up. This shaft, with an angle of gradient of nearly 70 degrees, definitely was not built by untrained soldiers; rather, it is the work of professional miners who used wooden platforms.[10]

Not far away from Castle Berwartstein, on the French side of the border, can be found Castle Alt-Windstein. The main castle is situated on the top of two steep rocks of red sandstone, running from north to south, and an outer bailey on the eastern foot of the rocks. In 1332, the castle was besieged by the archbishop of Strasbourg, the city of Hagenau, Hanemann von Lichtenberg and Landvogt Rudolf von Hohenberg. The siege lasted ten weeks; the besiegers built two "siege castles" (most probably only a stockade), and they used "quatuor machinis," i.e., four trebuchets, two "cattis," i.e., wooden protective roofs, and 80 "fossores," i.e., mine workers.[11]

These workers built a very impressive mine that can still be seen today. In the west of the southern half of the castle, a small kind of ravine leads up the hill—obviously built by the attackers who, while they built it, threw the earth on the southern side of the ravine to get protection. This ravine then descends into the sandstone and becomes a real mine, 2.4 × 1.8 meters wide, which leads up the hill to the main castle rock. Then it opens, and directly beside the mouth of the mine, the rock is broken through so that the eastern parts of the castle are completely defenseless. Probably a second part of the mine led to the main gate at the southern tip of the rock, but these parts have been destroyed by a modern road.

The fourth example from this area concerns Castle Löwenstein and shall show that we have to be careful when regarding only archaeological sources. Again, it is a castle situated on the top and sides of a rock of red sandstone.

It was besieged by the city of Strasbourg in 1386, and what is still visible in the area surrounding the castle is comparable to the situation in Alt-Windstein. The camp of the besiegers can be assumed in the north of the castle, near the neighboring Castle Hohenbourg. From there, a small ravine is still visible on the ground that leads directly to the ditch of Castle Löwenstein. However, in this case, it was definitely not the work of miners because the written sources tell us about the work of "Schanzgräber," i.e., workers who had special skills in digging and entrenching.[12]

In the British Isles, some mines that are quite similar to those described previously survived. A very famous example is a chalk-cut tunnel at Dover Castle, which may date from a siege in 1216.[13] In 1546, St. Andrew's Castle in Scotland was under siege by Regent Arran, whose troops built a siege mine. It is a "spacious stepped corridor" in the solid rock, big enough even for pack animals to remove stones. The defenders built two unsuccessful countermines until the third one broke through into the mine of the besiegers. After that, the mine was obviously useless and was abandoned. Unfortunately, there seem to be no written sources that could tell us who really did the work in the mines.[14]

An example that is very well documented in regard to written sources and archaeological findings alike is the siege of King John's Castle in Limerick, Ireland, in 1642. At the beginning of that year, many workers from the royal silver mines in Munster fled to Limerick; some were Irish, and some were English. In May 1642, the Catholic Army from Munster arrived in Limerick, and many of the English fled into the castle. As the besieging Irish army had no cannons, mining was one of the main features of the siege, but as many miners were in the castle, too, there was considerable countermining as well. Even before the beginning of the mining, the defenders of the castle had built a siege trench on the eastern side of the castle to prevent mines—an attempt which proved unsuccessful. Mining activity started alongside the eastern front of the castle on May 25, 1642, and in the south on June 1, 1642. Countermining began in the east on May 30, 1642, and in the south on June 2, 1642, immediately after the besieged received knowledge of what was going on. The workers advanced their mines at a rate of about 1.5 meters per day. On June 20, 1642, a breakthrough was achieved between Mine 2 and Countermine 3 on the eastern side, and in the following combat, several persons were injured or died. In the course of the siege, which lasted until the surrender of the Castle Garrison on June 23, 1642, after breaches were successfully made on the eastern side, eleven Irish mines and eight countermines were constructed.[15]

The methods used to build the mines are best described in the words of the archaeologist Kenneth Wiggins: "When a gallery was to be opened at the bottom of an entrance shaft, the first rectangular timber frame was established.

A frame was made up of four members: a baseplate, mortised at both ends, which was laid transversely across the floor of the mine; two vertical props for the sides, each with a foot tenon that was inserted into a baseplate mortise; a horizontal top-plate completed the frame by connecting the opposed pair of props and was secured by mortise-and-tenon joinery. The frames were installed along the length of a gallery at intervals of between 32 cm and 76 cm. The sectional dimensions of the galleries, controlled by the size of the timber frames, varied between 1.16 metres and 1.61 metres in width and by between 1.4 metres and 1.6 metres in height. To prevent subsidence, the overhead gaps between the frames were filled with slotted-in timber planks, supported by the top-plates, and the side gaps were often covered with pointed timber strips, inserted between adjacent pairs of props."[16]

The 17th century saw even more mining warfare and especially grand-scale actions at the border of Christendom where the Ottomans attacked. In the years from 1666 to 1669, the Ottomans attacked the Venetian town of Candia in Crete. After several attempts to storm the heavily fortified city had failed and had cost the attackers about 20,000 men, the besiegers started to build siege mines. What followed was mining warfare of a scale which had not been seen before. Big pairs of bellows and tubes were used to secure fresh air for the miners, pumps and tubes were used to keep the mines dry and in some parts, the mines were constructed with several stories. The attackers tried to blow up parts of the walls, and the defenders built countermines to blow the mines up or to set them under water. In 1669, when the defenders gave up, the balance was impressive—about 5,000 detonations of mines and more than 40 grand-scale fights in the darkness under the surface.[17]

Georg Rimpler (1636–1683) was a German engineer who took part in the defense of Candia. There, he learned many things that helped him to strengthen the fortifications of Vienna before the second Turkish siege of 1683, during which he died in the fighting after the blowing up of an Ottoman mine in front of the Löbelbastei.

In the course of the first Turkish siege of Vienna in 1529, the Ottomans had *in extenso* used siege mines to blow up the walls of the Kärntner Tor, and the defenders between them—miners from Tyrol—built countermines as well. Much fighting took place beneath the earth, but on October 12, 1529, the Ottomans succeeded in blowing a big breach in the city walls. Nevertheless, the following attack was beaten back by the Austrians, and the following day, the Sultan decided to withdraw because of the weather.[18]

In 1683, events repeated themselves on an even bigger scale. The Ottomans, who had special troops for mining, succeeded in blowing up several parts of the outer parts of Vienna city walls although the defenders had built countermines as well, and harsh fighting took place. However, at the very moment when the besiegers had finished five mines beneath the inner walls, the Battle of Vienna (Schlacht am Kahlenberg) was lost by the Sultan, who had to withdraw.[19]

One of the most fascinating examples of mining is the case of the so-called "crater episode" in the American Civil War. In the course of the war, and especially Grant's so-called Overland Campaign, warfare in the American Civil War became more and more static and culminated in the siege of Petersburg, Virginia, by northern forces beginning in June 1864. The southern forces had built formidable fortifications around the town while the northerners built many forts, and several times, they tried to break through into the town using heavy artillery bombardment. One part of the Confederate fortifications was "Elliot's Salient," a raised salient that reached as close as 140 meters to the front line of the besiegers. Henry Pleasants (1833–1880), commander of one of the Pennsylvania regiments lying in front of the salient, was, in civilian life, a mining engineer who built tunnels for a railway company. Pleasants had the idea to blow up the Confederate bastion by undermining, and General Ambrose E. Burnside (1824–1881) accepted his plans. Nonetheless, as the military engineers did not believe in the success of this operation executed by coal miners from the Pennsylvania regiments, they offered no assistance. The work began on June 25, 1864, and the mine was finished on July 17, 1864. It was 155 meters long, and fresh air for the workers was ensured by a ventilation shaft and a chimney. Beneath the Confederate bastion, the mine split into three small side branches to get more space for the powder. Beginning on July 23, 1864, the attackers started to fill the mine with 3.5 tons of black powder. Although the Confederates assumed the building of the mines and built countermines themselves, they did not find Pleasants' mine; they thought that the project had been abandoned after they could no longer detect any sound of sapping. Early in the morning on July 30, 1864, the mine was blown up, killing and wounding 278 Confederates before the Union attack began. The fighting that arose is known as the "Battle of the Crater," and the outcome was somewhat curious. As the northerners were as surprised by the result of the detonation as the Confederates were, they did not attack as planned. In addition, although General Beauregard had ordered the building of new fortifications 30 meters behind the salient after the first signs of the building of the mine, the result was nearly nothing.[20]

The climax of military mining was definitely in the First World War. Trench warfare, which emerged at nearly all fronts, had the effect that most tactics used were quite similar to the siege warfare of centuries before despite the more powerful weapons. Thus, it is not surprising that mining was one alternative to break the stalemate by blowing up parts of the enemies' trenches.

In the Royal Army, John Norton Griffiths (1871–1930) was very much engaged in building up tunneling companies. Norton Griffiths was an engineer in civil life who had participated in the building of sewers and underground railways, and in the beginning, some of the men whom he recruited were workers from his own firm. The tunneling companies were completely made up of volunteers—some coming from infantry units, but most coming directly from civilian mines; some of them were even too old to become soldiers, but allowances were made. By July 1916, there were 33 BEF tunneling companies— 25 British, three Canadian, four Australian and one from New Zealand.[21]

The most impressive examples of mines built by the BEF are those beneath Messines Ridge in Flanders. From the end of 1914 onward, the German army held the high ground around a salient in which the town of Ypres was situated. For the Allied forces, it was very important to drive the Germans away and conquer the high ground—not only to save Ypres but also to get a foothold for their own offensive. The first plans to try to build mines at Messines Ridge began in May 1915 and comprised six mines, but later, the number rose to 49 mines, which should have been built if manpower and time allowed. The main challenge was the geology of Flanders. While the upper strata were very wet and did not allow the building of big and long mines, the lower strata were quite dry because of the Flemish blue clay. Therefore, the miners had to sink shafts of, for example, 28 meters at Hill 60 before they could start digging the actual mine. Although machines like pumps were used by the BEF tunnelers, the main work had to be done by hand. The very reason for this fact was that the work had to be done as silently as possible because the Germans assumed that the British might build mines, and both sides tried to listen for the sound of the enemy's activity. For this purpose, the Australian tunnelers at Hill 60 even used a whole "network of dummy picks banging away at dead-end shallower projects [...] to keep the *Pioniere* off the scent."[22]

General Sir Herbert Plumer (1857–1932) gave the order for the attack at Messines Ridge on June 6, 1917. By this time, 21 mines were finished and filled with highly explosive ammonal. St. Eloi, for example, a mine built by Canadian tunnelers, was 42 meters deep, had a gallery with a length of more than 400 meters and was filled with more than 43 tons of explosives. At 3 o'clock in the morning of June 7, 1917, the mines were fired—the largest man-made pre-nuclear explosion, which could even be heard in London. Nineteen of the twenty-one mines exploded within 20 seconds and caused craters of diameters of up to 80 meters. The exact number of German soldiers killed by the mine explosions remains unclear, but, as so often in World War I, the following offensive did not have the decisive effects the British commanders had expected.[23]

Two mines did not detonate in June 1917—Birdcage III exploded in 1955 when struck by lightning, and the last one is still lost and assumed to be beneath a modern farm, but nobody knows for sure.[24]

Mining was not only confined to Flanders and the soft underground of blue clay. In the Alps, the fighting between Austria-Hungary and Italy from 1915 to 1918 sometimes took place in mountainous high grounds, often under alpinistic conditions, and it was static warfare, as on the Western Front. The Italian troops tried to conquer the Col di Lana and the surrounding mountains from 1915 onwards, but despite high casualties, they could not storm the top of the hill. As a result, an Italian officer, Gelasio Caetani (1877–1934), proposed to undermine the Austrian positions on the top and to blow them away with the help of this mine. The work had to be done by hand braces to avoid noise; however, the Austrians became suspicious and started to build a countermine. The Austrian countermine was fired too far away from the Italian mine, causing no damage. During the night of April 17–18, 1916, a blasting gelatin was fired in the Italian mine that was filled with five tons of gelignite, and the Austrians were forced to give up their positions. Regardless of these actions, again no breakthrough was reached because the Austrians could successfully defend the neighboring mountain.[25]

Another impressive example is the hill of Vauquois in the vicinity of Verdun, which was very important because of the possibility of watching the enemy's movements. On September 24, 1914, German troops conquered the hill without French resistance. Several French attacks had failed, but in March 1915, they were able to occupy the plateau of the hill (350 × 120 meters) with the meager rest of the village. The Germans also managed to hold their position on the northern side of the hill. From that time onwards, German engineer troops, reinforced with miners, started to build some sort of barracks into the rocks of the hill, and mining warfare started. At the end of the war, the German "barracks" were big enough for 2,200 soldiers; they had built 17 kilometers of mines inside the hill and the strongest mine they had blown up consisted of 60 tons of Westfalit, a special explosive used in civilian mining as well.[26]

These events were not the end of military mining despite the changes in warfare. In May 1954, during the siege of the French fortifications at Dien Bien Phu, the Vietnamese attackers blew up a mine at the beginning of the final attacks.[27] Once again, in the war against the American invaders, the Vietcong used tunnel systems—this time to hide troops and material. The tunnel system of Cu Chi, which became well-known because of the desperate fighting in the narrow tunnels, was so big and elaborate that the U.S. Army trained Special Forces to clear the tunnels—the so-called "tunnel rats." Nevertheless, the entrances to some of the tunnels were masked so well that even a U.S. headquarters was built on top of one of the entrances.[28]

From the 1970s onwards, several tunnels were discovered on the border between North and South Korea—most probably, they were built to allow troops from the north to surprise their enemy when an attack started.[29]

Of course, these kinds of tunnels could be used in the opposite way as well. In 1944, Allied prisoners of war in Stalag Luft III in Silesia built two tunnels to try to escape—this episode was the basis for the 1963 popular Hollywood film *The Great Escape*.[30] In 1993, while Sarajevo in Yugoslavia was besieged by Serbian troops, the besieged built the so-called "Sarajevo Tunnel," a communication line of 800 meters to secure contact to the outer world. A tunnel of 340 meters was about 1 meter wide and 1.5 meters high and was built beneath the airfield of the Sarajevo airport.

What do these examples tell us about the topic of interdependence between technology and war? Three aspects should be underlined in this regard:

- One big change in mining warfare occurred in the time after the middle of the 14th century, after the introduction of fire weapons and explosives: It was no longer necessary to get into a besieged castle or town by intensive digging to try to destroy the foundations of a wall. It was enough to get under the walls and place the explosives there, which would cause severe damage to any fortification—at least, as long as some specialist knew how to place and blow up the powder.
- Throughout the centuries, military mining was always the task of civilian miners. The rulers or generals used specialists who knew how to handle powder or who wrote and used theoretical treatises, but for the work in the tunnels, the rulers or generals most often resorted to the knowledge, skills and techniques of the civilian miners—in the Middle Ages, the 19th century and the First World War alike.
- Although civilian mining machines and new technologies appeared, especially in the late 19th and early 20th centuries, they were used only to a limited degree for military purposes; electrical pumps and things like that were used in the back parts of the mines and tunnels, but the work in the front parts, the real digging, had to be done by hand with tools known for centuries. This was so because of the noise the modern machines would have caused, which would have led to detection and destruction.

Summing up, one can say that the praxis of military mining—apart from the process of blowing up the mine with the help of explosives—did not change very much in the course of the centuries and remained a very conservative business—a miner from the siege of Desenberg Castle would most probably have been able to work equally well in the First World War.

NOTES

1. Paul Bentley Kern, *Ancient Siege Warfare* (Bloomington and Indianapolis: Indiana University Press, 1999), 51, 57; David Ussishkin, *The Conquest of Lachish by*

80   I. Ancient Rome and the Medieval Ages

Sennacherib (Tel Aviv University Publications of the Institute of Archaeology Number 6) (Tel Aviv: Institute of Archaeology of Tel Aviv University, 1982), 49–58.

2. Kern, *Warfare*, 252.

3. Kenneth Wiggins, *Anatomy of a Siege. King John's Castle*, Limerick, 1642 (Woodbridge: Boydell Press, 2001), 7.

4. Simon James, *The Excavations at Dura-Europos Conducted by Yale University and the French Academy of Inscriptions and Letters 1928 to 1937: Final Report VII: The Arms and Armour and other Military Equipment* (London: The British Museum Press, 2004), 30–39.

5. Cf. Cornelia Kneppe, and Hans-Werner Peine, *Der Desenberg bei Warburg, Kreis Höxter* (Münster: Altertumskommission für Westfalen, 2000).

6. Bernhard Schmeidler, ed., *Helmoldi Presbyteri Bozoviensis Cronica Slavorum* (Monumenta Germaniae Historica, Scriptores rerum Germanicarum in usum scholarum 32) (Hannover: Hahnsche Buchhandlung, 1937), 211; cf. Heinz Stoob, ed., *Helmold von Bosau. Slawenchronik* (Freiherr vom Stein-Gedächtnisausgabe 19) (Darmstadt: Wissenschaftliche Buchgesellschaft, 1973), 3.

7. K. Blaschke, "Verbreitung des Bergbaus im Mittelalter," in *Lexikon des Mittelalters* Bd. 1 (Darmstadt 1993), Sp. 1946–1947; cf. also Klaus Grewe, "Der Fulbert-Stollen am Laacher See. Eine Ingenieurleistung des hohen Mittelalters," in *Zeitschrift für Archäologie des Mittelalters* 7 (1979): 3–38.

8. Berrnhard Metz, "Dix chateaux des environs de Soultzbach," *Bulletin de l'Association pour la Sauvegarde de l'Architecture Medievale* 5 (Association pour la Sauvegarde de l'Architecture Medievale, 1978), 23–24; Philipp Jaffé, ed., "Ellenhardi Argentinensis annals et chronica. Ellenhardi chronicon—1299," in *Annales aevi Suevici* (Monumenta Germaniae Historica, Scriptores [in folio] 17), ed. Georg Heinrich Pertz (Hannover: Hahnsche Buchhandlung, 1861), 132–133; Philipp Jaffé, ed., "Annales Colmarienses, Basileenses, Chronicon Colmariense. Annales Colmarienses maiores a. 1277–1472," in *Annales aevi Suevici* (Monumenta Germaniae Historica, Scriptores [in folio] 17), ed. Georg Heinrich Pertz (Hannover: Hahnsche Buchhandlung, 1861), 217.

9. Henri Schoen, "Quelques sites de guerre de sape medievale des Vosges et du Wasgau," *Revue d'Alsace* 122 (1996): 127–130.

10. *Schoen guerre* 133–135; Alexander Thon and Rolf Übel, "Berwartstein," in *Pfälzisches Burgenlexikon* Bd. 1 A-E (Beiträge zur pfälzischen Geschichte 12.1), ed. Jürgen Keddigkeit et al. (Kaiserslautern: Institut für pfälzische Geschichte und Volkskunde, 2003), 258. Cf. Marie-Christine Bailly-Maitre, "Tradition et Innovation dans les Mines médiévales," in *L'Innovation technique au Moyen Age*, ed. Patrice Beck (Paris: Editions Errance, 1998), 99–107.

11. Schoen guerre 131, 134–135; Thomas Biller, *Die Burgengruppe Windstein: Untersuchungen zur hochmittelalterlichen Herrschaftsbildung und zur Typenentwicklung der Adelsburg im 12. u. 13. Jh.* (Veröffentlichungen der Abteilung Architektur des Kunsthistorischen Instituts der Universität zu Köln 30) (Köln: Kunsthistorisches Institut der Universität zu Köln, 1985), 81–85 und 381–382.

12. Alexander Thon, "'…daz huss ward gar zerrissen.' Belagerung und Untergang pfälzisch-elsässischer Burgen im Spätmittelalter," in *Burgen, Schlösser, Feste Häuser. Wohnen, Wehren und Wirtschaften auf Adelssitzen in der Pfalz und im Elsaß*, ed. Jürgen Keddigkeit (Kaiserslautern: Institut für pfälzische Geschichte und Volkskunde, 1997), 112–113; Jürgen Keddigkeit, Jean-Michel Rudrauf and René Kill, "Löwenstein (Lindenschmitt)," in *Pfälzisches Burgenlexikon* Bd. 3 I-N (Beiträge zur pfälzischen Geschichte 12.3), ed. Jürgen Keddigkeit et al. (Kaiserslautern: Institut für pfälzische Geschichte und Volkskunde, 2005), 467–468.

13. Kenneth Wiggins, *Siege Mines and Underground Warfare* (Shire Archaeology 84) (Princes Risborough: Shire, 2003), 15–16.
14. Chris Tabraham and Kirsty Owen, *St. Andrews Castle, Cathedral and Historic Burgh* (Edinburgh: Historic Scotland, 2010), 18–19.
15. Wiggins, *Anatomy of a Siege*.
16. Wiggins, *Siege Mines*, 37–38.
17. Christopher Duffy, *The Fortress in the Age of Vauban and Frederick the Great 1660–1789: Siege Warfare* Vol. II (London, Boston, Melbourne and Henley: Routledge and Kegan Paul, 1985), 218–221; Ekkehard Eickhoff, *Venedig, Wien und die Osmanen. Umbruch in Südosteuropa 1645–1700* (Stuttgart: Klett-Cotta, 2009), 214–221.
18. Walter Hummelberger, *Wiens erste Belagerung durch die Türken 1529* (Militärhistorische Schriftenreihe 33) (Wien: Österreichischer Bundesverlag, 1976).
19. Johannes Sachslehner, *Wien Anno 1683* (Wien: Pichler Verlag, 2006).
20. Earl J. Hess, *Into the Crater: The Mine Attack at Petersburg* (Columbia, SC: University of South Carolina Press, 2010).
21. Institute of Royal Engineers, ed., *Military Mining: The Work of the Royal Engineers in the European War, 1914–19* (Uckfield: Naval and Military Press, 2004), 1–8; Alexander Turner, *Messines 1917: The Zenith of Siege Warfare* (Campaign 225) (Oxford and Long Island City: Osprey Publishing, 2010), 22–23; cf. Ian Passingham, *Pillars of Fire. The Battle of Messines Ridge June 1917* (Stroud: Spellmount, 1998); Peter Barton, Peter Doyle and Johan Vandewalle, *Beneath Flanders Fields: The Tunnellers' War 1914–18* (Stroud: Spellmount, 2010); Simon Jones, *Underground Warfare 1914–1918* (Barnsley: Pen & Sword Military, 2010).
22. Turner, *Messines*, 39.
23. Passingham, *Pillars of Fire*, 134–186; Hew Strachan, *Der Erste Weltkrieg: Eine neue illustrierte Geschichte* (München: Pantheon Verlag, 2009), 308–309; Thorsten Loch, "Die Dritte Flandern-Schlacht," in *Der Erste Weltkrieg 1914–1918: Der deutsche Aufmarsch in ein kriegerisches Jahrhundert*, ed. Markus Pöhlmann et al. (München: Bucher Verlag, 2014), 261.
24. Turner, *Messines*, 92.
25. Robert Striffler, *Der Minenkrieg in Ladinien: Col di Lana 1915–1916* (Schriftenreihe zur Zeitgeschichte Tirols 10) (Nürnberg: Buchdienst Südtirol, 1996).
26. Adolf Buchner, *Der Minenkrieg auf Vauquois* (Deutenhausen: Adolf Buchner, 1982).
27. Jules Roy, *Der Fall von Dien Bien Phu. Indochina—der Anfang vom Ende* (Genf: Edito-Service, no year available), 323–324 and 328; James A. Warren, *Giap. The General who defeated America in Vietnam* (New York: Palgrave Macmillan, 2013), 119.
28. Tom Mangold and John Penycate, *The Tunnels of Cu Chi. A Harrowing Account of America's "Tunnel Rats" in the Underground Battlefields of Vietnam* (New York: Random House, 1985); Gordon L. Rottman, *Viet Cong and NVA Tunnels and Fortifications of the Vietnam War* (Fortress 48) (Oxford and New York: Osprey Publishing, 2006); Gordon L. Rottman, *Tunnel Rat in Vietnam* (Warrior 161) (Oxford and Long Island City: Osprey Publishing, 2012).
29. Bernd Stöver, *Geschichte des Koreakriegs: Schlachtfeld der Supermächte und ungelöster Konflikt* (München: Verlag C.H. Beck, 2013), 179.
30. Peter Doyle, Lawrence Babits and Jamie Pringle, "'For you the War is Over': Finding the Great Escape Tunnel at Stalag Luft III," in *Fields of Conflict. Battlefield Archaeology from the Roman Empire to the Korean War*, ed. Douglas Scott et al. (Washington, D.C.: Potomac Books, 2009), 398–416.

Works Cited

Bailly-Maitre, Marie-Christine. "Tradition et Innovation dans les Mines médiévales," in *L'Innovation technique au Moyen Age*, ed. Patrice Beck. Paris: Editions Errance, 1998, 99–107.
Barton, Peter, Peter Doyle, and Johan Vandewalle. *Beneath Flanders Fields: The Tunnellers' War 1914–18*. Stroud: Spellmount, 2010.
Biller, Thomas. *Die Burgengruppe Windstein: Untersuchungen zur hochmittelalterlichen Herrschaftsbildung und zur Typenentwicklung der Adelsburg im 12. u. 13. Jh. (Veröffentlichungen der Abteilung Architektur des Kunsthistorischen Instituts der Universität zu Köln 30)*. Köln: Kunsthistorisches Institut der Universität zu Köln, 1985.
Blaschke, K."Verbreitung des Bergbaus im Mittelalter," in *Lexikon des Mittelalters Bd. 1*. Darmstadt, 1993, Sp. 1946–1947.
Buchner, Adolf. *Der Minenkrieg auf Vauquois*. Deutenhausen: Adolf Buchner, 1982.
Doyle, Peter; Babits, Lawrence and Pringle, Jamie. "'For You the War is Over': Finding the Great Escape Tunnel at Stalag Luft III," in *Fields of Conflict: Battlefield Archaeology from the Roman Empire to the Korean War*, ed. Douglas Scott et al. Washington, D.C.: Potomac Books, 2009, 398–416.
Duffy, Christopher. *The Fortress in the Age of Vauban and Frederick the Great 1660–1789: Siege Warfare Volume II*. London, Boston, Melbourne and Henley: Routledge and Kegan Paul, 1985.
Eickhoff, Ekkehard. *Venedig, Wien und die Osmanen: Umbruch in Südosteuropa 1645–1700*. Stuttgart: Klett-Cotta, 2009.
Grewe, Klaus. "Der Fulbert-Stollen am Laacher See. Eine Ingenieurleistung des hohen Mittelalters," in *Zeitschrift für Archäologie des Mittelalters* 7 (1979): 3–38.
Hess, Earl J. *Into the Crater. The Mine Attack at Petersburg*. Columbia, SC: University of South Carolina Press, 2010.
Hummelberger, Walter. *Wiens erste Belagerung durch die Türken 1529 (Militärhistorische Schriftenreihe 33)*. Wien: Österreichischer Bundesverlag, 1976.
Institute of Royal Engineers, ed., *Military Mining. The Work of the Royal Engineers in the European War, 1914–19*. Uckfield: Naval and Military Press, 2004.
Jaffé, Philipp, ed. "Annales Colmarienses, Basileenses, Chronicon Colmariense. Annales Colmarienses maiores a. 1277–1472," in *Annales aevi Suevici (Monumenta Germaniae Historica, Scriptores [in folio] 17)*, ed. Georg Heinrich Pertz. Hannover: Hahnsche Buchhandlung, 1861.
Jaffé, Philipp, ed. "Ellenhardi Argentinensis annals et chronica. Ellenhardi chronicon—1299," in *Annales aevi Suevici (Monumenta Germaniae Historica, Scriptores [in folio] 17)*, ed. Georg Heinrich Pertz. Hannover: Hahnsche Buchhandlung, 1861.
James, Simon. *The Excavations at Dura-Europos Conducted by Yale University and the French Academy of Inscriptions and Letters 1928 to 1937: Final Report VII: The Arms and Armour and other Military Equipment*. London: British Museum Press, 2004.
Jones, Simon. *Underground Warfare 1914–1918*. Barnsley: Pen & Sword Military, 2010.
Kern, Paul Bentley. *Ancient Siege Warfare*. Bloomington and Indianapolis: Indiana University Press 1999.
Keddigkeit, Jürgen, Jean-Michel Rudrauf, and René Kill. "Löwenstein (Lindenschmitt),"

in *Pfälzisches Burgenlexikon Bd. 3 I-N (Beiträge zur pfälzischen Geschichte 12.3)*, ed. Jürgen Keddigkeit et al. Kaiserslautern: Institut für pfälzische Geschichte und Volkskunde, 2005.
Kneppe, Cornelia, and Hans-Werner Peine. *Der Desenberg bei Warburg, Kreis Höxter (Frühe Burgen in Westfalen 16)*, Münster: Altertumskommission für Westfalen, 2000.
Loch, Thorsten. "Die Dritte Flandern-Schlacht," in *Der Erste Weltkrieg 1914–1918: Der deutsche Aufmarsch in ein kriegerisches Jahrhundert*, ed. Markus Pöhlmann et al. München: Bucher Verlag, 2014.
Mangold, Tom and Penycate, John. *The Tunnels of Cu Chi: A Harrowing Account of America's "Tunnel Rats" in the Underground Battlefields of Vietnam*. New York: Random House, 1985.
Metz, Bernhard. "Dix chateaux des environs de Soultzbach," *Bulletin de l'Association pour la Sauvegarde de l'Architecture Medievale 5*. Association pour la Sauvegarde de l'Architecture Medievale, 1978.
Passingham, Ian. *Pillars of Fire: The Battle of Messines Ridge June 1917*. Stroud: Spellmount, 1998.
Rottman, Gordon L. *Tunnel Rat in Vietnam (Warrior 161)*. Oxford and Long Island City: Osprey Publishing, 2012.
Rottman, Gordon L. *Viet Cong and NVA Tunnels and Fortifications of the Vietnam War (Fortress 48)*. Oxford and New York: Osprey Publishing, 2006.
Roy, Jules. *Der Fall von Dien Bien Phu: Indochina—der Anfang vom Ende*. Genf: Edito-Service, no year available.
Sachslehner, Johannes. *Wien Anno 1683*. Wien: Pichler Verlag, 2006.
Schmeidler, Bernhard, ed. *Helmoldi Presbyteri Bozoviensis Cronica Slavorum (Monumenta Germaniae Historica, Scriptores rerum Germanicarum in usum scholarum 32)*. Hannover: Hahnsche Buchhandlung, 1937.
Schoen, Henri. "Quelques sites de guerre de sape medievale des Vosges et du Wasgau," *Revue d'Alsace 122* (1996): 127–130.
Stoob, Heinz, ed. *Helmold von Bosau: Slawenchronik (Freiherr vom Stein-Gedächtnisausgabe 19)*. Darmstadt: Wissenschaftliche Buchgesellschaft, 1973.
Stöver, Bernd. *Geschichte des Koreakriegs: Schlachtfeld der Supermächte und ungelöster Konflikt*. München: Verlag C.H. Beck, 2013.
Strachan, Hew. *Der Erste Weltkrieg: Eine neue illustrierte Geschichte*. München: Pantheon Verlag, 2009.
Striffler, Robert. *Der Minenkrieg in Ladinien: Col di Lana 1915–1916 (Schriftenreihe zur Zeitgeschichte Tirols 10)*. Nürnberg: Buchdienst Südtirol, 1996.
Tabraham, Chris, and Kirsty Owen. *St Andrews Castle, Cathedral and Historic Burgh*. Edinburgh: Historic Scotland, 2010.
Turner, Alexander. *Messines 1917: The Zenith of Siege Warfare (Campaign 225)*. Oxford and Long Island City: Osprey Publishing, 2010.
Thon, Alexander and Übel, Rolf. "Berwartstein," in *Pfälzisches Burgenlexikon Bd. 1 A-E (Beiträge zur pfälzischen Geschichte 12.1)*, ed. Jürgen Keddigkeit, et al. Kaiserslautern: Institut für pfälzische Geschichte und Volkskunde, 2003.
Thon, Alexander. "'...daz huss ward gar zerrissen.' Belagerung und Untergang pfälzisch-elsässischer Burgen im Spätmittelalter," in *Burgen, Schlösser, Feste Häuser. Wohnen, Wehren und Wirtschaften auf Adelssitzen in der Pfalz und im Elsaß*, ed. Jürgen Keddigkeit. Kaiserslautern: Institut für pfälzische Geschichte und Volkskunde, 1997.
Ussishkin, David. *The Conquest of Lachish by Sennacherib (Tel Aviv University Publications*

of the Institute of Archaeology Number 6). Tel Aviv: Institute of Archaeology of Tel Aviv University, 1982.

Warren, James A. *Giap: The General who Defeated America in Vietnam*. New York: Palgrave Macmillan, 2013.

Wiggins, Kenneth. *Anatomy of a Siege: King John's Castle, Limerick, 1642*. Woodbridge: Boydell Press, 2001.

Wiggins, Kenneth. *Siege Mines and Underground Warfare (Shire Archaeology 84)*. Princes Risborough: Shire, 2003.

Part II.
The Age of the World Wars

The German Navy League, Navalism and the Perception of the Imperial German Navy as a Technological Masterpiece, 1898–1914

Sebastian Diziol

In the two decades prior to the First World War, the traditional militarism of the *Bürgertum* of the German Reich was supplemented, if not superseded, in various degrees by navalism. This constituted a new phenomenon in Germany, which had, apart from the Hanse, hardly any maritime tradition to speak of.[1] Even so, with the large-scale build-up plan for the German navy under Wilhelm II and Alfred von Tirpitz and the subsequent naval arms race with Great Britain and other great powers, the navy became an increasingly prominent factor of military, political, social, cultural and even private life in Germany. This success was closely intertwined with the thoroughly modern appeal of the technology, the impressive and awe-inspiring battleships.

While there have been many historical enquiries into the decision-making process around the so-called Tirpitz Plan on the highest military and political levels in Germany and abroad,[2] there has hardly been any study on the massive cultural impact of this new navalism.[3] The term navalism has usually been used by historians to describe a certain mode of strategic thought by the military and political elites. Similar to the term militarism,[4] this article defines navalism as a mental phenomenon that describes the transfer of hierarchical systems, patterns of behavior and moral concepts inherent to the navy, the state, politics, society and culture.

The effects of this new phenomenon, its proliferation, attractiveness, contents and concepts can exemplarily be analyzed in the German Navy

League (GNL),[5] one of the main actors of German naval propaganda. Founded in 1898 with the help of the German Imperial Navy Office and industrialists, it quickly became the largest national propaganda league in Germany, counting up to 330,000 (mostly middle-class) members in 1913. The rank and file members soon realized that they were merely lobbying for the profit interests of industrialists like Friedrich Alfred Krupp and replaced the league's leadership with more independent men in 1900, with Otto Fürst zu Salm-Horstmar as the new president. They decentralized the GNL, which had up to 3,800 local branches distributed all over the Reich, and gave the rank-and-file members more possibilities for participation. The propaganda, which used all mediums known at the time, became more radical and at times even opposed the plans of Tirpitz and Wilhelm II. After massive discussions about the course of the league, both internally and publicly, the radical leaders, Salm-Horstmar, August Keim and Wilhelm Menges, were forced to resign in 1908 and were replaced by more moderate men. The former admiral Hans von Koester was elected president. The league now worked more closely together with the Imperial Navy Office and did not openly oppose their plans anymore while still making its own demands. Even though the GNL was no longer as influential in the shaping of the navy bills as it had been in the years before 1908, it had arrived in the national mainstream: it recruited more members than ever before, and its propaganda was even more active and was widely accepted by the bourgeois society.

The league's propaganda was usually most active in the months before new naval bills were passed in the Reichstag in order to voice their demands and to influence the public opinion in favor of a larger navy. The league, however, was also busy when there was not an immediate bill ahead, and they were not concentrating on specific demands for more ships or better armament, but dealing more generally with the alleged importance of sea power for the Reich. Therefore, the GNL's propaganda had a huge influence not only on the military and political elites in their naval armament plans, but also on the political mentalities of the general public, especially the middle classes.

By analyzing the propaganda of the German Navy League, this essay aims to identify the contents and the attractiveness of navalism in the German *Bürgertum* prior to 1914, which was closely connected to the notion of modernity and progressiveness of the technology of the navy. The league established, in its propaganda, an interconnected system of new national symbols, centered on the navy and oriented towards the future. The system consisted of the symbols fleet, Kaiser, world policy, flag, sea, Germans abroad and "blaue Jungs," i.e., the officers and the crews of the navy.

Before these symbols are analyzed, it is necessary to look at the propaganda methods used by the league as well as the participation of the rank-and-file members in shaping and distributing the propaganda. The national symbols established by the league were not following a master plan but evolved slowly from internal discourse between the members. As an example, the symbol "blaue Jungs," which was the most exclusive element in the system, will be analyzed more closely below, taking particular interest in its inherent concept of gender roles and their alleged mastery of modern technology. As such, this paper is not so much interested in the actual warfare technology but in the perception of it, which had a massive influence on the political mentalities of the *Bürgertum* in the years prior to World War II.

The German Navy League used every method known at the time and even introduced new and thoroughly modern media for its propaganda. The most important propaganda method was the league's monthly journal *Die Flotte*, which had a circulation of up to 375,000 copies and was regularly sent to every member. It consisted of articles, news from the local branches and short stories, often written by members of the league, which played a huge role in the establishment of the national symbols. Most of the local branches hosted lectures and speeches about naval subjects, celebrated festive events with music and dance, and offered small recreational day-trips, and many staged self-written naval plays. The audience ranged from about ten people in small villages to up to 2,000 in large cities, including members of the regional government, military officials and even members of the Federal princes' families. From 1901, as one of the first organizations worldwide, the GNL also used large-scale film propaganda, showing short films of the navy to up to 50,000 inhabitants of one city in a week.[6] In a time when recreational travel was not yet affordable or common for the middle-classes, the league offered relatively cheap week-long propaganda trips to the German coast, with visits to the harbors in Hamburg, Kiel and Wilhelmshaven, and to battleships and shipyards. It also sent several thousand schoolboys and 200 teachers each year to the coast on special trips. Additionally, the GNL published flyers, brochures, books and travel guides to the German coast, posters, and pictures of vessels and the Kaiser, as well as a guide for boys about potential careers in the navy.

In conclusion, it can be said that the propaganda not only dealt with modern technology, i.e., battleships, but also used and introduced the latest technology as a means for the propaganda, which not only attracted more interest among society but also gave the league the aura of being thoroughly modern and future-oriented itself.

Even though the league was dominated by men and until 1914 there was not a single woman holding an office, female members as well as wives and daughters of male members played an active role on a smaller scale in the shaping and distributing of the league's propaganda, and therefore, the system of national symbols. They wrote short stories published in the *Flotte*, wrote, staged and starred in plays in local branches and held charity meetings.

From the mid–1890s, there had been a shift in German nationalism. Before, the unification had been seen as the culmination, if not the end point, of German history. This was reflected by the Bismarckian foreign policy of saturation, with Europe being the focal point. The 1890s saw the coming of age of a generation for whom the unification was self-evident and who saw it as a starting point from which to achieve something bigger, to become a major world power. Together with the booming German economy and the technical progress made in all areas of everyday life, the Reich was bursting with self-confidence. The focal point for its foreign policy was no longer Europe, but overseas. The traditional national symbols of the Reich, which were all oriented at the past, the wars against Napoleon, the wars of unification and the army, could not display Germany's new expansionism or its grasp for world power.

Therefore, symbolic struggles[7] emerged for the establishment of new national symbols directed towards the future of the Reich as a major world power. The German Navy League was one of the most successful actors in these symbolic struggles. In the internal discourse among the members and in its propaganda, there slowly emerged a system of new and thoroughly modern national symbols, which were oriented at the major zeitgeist phenomenon of the time: the navy, which reflected the military and economic and technological strength of the Reich like nothing else. The GNL gave traditional symbols like the flag new meanings and introduced new ones like the "blaue Jungs." The symbolic system was heavily interconnected; every element of it referred to every other, so that everybody who believed in one of the symbols would automatically, voluntarily or involuntarily, by acclamation also support all the others.

The navy itself stood at the center of the symbolic system. In the propaganda of the league, the navy was the weapon of the future, which made overseas trade, overseas expansion and world policy possible in the first place. It was portrayed as a major technological achievement in its own right: "A battleship of the present represents an ingenious masterpiece of technology, currently there is hardly any bigger technological achievement that human beings can put together in the confined space of 120 metres in lengths and 23 metres in width."[8] As the general belief in technological progress was still mainly unbroken in the decades before 1914, new technologies and groundbreaking technological achievements were important for the national prestige in the peaceful competition among the nations. In that sense, in the reading of the league, the navy added as much if not more to Germany's national prestige as, for example, the Eiffel Tower to the French. Countless articles about the latest developments in the technology of battleships were published in the league's journal, most often written by experts and engineers.[9] The journal also participated in discussions about future technologies of the navy that were just being tested, like submarines.[10]

The propaganda of the GNL portrayed the navy as thoroughly modern and connected it closely to the future of the Reich itself. With a strong navy, Germany would rise to become a major world power; without it, it would lose its power status even in Europe. Accordingly, the league's propaganda identified not the unification in 1871 but the passing of the first navy bill in the Reichstag in 1898 as the culmination of German history in the 19th century.

Above the symbol "navy," stood the symbol "Kaiser," a traditional symbol, which the GNL charged with new dimensions of meaning. Its propaganda closely connected it to the charismatic personality and the popular image of Wilhelm II.[11] The Kaiser in the league's reading was no longer only the warrantor of the existence of the German Reich in central Europe but interpreted as personification of the nation itself, as the youthful visionary and leader to a glorious future. The league's propaganda celebrated the great progress Germany had allegedly made in all areas of economic, technological, military, political and cultural life in the reign of Wilhelm II. As his major achievement, as his life's work, however, it identified the naval armament. It portrayed him as the visionary who had very early recognized the alleged importance of a strong navy and who had tirelessly worked against all odds and resistances to spread the understanding of the assumed necessity of sea power to the people and the Reichstag.[12] The GNL presented Wilhelm II as the father and builder of the German navy: "If today Germany's flag waves above a modern fleet, which in all its aspects is the work of Your Majesty, it befits the German Navy League to express its deep gratitude for that in the name of the German people."[13]

The symbol had a strong antidemocratic subtext and emphasized the Caesarism of Wilhelm's rule, as the GNL demanded that the people had to follow the Kaiser's leadership and stand united with him against the unloved Reichstag and the despised party politics. At the same time, the Navy League created the image of a close contiguousness among its members, and the Kaiser himself presented the league as the foremost collaborator of Wilhelm II in spreading the understanding of the alleged necessity of a strong navy to the people. The visible symbol for this pretended contiguousness was Prince Heinrich, the brother of the Kaiser, who was protector of the GNL. The members could picture themselves as national elite who worked closely together with the visionary Wilhelm II towards a glorious future of the Reich as a major world power. In order to make this alleged close connection between the league and the Hohenzollern family visible, the members regularly sent goodwill telegrams to the Kaiser and his brother from their meetings, thereby giving *de facto* meaningless get-togethers in a tiny village the aura of an assembly of national importance.

The element "world policy" was situated at the head of the league's system of national symbols. Even though it represented the destination the GNL envisioned for the future of the Reich, it never became quite clear what exactly world policy meant. The term always stayed diffuse and had to be given meaning by the recipient of the league's propaganda. The closest the GNL ever came to a definition of the term was "to pursue world policy does not mean to be jack-of-all-the-world's-trades but to guard Germany's commerce and its merchant navy against wrongful conduct, affronts and vexations, to protect every German subject overseas, no matter if he is a businessman a pioneer for German spiritual and cultural life."[14] This ambiguous use of the term made the GNL attractive to the whole spectrum of the political right; proponents of an informal, economically motivated world policy could identify with the symbol as well as could those who were in favor of a more aggressive, culturally motivated formal interpretation of the concept. The only point the GNL always stressed was that everybody who supported German world policy, and the league left no doubt that the Reich had no other choice,[15] had to be also in favor of sea power, as a strong navy was seen as the condition for world policy.

The sea itself was the next element in the symbolic system of the GNL. In its propaganda, the sea appeared as the highway, the battlefield, and the realm of the future, which therefore would belong to the nation controlling the oceans. The league gave the sea a mythical as well as cathartic quality as both origin and aim of the German people, who, in the GNL's reading, had a deeply rooted desire for it that had been asleep for centuries and was now awakening again. "There is no new world to explore anymore, but on the sea lies the new German Reich, in which the two-headed dragon of the old one— fraternal strife and poverty—does not exist any longer. Not only will the general welfare, but also the feeling of togetherness rise through extensive overseas commerce and overseas possessions."[16]

The flag of the German Reich was another symbol to which the GNL gave new meaning. The colors black, white and red had been introduced by Bismarck in 1866, out of the sheer necessity of having a common flag for the merchant vessels. He consciously chose those colors, as they had no real tradition. Accordingly, in the first decades after 1871, this flag hardly aroused any emotions in the subjects, who still identified with the flags of their respective counties.[17] It was not until 1892 that Wilhelm II officially announced the colors to be the national flag of the Reich. The GNL was anxious to give the colors black, white and red real meaning to make the flag an object of identification, positive emotion and integration: "This flag [black-white-red] is sometimes utterly described as [a] merchant flag. To us, however, there seems no doubt that the term 'national flag' is the only rightful and dignified name."[18] In many league meetings, the members sang the so-called *Flag Song* together, which pledged allegiance to the flag as well as the fatherland and promised to defend it against any foes. In its propaganda, it invented a tradition by publishing articles about the heraldry of the flag.[19] More importantly, however, was that the GNL tied the flag closely to the navy and the sea, which had been its primordial use.

In this specific reading, the nation, represented by the flag, evolved out of the merchant navy, which carried it around the whole world, adding to German wealth, power and prestige. For Germans worldwide, the flag would convey a sense of belonging, of home and security:

> The flags of the homeland wave cheerfully above consulates and navy vessels in foreign countries, heightening the spirits of every German abroad for he knows that he is not unprotected in the face of the arbitrariness of foreigners. There is no day more beautiful for the German abroad than when a German warship gives him the exhilarating feeling to be a member of a great, powerful people, when he is able to shake hands with the German crew and feels that the plank below his feet is German soil, even at the most remote shore.[20]

This connected the flag with the next symbol, the Germans abroad. While in reality, the main feature of the German subjects who lived all over the globe was their heterogeneity,[21] the GNL portrayed them as a more or less homogeneous group with similar values, interests and self-perceptions, who were important protagonists of German world power. It called them bearers of Germandom and agents of German overseas trade who had to be protected by the fatherland, thereby constructing an argument for more navy vessels.

While many other symbols like "Kaiser" and "flag" had been traditional national symbols to which the GNL gave new dimensions of meaning, the symbol "blaue Jungs" was entirely new and created by the GNL. It acted as a role model for "the perfect German" in politics, society and private life. The symbol thereby helped in shaping the self-perception of the *Bürgertum* as well as defining the national identity in the decades prior to the First World War. The "blaue Jungs" stood for youthfulness, for the beginning of a great career and for marching self-confidently into an open, long and promising future. In the reading of the league's propaganda, they were full of strength, freshness, vitality and zest for action; they mastered the modern technology on board the battleships to perfection. On a meta-level, they embodied the "young" German Reich and were the immediate personification of the navy.

One of the major tools for the distribution of the symbol used by the GNL, therefore, was simply to tell stories about it in articles and short stories published in the monthly journal or the league's calendar, in theatre plays staged by the local branches, in songs sung at meetings and in films. The protagonists of those stories, however, were not so much well-invented, diverse and complex characters but rather always followed the same clichés.

Two dimensions of meaning were inherent in this symbol, and there were two possibilities of reading it: a "masculine" and a "feminine" one. While the masculine dimension was supposed to address teenage boys and men, the feminine dimension was directed to teenage girls and women. Both dimensions consciously fulfilled certain desires, created role-models and offered projection screens for hopes, wishes and dreams.

Generally speaking, the GNL presented the members of the navy as archetypes for boys and men on the one hand and as objects of lust and desire for girls and women. In both dimensions, they were portrayed as the heroes of the navy who were supposed to facilitate the identification with the fleet as well as the political ideas and aims of the GNL. On the masculine dimension, they gave a human touch to the otherwise cold technology of the navy vessels; on the feminine dimension, they charged them with eroticism.

Three main prototypes of "blaue Jungs" can be found in the League's propaganda: naval cadets in the bloom of their youth, airily and boisterous and with a zest for action, naval officers in the prime of their age, experienced, sophisticated, responsible and marriageable and last but not least, old captains, fulfilling every cliché of the sea dog, being intelligent if not wise, hard-bitten and taciturn. Their physical appearance followed the aesthetical ideal of the time and always hinted at their Germanic parentage: they were invariably tall, strong, slim, blonde and blue-eyed.

The major attribute given to the "blaue Jungs" by the GNL was their alleged faithfulness, which was closely connected to the term "duty." The faithfulness of the "blaue Jungs" belonged first and foremost to the Kaiser, the flag and the *Vaterland*. Second, came their faithfulness to their fellow soldiers and only third, came their fidelity to a woman. In the gender roles imagined by the political right at the time, the family was very important, however, it was never allowed to "chain" the man to his home or to question his duty to the nation and the military, to whom his foremost loyalty belonged.[22]

The "blaue Jungs" were also portrayed as having complete mastery of the modern, highly complex technology of the battleships. This characterization is most evident in the short story, "Wir im Turme" (We in the gun turret), published in *Die Flotte* in 1911, in which the crew of a turret is portrayed during a maneuver: "The crew became more secure, more brisk and more skillful with every shot. They worked in breathless fervor but without haste [...] eager not to make even the smallest mistake."[23] The emphasis of the technical expertise of the "blaue Jungs" implied that they would not have a problem in finding a job after their military service, as technicians and engineers were highly asked for in the industry. In this short story, the turret itself was personified as a living creature, with which the "blaue Jungs" were strongly connected:

> We got used to our turret, and when his huge body quiveringly lifted and lowered, when it groaned and moaned, when it exhalated toxic gases and filled the whole room with its steamily breath, when it hissingly recoiled just to glide back again ponderously, when it obeyed our cues and commands, spitting its projectiles just as far as we ordered, it seemed to us to be a living creature, which wanted to be treated well and which had its moods.... And I thought I sometimes saw Salchow fondling it, saw Anders snubbing it earnestly. When we looked through its soul, enquiringly and exploratory, like the artillerist does, through the long, cold ordnance, we learned to read the movements of its soul; We recognized when the monster did not feel quite well in its innermost body, slowly recognized the movements of his soul [...] To work with it was pure lust for us.[24]

This personification of the turret is charged with a strong sexual subtext: the "lust" of the "blaue Jungs" was not fulfilled by the (physical) love of a woman but by the turret. The experienced bodies of the crew merge with the "lifting and lowering, moaning and groaning" body of the machine, making modern warfare technology humane and desirable in every sense of the word.

In the late 19th century, when women began to demand an equal place and status in society as men, a crisis of masculinity emerged.[25] The GNL portrayed the life on board the ships of the Imperial Navy as an exclusively masculine sphere in which the traditional image of masculinity was still intact and to which women had no access.[26]

The feminine dimension portrayed the "blaue Jungs" as perfect lovers and husbands due to their sexual attractiveness and faithfulness as well as perfect sons-in-law thanks to their honor and sophistication. It also showed the women their place and role in society, which in the league's reading, was to support the soldiers of the navy, offer them recreation and provide them with a comfortable home for the best of the "blaue Jungs" and the best of the nation, which they embodied.

This complex and interwoven system of new national symbols propagated by the German Navy League can be seen as the core of the mental phenomenon navalism in Wilhelmine Germany. While German militarism was grounded in the experience of strength—Germany had the strongest army worldwide—navalism, in contrast, was grounded in the experience of weakness, as the Reich had only a marginal fleet compared to Great Britain. The attractiveness of navalism, therefore, lay in giving a strong promise directed to the future: it did not represent the saturated continental foreign policy of Bismarckian Germany but the Reich's grasp for world power. It was reflationary, energetic, progressive, aggressive and genuinely modern. While militarism was stagnant, inherent in navalism was a strong dynamic. At the same time, it conveyed a promise of departure, adventure, exoticism and wanderlust while implying a minimum of the risks usually inherent in those terms thanks to the alleged strength and technical superiority of the German navy.

NOTES

1. John B. Hattendorf, "Deutschland und die See. Historische Wurzeln deutscher Seestreitkräfte bis 1815," in *Deutsche Marinen im Wandel: Vom Symbol nationaler Einheit zum Instrument internationaler Sicherheit*, ed. Werner Rahn (München: Oldenbourg, 2005), 17–40.

2. Amongst the most important studies are Eckart Kehr, *Schlachtflottenbau und Parteipolitik 1894–1901: Versuch eines Querschnitts durch die innenpolitischen, sozialen und ideologischen Voraussetzungen des deutschen Imperialismus* (Berlin: Ebering, 1930); Volker R. Berghahn, *Der Tirpitz-Plan: Genesis und Verfall einer innenpolitischen Krisenstrategie unter Wilhelm II* (Düsseldorf: Droste, 1971); Rolf Hobson, *Imperialism at Sea: Naval Strategic Thought, the Ideology of Sea Power, and the Tirpitz Plan 1875 bis 1914* (Boston: Brill, 2004); Michael Epkenhans, *Die wilhelminische Flottenrüstung 1908–1914: Weltmachtstreben, industrieller Fortschritt, soziale Integration* (München: Oldenbourg, 1991).

3. The only exceptions are Jan Rüger, *The Great Naval Game: Britain and Germany in the Age of Empire* (Cambridge: Cambridge University Press, 2007); Sebastian Diziol, "'Deutsche, werdet Mitglieder des Vaterlandes!' Der Deutsche Flottenverein 1898–1934" (Ph.D. diss., University of Hamburg, 2013); the studies W. Mark Hamilton, *The Nation and the Navy: Methods and Organization of British Navalist Propaganda, 1889–1914* (New York, London: Garland, 1986) and W. Mark Hamilton, "The 'New Navalism' and the British Navy League, 1895–1914," *Mariners Mirror* 64, no. 1 (1978): 37–44 look at navalism in Great Britain from a more cultural historical point of view.

4. Wolfram Wette, *Militarismus und Pazifismus: Auseinandersetzungen mit den deutschen Kriegen* (Bremen: Donat, 1991); Wolfram Wette, *Militarismus in Deutschland: Geschichte einer kriegerischen Kultur* (Frankfurt a.M.: Fischer-Taschenbuch-Verlag, 2008); Stig Förster, "Militär und Militarismus im Deutschen Kaiserreich: Versuch einer differenzierten Betrachtung," in *Militarismus in Deutschland 1871 bis 1945: Zeitgenössische Analysen und Kritik*, ed. Wolfram Wette, 63–80 (Münster, London: Lit, 1999).

5. Konrad Schilling, *Beiträge zu einer Geschichte des radikalen Nationalismus in der Wilhelminischen Ära 1890–1909: Die Entstehung des radikalen Nationalismus, seine Einflussnahme auf die innere und äußere Politik des Deutschen Reiches und die Stellung von Regierung und Reichstag zu seiner politischen und publizistischen Aktivität* (Köln: Gouder u. Hansen, 1968), 179–371; Geoff Eley, "Reshaping the Right: Radical Nationalism and the German Navy League 1898–1908," *Historical Journal* 21, no. 2 (1978): 327–354; Geoff Eley, *Reshaping the German Right: Radical Nationalism and Political Change after Bismarck* (New Haven, London: Yale University Press, 1980); Wilhelm Deist, *Flottenpolitik und Flottenpropaganda: Das Nachrichtenbureau des Reichsmarineamtes 1897–1914* (Stuttgart: DVA, 1976), 147–247; Diziol, *Flottenverein*.

6. Martin Loiperdinger, "The Beginnings of German Film Propaganda: The Navy League as travelling Exhibitor," *Historical Journal of Film, Radio and Television* 22, no. 3 (2002): 305–313.

7. For the theoretical background of political symbols and symbolic struggles see Gerhard Göhler, "Der Zusammenhang von Institution, Macht und Repräsentation," in *Institution, Macht, Repräsentation: Wofür politische Institutionen stehen und*

wie sie wirken, ed. Gerhard Göhler (Baden-Baden: Nomos-Verlags-Gesellschaft, 1997), 11–65.

    8. "Der Wandel im Bau von Kriegsschiffen während des 19. Jahrhunderts," in *Die Flotte*, Feb. 1903, 24, my translation.

    9. See for example "Die Krahne im Werftbetrieb; Deutsche Riesenkrahne; Der größte Krahn der Welt," in *Die Flotte*, March 1902, 35–38; "Die Dampfturbinen," in *Die Flotte*, March 1904, 37–39; "Marinegeschütze und deren Munititon," in *Die Flotte*, Juni 1904, 91–93; "Über ein neues Geschützsystem," in *Die Flotte*, Oct. 1904, 162; "Die Chemie im Dienste der Schifffahrt," in *Die Flotte*, Oct. 1907, 150–152; "Beton-Panzerplatten," in *Die Flotte*, July 1908, 102–103; "Die Entwicklung der Schiffsturbine," in *Die Flotte*, Dec. 1910, 197–201.

    10. See for example "Von den Unterseebooten der Gegenwart," in *Die Flotte*, Feb. 1905, 21–22; "Die Entwickelung und der jetzige Stand des Unterseebootwesens," in *Die Flotte*, Nov. 1908, 164–166; "Im Unterseeboot, von Korvettenkapitän a.D. Graf Bernstorff," in *Die Flotte*, Nov. 1910, 179–180;

    11. See for example Elisabeth Fehrenbach, *Wandlungen des deutschen Kaisergedankens 1871–1918* (München, Wien: Oldenbourg, 1969); Michael A. Obst, *"Einer nur ist Herr im Reiche": Kaiser Wilhelm II. als politischer Redner* (Paderborn: Schöningh, 2010); Alexander König, *Wie mächtig war der Kaiser? Kaiser Wilhelm II. zwischen Königsmechanismus und Polykratie von 1908 bis 1914* (Stuttgart: Steiner, 2009); Wolfgang König, *Wilhelm II. und die Moderne: Der Kaiser und die technisch-industrielle Welt* (Paderborn: Schöningh, 2007); the most important biography about the last Kaiser is Röhl: John C. G. Röhl, *Wilhelm II.: Die Jugend des Kaisers 1859–1888* (München: Beck, 1993); John C. G. Röhl, *Wilhelm II.: Der Aufbau der persönlichen Monarchie 1888–1900* (München: Beck, 2001); John C. G. Röhl, *Wilhelm II.: Der Weg in den Abgrund 1900–1941* (München: Beck, 2008).

    12. See for example "Der Kaiser und die Flotte," in *Die Flotte*, June 1913, 98–102.

    13. "Glückwunschurkunde," in *Die Flotte*, June 1913, 99, my translation.

    14. "Dortmund als Industrie- und Handelsstadt und sein Anteil am Welthandel," in *Die Flotte*, Sept. 1910, 147.

    15. See for example ibid; "Weltmächte der Gegenwart," in *Die Flotte*, Jan. 1911, 5–6; "Imperialismus und Flottenpolitik," in *Die Flotte*, Jan. 1914, 1–3.

    16. "Die geschichtliche Entwickelung der deutschen Seemacht: Festrede, gehalten anlässlich der Hauptversammlung des DFV am 28.3. zu München von Prof. Ritter von Heigel," in *Die Flotte*, Mai 1903, 81, my translation.

    17. Hans Hattenhauer, *Deutsche Nationalsymbole: Geschichte und Bedeutung*, 4th edition (München: Olzog, 2006) 41–44; Karlheinz Weißmann, *Schwarze Fahnen, Runenzeichen: Die Entwicklung der politischen Symbolik der deutschen Rechten zwischen 1890 und 1945* (Düsseldorf: Droste, 1991), 23–24; Elisabeth Fehrenbach, "Über die Bedeutung der politischen Symbole im Nationalstaat," *Historische Zeitschrift* 213 (1971): 296–357, 344–345; Bernd Buchner, *Um nationale und republikanische Identität: Die deutsche Sozialdemokratie und der Kampf um die politischen Symbole in der Weimarer Republik* (Bonn: Dietz, 2001), 65–68.

    18. "Die deutsche Kriegs- und Handelsflagge, ihre Geschichte und ihre Heraldik," in *Die Flotte*, March 1901, 43–45; see also "Kommandozeichen," in *Die Flotte*, Dec. 1906, 180–181; "Flagge und Wimpel," in *Die Flotte*, June 1908, 87.

    19. See for example "Die deutsche Kriegs- und Handelsflagge, ihre Geschichte und ihre Heraldik," in *Die Flotte*, March 1901, 43–45; "Kommandozeichen," in *Die Flotte*, Dec. 1906, 180–181; "Flagge und Wimpel," in *Die Flotte*, June 1908, 87.

    20. "Das Deutschtum in Südamerika," in *Die Flotte*, Feb. 1902, 17, my translation.

II. The Age of the World Wars

21. See for example Klaus J. Bade, ed., *Deutsche im Ausland, Fremde in Deutschland: Migration in Geschichte und Gegenwart* (München: Beck, 1992), 135–230; Sebastian Conrad and Philipp Ther, "On the Move: Mobility, Migration, and Nation 1880–1948," in *The Oxford Handbook of Modern German History*, edited by Helmut Walser Smith, 573–590 (Oxford: Oxford University Press, 2011), 574–578.

22. René Schilling, *"Kriegshelden": Deutungsmuster heroischer Männlichkeit in Deutschland 1813–1945* (Paderborn: Schöningh, 2002), 205.

23. "Wir im Turm," in *Die Flotte*, March 1911, 1–2, my translation; for information on the technology and the handling of turrets see Peter Max Gutzwiller, *Die deutschen Kriegsmarinen im 19. Jahrhundert. Fakten, Daten, Zusammenhänge* (Berlin: Duncker & Humblot, 2014), 314–324.

24. "Wir im Turm," in *Die Flotte*, March 1911, 1–2, my translation.

25. René Schilling, *"Kriegshelden": Deutungsmuster heroischer Männlichkeit in Deutschland 1813–1945* (Paderborn: Schöningh, 2002), 205.

26. See for example "Der imitierte Fähnrich zur See," in *Die Flotte*, April 1904; "Der Messingschornstein," in *Die Flotte*, Feb. 1914, 3.

Works Cited

Bade, Klaus J., ed. *Deutsche im Ausland, Fremde in Deutschland: Migration in Geschichte und Gegenwart*. München: Beck, 1992.

Berghahn, Volker R. *Der Tirpitz-Plan: Genesis und Verfall einer innenpolitischen Krisenstrategie unter Wilhelm II.* Düsseldorf: Droste, 1971.

Buchner, Bernd. *Um nationale und republikanische Identität: Die deutsche Sozialdemokratie und der Kampf um die politischen Symbole in der Weimarer Republik*. Bonn: Dietz, 2001.

Conrad, Sebastian, and Philpp Ther. "On the Move: Mobility, Migration, and Nation 1880–1948," in *The Oxford Handbook of Modern German History*, edited by Helmut Walser Smith. Oxford: Oxford University Press, 2011, 573–590.

Deist, Wilhelm. *Flottenpolitik und Flottenpropaganda: Das Nachrichtenbureau des Reichsmarineamtes 1897–1914*. Stuttgart: DVA, 1976.

Diziol, Sebastian. "'Deutsche, werdet Mitglieder des Vaterlandes!' Der Deutsche Flottenverein 1898–1934." Ph.D. diss., University of Hamburg, 2013.

Eley, Geoff. "The German Navy League in German Politics 1898–1914." Ph.D. diss., University of Sussex, 1974.

Eley, Geoff. "Reshaping the Right: Radical Nationalism and the German Navy League 1898–1908," *Historical Journal* 21, no. 2 (1978): 327–354.

Eley, Geoff. *Reshaping the German Right: Radical Nationalism and Political Change after Bismarck*. New Haven, London: Yale University Press, 1980.

Epkenhans, Michael. *Die wilhelminische Flottenrüstung 1908–1914: Weltmachtstreben, industrieller Fortschritt, soziale Integration*. München: Oldenbourg, 1991.

Fehrenbach, Elisabeth. *Wandlungen des deutschen Kaisergedankens 1871–1918*. München, Wien: Oldenbourg, 1969.

Fehrenbach, Elisabeth. "Über die Bedeutung der politischen Symbole im Nationalstaat," *Historische Zeitschrift* 213 (1971): 296–357.

Förster, Stig. "Militär und Militarismus im Deutschen Kaiserreich: Versuch einer differenzierten Betrachtung," in *Militarismus in Deutschland 1871 bis 1945: Zeitgenössische Analysen und Kritik*, ed. Wolfram Wette. Münster, London: Lit, 1999, 63–80.

Göhler, Gerhard. "Der Zusammenhang von Institution, Macht und Repräsentation," in *Institution, Macht, Repräsentation: Wofür politische Institutionen stehen und*

wie sie wirken, ed. Gerhard Göhler. Baden-Baden: Nomos-Verlags-Gesellschaft, 1997, 11–65.
Gutzwiller, Peter Max. *Die deutschen Kriegsmarinen im 19. Jahrhundert. Fakten, Daten, Zusammenhänge.* Berlin: Duncker & Humblot 2014.
Hamilton, W. Mark. "The 'New Navalism' and the British Navy League, 1895–1914." *Mariners Mirror* 64, no. 1 (1978): 37–44.
Hamilton, W. Mark. *The Nation and the Navy: Methods and Organization of British Navalist Propaganda, 1889–1914.* New York, London: Garland, 1986.
Hattendorf, John B. "Deutschland und die See. Historische Wurzeln deutscher Seestreitkräfte bis 1815," in *Deutsche Marinen im Wandel: Vom Symbol nationaler Einheit zum Instrument internationaler Sicherheit,* ed. Werner Rahn. München: Oldenbourg, 2005, 17–40.
Hattenhauer, Hans. *Deutsche Nationalsymbole: Geschichte und Bedeutung,* 4th edition. München: Olzog, 2006.
Hobson, Rolf. *Imperialism at Sea: Naval Strategic Thought, the Ideology of Sea Power, and the Tirpitz Plan 1875 bis 1914.* Boston: Brill, 2004.
Kehr, Eckart. *Schlachtflottenbau und Parteipolitik 1894–1901: Versuch eines Querschnitts durch die innenpolitischen, sozialen und ideologischen Vorraussetzungen des deutschen Imperialismus.* Berlin: Ebering, 1930.
König, Alexander. *Wie mächtig war der Kaiser? Kaiser Wilhelm II. zwischen Königsmechanismus und Polykratie von 1908 bis 1914.* Stuttgart: Steiner, 2009.
König, Wolfgang. *Wilhelm II. und die Moderne: Der Kaiser und die technischindustrielle Welt.* Paderborn: Schöningh, 2007.
Loiperdinger, Martin. "The Beginnings of German Film Propaganda: The Navy League as travelling Exhibitor," *Historical Journal of Film, Radio and Television* 22, no. 3 (2002): 305–313.
Obst, Michael A. *"Einer nur ist Herr im Reiche": Kaiser Wilhelm II. als politischer Redner.* Paderborn: Schöningh, 2010.
Röhl, John C.G. *Wilhelm II.: Die Jugend des Kaisers 1859–1888.* München: Beck, 1993.
Röhl, John C.G. *Wilhelm II.: Der Aufbau der persönlichen Monarchie 1888–1900.* München: Beck, 2001.
Röhl, John C.G. *Wilhelm II.: Der Weg in den Abgrund 1900–1941.* München: Beck, 2008.
Rüger, Jan. *The Great Naval Game: Britain and Germany in the Age of Empire.* Cambridge: Cambridge University Press, 2007.
Schilling, Konrad. *Beiträge zu einer Geschichte des radikalen Nationalismus in der Wilhelminischen Ära 1890–1909: Die Entstehung des radikalen Nationalismus, seine Einflussnahme auf die innere und äußere Politik des Deutschen Reiches und die Stellung von Regierung und Reichstag zu seiner politischen und publizistischen Aktivität.* Köln: Gouder u. Hansen, 1968.
Schilling, René. *"Kriegshelden": Deutungsmuster heroischer Männlichkeit in Deutschland 1813–1945.* Paderborn: Schöningh, 2002.
Weißmann, Karlheinz. *Schwarze Fahnen, Runenzeichen: Die Entwicklung der politischen Symbolik der deutschen Rechten zwischen 1890 und 1945.* Düsseldorf: Droste, 1991.
Wette, Wolfram. *Militarismus und Pazifismus: Auseinandersetzungen mit den deutschen Kriegen.* Bremen: Donat, 1991.
Wette, Wolfram. *Militarismus in Deutschland: Geschichte einer kriegerischen Kultur.* Frankfurt a.M.: Fischer-Taschenbuch-Verlag, 2008.

The Soviet Propaganda Film as an Instrument of Warfare
Sergey Eisenstein's Montage Technique and the "Global Civil War of Ideologies"

GERRIT DWOROK

From a certain historical point of view, the end of World War I was the beginning of a war after the war. President Wilson's concept of the self-determination of peoples evoked and reinforced unrealizable hopes, which again unintentionally led to nationalistic fights and ethnic clashes of an extreme degree.[1] Moreover, the uprising thinking in strongly ideological terms ushered in a new epoch: a *global civil war of ideologies*.[2] The liberal "western" nation-states stood against the Bolshevist utopia of a non-capitalistic, socialist world. In addition to this, power-gaining fascist movements demonized both liberal as well as communist ideologies, attacking democratic and leftist parties at the same time.

In this global conflict, the key actors battled for their own conception of a society's political and socio-economic order. They all had a strong sense of mission and competed for the souls and minds not only of their own people but also of the "world's society." Within this struggle, propaganda, which already had shown its potential in World War I, became a major instrument of ideological warfare.

In a general view, this paper deals with propaganda as a technique of confirming dominion and exporting ideology. A special focus is put on propaganda films as a new type of media with high impact on leading politicians and the slowly arising mass audience. As significant examples, the text examines Sergey Eisenstein's films *Battleship Potemkin* and *October*. The major issues of this survey are these questions: To what extent was Eisenstein involved in Soviet propaganda campaigns, and how did his use of montage style, "an editing technique in which shots are juxtaposed in an often fast-paced fashion that compresses time and conveys a lot of information in a relatively short period," influence contemporary concepts of the "bourgeois" enemy?[3]

Approaching the "age of extremes": The Soviet Policy of Agitprop

The 20th century began with two fulminant outbursts of violence. In 1914, European politicians initially were not willing and finally not able to prevent the outbreak of World War I, a fact that eventually caused almost 10 million dead and more than 20 million wounded.[4] Besides this disaster, which John F. Kennan once described as the "great seminal catastrophe of this century,"[5] other events shook the world not less than the so-called Great War: Vladimir Ilyitsch Lenin's Bolshevik Revolution in 1917, followed by the immensely brutal Russian Civil War in the period between November 1917 and October 1922.[6]

In both conflicts, propaganda was considered as a key to military success. Until the end of the 19th century, the term was used in a neutral way. Back then, it described the act of distributing political ideas and religious beliefs. However, in World War I, propaganda appeared as a more lurid business. In the early 20th century, it had already transformed into an "attempt to influence the public opinions of an audience through the transmission of ideas and values."[7] Improved by politicians and military authorities, it soon became an instrument for recruiting soldiers and mobilizing the home front, for example, when allied propaganda misleadingly used pictures of a Russian pogrom to illustrate German cruelty or when German propaganda untruthfully claimed that Nürnberg had been bombed by the French air force in 1914.[8] Finally, in the aftermath of the war, propaganda belonged to the standard means of a democratic as well as a totalitarian policy, not being disavowed until the end of World War II.[9]

For the Bolshevik movement, propaganda played an extraordinarily decisive role since it seemed to be a promising opportunity to establish the Marxist-Leninist ideology in the Russian society. In the long run, Lenin and his Bolshevik followers attempted to shape new men, thereby creating a utopia that particularly seemed to require the professional use of mass manipulation. According to Lenin, who developed his vision of professional propaganda in three programmatic papers (*S čego načat'?* [1901]; *Čto delat'?* [1902]; *Partijnaja organizacija i partijnaja literatura* [1905]), political indoctrination had to be an exclusive issue of the Bolshevik party since the crowd was not capable of developing revolutionary awareness on its own. Theoretically, propaganda was distinguished from agitation. Whereas the latter concept referred to practical action in terms of the Communist Party (pointing at *emotio*), propaganda seemed to be a more sophisticated concept dealing with all possible means of influencing henchmen as defined by the Marxist-Leninist ideology (pointing at the communist understanding of *ratio*). As Georgi Plechanov stated in 1891, the *agitator* presents only few ideas to a mass audience in order to make people act. The *propagandist*, on the contrary, introduces many communist ideas to a small group of comrades in order to raise their political awareness.[10] In practice, one could not separate those two kinds of indoctrinating PR from each other. Thus, the Bolsheviks established a comprehensive, statewide *Department for Agitation and Propaganda* in 1920.[11] From this time on, agitprop, the institutionalized mixture of interactive action and theory, was an inherent part of communist policy. One of the founders was Sergey Chakhotin, a scholar of Ivan Pavlov, who is known for being the father of Classical Conditioning. The newly-shaped department would combine psychological studies with political ideology in order to support all sorts of Soviet propaganda.[12] In this regard, cinematic pictures attracted special notice. In 1918, when communist leaders organized official festivities to commemorate the October Revolution in Leningrad, films had already been in the field.[13] Lenin himself realized the forward-looking qualities of the new medium. Whereas the last Russian Tsar, Nicholas II, considered cinema to be "an empty, totally useless, and even harmful form of entertainment," Lenin maintained in 1922: "Of all the arts, for us the cinema is the most important."[14] There were mainly two reasons for taking his words into account. Firstly, the Bolsheviks needed an efficient way to spread their ideology especially in rural areas, in which scarcely anybody was capable of reading. The communist education of the Russian (and all the other) peasants in the territories of the later Soviet Union was one of the most striking conditions for the communist party to be successful.[15] Secondly, they needed convincing arguments in the threatening state of civil war. A rapidly changing front demanded flexibility and skills to mobilize combatants against the *Whites* within a short period of time. For this purpose, agitpunkty (agitational centers) were installed in strategic places along the railways or in bigger settlements. In addition to this, Bolshevik propaganda trains crossed the land and brought manipulative media to remote places of Russia. As stated by Richard Taylor, "it was the cinema that helped to make visits of the trains memorable, for most peasants had never before seen a moving picture."[16]

Despite the Red Army's carrying of the day in the Russian Civil War, the Bolsheviks did not manage to gain full control of all peoples and social classes within their claimed dominion. That, as well as the overbearance of the upcoming Soviet system, caused a strong request by the communist leaders to reinforce the policy of agitprop (Lenin died in 1924 and was succeeded by Joseph Stalin). In this context, the Soviet film industry was strongly pushed, which enabled vanguard directors like Lev Kuleschov, Vsevolod Pudovkin and Sergey Eisenstein to tap their full potential.[17]

Soviet Vanguard and the Propagandistic Character of Cinematic Theory

The stunning rise of Soviet cinema and its biggest film company, Mosfilm, might be explained in two ways: it was an artistic countermovement against the predominance of Hollywood as well as a part of Soviet agitprop policy in times of the global civil war of ideologies.[18]

Referring to the first aspect, we have to focus on two different concepts of movie-making. In the second decade of the 20th century, American cinema was highly influenced by the artistic approaches of David Wark Griffith. Having gained considerable fame with his blockbuster *Birth of a Nation* in 1915, Griffith was the man to experiment with various cinematic techniques in order to refine the new medium. His artistic masterpiece, *Intolerance* (1916), was a financial disaster, but Griffith's usage of montage style can be considered a cornerstone of film history. Cutting shots in contrastive as well as parallel order, the American director managed to combine different lines of action in a highly appealing manner. By doing so, Griffith (and several colleagues) shaped an "American grammar" of composition, stressing the ideas of organic narration and inner coherence.[19]

While these ideas became fixed standards of Hollywood movie-making, Soviet vanguard artists laid down their own theories of cinematic pictures and opposed the American concept of an organic flow of shots.[20] In the early 20th century, Russian artists had already gained leading positions and global reputation in the aesthetic fields of literature, fine arts and music.[21] Then, in the 1920s, a group of young Soviet avant-gardists was about to update this success story by creating a theoretical and practical framework for the juvenescent film medium.[22] Directors like Lev Kuleschov, Vsevolod Pudovkin and Sergey Eisenstein considered movie-making to be an interdependent process combining theory and handcraft. They were willing to support the Bolshevik movement by sketching a reliable historical perspective on the revolutionary past within the meaning of the communist party.[23] Because of their pioneering academic essays and political films, they were labeled as revolutionary directors.

Above all, it was the oeuvre of Sergey Eisenstein that attracted attention throughout the world. Born into a bourgeois family in 1898 (Riga), young Eisenstein soon took an exceptional path. During the October Revolution, he got in touch with the Bolshevik movement, and in 1918, he became a member of the Red Army. The committed communist participated in the Russian Civil War, agitating for Soviet propaganda units. When the war was over, he studied dramatics and simultaneously took his first steps in directing plays that were complemented by short movie sequences.[24] Moreover, he contemplated ways to exert ideological influence on society by means of modern mass media. Eisenstein realized the ambivalence of motion pictures, spotting their artistic as well as political potential. He considered cinema to be not only a highly expressive art form, but also an intellectual tool to examine and affect the community. Thus, he stated, a director had to perform a "dual activity, combining creative and analyzing work" at the same time.[25] In matters of Marxist ideology, the result of this "dual activity" had to be artwork that insistently illustrated the concept of dialectics.[26] Indeed, Eisenstein regarded no theory of movie making as more suited to the realization of this vision than his conception of montage technique.

"To what benefit directors use montage style," Eisenstein asked retrospectively in 1938. Joining different pictures or sequences by means of montage, he answered, enables producers to illustrate a dialectic overall view on social inequities.[27] In his visionary manifesto, *Montaž attrakcionov* (*Montage of Attractions*, 1923), the Soviet vanguard artist even argued that movies would gain the power to convey revolutionary insight to the audience if contrastive pictures were assembled in a shocking way. With respect to this, montage style was considered to be an immediate expression of the revolutionary relationship with the world.[28] This was quite a quixotic assumption and posed an important question: how could movies break down complex issues of Marxist ideology into generally intelligible messages? Eisenstein resolved this problem by evolving the technical concept of pars pro toto. In other words, he used suggestive close-ups in order to symbolize and reflect on social conditions.

In *Battleship Potemkin*, for example, a naval surgeon and his pair of pince-nez stand for the aristocratic officer corps—one of the leading bourgeois castes of the tsarist regime. The mentioned pince-nez picture is part of a sequence that clearly had a tendentious political intent: a group of angered Russian sailormen complains about a piece of rotten meat but is not taken seriously by the responsible superior.[29] By means of this montage, Eisenstein pointed at the inhuman conditions the laboring classes were suffering from in Russian Tsardom.[30] Stressing the social gap between the people of Russia and the predominant authorities, the director alluded to one of the fundamental contrasts of the pre–Bolshevik era in order to legitimate leftist revolutions as well as to convert the contemporary audience to the dialectic concept of Marxism. Eisenstein's movies are full of such allusions and it was his usage of pars pro toto that constituted their propagandistic potential.

Another aspect that came along with Soviet montage theory was the subordination of the actors. Quite contrary to Hollywood directors, who emphasized the individuality of their protagonists, Eisenstein stressed the prominence of the mass. His star was the dynamically moving crowd, not a famous actor.[31] In *October*, for instance, he was able to fall back on more than 5,000 extras to illustrate the revolutionary agitation of laborers in St. Petersburg. This was an enormous contingent for the cinema of the 1920s, by which the contemporary audience must have been fairly impressed. Not least because of this, Eisenstein held on to the idea of collectivism. Thus, even in historical movies like *Alexander Nevski*, which thematically referred to a single hero, he displayed overwhelming crowds to emphasize both Russian and communist companionship at the same time.

Concluding this thought, we can state that Sergey Eisenstein's theoretical concepts of montage style are to be interpreted not only as milestones of cinematic history but also as basic texts of Bolshevik propaganda. After all, that is the reason why movies like *Battleship Potemkin*, *October* and *Alexander Nevski* vociferously propagated the ideas of revolutionary heroism and companionate communism. Besides the director's lust for creating artistic values, such motion pictures were shot to indoctrinate the increasing number of Soviet movie-goers. However, an important question remains: To what extent could vanguard art actually win people over to the idea of Bolshevism?

Forming Concepts of the Enemy: Battleship Potemkin *and* October

In his scientific survey on *The Russian Revolution*, Steve A. Smith argues that Eisenstein's cinematic montages overstrained plenty of the Soviet leaders as well as the unexercised Russian audience. For this reason, the success of avant-garde movies had been strongly limited.[32] To some extent, I agree with this evaluation. Certainly, only few coevals were able to decode all the ideological symbolism Eisenstein was making use of in his motion pictures. In addition to this, Stalin himself definitely had severe objections to the formalistic approaches of Eisenstein and his avant-gardist colleagues even though most of the film directors bowed to the dictator regularly.[33] However, the efficacy of Eisenstein's pars pro toto montages must not be underestimated since they performed an important task of Stalinist propaganda: the figurative formation of the bourgeois enemy. In the following, two examples will help to outline this aspect.

Firstly, let us focus on *Battleship Potemkin*. The historical background of the movie, which is set in and around Odessa, is the Russian Revolution in 1905. Because of the Russian-Japanese War, especially in reaction to the total defeat of the Tsarist pacific fleet in the naval battle of Tsushima (May 27/28,

1905), social and political conflicts within Russian society increased dramatically at that time. There had already been riots in Odessa, when upset sailors on the warship *Potemkin* (which was located in the Black Sea) started a mutiny due to the men's discontent with the food supply (June 27, 1905). Nevertheless, it was not until the warship had dropped anchor in the harbor of Odessa and the news about the rebellion had spread out over the city, that this unrest intensified severely. In order to dissolve the rioting, local Cossacks were commanded to attack the enraged but unarmed crowd, which ended in a terrible bloodbath.

However, the warship *Potemkin* did not intervene since the naval mutiny and the riots in town had barely been coordinated.[34] In the movie, Eisenstein tells a slightly different story. The people of Odessa take notice of the mutiny on *Potemkin* (which technically wasn't a battleship, but a warship) and join in solidarity with the sailors in public. A jolly and peaceful assembly on the harbor steps is disbanded by Tsarist troops, who disperse the crowd by utterly brutal means. Finally, the intervention of the battleship's cannons brings the massacre to an end.

Due to the impressive work of montage, Eisenstein's stairsteps scene has become famous around the world; several motion pictures have referred to it. Likewise, however, the propagandistic content of the movie is also important. The director emphasized the antagonism of good and evil, contrasting the general public with the potentates of monarchist Russia. By presenting the Cossacks as a murdering apparatus, which blazes its destructive trail down the stairs of Odessa, Eisenstein connoted Tsarism with the policy of oppression, injustice and murder. There seemed to be no way out: A mother who wants to protect her child from the trigger-happy soldiers is gunned down without mercy. Even her little baby falls victim to the violence by being pushed down the steps in its baby carriage.[35]

What was the point of Eisenstein's detailed depiction of this cruelty? Certainly, he did not want to present ordinary history. He rather aimed at creating ideological symbolism. Thus, Eisenstein's motion picture should be interpreted not as a historical approach but as an exemplary history of just revolution.[36] With regard to this, it must not be forgotten that *Battleship Potemkin* was released only three years after the Russian Civil War. Emphasizing the brutality of the Tsarist troops, Eisenstein clearly alluded to the White party. Taking this into account, we can state that Eisenstein's movie was not only an artistic legitimation for the issue of revolution but also a pictographic strike against the conservative enemies of the Bolshevik party.[37]

Let us move on to the second example. With his revolutionary epic, *October*, Sergey Eisenstein managed to shoot a fictional motion picture, which some people up to the present day consider to be documental material. Not only for this reason can there be no doubt that *October* is the most "popular historical reminiscence of the October Revolution."³⁸ What was the director's motivation to release that movie? Well, being an expert on the revolutionary subject, he was instructed to do so by the Soviet authorities—and he had no doubts concerning this task.³⁹ The movie does not display historical truth, it rather illustrates the contemporary Bolshevik view on the revolution. Thus, Eisenstein again acted his part in the Soviet play of indoctrination.

One of the most striking scenes of the movie regarding the issue of communist propaganda is the assassination of a young Bolshevik during an escalating leftist demonstration in St. Petersburg. As troops sent out by the provisional government (under the command of Alexander Kerenski) forcibly disperse the protesters in the streets of the capital, the young man attempts to hide himself in order to rescue a communist banner. He approaches a boardwalk and encounters a kissing couple, whereupon the uniformed male kisser turns out to be one of the government's men. The soldier overpowers the young Bolshevik and delivers him to a mob of wealthy women who gradually kill the boy by battering him relentlessly with their parasols. Initially, the well-heeled girlfriend of the soldier only watches the bloody deed, but after a while she joins the mob to take part in the massacre. Finally, the dead body slips into the water, and amused witnesses—for example an elderly man wearing a bowler hat—applaud enthusiastically.⁴⁰

The aforementioned scene appears to depict a subplot, but actually, it is one of the key propaganda sequences in the movie, as it shows close-ups that are eye-catching as well as repellant at the same time. Here again, Eisenstein effectively uses the technique of pars pro toto in order to affect the viewer's perception of the world. The characters portrayed in that sequence are stereotypical examples of the Bolshevik view *on* the bourgeois. According to Eisenstein, they appeared to be wealthy, brutal, barbarous, and, above all, a serious threat to communist society. By illustrating these character traits and by linking them to the concept of the bourgeois class, Eisenstein not only helped the Soviet leaders to establish the biased worldview of Marxism-Leninism in Russian society but also provided communists around the world with ammunition for their "mission" in the global civil war of ideologies.

Conclusion

Sergey Eisenstein's cinematic work decisively influenced the development of film and photography. His concept of montage is rightly considered a milestone of film history. To Eisenstein, cinema was a medium of unique expressiveness and he helped to enforce its global acceptance as a new form of art.

However, a historical retrospect of Eisenstein would fail if the political quality of his motion pictures was not taken into account. The artist was an ardent worshipper of the idea of Marxism-Leninism as well as a reliable supporter of Bolshevik policy. His radically formalistic attitude towards arts brought him into conflict with Stalin more than once, but eventually, he always submitted to the dictator and the party line. Eisenstein's movies *Battleship Potemkin* and *October* are full of propagandistic contents and ideological allusions. They illustrate stereotypical characters such as the bourgeois citizen and the aristocratic officer. Using montage style and the concept of pars pro toto, Eisenstein convincingly managed to portray representatives of a social and political order, which the Soviets intended to destroy.

With respect to this, one question remains to be answered: Is it really appropriate to define Eisenstein's montage technique as a propagandistic weapon, an instrument of warfare in times of a global civil war of ideologies? A statement made in 1933 should help us find an answer. At that time, Joseph Goebbels stated in reference to *Battleship Potemkin*: "It is a fantastically well-made film and displays considerable cinematic artistry. The decisive factor is its orientation. Someone with no firm ideological convictions could be turned into a Bolshevik by this film. This proves that a political outlook can be very well contained in a work of art and that even the worst outlook can be conveyed if this is done through the medium of an outstanding work of art."[41]

Notes

1. Jörg Fisch, *Das Selbstbestimmungsrecht der Völker: Die Domestizierung einer Illusion* (München: Beck, 2010), 144–200.

2. The term "Weltbürgerkrieg" (German for global civil war) had been used by Ernst Jünger and Carl Schmidt at first. But it was Ernst Nolte who introduced it to historiography in 1987. To a certain extent, also Eric Hobsbawm made use of it writing about the 20th century as an "Age of Extremes." The striking aspect of the term is the idea that there was a worldwide, transnational civil war between 1917 and 1945—a war between political systems (democratic constitutional states vs. totalitarian states) and ideologies (democracy vs. fascism vs. communism). Enzo Traverso, "Der neue Antikommunismus: Nolte, Furet und Courtois interpretieren die Geschichte des 20. Jahrhunderts" in *Zeitgeschichte, Wissenschaft und Politik: Der "Historikerstreit"—20 Jahre danach*, ed. Volker Kronenberg (Wiesbaden: VS Verlag, 2008), 67–90, especially 68.

Also Eric Hobsbawm, *Age of Extremes: The Short Twentieth Century* (London: Penguin, 1994); Thomas Nipperdey, Anselm Doering-Manteuffel and Hans-Ulrich Thamer, ed., *Weltbürgerkrieg der Ideologien: Antworten an Ernst Nolte* (Berlin: Propyläen, 1993); Ernst Nolte, *Der europäische Bürgerkrieg 1917–1945: Nationalsozialismus—Bolschewismus* (Frankfurt am Main: Herbig, 1987); Enzo Traverso, *Im Bann der Gewalt: Der europäische Bürgerkrieg 1914–1945* (München: Siedler, 2008).

3. Complete definition: "A montage is a single pictorial composition made by juxtaposing or superimposing many pictures or designs. In filmmaking, a montage is an editing technique in which shots are juxtaposed in an often fast-paced fashion that compresses time and conveys a lot of information in a relatively short period."

Cf. http://www.elementsofcinema.com/editing/montage.html (Last access, 23 July 2014).
    4. For the data see Rainer Rother, ed., *Der Weltkrieg: Ereignis und Erinnerung 1914-1918* (Berlin: Edition Minerva, 2004), 176-197.
    A new discussion on the reasons for the outbreak of World War I accompanied the release of Christopher Clark's *Sleepwalkers*. Christopher Clark, *The Sleepwalkers: How Europe Went to War in 1914* (London: Allen Lane, 2012).
    5. George F. Kennan, *The Decline of Bismarck's European Order: Franco-Russian Relations 1875-1890* (Princeton: Princeton University Press, 1980), 3.
    6. Jörg Baberowski, *Der rote Terror: Die Geschichte des Stalinismus* (Frankfurt am Main: Fischer, 2007), 34-53.
    7. Richard Taylor, *Film Propaganda: Soviet Russia and Nazi Germany* (London: Croom Helm, 1979), 28.
    8. Michael Jeismann, "Propaganda" in *Enzyklopädie Erster Weltkrieg*, ed. Gerhard Hirschfeld, Gerd Krumeich and Irina Renz (Paderborn, et al.: Ferdinand Schoeningh, 2009), 198-209, especially 200.
    9. Toby Clark, *Kunst und Propaganda: Das politische Bild im 20. Jahrhundert* (Köln: Dumont, 1997), 7-8.
    10. Lenin adopted Plechanov's distinction between agitation and propaganda. Cf. Ingo Grabowsky, *Agitprop in der Sowjetunion: Die Abteilung für Agitation und Propaganda 1920-1928* (Freiburg: Projektverlag, 2004), 137.
    11. The Russian term for this department was otdel agitatsii i propagandy.
    12. Stephane Courtois, ed., *Das Handbuch des Kommunismus: Geschichte—Ideen—Köpfe* (München: Piper, 2010), 160.
    13. Alexander Rabinowitsch, *Die Sowjetmacht: Das erste Jahr* (Essen: Mehring, 2014), 493.
    14. Cf. Taylor, *Film Propaganda*, 35 and 44.
    15. Problems regarding the confirmation of Soviet dominion in the rural circumference of Russia are discussed by Baberowski, *Der rote Terror*, 61-69.
    16. Cf. Taylor, *Film Propaganda*, 49.
    17. Janina Urussowa, "Lev Kuleschov, Vsevolod Pudovkin, Sergei Eisenstein" in *Medienwissenschaft: Ein Handbuch zur Entwicklung der Medien und Kommunikationsformen*, vol. 2., ed. Joachim-Felix Leonhard (New York: de Gruyter, 2001), 1185-1198, especially 1185.
    18. Lisa Gotto, "Konflikt und Kollision" in *Eisenstein Reader: Die wichtigsten Schriften zum Film*, ed. Lisa Gotto (Leipzig: Henschel, 2011), 10-19, especially 15.
    19. James Monaco, Film verstehen. Geschichte und Theorie des Films und der neuen Medien (Reinbek bei Hamburg: Rowohlt, 2000), 219.
    20. Hans-Goerg Soeffner and Jürgen Raab, "Sehtechniken. Die Medialisierung des Sehens: Schnitt und Montage als Ästhetisierungsmittel medialer Kommunikation," in *Technik und Sozialtheorie*, ed. Werner Rammert (Frankfurt am Main/New York: Campus, 1998), 121-148, especially 139.
    The most important differences between American and Soviet ideas of movie making are described by Sergey Eisenstein, "Dickens, Griffith und wir" in *Eisenstein Reader: Die wichtigsten Schriften zum Film*, ed. Lisa Gotto (Leipzig: Henschel, 2011), 84-151, especially 150.
    21. Regarding the rise of Russian avant-garde art cf. Jewgeni Kowtun, *Die russische Avantgarde der 1920er Jahre* (Bournemouth: Parkstone/Aurora, 1996).
    22. Concerning the Soviet vanguard cinema of the 1920s, it has to be stated that there has also been an influential vanguard film movement in other European countries

like France and Germany. A historical classification is given by Sigrid Lange, *Einführung in die Filmwissenschaft* (Darmstadt: WBG, 2007), 126–131.
   23. Rainer Rother, "*Panzerkreuzer Potemkin*" in *Der Filmkanon: 35 Filme, die Sie kennen müssen,* ed. Alfred Holighaus (Bonn: BpB, 2005), 27–34.
   24. Bernhard Schalhorn, "Eisenstein" in *Historisches Lexikon der Sowjetunion 1917/22 bis 1991,* ed. Hans-Joachim Torke (München: Beck, 1993), 77.
   25. Sergey Eisenstein, "Wie ich Regisseur wurde," in *Eisenstein Reader: Die wichtigsten Schriften zum Film,* ed. Lisa Gotto (Leipzig: Henschel, 2011), 226–236, especially 235.
   26. Lisa Gotto, *Konflikt und Kollision*, 15.
   27. Sergey Eisenstein, "Montage" in *Eisenstein Reader: Die wichtigsten Schriften zum Film,* ed. Lisa Gotto (Leipzig: Henschel, 2011), 38–83, especially 38 and 42.
   28. Christine Engel, *Geschichte des sowjetischen und russischen Films* (Stuttgart/Weimar: Metzler, 1999), 30.
   29. Compare Sergey Eisenstein, *Battleship Potemkin* (1925), https://www.youtube.com/watch?v=UNT6xyopdBs (Minutes: 5.15- 7.50)
   30. Sergey Eisenstein, "Zwölf Apostel," in *Eisenstein Reader: Die wichtigsten Schriften zum Film,* ed. Lisa Gotto (Leipzig: Henschel, 2011),198–225, especially 220.
   31. David Priestland, *Weltgeschichte des Kommunismus: Von der Französischen Revolution bis heute* (München: Siedler, 2009), 175.
   32. Steve A. Smith, *Die russische Revolution* (Stuttgart: Reclam, 2011), 224.
   33. A turning point of Soviet cultural and educational policy was the year 1937. Mass prosecution, ideological terror and censorship were the inglorious steps that Stalin and his fellowmen took at that time. Eisenstein was one of the victims, but he managed to survive by criticizing himself in public and subordinating himself to the Stalinist ideal of culture and art. Cf. Karl Schlögel, *Terror und Traum: Moskau 1937* (Bonn: BpB, 2008), 493.
   34. Geoffrey Hosking, *Russland: Nation und Imperium 1552–1917* (Berlin: BvT, 2003), 462.
   35. Compare Sergey Eisenstein. *Battleship Potemkin* (1925), https://www.youtube.com/watch?v=UNT6xyopdBs (Minutes: 46,34–54,15).
   36. Eisenstein, *Zwölf Apostel,* 220–222.
   37. Nolte, *Der europäische Bürgerkrieg,* 249.
   38. Cf. Dietrich Beyrau, *Petrograd: 25 Oktober 1917: Die russische Revolution und der Aufstieg des Kommunismus* (München: DTV, 2001), 7.
   39. Taylor, *Propaganda and Film,* 92–93.
   40. Compare Sergey Eisenstein. October. Ten days that shook the world (1927), https://www.youtube.com/watch?v=k62eaN9-TLY (Minutes: 15.45–1913).
   41. Quotation from Richard Taylor, *The Battleship Potemkin* (London: I.B. Tauris, 2000), 112.

WORKS CITED

Baberowski, Jörg. *Der rote Terror: Die Geschichte des Stalinismus.* Frankfurt am Main: Fischer, 2007.
Beyrau, Dietrich. *Petrograd: 25. Oktober 1917: Die russische Revolution und der Aufstieg des Kommunismus.* München: DTV, 2001.
Clark, Christopher. *The Sleepwalkers: How Europe Went to War in 1914.* London: Allen Lane, 2012.
Clark, Toby. *Kunst und Propaganda: Das politische Bild im 20. Jahrhundert.* Köln: Dumont, 1997.

Courtois, Stephane, ed. *Das Handbuch des Kommunismus: Geschichte—Ideen—Köpfe*. München: Piper, 2010.
Eisenstein, Sergey. *Battleship Potemkin* (1925), https://www.youtube.com/watch?v=UNT6xyopdBs.
Eisenstein, Sergey. "Dickens, Griffith und wir," in Eisenstein Reader: Die wichtigsten Schriften zum Film, ed. Lisa Gotto. Leipzig: Henschel, 2011, 84–151.
Eisenstein, Sergey. "Montage," in *Eisenstein Reader. Die wichtigsten Schriften zum Film*, ed. Lisa Gotto. Leipzig: Henschel, 2011, 38–83.
Eisenstein, Sergey. *October: Ten Days that Shook the World* (1927), https://www.youtube.com/watch?v=k62eaN9-TLY.
Eisenstein, Sergey. "Wie ich Regisseur wurde," in *Eisenstein Reader: Die wichtigsten Schriften zum Film*, ed. Lisa Gotto. Leipzig: Henschel, 2011, 226–236.
Eisenstein, Sergey. "Zwölf Apostel," in *Eisenstein Reader: Die wichtigsten Schriften zum Film*, ed. Lisa Gotto. Leipzig: Henschel, 2011, 198–225.
Engel, Christine. *Geschichte des sowjetischen und russischen Films*. Stuttgart/Weimar: Metzler, 1999.
Fisch, Jörg. *Das Selbstbestimmungsrecht der Völker: Die Domestizierung einer Illusion*. München: Beck, 2010, 144–200.
Gotto, Lisa. "Konflikt und Kollision," in *Eisenstein Reader: Die wichtigsten Schriften zum Film*, ed. Lisa Gotto. Leipzig: Henschel, 2011, 10–19.
Grabowsky, Ingo. *Agitprop in der Sowjetunion: Die Abteilung für Agitation und Propaganda 1920-1928*. Freiburg: Projektverlag, 2004.
Hobsbawm, Eric. *Age of Extremes. The Short Twentieth Century*. London: Penguin, 1994.
Hosking, Geoffrey. *Russland: Nation und Imperium 1552-1917*. Berlin: BvT, 2003.
Jeismann, Michael. "Propaganda," in *Enzyklopädie Erster Weltkrieg*, ed. Gerhard Hirschfeld, Gerd Krumeich and Irina Renz. Paderborn et al.: Ferdinand Schoeningh, 2009, 198–209.
Kennan, George F. *The Decline of Bismarck's European Order: Franco-Russian Relations 1875-1890*. Princeton: Princeton University Press, 1980.
Kowtun, Jewgeni. *Die russische Avantgarde der 1920er Jahre*. Bournemouth: Parkstone/Aurora, 1996.
Lange, Sigrid. *Einführung in die Filmwissenschaft*. Darmstadt: WBG, 2007.
Monaco, James. *Film verstehen. Geschichte und Theorie des Films und der neuen Medien*. Reinbek bei Hamburg: Rowohlt, 2000, 219.
Nipperdey, Thomas; Doering-Manteuffel, Anselm and Thamer, Hans-Ulrich, ed. *Weltbürgerkrieg der Ideologien: Antworten an Ernst Nolte*. Berlin: Propyläen, 1993.
Nolte, Ernst. *Der europäische Bürgerkrieg 1917-1945: Nationalsozialismus—Bolschewismus*. Frankfurt am Main: Herbig, 1987.
Priestland, David. *Weltgeschichte des Kommunismus. Von der Französischen Revolution bis heute*. München: Siedler, 2009.
Rabinowitsch, Alexander. *Die Sowjetmacht: Das erste Jahr*. Essen: Mehring, 2010, 493.
Rother, Rainer. "Panzerkreuzer *Potemkin*" in *Der Filmkanon. 35 Filme, die Sie kennen müssen*, ed. Alfred Holighaus. Bonn: BpB, 2005.
Rother, Rainer, ed. *Der Weltkrieg: Ereignis und Erinnerung 1914-1918*. Berlin: Edition Minerva, 2004.
Schalhorn, Bernhard. "Eisenstein," in *Historisches Lexikon der Sowjetunion 1917/22 bis 1991*, ed. Hans-Joachim Torke. München: Beck, 1993, 77.
Schlögel, Karl. *Terror und Traum: Moskau 1937*. Bonn: BpB, 2008.
Smith, Steve A. *Die russische Revolution*. Stuttgart: Reclam, 2011.

Soeffner, Hans-Goerg and Raab, Jürgen. "Sehtechniken. Die Medialisierung des Sehens: Schnitt und Montage als Ästhetisierungsmittel medialer Kommunikation," in *Technik und Sozialtheorie*, ed. Werner Rammert. Frankfurt am Main/ New York: Campus, 1998, 121-148.

Taylor, Richard. *Film Propaganda: Soviet Russia and Nazi Germany*. London: Croom Helm, 1979.

Taylor, Richard. *The Battleship Potemkin*. London: I.B. Tauris, 2000.

Traverso, Enzo. "Der neue Antikommunismus: Nolte, Furet und Courtois interpretieren die Geschichte des 20. Jahrhunderts," in *Zeitgeschichte, Wissenschaft und Politik: Der "Historikerstreit"—20 Jahre danach*, ed. Volker Kronenberg. Wiesbaden: VS Verlag, 2008, 67-90.

Traverso, Enzo. *Im Bann der Gewalt: Der europäische Bürgerkrieg 1914-1945*. München: Siedler, 2008.

Urussowa, Janina. "Lev Kuleschov, Vsevolod Pudovkin, Sergei Eisenstein," in *Medienwissenschaft: Ein Handbuch zur Entwicklung der Medien und Kommunikationsformen*, vol. 2., ed. Joachim-Felix Leonhard. New York: de Gruyter, 2001, 1185-1198.

Four Technical Artifacts of the Great War

KURT MÖSER

The centennial of the Great War would be an obvious starting point for remarks on the subject of technology and war, but this war has a special significance for this crucial relationship. There seems to be a common view among historians that technology has played a more decisive—and more deadly—role than in other wars. The Great War presents, in this respect, a challenge with which one has to come to terms. It has been dubbed the "machinist's war" or the "worker's war." Its type of technologically dominated battle was called the "storm of steel," the "Materialschlacht," in which death became mechanized. The debate about the role of technology in modern battles began in Germany already during the war, but it became a public issue immediately after its end. Typically for this is Max Schwarte's "Technik im Weltkriege" (1920).[1] This is the central work focusing on seeing the underestimation of technology as the main reason for the German defeat, claiming that Germany has focused too much on traditional courage, whereas the Allies had rightly concentrated on "blood-saving" by focusing on mass-produced and mass-employed technology. In this context of reasoning, right from the start, even in the war, objects of military technology were loaded with significance for morality and dishonesty and for victory and defeat. Particularly, tanks, heavy artillery, gas warfare or the machine gun were put in the center of military significance and of cultural meaning as well.

This focus on technological objects in terms of military and cultural significance does legitimate a closer view on artifacts of military technology. This approach, which is somewhat emphatically claimed to be a "material turn," can contribute significantly to the military and social history of warfare and to the subject of the workshop—but only if objects are placed into context; if they are placed in narratives, contemporary as well as actual; and if they are seen in their functionality as well as in their symbolic value.

This entails "wrenching" some of these objects of military technology out of the hands of collectors and specialists of military hardware and into the working field of academic historians. There are, of course, museums that do work with these objects professionally; they have done it for a long time, and they do it well, by collecting, preserving, interpreting and using them as tools to communicate meaning. Objects in the case of research-orientated museums are firstly sources to be interpreted and related to a broader view, and secondly, they are media to show, teach and, of course, entertain and/or amuse. For historians, learning from this object-focused, material approach of museums, there seem to be opportunities to open up their methodical range as well as their viewpoints. There is an ongoing discussion as to how objects relate to history, which I would like to boil down to the following alternatives:

- History *from* things, meaning that artifacts are mainly used as sources. In this approach "artefacts are used as raw materials for the discipline of history of and for the interpretation of the past."
- History *of* things, coming to terms with the meaning and the position of artifacts, or as Gieorgio Riello puts it, "the historical analysis of the relationship between objects, people and their representations."[2]

Looking at some new approaches, there seems to be an additional way to relate objects to history. Riello has suggested that yet another relationship—namely history *and* things—has to be explored. This approach claims that neither are things in a servile position to historiography, nor is historiography a purely interpretative tool for understanding and interpreting objects. Instead, there can be a looser relationship of things and history. Things have, as we know, a "social life"[3] and can be re-evaluated and re-contextualized in ways not or only loosely connected with historical narratives. This approach not only allows but also requires a freer interpretation, questioning the coherence of narratives and relationships. Again, as Riello explains: "Historians tend to present history as a well-woven tablecloth, covering all corners. Objects show how history instead [is] a rather loosely woven net that sometimes retains—but often is unable to "catch"—concepts, people, events and explanations."[4]

To find a pragmatic approach towards this somewhat seemingly opaque relationship, a more straightforward distinction can help. Firstly, objects have an instrumental character and practical and pragmatic functions, but there must be caution: Functions are not in a fixed or straightforward relationship to the artifact but can be—and mostly are—attributed to them. Secondly, objects have a character as signs, and these are always situated in social and cultural contexts and have to be decoded in their specific contexts of usage and reception. Moreover, these sign elements form narratives around and together with the objects.[5]

For historians, there has to be a crucial decision to perform which, traditionally, has variously been made by academic museum curators and "traditional" research-based historians. This decision is whether to place historical narratives in the center and to use objects as tools to understand and narrate these objects or to place objects in the center and use historical narratives as tools to understand, interpret and communicate these objects. I suggest opening up this seemingly clear-cut alternative—which is routinely done by historians combining museum and university backgrounds—and practice observing a less strict relationship between history and objects.

Getting closer to the subject of the workshop, war and technology, a glimpse of military history shows that this sub-field has always relied heavily on hardware. Weapons, equipment and systems held and still hold a great attraction for experts and the vast and diverse part of the public interested in military history. In addition, there has been a long tradition in analyzing and signifying artifacts related to war and the military. In the case of the Great War, such diverse artifacts as tanks, gas masks, machine guns and their significant parts hold special fascinations. For example, a sighting and aiming telescope for the famous machine gun 08, the "Spandau," can demonstrate or re-create the sight and vision of a machine gunner, adding a sensual, visual dimension to contextually-based fascination or horror, creating or exploring an aura around the object.

Of course, I am building on this tradition of constructing and exploiting significance, meaning and attributed values, but I suggest modifying this approach. For that I am relying on the works of scholars who have transformed military history from the 1970s and in the past 30 years. There are some groundbreaking works that often take the Great War in focus: There is Paul Fussel's *The Great War and Modern Memory* (1979), which provided an approach of cultural and literature history[6]; Martin Middlebrook's *The First Day at the Somme* (1971),[7] a seminal work closely linked with the rise of oral history and "history from below" as methods of academic historiography; and John Keegan's *The Face of Battle* (1976),[8] dealing with the battles of Agincourt, Waterloo and the Somme in a novel way. Keegan goes far beyond the analysis of his sample battles in questioning the approach of military historians and advocating a much closer look at the individual experience of combatants and the basic level of conflict. He also takes a new view on military technology as well, establishing types of confrontation and fighting with and against weapons systems.

From the side of the role of artifacts in social and cultural history, in the 1980s, a new appreciation of things in the life of man and as subjects for historical scrutiny appeared. Here, Arjun Appadurais' book, *The Social Life of Things* (1988),[9] broke new ground. It fit into another trend of the history of technology, that is, the stress on usage and the role of relevant user groups in dealing with developing and changing technologies. This "social construction" of technologies presented first by Wibe Bijker in his book,[10] attempts to assess the framing of technologies in social contexts and offers methods to analyze the interplay of technology and its users. Museums have contributed to a new assessment of artifacts, too. The Nuremberg Centrum Industriekultur developed in 1983 the concept of "industrielle Leitfossilien" ("industrial guide fossils" or "index fossils"), significant for identifying typical aspects of technology cultures.

Having these and other methodological approaches in mind, to which I am indebted, I try to look at four artifacts of the Great War. In particular, the "social construction" concept offers good chances to find out which role certain technologies played for users—and for those at the receiving end, suffering or being terrorized.

It has been stressed that objects of technology and technological systems cannot be viewed and analyzed in an isolated way but have to be placed in military usage contexts. Max Boot in *War Made New* (2006)[11] has stressed the fact that there is never just a new technology introduced for military employment and purposes, never a singular "technological revolution" but always a "revolution in military affairs" ("RMA"). Any new technology is, he proposes, embedded in a system of real—and imagined—usage, a doctrine for employing it. There also has to be integration into military organizational structures either by integrating into existing unit structures or by creating new ones. Moreover, often technologies have to be positioned within the military hierarchy beckoning the question who is in charge of them and within a framework of training, learning and employment. Max Boot argues that there is no singular new weapon without a systemic, doctrinal and organizational frame in which to embed it. There is—here I extend the suggestions of Max Boot—very often a narrative about the potential and the capabilities of the new technology or weapon. Both the users and those who suffer from them can work on those narratives and change them. For instance, the stories of what the new tanks could do were different when told in 1916 by the proponents of the new weapon and by the Tank Corps officers, or by German soldiers first encountering them. Narratives can do many things: they can instill pride in a new weapon, confidence in the "war chariots" or as in the case of German infantry soldiers, "tank horror" ("Tankschrecken").

There has existed a long tradition of seeing and communicating military technology not only in terms of functionality but also with a symbolic and even aesthetic value. Martin van Creveld in *The Culture of War* (2008)[12] stressed the cultural role of military objects, which are by no means just a matter of crude effectiveness but loaded with meanings, connotations, and cultural significance, and all of this happens in specific periods over time. In some cases, the cultural attributions are renewed and re-valued and deeply embedded in national cultural codes.

When technology—however charged it may be—is employed under real, practical conditions, there will often be a transformation of function and usage. For instance, the airplane was before 1914 militarily-socially constructed as a spotter plane, simply lifting the eyes of observing officers higher. Soon, though, it was transformed into several new usages: fighter, day and night bomber, photo reconnaissance plane, and trench fighter planes. This was done by "relevant user groups" mostly in an improvised way from "bottom up" by the actual users and not planned top-down by staff officers or military planners.[13] This transformation entails a transformation of the narratives: The technology can become symbolic and representative, placing it in new social, military and aesthetic contexts. The symbolic character thus can change over time, and it can influence or even transform the functional employment of a technology.

These processes thus sketched can be observed in all of the four artifacts I am going to present. In selecting the artifacts (under the headline "objects and history"), my artifacts or military technologies have to have—on top of their functional significance—a symbolic character. They have to be (a) significant for the character of the Great War from our own historic perspective, when analyzing them with the tools of a historian, but (b) symbolic also in contemporary contexts—that is, already in the war they must have become loaded with meaning and charged symbolic value. To sum up, the objects I have selected are significant in three ways: for their functional role in the First World War, for their symbolic significance as seen during the war in contemporary communicative contexts and for their historic significance for the military and social history of the period. This retrospective symbolic dimension (or what historians see and construct as symbolic) makes a historical narrative. I have chosen four objects, both weapons and equipment pieces, which seem in some cases very straightforward, mundane and not connected with any modernizing "revolution in military affairs" (RMA), but with closer inspection, they reveal their role as means for an "inroad into modernism" that the Great War provided in several fields.

First: The Army Spade

This piece of equipment was introduced in the German Army in 1898 at first for machine gunners, the M.G. being at that time seen as a purely defensive weapon. In a culture where the offensive—on the strategic, operational and tactical level—was seen as the foremost, most effective and most honorific approach to the battle, any preparation of the defensive had an even morally dubious tinge. When the "entrenching tool" was issued to ordinary infantry privates before 1914, it could be interpreted as a tentative appreciation of the German high command of the new firepower by repeating rifles with high accuracy and high shooting frequency. Still, any digging was seen only as an auxiliary and temporary measure, just preparing for renewed attack. Despite the appreciation of the new type of warfare, defensive actions seem to have been trained only reluctantly in maneuvers before the War, tying in with a tendency to "Dekorationsmilitarismus," meaning that German militarism was more for display than for functionality in a future war. The entrenching spade was carried per regulation by the German infantryman in combination with the bayonet. Thus, ironically, the typical offensive and defensive tools were holstered together. The German army regulation of 1906 showed the fundamental ambivalence towards the spade. It warned against extensive digging in the field in order not to spoil the principle of the offensive.[14] Even so, the German infantry in 1914 was the only one of the European armies equipped completely with an "entrenching tool."

Nonetheless, the unloved defensive action proved to be crucial after the first phase of movement warfare and in defensive periods of attacks. As soon as the offensives petered out (which they did regularly), the troops were expected quickly to "dig in" for some shelter in a race against the opponent's artillery and the "Gegenstoß" (counterattack). Typically, for fast digging under enemy fire, the German spade proved to be a lifesaving tool. Thus, it was an object for strengthening the defensive, being closely linked with trench warfare and the "Materialschlacht" as it developed after 1914. Particularly in the middle phase of the war, extensive earthworks and excavations were worked mostly by hand labor and with spades. Even during the war, the spade transformed into a symbol of the "work war" and of the troglodyte life in deep caverns, dark and close to the earth, as described by Paul Fussell.[15]

However, the spade acquired an additional and somewhat contradictory coding during the war. On one hand, in the subterranean "troglodyte world" pierced by trench raids, the spade became a weapon in close-range fighting. By regulation, one edge had to be sharpened to transform the spade into a deadly close fighting weapon. Together with bayonets, maces or clubs that were either issued or acquired by own initiative, these weapons harked back to archaic forms of conflict within the emphatically modern and modernizing type of fighting. Thus, quite differing forms of warfare developed, parallel and overlapping, in the "Materialschlacht."

The peaceful coding of the spade is linked with the companies made up of conscientious objectors who were allowed to do duty within the military but without weapons. These "Armierungssoldaten," called "Schipper" (shovelers), were employed as construction workers mostly behind the front for "Schanzen" (digging work), showing their pacifist and reluctant attitude to war work by resembling civil workers. Typically, an "Armierungsssoldat" is the hero of Stefan Zweig's pacifist novel *Erziehung vor Verdun* (1935).[16]

Still another, re-militarized coding appeared in the inter-war period. From the early 1920s onwards, there was a movement of young men, often students, to work on the fields, on drainage or melioration projects. Their motive ranged from the idealistic, aiming at working together and side by side with the "common worker" and supplementing their intellectual approach, to the political and militaristic. This was mostly done by former members of the right-wing "Freikorps," who often went to farmers after being disbanded and finding, in common spadework, the sought-after cohesion, comradeship and solidarity, as in fighting before. The "Freiwillige Arbeitsdienst" (FAD—volunteer work organization) of the Weimar Republic, which was transformed after 1933 into the compulsory "Reichsarbeitdienst," provided young men before their military service with pre-military education. The tool for this was the spade. It was treated like a rifle, polished, cherished and presented. With the spade, they had to perform gun drills, thus educating future Wehrmacht soldiers by and with the spade for their soldiering. At the same time, it could become a tool for punishment by digging. The victims of the early concentration camps became "Moorsoldaten" (swamp soldiers), carrying their spade into the moor for hard labor:

> Hier in dieser öden Heide
> Ist das Lager aufgebaut,
> Wo wir fern von jeder Freude
> Hinter Stacheldraht verstaut
> Wir sind die Moorsoldaten
> Und ziehen mit den Spaten
> Ins Moor.

> Here inside this barren marshland
> the camp is built up,
> Where we are, far from any joy,
> stowed away behind barbed wire.
> We are the bog soldiers
> And we are marching with our spade; into the bog
> We are Bog soldiers
> And we are marching with our spade; into the bog.

Second: The Sea Mine

The naval mine was by no means new when the war broke out. Its significance for naval warfare could be observed during the Russo-Japanese war of 1904/05 when ships of both combatant navies were destroyed by mines anchored at fixed places. By 1900, the technology of the self-acting anchoring in predetermined depths after being dropped overboard, which could be done from nearly any vessel, was well established. Nevertheless, a thorough preparation for clearing was lacking. In principle, this was not too difficult. Two fishing boats, trawlers or drifters, working in pairs, towed a line that cut through the anchoring line of the mine that surfaced then and could be disposed of by gunfire. The British Navy relied heavily on fishing vessels drafted together with their civilian crew with a single Naval Volunteer Reserve officer, often a yachtsman.

This somewhat amateurish approach, showing the disregard for mine warfare and mine clearing before 1914, is starkly contrasted with the thorough and enthusiastic preparation for torpedo warfare. Here, literally hundreds of torpedo boats were commissioned, incorporating the latest technologies of turbines, forced draught and hull optimization for very high speeds and preparing daring offensive action against enemy battleships. The "cavalry of the seas," as surface torpedo vessels were dubbed, became the epitome of the offensive spirit, attracting eager young officers, whereas mining and antimine warfare was linked to an aversion against warfare "below the belt" and stealthy and defensive weapons.

Thus, skepticism against the defensive on land and a lack of preparation for it was mirrored in naval warfare. Here, too, offensive weapons were as overestimated as the stress on building battle fleets, stimulated by an influential and widely-read book by Alfred Thayer Mahan.[18] This tied in well with the symbolic role of big warships in Imperialistic power projection. Mine warfare, in contrast, was largely underestimated mainly because of its seemingly unheroic, inhuman and morally dubious image. In the mine-dominated naval war, a parallel situation emerged as to what happened in the land battles: There was no longer room for individual heroism. Consequently, there were no proper precautions, in contrast to the obsession with attack torpedoes and the building of vast fleets of torpedo boats.

However, there were two types of mining warfare: first, with a defensive aim, by creating zones of interdiction and maximal danger for the enemy, for instance around naval bases or in front of beaches threatened by landings and second, with an offensive aim by creating a randomized threat, an unseen danger at unexpected places. Both types of mine warfare were seen—even by contemporaries—as typical for the specifics of warfare in this industrialized war, by the creation of spaces that meant highest danger and of lethal zones potentially not to be used at all. Then, there was the creation of randomized danger, of lethality that could strike at any moment without warning. Both types created typical expectations and typical fear: the horror of having to enter lethal spaces and the fear of being threatened at any time. Sea mines thus fitted in the same danger structure as the lethal zones of the land battles in the Great War, in which danger zones were characteristic: the mustard gas "interdiction zones," where nobody who was not fully protected could exist; the vast zones of barbed wire; the high explosives of artillery barrages; or the lethal lead cones of machine weapons.

Like on land, naval leaders were forced to learn and to deal with the unloved and underestimated strengthened defensive. The textbook case, in the case of sea mining warfare, is the first phase of the combined British and French attack at Gallipoli in 1915. When encountering minefields defended by Ottoman forts and German-led field artillery, the drifters, hastily ordered from Britain with their civilian crew, proved to be unable to clear the mines despite renewed efforts. Now, the failure to develop a proper naval clearing system proved to be decisive. On March 18, 1915, on a minefield of (probably) less than thirty mines that went undetected, two British and one French pre-dreadnought battleships were sunk, and one battlecruiser and two battleships were severely damaged.[19] This ignominious (and decisive) defeat was caused by a small minelayer of 365 tons, built in Kiel in 1913 and given to the Ottoman fleet, the *Nusret*. Thus, Istanbul was not taken; a notorious stalemate on land developed, the naval secretary, Winston Churchill, had to step down and Turkey defended Gallipoli successfully. The impact on Turkish identity and the evolvement of a military hero, Mustapha Kemal, cannot be underestimated.

This is proof of the severe neglect of mining warfare and of the lack of anticipation. The sea mine proved to be as revolutionizing to naval warfare in the Great War as the role of defensive weapons in the trench war on land. I should have presented Nusret, rather than the sea mine in general, as a significant object, a representation of a spectacular unsymmetrical action as well as a symbolic artifact for a significant type of warfare, and a weapon closely linked with Turkish national identity and pride. A replica of the *Nusret* is displayed in the war museum in Canakkale, and the original wreck is lying in Tarsus, awaiting restoration. To me, this seems like an important, small ship that changed history.

Third: The Aerial Camera

In 1914, aerial observation was universally done by an officer in the rear seat of an airplane, sketching what he saw with blue pencil on a map and reporting, personally, after the landing. In 1918, a sophisticated system of acquiring photographs from high-flying planes in great numbers, totally surveying the battle zones and their area, ensured that information was interpreted and delivered to the military planners very fast.

120 II. The Age of the World Wars

This sums up the fast development from personal to complex mechanical acquisition and distribution of images. The aerial camera was the tool for this significant process, being positioned in the center, but, as a "revolution in military affairs," part of a systemic technological change. Many innovations and new practices were introduced around aerial photography, for instance, stereo cameras to record the height of objects and serial photographing to create continuous strips, so-called "Reihenmeßkammern." The task of serial photography had to be done regularly by repeating reconnaissance flights often to acquire recurring photographs in order to record any changes. In particular, the semi-automated version, the "Reihenbildkamera" (strip photograph camera), has to be mentioned here. Also, there were technical means for acquiring vertical, un-distorted views from above. In 1916, the Austro-Hungarian monarchy had vertical camera axis aerial photos taken above Italy for map-making. Photographs taken at 15,000 feet could be blown up to show footprints in the mud.[20] From 1916 at the latest, comprehensive aerial observation and documentation were necessities for military action, not only for the offensive.

Systems of rushing the plates for development and to the decision makers were soon developed in order to create near real-time intelligence. This had to be repeated continuously. In addition, a new art, that of interpreting, had to evolve. There were new qualities required for interpreting and signifying the pictorial records, which was done among the Allies by women. These required new ways of seeing and recognizing and interpreting patterns.

At the same time, the aesthetic qualities of aerial photos were recognized and admired, for this was not a matter of a small modernizing elite. What was seen, in the first place, as a highly irritating and uncommon view became popular and accessible for a broad public in the war. Popular war media—in Germany, for instance, the serial *Der Große Krieg*—regularly printed aerial photographs and familiarized an interested and curious public with this imagery. A new aesthetics of the view of the war from above was established.[21] At the same time, camouflage was developed as a reaction, employing artists on both sides. The anticipated and communicated view from the air changed the perception of the world and has been related to the development and also the appreciation of abstract visual art.[22]

On the materiel level, new types of high altitude recce planes were introduced. Up to 1917, engines losing power in heights above 5,000 meters, thus preventing the reaching of higher altitudes, presented the main problem. Then, supercharged engines or those with special altitude carburetors came into use. This high technology produced significant forward linkages for civilian technology development after 1918. The pilots and observers, enduring long flights as high as eight kilometers "deep in the rear of the Enemy"[23] and virtually unreachable by air defense, had to develop special physical and psychological stamina, aided by oxygen supply and heated clothing.

The new type of "Arbeitsflieger," the "working flyers"—not a single pilot but a two-man crew in close cooperation—had to develop new types of heroism, not by heroic aerial combat like the famed "aces" but by fulfilling stoically a hazardous task requiring stamina and endurance in heights that were physically dangerous in themselves. Thus, the crew became typically "modern heroes".[24] The high-tech high altitude airplane and the high-tech altitude automated serial camera with vertical focal correction formed a specifically modern military technology system, geared for a (potentially) total high-tech mechanical view from above. This was cutting-edge aircraft and optical technology with the crew working on visual modernization. Thus, this new technologically-generated perspective integrated a new view into total war.

As a result, in the late war and afterwards, the aerial photographer took a place in popular iconography and imaging. He represented an entirely new pattern of heroism, battling not the foe but icy cold and dangerous heights, fulfilling his task by all means and sacrifices. This new functional heroism for the acquisition of images entailed avoiding fighting and subordinating everything to serve the mechanical recording apparatus. The photographer, part of a complex imaging system, was the fallible human eye behind the infallible technical lens eye.

This, again, casts a long shadow on the inter-war era. Ernst Jünger chose the aerial photograph as an example for his Arbeiter ("worker"), a new type of technologically-optimized man. This tied in with the image of the photographer as an aesthetic paragon. The "mechanical eye," the "kino-glaz" or camera eye, conceptualized, for instance, by Tsiga Vertov, became the "culture of cool" between the wars in which Helmut Lethen described[25] the mechanical view from above, and its protagonists became a cultural icon, being integrated into a narrative of trans-human mechanization of the senses.

Fourth: The Optical Signaling Apparatus

The First World War was a war fought generally without effective control or real-time command on the battlefield. The American forces named "C3I"— command, control, communication and information—was maintained with difficulties in defensive situations. However, even there, barrages and other forms of interdiction and isolation could lead to a breakdown by cutting telegraph wires or killing messengers. C3I, nevertheless, was an even more serious structural hazard of the operative and tactical offensive, leading again to favoring the defender. Once an attack was on, there were no proper communications between the forward and the rear areas. Planting a higher commanding officer, the "KTK" (Kampftruppenkommandeur, leader of fighting troops), from 1917 onward, the German Army did not manage to ease the problem because even officers in this function perceived little beyond their radius from a dugout. All other means were either imperfect, prone to delay or hazardous for the troops: carrier pigeons, markers, flags and, foremost, runners. The obvious technology necessary for bridging the "offensive gap" would have been wireless, but a portable field radio set was not yet fit by far for being used in the "forward edge of battle zone"—again, a NATO term. There was, in addition, a "real-time" problem. It was close to impossible in fast-moving battle situations to keep track of one's own troops without delay.

Here, the signaling lamp comes into the story. In 1916, lacking a true communications revolution, the German army introduced a flash-signaling lamp, named the "MBlink16," designed to be carried into the forward trenches and used by attacking troops. This was a direct reaction to fundamental problems in battlefield communications. The Blinkgerät, with its electric bulb powered by storage accumulators or pedal-driven generators and use of Morse flashes, had to fulfill the task, which later electronic wireless devices had to perform. Thus, it can be described as a typical bridge technology, not quite optimal for the task of providing real-time information across the battlefield but the most adaptable available. Flashlights were a typical stopgap means of solving the communication problem in the industrial battle zone. They were an "in between" technology, between impractical wire phones and not yet practical battlefield wireless apparatus. Again, as in the case of the spade, innovative and older technologies characterized the Great War.

The MBlink16 became mainly a piece of equipment that the German Army employed increasingly with attacking units, especially the storm troops. These smallish groups, highly coherent with a variety of weapons and equipment employed in a shared division of labor, formed the spearhead of raids and offensives from 1917. The Blinkgerät, thus, became an example (and a symbol) of the technological arming of the smaller, more mobile and more independent fighting groups with an increasing bias toward technology and "force multipliers."

Despite some hazards in its use by attracting enemy observation, the "Blinkgerät" proved to be a technology, in many cases, able to keep up communications not only between troops on the ground and the rear but also between troops and airplanes. Here, especially, the "Schlachtflieger" (battle-planes), which were employed in the last year of the war for strafing and communication, used the standard signaling lamp extensively. Ground-to-air and air-to-ground signaling was an invaluable instrument for the new type of three-dimensional battlefield, which emerged slowly in the last months of the war.[26]

Similarly to the aerial camera, surplus signaling lamps again were loaded symbolically between the wars. They were used by paramilitary youth groups in the 1920s. In contrast to the "Wandervogel" and other youth groups of the Lebensreformbewegung before the war, which despised technology in favor of the simpler, pre-industrial lifestyle, many of these more recent groups came to appreciate and develop a fascination for technology, modifying the previously anti-technologically orientated youth movement. Additionally, the war and the experience of the bitter defeat symbolized by the Versailles treaty fueled a militarization and "technization" of these groups. They saw themselves as spearheads of a new fighting elite, incorporating technology into traditional soldierly qualities and providing military training that was officially forbidden in order to avenge Germany's humiliation. They were substituting "Geländespiele" with military technology for compulsory military service.

There is a well-researched field of militarized youth groups in Heidelberg,[27] which used the MBlink16 and surplus other signaling apparatus together with self-constructed "Blinkgeräte." Felix Wankel, later famous for the invention of the rotary internal combustion engine, founded and led several paramilitary youth cells from 1921. There, the military training of small units was done with an emphasis on communication technology and mobility. Within these groups, special departments for optical communication, for instance, the "Bliab" ("Blinkerabteilung" = flashing department), were formed. These technologically-minded paramilitary youth groups set the pattern for and in some cases formed the core of the later Hitler Youth and their technology departments.

One of the questions researchers of technology and war have asked regarding the role of the First World War is, was it a modernizing agent, or did earlier developments simply come to the surface? Was it the motor or the executor of techno-social-military change and its symbolic and cultural representations? When looking at my four significant objects which I have presented, characterized by functional as well as different symbolical values, there is no straightforward answer. Their significance reaches from the "Shock of the Old" (David Edgerton) of the spade as a weapon to the high-tech imaging system of the aerial camera. This points toward a fundamental ambivalence of technology in the Great War, which in its complexity cannot be explored deeper here.

NOTES

1. Max Schwarte, *Technik im Weltkriege* (Berlin: Mittler, 1920).
2. Giorgio Riello, *Things That Shape History: Material Culture and Historical Narratives* (London: Routledge, 2009), 25.
3. See Arjun Appadurai, *The Social Life of Things* (Cambridge: Cambridge University Press 1986), 3–63.
4. Riello, *Things*, 43.

II. The Age of the World Wars

5. Helmut Trischler, and Hans Holzer, "Die symbolische Dimension des Artefakts: Der Doppeldecker der Gebrüder Wright und der Beginn der Motorluftfahrt in Deutschland," in *Circa 1903: Artefakte in der Gründungszeit des Deutschen Museums* ed. Ulf Hashagen, Oskar Blumtritt, and Helmut Trischler (München: Deutsches Museum, 2003), 226-250.
6. Paul Fussell, *The Great War and Modern Memory* (New York: Oxford University Press, 1979).
7. Martin Middlebrook, *The First Day at the Somme: 1 July 1916* (London: Penguin: 2011).
8. John Keegan, *The Face of Battle. A Study of Agincourt, Waterloo, and the Somme* (London : Penguin, 1976).
9. Appadurai, *Social Life*, 3-63.
10. Wibe E. Bijker, Thomas P. Hughes and Trevor J. Pinch (ed.), *The Social Construction of Technological Systems: New Directions in the Sociology and History of Technology* (Cambridge, MA: MIT Press, 1987); Wibe E. Bijker, *Of Bicycles, Bakelite, and Bulbs: Towards a Theory of Sociotechnical Change* (Cambridge (Mass.), London: MIT Press, 1997).
11. Max Boot, *War made New: Technology, Warfare, and the Course of History, 1500 to today* (London: Penguin, 2006).
12. Martin van Creveld, *The Culture of War* (New York: Presidio Press, 2008).
13. See Kurt Möser, "Schlachtflieger 1918—ein technisches Waffensystem im Kontext," *Technikgeschichte* 77 (2010): 185-230.
14. Bruno Cabanes, and Anne Duménil (ed.), *Der Erste Weltkrieg: Eine europäische Katastrophe* (Bonn: Theiss, Konrad, 2013), 80.
15. Fussell, *Great War*.
16. Arnold Zweig, *Erziehung vor Verdun* (Amsterdam: Querido, 1935).
17. http://www.diz-emslandlager.de/moorlied.htm (Last access, 3 May 2014).
18. Alfred Thayer Mahan, *The Influence of Sea Power upon History, 1660-1873* (New York: Little, Brown & Co., 1890).
19. Harvey Broadbent, *Gallipoli: The Fatal Shore* (Camberwell, Vic.: Penguin Australia, 2005).
20. http://employees.oneonta.edu/baumanpr/geosat2/RSHistory/HistoryRSPart1.htm (Last access, 3 May 2014).
21. Kurt Möser, "Fliegerblick 1914," *Journal of New Frontiers in Spatial Concepts* 1 (2009): 99-106, http://ejournal.uvka.de/spatialconcepts/wp-content/uploads/2009/05/spatialconcepts_article_858.pdf (Last access, 15 July 2014).
22. Kurt Möser, *Fahren und Fliegen in Frieden und Krieg: Kulturen individueller Mobilitätsmaschinen 1880—1930* (Heidelberg u.a.: verlag regionalkultur, 2009).
23. See the autobiography of Friedrich Wilhelm Radenbach, *Weit im Rücken des Feindes: Kriegserlebnisse eines Fernaufklärers* (Berlin: Traditions-Verlag Kolk & Co., 1938).
24. Christian Kehrt, *Moderne Helden: Die Technikerfahrungen deutscher Militärpiloten 1910—1945* (Paderborn u.a.: Schöningh, 2010).
25. Helmut Lethen, *Verhaltenslehren der Kälte. Lebensversuche zwischen den Kriegen* (Frankfurt a.M.: Suhrkamp, 1994).
26. Möser, *Schlachtflieger* 1918, 185-230.
27. Kurt Möser, "Lili, Flutsch und Teufelskäfer: Die unbekannteren Entwicklungsarbeiten Felix Wankels in Heidelberg 1915-31," in *Pioniere aus Wirtschaft und Technik in Heidelberg, ed.* Blum, Peter (Aachen: Shaker, 1999), 42-53; Sascha Becker, *Spiel, Technik und Krieg: Das "Maschinenspielkind" Felix Wankel und der Nationalsozialismus 1918-1950* (Marburg, 2013).

Works Cited

Appadurai, Arjun. *The Social Life of Things*. Cambridge: Cambridge University Press 1986.
Becker, Sascha. *Spiel, Technik und Krieg: Das "Maschinenspielkind" Felix Wankel und der Nationalsozialismus 1918–1950*. Marburg: Tectum Verlag, 2013.
Bijker, Wibe E. *Of Bicycles, Bakelite, and Bulbs: Towards a Theory of Sociotechnical Change*. Cambridge (Mass.), London: MIT Press, 1997.
Bijker, Wibe E., Hughes, Thomas P. and Pinch, Trevor J., ed. *The Social Construction of Technological Systems: New Directions in the Sociology and History of Technology*. Cambridge, MA: MIT Press, 1987.
Boot, Max. *War Made New: Technology, Warfare, and the Course of History, 1500 to Today*. London: Penguin, 2006.
Broadbent, Harvey. *Gallipoli: The Fatal Shore*. Camberwell, Vic.: Penguin Australia, 2005.
Cabanes, Bruno, and Anne Duménil, ed. *Der Erste Weltkrieg: Eine europäische Katastrophe*. Bonn: Theiss, Konrad, 2013.
Creveld, Martin van. *The Culture of War*. New York: Presidio Press, 2008.
Fussell, Paul. *The Great War and Modern Memory*. New York: Oxford University Press, 1979.
Keegan, John. *The Face of Battle: A Study of Agincourt, Waterloo, and the Somme*. London: Penguin, 1976.
Kehrt, Christian. *Moderne Helden: Die Technikerfahrungen deutscher Militärpiloten 1910–1945*. Paderborn u.a.: Schöningh, 2010.
Lethen, Helmut. *Verhaltenslehren der Kälte: Lebensversuche zwischen den Kriegen*. Frankfurt a.M.: Suhrkamp, 1994.
Middlebrook, Martin. *The First Day at the Somme: 1 July 1916*. London: Penguin: 2011.
Mahan, Alfred Thayer. *The Influence of Sea Power Upon History, 1660–1873*. New York: Little, Brown & Co., 1890.
Möser, Kurt. *Fahren und Fliegen in Frieden und Krieg: Kulturen individueller Mobilitätsmaschinen 1880–1930*. Heidelberg u.a.: verlag regionalkultur, 2009.
Möser, Kurt. "Fliegerblick 1914," *Journal of New Frontiers in Spatial Concepts* 1 (2009): 99–106.
Möser, Kurt. "Lili, Flutsch und Teufelskäfer. Die unbekannteren Entwicklungsarbeiten Felix Wankels in Heidelberg 1915–31," *Pioniere aus Wirtschaft und Technik in Heidelberg*, ed. Peter Blum. Aachen: Shaker Verlag GmbH, 1999, 42–53.
Möser, Kurt. "Schlachtflieger 1918—ein technisches Waffensystem im Kontext," *Technikgeschichte* 77 (2010): 185–230.
Radenbach, Friedrich Wilhelm. *Weit im Rücken des Feindes: Kriegserlebnisse eines Fernaufklärers*. Berlin: Traditions-Verlag Kolk, 1938.
Riello, Giorgio. *Things that Shape History: Material Culture and Historical Narratives*. London: Routledge, 2009.
Schwarte, Max. *Technik im Weltkriege*. Berlin: Mittler, 1920.
Trischler, Helmut, and Hans Holzer. "Die symbolische Dimension des Artefakts: Der Doppeldecker der Gebrüder Wright und der Beginn der Motorluftfahrt in Deutschland," *Circa 1903: Artefakte in der Gründungszeit des Deutschen Museums*, ed. Ulf Hashagen, Oskar Blumtritt and Helmut Trischler. München: Deutsches Museum, 2003, 226–250.
Zweig, Arnold. *Erziehung vor Verdun*. Amsterdam: Querido, 1935.

The Special Operations Executive (SOE) and the Use and Abuse of Peacetime Technology, 1940–45
A Case Study of Unconventional Warfare

RODERICK BAILEY

The Special Operations Executive (SOE) was a secret British organization set up early in the Second World War to encourage subversion and carry out sabotage inside enemy territory. Disbanded in 1946, it had become, by the end of the war, one of the Allies' principal means of waging irregular warfare; it had also secured a global reach: mostly dropped by parachute or sent in by sea, SOE operatives worked alongside resistance movements in almost every major theatre in which the Allies were engaged against the Axis powers. Drawing on declassified files and the recorded testimonies of former personnel, what follows seeks to highlight SOE's unusual use in its unique brand of unconventional warfare, of civilian, peacetime, technology. More specifically, it demonstrates how modern advances in such technology were used to disguise specialist weapons and pieces of equipment, even agents themselves, in order to aid their deployment against the enemy. It also suggests that, while such modes of warfare may have been legal then, some might be viewed differently if practiced today. This chapter begins with a brief introduction to SOE and its wartime role, to place those topics in context.

The SOE was established in July 1940 when Britain was in a dark place. Europe was under growing Axis control and occupation. France, Belgium, Holland, Luxembourg, Denmark and Norway had all been overrun. British forces had been almost totally ejected from the Continent, there were no strong toeholds left, and the search was on for effective ways of striking back. One idea, which was partly the brainchild of a Member of Parliament for the Labour Party, Hugh Dalton (1887–1962), who would be appointed the first Cabinet Minister responsible for SOE, was to strike behind the enemy's lines and encourage threatened and occupied populations to resist. In the course of the next five years, SOE became the principal British organization engaged in working secretly inside enemy-occupied Europe. In many countries, it would play the principal Allied role, occupying a superior position (in terms of agents on the ground and influence with resistance groups) even to the American Office of Strategic Services, which was, roughly, the combined equivalent of SOE and Britain's Secret Intelligence Service and a precursor to the CIA.

One of the main methods by which SOE sought to go about its tasks was by sending out agents to operate clandestinely in enemy territory, where they would seek to sabotage enemy installations and infrastructure and work side-by-side with local resistance movements. Today, at least in Britain, the popular image of SOE remains dominated by stories of its agents in Occupied France (those agents included most of SOE's women agents). The reality is different. SOE became active on a global scale. France was an important area of operations, and several dozen women agents did operate there, but thousands of SOE operatives, almost all of them men, ended up working in every enemy-occupied country in Europe and as far afield as Japanese-occupied Burma and Malaya. The local groups they supported were also diverse, ranging from communist partisans in the Balkans, for example, to headhunting tribes in the Japanese-occupied jungles of Borneo. Agents destined for work in enemy territory received specialist training in various techniques and also had different roles. Some had command roles, where they were responsible for building up and organizing local resistance. Some were sabotage specialists and weapons instructors. Some operated secret radio sets that were essential for sending back reports to SOE headquarters and calling in deliveries of reinforcements and supplies.[1]

When it reached its peak strength in the middle of 1944, SOE employed around 13,000 personnel. Of these, about 5,000 were agents either in training or deployed in the field. The remaining personnel were engaged in a wide range of support activity from instructing prospective agents at secluded training schools, to the manning of secret stations devoted to exchanging radio messages with the field and to routine administration at SOE headquarters. They also included men and women devoted to the invention and production of specialist weapons and equipment to assist SOE agents in their work.

SOE had several research and development stations that were dedicated

II. The Age of the World Wars

to that technical support work.[2] Each was housed in conditions of great secrecy in various suitable premises around Britain. Much of the material produced in these establishments took the form of weapons and other equipment designed specifically for clandestine and irregular warfare: from "Sleeve-guns" (single-shot weapons designed for carrying and concealing inside the arm of a coat) to "Sleeping Beauties" (motorized submersible one-man canoes developed for a diver to conduct clandestine reconnaissance and raids). Many of the responsible innovators and designers were gunsmiths, engineers, explosives experts and the like.

SOE also identified a vital need to disguise material to ensure that it blended in with local environments and that it could be delivered, stored and moved undetectably. To accomplish this, SOE created a section devoted to "camouflage," as it termed it. Located just north of London on the Barnet bypass, the establishment where the Camouflage Section was based was code-named Station XV. It was housed in premises in and around a former roadhouse (i.e., a motel) called The Thatched Barn, which became another name that SOE used for it. For a long time, the British officer in charge was J. Elder Wills (1900–1970), who, before the war, had had a career in the film business. Like Wills, the men and women whom SOE recruited and employed at Station XV often

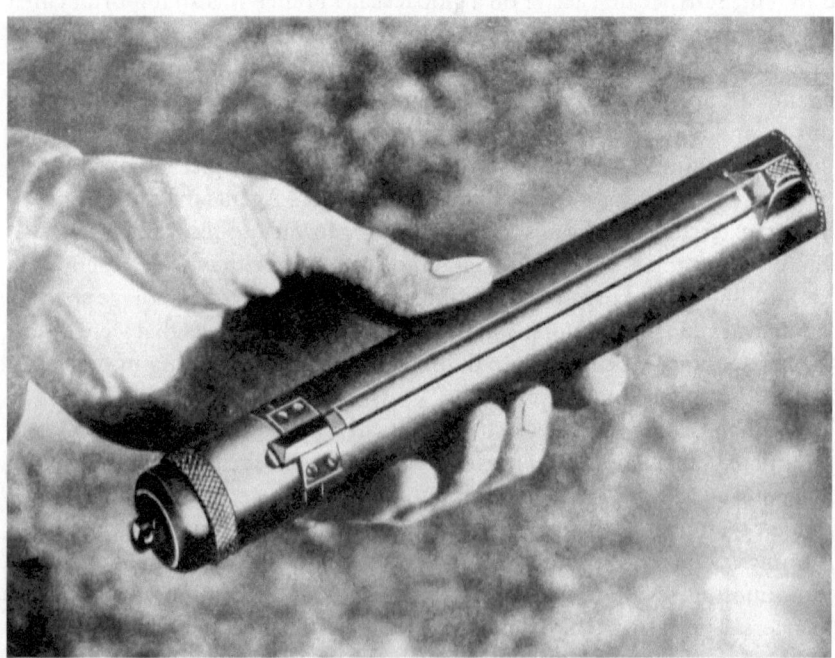

SOE-developed Sleeve Gun (source: "Descriptive Catalogue of Special Devices and Supplies," 1944, NARA RG 226, Entry 134, Box 41).

had very different backgrounds from those tasked with inventing and developing weaponry. Many had also worked during peacetime for the film industry, as plasterers, carpenters, props experts, hairdressers, make-up artists and so on.

The paramount aim of camouflage work was to maximize an agent's chances of surviving in the field and carrying out his or her job. It could mean providing them with convincing clothes and personal items from the countries to which they were going: French-made shirts for France, for instance, complete with all the correct labels. It could mean altering their looks by changing hairstyles and adding make-up. On occasion, efforts at camouflaging an agent's physical appearance could also require the assistance of professionals skilled in modern medical techniques. Among the medical men employed by SOE was a dental surgeon who, with his assistants, did more than maintain agents' dental health. Another of his roles was to ensure that, if examined in an enemy country, an agent's mouth would not betray evidence of having received dental treatment in Britain. SOE could also provide different types of caps with relative ease, and there is a recorded case of an agent going into Nazi-occupied Denmark with a gold tooth concealed beneath a porcelain cap. SOE also developed a gold cap that an agent could carry in his pocket ready for easy and immediate use: if he suddenly felt the need to look a little different, he could take it out and slip it over an existing tooth. SOE's dental personnel were also able to add temporary bulk to the inside of mouths to deliberately distort the shape of a face.

The idea behind disguising agents' mouths was of course so that they could go into enemy territory without fear of standing out as outsiders or being recognized by people who had known them previously (many SOE recruits were natives of the countries to which they were returning to work as clandestine agents). However, medical assistance with disguises went beyond dentistry. SOE also arranged for several agents to be on the receiving end of modern techniques in facial surgery in order to change prominent and distinguishing physical features. As with dentistry, this surgery had to be out-sourced since SOE's permanent medical staff lacked the necessary skills to do it themselves. In this case, it was given to professional plastic surgeons.

As well as working to develop efficient ways of disguising the true identities of agents, SOE sought also to explore the ways and means of concealing essential equipment within everyday objects that no one would suspect of any nefarious dual purpose. Staff employed on these tasks at Station XV could be extremely imaginative, as demonstrated by a contemporary catalogue, complete with illustrations, of SOE's various inventions and devices.[3] Items for concealing secret documents ranged from the hollowed-out corks of winebottles to hollow door-keys, pencils, toothbrushes, toothpaste tubes, chess-sets, shaving sets and cotton-reels. For hiding wireless sets and similarly large equipment on enemy shores for resistance fighters to recover and use, hollow "rocks" were made of plaster and painted to fit the appropriate coastline. (SOE found a plethora of ways of concealing wireless sets: from tins of tea to boxes of artists' paint.) Plaster casts of logs, again hollowed-out and suitably presented, were invented for similar storage purposes, as were carefully converted fish barrels, metal flagons, oil drums, packing cases, cement bags, pieces of driftwood and even plaster casts of fruit and vegetables. On display today in London's Imperial War Museum are a pair of SOE-manufactured shoes designed with the imprint of the sole of a human foot; these were invented in the hope of allowing the booted tread of agents fighting the Japanese to blend convincingly with those of native populations in the Far East.

Perhaps the most famous of SOE's inventions—the one that, since the war, has become most publicly associated with the ingenuity of its research and development staff—was the explosive rat. The idea here was simple: take the skin of a rat; fill it with an explosive and a detonator; then leave it in a suitable spot to go off on its own or be helped on its way by, for example, a factory workman pitching it innocently into a factory boiler as a run-of-the-mill dead rodent. SOE also produced pieces of heat-operated "explosive coal" to perform a similar role. Hollowed-out and filled with explosives, these were designed to explode when shoveled by unsuspecting stokers into the boilers that fueled the engines of enemy ships and trains. Then there were "tyre-bursters," which were small explosive charges designed to be scattered over roads and tracks in the hope of enemy vehicles driving over and detonating them. SOE could camouflage these as a host of different objects in plaster or papier-mâché form, including stones and rock fragments, coal, cork, pieces of mud and brick, and horse, mule and dog excrement. "They weren't terribly powerful," remembered one SOE operative who had scattered tyre-bursters disguised as mule droppings over roads in mainland Greece, "they would [only] blow the wheel off a truck, but they irritated the Germans. And the Germans twigged what was going on and what was good to see on the roads was that the Germans had fatigue parties of soldiers sweeping the roads, sweeping the shit off, because they were covered with mule shit."[4]

To disguise weapons and equipment, SOE went further than using rocks, rats, driftwood and dung. It also made use of popular items of modern civilian technology by deliberately exploiting their original intention and peaceful appearance. Easily carried and unlikely to arouse suspicion, portable gramophones, for example, were used to conceal clandestine radio sets. "This concealment is only for carrying purposes," the SOE catalogue adds, "and the wireless set must be taken out of the gramophone and assembled for working. Wherever possible the gramophone is made to play and appropriate records are supplied." Also used for hiding radio sets were adding machines (i.e., early calculators), domestic radio sets, clocks and vacuum cleaners. "The [vacuum] cleaner can be 'plugged in' and although not actually operating as a cleaner the noise produced will give all the appearance of it doing so. If an agent was stopped while carrying the cleaner in the street it would be normal to tell a story that it was being taken for repair, or to be sold."[5]

SOE did not stop at employing modern technology to disguise radio sets; it also sought to exploit its often peaceful and mundane appearance in order to deliberately inflict harm. To initiate the detonation of explosives beneath a railway line, for example, SOE manufactured dummy fog signals. These had the appearance of real fog signals, which were peaceful devices designed to be clipped to a line of rail to warn train drivers of fog ahead. SOE's version was designed to be crushed by the pressure of an incoming train and thus ignite hidden charges.

Dummy fog signals, which were used extensively by SOE agents tasked with sabotaging trains, caused damage indirectly and at a distance. Other everyday objects were selected for their ability to disguise explosive devices designed to cause death and destruction at much closer quarters. Some were not necessarily examples of modern technological progress. Glass Chianti bottles, which were redesigned in celluloid form to hold a bomb timed to go off when an agent had withdrawn to a safe-enough distance, had been around for hundreds of years. Explosive-filled reproductions of Balinese woodcarvings, designed for selling as souvenirs to unwitting Japanese troops, exploited traditions that had been around for much longer. Using wood and plaster, Station XV even made faithful copies of Chinese stone lanterns.

According to the SOE catalogue, these could then be "filled with H.E. [high explosive] and

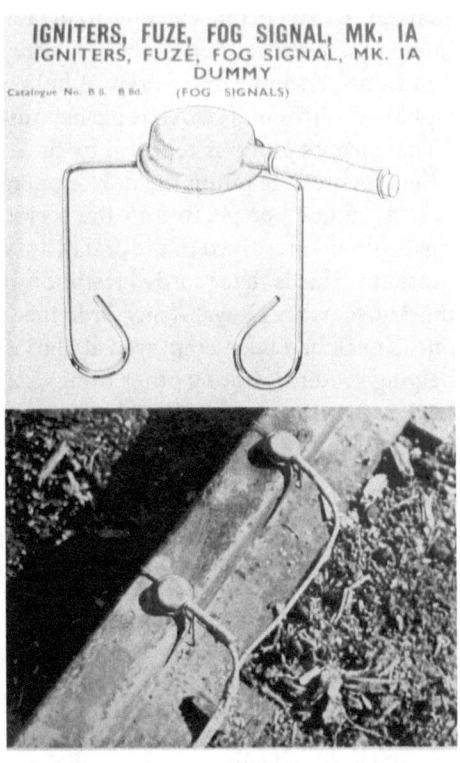

SOE-developed Dummy Fog Signals (source: "Descriptive Catalogue of Special Devices and Supplies," 1944, NARA RG 226, Entry 134, Box 41).

fitted with [a] delayed action fuse or anti-removal switch." The lantern could also be disassembled into various exploding parts to give the impression that it had fallen over and broken up. Use was made, too, of the invention of the modern printing press. "The Explosive Book is a booby trap which may be placed on any flat surface preferably among other books on a table top," says the catalogue. "The inside of the book is cut away in order to leave sufficient space for a lb. or more of P.E. [plastic explosive] [...] The covers are fixed so that any attempt to open the book will cause lifting of the volume and immediate action of the fuse."[6]

Other devices, though, took advantage of much more recent innovations. One was a torch (i.e., a flashlight) that doubled as a hand grenade. "A German pattern torch of the Daimon variety is used as an explosive device," the SOE catalogue explains. "Two of the three batteries normally present in the torch are removed, their place being taken by a cylindrical, deeply grooved bomb filled with Baratol. The normal switch on the outside of the torch has been adapted so that current can flow to the torch bulb, or, after removal of a small safety pin, to the igniter." Another example was a bicycle pump designed to be an anti-personnel booby trap. "A hollow brass cylinder filled with explosive and fitted with a pull switch is pushed inside the barrel of a bicycle pump [...] The enemy's pump is replaced by the explosive one and his tyres deflated. When he uses the pump the device operates."[7]

A unique perspective on the secret manufacture of objects like these can be found preserved in the oral history archives of London's Imperial War Museum. This is the recorded testimony of Jack Knock, a former sergeant in the British Army's Royal Army Ordnance Corps. In 1944, at the age of twenty-one, Knock had been employed at Station XV as an ammunitions examiner, helping produce, among other things, explosive bicycle pumps and torches. In the recording, he explains their purpose:

> French children or Frenchmen, they used to take the bicycle pumps off Germans' bicycles—because the Germans were great ones for using bicycles at one time—and then they would replace this pump that they had stolen with one we'd made to the exact specification.... [Then] they would let the German's tyre down, one tyre or two tyres, the German would come along, take his pump, and the first pump he gave, of course, he would blow his hands off.
>
> The same principle applied with torches.... You would remove the German's torch and put yours back in its place and the poor sod would again lose his hands [when he switched it on] [...]
>
> You [also] had a material that you put inside soap that will explode with contact with water.... They could wash their hands a dozen times and nothing would happen, but they'd wash their hands the next time and a piece of this would be exposed to the air and water and would explode.

Knock's testimony is particularly interesting because he also talks about the ethical dilemmas with which, he said, he had found himself confronted. "It's an awfully dirty trick if you come to think of it," he comments about the way in which the pumps were used.

> I didn't lose very much sleep about it [...] [But] to my mind ... we were maiming people [...] we were taking away their hands or their arms, their means of sustenance. Although they were German soldiers at the time, they were going to live; they were the enemy, but even so [...]
> Quite honestly, it is this sort of thing that is in my mind and was in my mind in those days. It was a hurdle to get over and one that I still remember. I still remember being in this shed [...] doing these jobs that I was doing, and knowing what was likely to happen as a result of the jobs I was doing, and not quite liking it.

Knock adds that, "because so many of the things were against the Geneva Convention that we did," he was told by SOE that the British Army was not funding the work, to make him feel better about taking part in it.

> I was quite willing to believe that the British Army wouldn't indulge in such things even if the German Army did, which was very naïve of me. I've no doubt it was the British Army, but people would have preferred, then, not to have us mixed up with atrocities; and some of the things we did could be termed atrocities, they couldn't be termed warfare, not blowing up people with torches.[8]

When considering Knock's testimony, it is important to keep in mind the potential pitfalls and weaknesses of oral interviewing and of memories recalled long after the event concerned. For example, a distinction may need to be made between explosive bicycle pumps and explosive torches: the former was certainly meant to act as a booby trap; torches, on the other hand, seem to have been developed in order to be thrown like grenades. Care must also be taken not to exaggerate the scale on which items like these were produced and used. While some items were manufactured in vast numbers (between 1941 and the end of December 1944, according to its files, SOE produced three-and-a-half tons' worth of explosive coal and 185,183 tyrebursters), others were made in much smaller quantities (during the same period, 138 explosive bicycle pumps and 50 explosive torches were produced).[9] The extensive use of explosive coal and tyre-bursters is also matter of documentary record: 8,200 were dispatched to British personnel for employment in enemy-occupied Albania alone.[10] Evidence seems to be lacking of concrete instances where explosive pumps and torches were even used.

Indeed, it is a fact that some much-publicized SOE inventions were never used aggressively against the enemy or even considered sufficiently efficient to be deployed. "The camouflage department," writes Professor M.R.D. Foot (1919–2012), the acclaimed historian of SOE, "was particularly proud of its dead rat, plastic [explosive]-stuffed, with a fuse that was armed by the action of a stoker shoveling it into a ship's boiler."[11] As proud as it may have been, only 100 explosive rats were ever prepared, according to SOE records, and no evidence exists of any of them actually seeing action beyond one container-full that fell immediately into enemy hands after being dropped by a parachute. (Unexpectedly, that discovery was still considered to have contributed indirectly to SOE's war effort. "It was a device with a limited operational use, and the happy discovery of it by the enemy was considered more advantageous to us," SOE's files explain. "[It] had an extraordinary moral effect and the device was exhibited at all German Military Schools, a wide search being organized to find the 'hundreds of rats' which the enemy believed were distributed on the Continent. The trouble caused to them was a much greater success to us than if the rats had actually been used. It is obvious that in the latter case no evidence would have remained, and the enemy would not have discovered their existence.")[12]

A note among the files of the American Office of Strategic Services (OSS), which was, more or less, the wartime combined equivalent of SOE and MI6, casts doubt on the operational effectiveness of several other items. "Not successful even with hinged toe," OSS recorded of the "native footprint maker" with which SOE had been experimenting: "Imprint uneven." "Poor," OSS observed of a painted, lacquered, and explosive-filled Buddha. "Easily spotted as imitation [...] Can't guarantee you can get your man to hover over the Buddha at the time of explosion."[13]

Care should also be taken with Knock's comments about the Geneva Convention. No international legislation existed during the Second World War that specifically outlawed the use of booby traps like exploding bicycle pumps. Nevertheless, it is the case that SOE's use of at least some of these devices, which were used to lull an unsuspecting enemy into a false sense of security in order to hurt, kill or otherwise inconvenience them, would be outlawed today. Explosive pumps and soap contravene Protocol II of the UN Convention on Prohibitions or Restrictions on the Use of Certain Conventional Weapons, a 1980 annex to the Geneva Conventions of 1949.[14] Another SOE creation, the "explosive food tin," would, today, contravene Protocol II on the additional ground that that particular booby trap interfered with the enemy's food and drink. The idea with this device took advantage of the everyday practice of storing food in sealed tins (a nineteenth century invention). SOE would fill a tin with plastic explosive and prime it to explode when opened. "The tin [thus] prepared," explains a note among SOE's records, "may be left in billets, kitchens, etc., where hostile troops can find it. Easing the lid permits the release switch to operate."[15] (Between 1941 and the end of 1944, Station XV produced twenty-four of these.) An exploding Buddha would also now contravene Protocol II, which prohibits booby traps associated with places of worship and objects of a religious nature.

"As man acquired defensive methods, and became more and more civilized, his instinctive desire to hide as a means of preservation gradually dwindled, and finally disappeared," reads an introductory note in SOE's files to the work of its Camouflage Section. "It was modern warfare that reawakened these lost instincts, and brought him again the imperative need of concealment."[16] However, as the character of modern warfare changes (and man, at times, becomes less civilized when waging it), so, too, do perceptions of what forms of warfare are ethically and legally sound. Given that the work of SOE's agents in enemy-occupied Europe is often presented in film and fiction—and in a lot of bad history writing—as wholly admirable and heroic, it may be sensible to keep in mind that, while many of its secret inventions remain examples of considerable ingenuity, the death and destruction inflicted by some of them could, if repeated today, be classified as atrocities and crimes.

NOTES

  1. For the best introduction to SOE's work, see W.J.M. Mackenzie, *The Secret History of SOE: Special Operations Executive 1940–1945* (London: St. Ermin's, 2000). Mackenzie had been commissioned at the end of the war to write an in-house history of SOE for the Cabinet Office. With access to SOE's surviving records, he completed his task in the late 1940s. His text remained secret for the next half century.

  2. For a thorough study of SOE's research and development work, see F. Boyce and D. Everett, *SOE: The Scientific Secrets* (Stroud: Sutton, 2003), which draws on SOE's own records and the memories and papers of participants.

  3. "Descriptive Catalogue of Special Devices and Supplies," Copy No. 148, Vol. 2, 1945, TNA HS 7/28. The catalogue has been published (with an introduction by me) as *Secret Agent's Handbook: The Top Secret Manual of Wartime Weapons, Gadgets, Disguises and Devices* (London: Max Press, 2008).

  4. Lieutenant Colonel Brian Dillon. Sound archive interview no. 23787, Imperial War Museum.

  5. "Descriptive Catalogue of Special Devices and Supplies," Copy No. 148, Vol. 2, 1945, TNA HS 7/28.

  6. "Descriptive Catalogue of Special Devices and Supplies," Copy No. 148, Vol. 2, 1945, TNA HS 7/28.

  7. Ibid.

  8. Sergeant Jack Knock. Sound archive interview no. 11471, Imperial War Museum. Knock was correct to remember explosive soap as having been produced at Station XV. It was known as "Incendiary Soap." "A hollow cast is made of a cake of soap," explains the SOE catalogue. The cavity is filled with pure metallic sodium and the joint is carefully sealed up with soap, so that the join cannot be seen. When the soap covering of the sodium wears thin through use, moisture seeps through causing it to ignite and burn fiercely. The device can cause a great deal of injury to the hands or face." The catalogue also mentions a related invention, the "Incendiary Shaving Brush." "A normal shaving brush handle is hollowed out and filled with pure metallic sodium. A small hole is bored in the stub of the hairs of the brush to allow water to seep through, and when the brush is used the sodium is ignited by contact with the water." "Descriptive Catalogue of Special Devices and Supplies," TNA HS 7/28.

  9. "History and Development of the Camouflage Section, 1941–1945," TNA HS 7/49.

10. "History of the Allied Military Mission, Albania, 1942–1945," TNA HS 7/70.
11. M.R.D. Foot, *Resistance: An Analysis of European Resistance to Nazism, 1940–1945* (London: Eyre Methuen, 1976), 46.
12. "History and Development of the Camouflage Section, 1941–1945" TNA HS 7/49.
13. Major G. Watts Hill to Major Sam G. Lucy, 26 September 1944, NARA RG 226, Entry 134, Box 49, Folder 505.
14. "Protocol (II) on Prohibitions or Restrictions on the Use of Mines, Booby-Traps and Other Devices. Geneva," 10 October 1980. Its provisions were amended and strengthened on 3 May 1996. For more on the 1980 Protocol, see, for example: http://www.icrc.org/applic/ihl/ihl.nsf/INTRO/510 (Last access, 15 January 2015).
15. "History and Development of the Camouflage Section, 1941–1945" TNA HS 7/49.
16. Ibid.

Works Cited

Boyce, F., and D. Everett. *SOE: The Scientific Secrets*. Stroud: Sutton, 2003.
"Descriptive Catalogue of Special Devices and Supplies," Copy No. 148, Vol. 2, 1945, TNA HS 7/28. *Secret Agent's Handbook: The Top Secret Manual of Wartime Weapons, Gadgets, Disguises and Devices*. London: Max Press, 2008.
Dillon, Lieutenant Colonel Brian. Sound archive interview no. 23787, Imperial War Museum.
Foot, M.R.D. *Resistance: An Analysis of European Resistance to Nazism, 1940–1945*. London: Eyre Methuen, 1976.
"History and Development of the Camouflage Section, 1941–1945," TNA HS 7/49.
"History of the Allied Military Mission, Albania, 1942–1945," TNA HS 7/70.
Mackenzie, W.J.M. *The Secret History of SOE: Special Operations Executive 1940–1945*. London: St. Ermin's, 2000.
"Protocol (II) on Prohibitions or Restrictions on the Use of Mines, Booby-Traps and Other Devices. Geneva," 10 October 1980.
Major G. Watts Hill to Major Sam G. Lucy, 26 September 1944, NARA RG 226, Entry 134, Box 49, Folder 505.

The Liberal Attraction to Technological Progress and the RAF

Tomáš Kučera

During the Second World War, the Royal Air Force (RAF) and the U.S. Army Air Force (USAAF) put an enormous effort into the destruction of German cities, including the ill-known bombing of Dresden in February 1945. In total, the strategic bombing campaign of the Allies resulted in about 300,000 fatalities, most of them civilians, and another 780,000 Germans seriously injured.[1] As it was later proved by the U.S. Strategic Bombing Survey, this carnage had little, or maybe even negative, strategic effect.[2] Moreover, the indiscriminate bombing of German cities at the end of the war significantly violated basic ethical principles that Western liberal people held dear.

Paradoxically, it was the liberal character of the UK defense policy, as this chapter is set to propose, that brought about this resort to indiscriminate area bombing. Although discrimination of combatants and civilians and immunity of the latter are one of the strongest imperatives of liberal ethics of war, among the bedrock attributes of liberal philosophy are also the "Whiggish" notions of humankind's progress, advancement and amelioration. This essay thus attempts to show the significance of liberal ethical and philosophical tradition in the interwar development of the RAF and its Bomber Command that resulted in the wartime strategic bombing campaign against the civilian population of Germany.

David Edgerton, referring to his concept of "liberal militarism," has provided a persuasive argument that the military sector in Britain has been deeply suffused with "the scientific, technological and industrial spirit."[3] In Edgerton's view, the capital intensive strategy, based on exploitation of science and technology, is a specifically liberal approach, for it rested on the view of the British elite that the UK's power was and should be based primarily on economy, industry and commerce, to which the purpose of the armed forces was subordinated. Given that Britain was a rather small nation in comparison with other great powers, it was a rational strategy to exploit its relative strength in science and technology without undermining the base of this strength by sending industrial workers into mass armies.[4]

It is hard to deny that preferring utilization of the scientific and industrial output to fielding mass armies must have appeared as an unequivocally rational and preferable strategy. Nevertheless, such a simple cost-benefit explanation cannot reveal the full picture. This essay will hence try to contribute to the understanding of this issue by interpreting the ascendency of the RAF as a manifestation of liberal ethical and philosophical tradition that had been ingrained in British society. To carry out this aim, this chapter is structured into three sections. In the first section, two liberal imperatives— the norm about the immunity of innocent civilians and the attraction to technological and scientific progress—are presented. These liberal imperatives play a crucial role in the following narrative. The following section offers an explanation of how the liberal propensity to scientific and technological progress became promoted into the rather conservative military realm in the UK. It is argued here that the specificity of the British civil-military relations enabled the civilian authorities, namely the Cabinet and the Treasury, to advance their own views on military strategy. The solution of strategic problems through utilization of technology was thus considered preferable to traditional military solutions. The last section is then concerned with the ethical conflict that emerged in the actual use of the bomber for the purpose of imperial policing and, more significantly, in the area bombing campaign against Germany.

Liberal Imperatives

It is essential for liberal ethics of war that distinctions are made not only between combatants and non-combatants but also between those guilty of causing the war and innocent victims. In the liberal eyes, the genuine enemy is only a limited group of people who bear responsibility for the war. All other classes of citizens of the enemy state are not regarded as guilty by the crime of aggression. As Micheal Walzer stated in his seminal book on just wars, "civilians on both sides are innocent, equally innocent, and never legitimate military targets."[5] Walzer's idea has been a recurring theme throughout the liberal philosophical tradition. Thus, John Locke insisted that no punishment can be inflicted on any but those responsible for the war:

It is the unjust use of force, then, that puts a man into the state of war with another, and thereby he that is guilty of it makes a forfeiture of his life.... But because the miscarriages of the father are no faults of the children, who may be rational and peaceable, notwithstanding the brutishness and injustice of the father, the father, by his miscarriages and violence, can forfeit but his own life, and involves not his children in his guilt or destruction.[6]

Moreover, Locke argued that when it came to compensations for the damages caused by the war, the innocent citizens of the vanquished aggressive state have a strong counter-claim over the winning side that fought for a just cause.[7] In a clear and explicit way, this idea was expressed by Immanuel Kant, too. He stated, "It is allowed in war to demand exactions and contributions from the defeated enemy, but one may not plunder the people, that is, take forcibly from individuals what is their own (for that would be robbery, since it was not the defeated people, but rather the state that rules the people, which waged war *through the people*)."[8] In Locke's and Kant's thinking thus come the origins of the liberal assumption that citizens of the state which committed a crime of aggression were victims of the crime to the same extent as the people in the offended state.

Another bedrock attribute of liberalism is the notion of humankind's progress, advancement and amelioration. Liberal thinking completely seized the Enlightenment notion of progress so that an optimistic outlook towards scientific discoveries and inventions can be rightly regarded as something characteristic to liberal societies. Consequently, military affairs are not excluded from the liberal belief in improvement through science and technology. To Kant, for example, military competencies were by no means natural; on the contrary, military skills and capabilities "were intended to be entirely products of their own efforts."[9] Similarly, according to James Mill, "one of the first applications of knowledge is to improve the military art."[10]

This chapter is set to focus its attention to the role of norms and ideological assumptions in the military strategy of the United Kingdom. To be slightly more down to earth, it is argued here that the liberal notion of progress could find its way into strategic decision-making due to the general mistrust of liberalism towards the military and exclusive military solutions to the problems of defense and war. If the security of the state and society is seen to be threatened, liberalism prescribes that it ought to be the strength of society as a whole—not only its military qualities—that needs to be utilized for the purpose of defense.

Materialization of Liberal Imperatives

The aspect of liberal antimilitarism plays a crucial role in understanding how the idea of technological and scientific progress expanded from the realm

II. The Age of the World Wars

of general society into the UK defense policy. That this transmission may face considerable obstacles stems from the fact that a deep expertise in military affairs is usually crucial in decision-making on this issue and, moreover, the question of weapon development and procurement often falls within the authority of the military itself.

In fact, there is a strong predisposition in military institutions in general to develop institutional cultures that tend to oppose any radical innovations.[11] As Jonathan Shimshoni puts it, militaries, like any other large bureaucratic organizations and even more, are normally conservative:

> [T]hey reduce uncertainty by adhering to standard operating procedures, sticking to the tried and true, and learning in a process that is linear, sequential, and cybernetic.... The simultaneous orientation towards promotion and discipline make the socialization to the "particular way of doing business" natural to army officers. Changing the way of doing business is not likely in a hierarchical organization whose leaders reached the top by virtue of success in the past. The way of the past is the way in which they are experts, and the source of their authority.[12]

According to various accounts, the 20th century British Army was a case in point. Illustrative is the debate on offense versus defense between 1900 and 1914. The army accepted that new weapons were more efficient and destructive, yet instead of adopting a doctrine that would suit the new battlefield conditions, the army sought to overcome the full implications of technology by emphasizing the moral and psychological qualities of the individual.[13] T.H.E. Travers explicates this occurrence by the fact that the officer corps of the British army in Victorian and Edwardian times was recruited from the conservative elements of British society. Individual moral qualities and above all "character," the major aim of public-school education, was a defining characteristic of this class. However, "if firepower and technology were required rather than character," then the training, present role and the social and political status of the officer class were obsolete. Therefore, notes Travers, "it was necessary to ignore the full impact of the [modern military technology] and insist on the moral qualities of war."[14]

Elizabeth Kier demonstrates that this kind of conservatism did not disappear after the First World War. On the contrary, "the absence of army reform meant that during the 1920s and 1930s the British army had an organizational culture that predated the modern era."[15] She argues that this "gentleman-officer" culture was detrimental to the development of armored warfare in the British army. Whereas in the aftermath of the First World War, the British army was in the lead of the development of the tank, a rather traditional doctrine of mechanized warfare was adopted by the 1930s. Although by the end of the 1930s, the army motorized most of its units and formed the Mobile Division, the approach to fighting remained unchanged. The main role of the tank was to support the infantry, and the Mobile Division was supposed to take the role of the old Cavalry Division before mechanization.[16]

How could it, then, happen that despite the military conservatism, the British military strategy became characteristic for its radical utilization of emerging technologies? Liberalism, as an antimilitaristic ideology, tends to be cautious about the military's authority, as the history of civil-military relations in the UK very clearly demonstrates. Not only was it the case that the British constitutional system placed the military under very strict civilian control of Parliament, *de jure*, and the government, *de facto*, but also the military's authority to give advice in strategic matters was by no means exclusive. As one pre-1914 critic of the British military system commented, "the opinion is not uncommon in England that members of Parliament and journalists are far more capable of organizing an army than even the most experienced soldier."[17] Indeed, this inclusivity of the strategic debate, the constitutional subordination of the military services to politicians and, in addition, the existence of, from 1918 on, three competitor services effectively enabled the technologically driven "liberal militarism," as Edgerton calls it, to happen.

One of the major technological breakthroughs in the First World War, the tank, was ushered into the army's services via the navy. Not only was it the case that the navy, as a technically oriented branch, presented a more fertile ground for technological innovations, the separate existence of the two services enabled progressively-minded politicians, such as Winston Churchill (1874–1965) in this case, to find organizational support for the development of a new technology. After the RAF was established in 1918, three armed services with diverse views on strategic priorities were competing for limited resources. This divergence of outlooks was particularly striking in the interwar period. The army had the needs of imperial policing and the preparation for another continental war in mind, while the navy emphasized the threat posed by Japan to the British Far-East possessions, and the air force's doctrine of strategic bombing promised the possibility of deterring a major war on the Continent from breaking out. Moreover, the RAF challenged the army's indispensability in imperial policing when it offered air policing as a dramatically cheaper alternative to the army's counter-insurgency approach.[18]

With this range of strategic options and in the absence of a unifying and over-arching ministry of defense, the Cabinet and the Treasury, the most powerful department in the process of articulating strategic policies, wielded the real power to settle strategic priorities.[19] Financial control and decision-making to allocate scarce resources were the main sources of power of the Treasury and the Cabinet. As C.I. Hamilton notes, even before 1914, financial control imposed by the Treasury over the navy's expenditures provided the Treasury officials with "the power of helping to shape policy, even in a detailed way."[20] The need to stabilize the government's budget after the end of the First World

War forced the Treasury to pursue an active policy towards the services, including formulation of its own strategic policy.[21] Both the Treasury and the Cabinet in the interwar period strongly favored air power and mechanization, for these were viewed as the most cost-effective ways, in terms of manpower and financial resources, to attain the strategic needs of the United Kingdom.[22] The very same reasons drove the Cabinet in the 1950s towards placing the nuclear deterrent, despite Chiefs of Staff's objections, at the center of the UK's military strategy.[23]

In addition to the plurality of official military expertise, the voices from outside the military organizations were by no means marginal. Basil Liddell Hart (1895–1970), a liberal military thinker and the most prolific advocate of mechanization and modernization of the armed forces in the first half of the 20th Century, was notably shaping, through his leading articles in the *Times* and other publications, the public and political discourse on Britain's military transformation and military strategy. From the late 1930s onwards, Liddell Hart was frequently quoted as an authoritative source on strategic and military issues in Parliamentary debates.[24] Moreover, the extent to which Liddell Hart's counsel was sought by Leslie Hore-Belisha (1893–1957), Secretary of State for War, 1937–40, caused a great resentment with the Chief of the Imperial General Staff of those years, Lord Gort (1886–1946).[25]

Because of the novelty of the bomber in the interwar period, the exclusivity of the official military expertise could be relatively easily contested. As Stanley Baldwin (1867–1947), leader of the Conservative party during most of the interwar period, had remarked in the House of Commons in November 1932, the proverbial "man in the street probably realized that "the bomber will always get through."[26] H.G. Wells' novel and film (*Shape of*) *Things to Come*[27] visualized not only the catastrophic consequences of modern warfare but also the hope that progress, including technological advancement in aviation, would bring peace. The peace-making capacity of the air force was also stressed by the advocates of the concept of International Air Police, which even became a part of the disarmament proposal presented by French Prime Minister Éduard Herriot (1872–1957) in 1932.[28] As Lord Davies put it, "there can be no question of [the airplane's] vital importance in war and of its efficiency as a "policeman." "[U]nder the control of the international authority the aeroplane may become the emissary of justice."[29] The scientific progress in aviation was seen to provide the opportunity, and now the statesmen and politicians were called "to march abreast of the scientific researchers."[30]

A Moral Paradox of the "British Way of Warfare"

The liberal enthusiasm for scientific and technological solutions to defense and war is not confined only to the introduction of new technology into the military but is also intrinsically related to a specific strategic logic. In the liberal eyes, the peacetime focus on scientific and technological progress in military affairs is justifiable only as long as it can prevent war, or if a war breaks out, it can bring the war to a quick and, in terms of lives, inexpensive conclusion. The rejection of the Clausewitzian decisive battle is at the very core of this liberal enthusiasm for advanced military technology. Such was argued by John Stuart Mill in 1867 when international convention was to prohibit the use of warships against civilian merchant ships of the enemy nation:

> a strange gain to humanity if the merchants, manufacturers, and agriculturists of the world lost nothing by a state of war, and had no pecuniary interest in preventing it except the increase of their taxes [...] How war is to be humanised by shooting at men's bodies instead of taking their property, I confess, surprises me.[31]

The threat to or actual targeting of economic power and the will of civilians was believed to be the future way effectively to avoid carnage on a battlefield. A major proponent of this strategy in the interwar period was Liddell Hart. He referred to this strategy as the "British way of warfare" and explained that "Britain never had the power to achieve outright victory over a great continental state. Her real power lay in her capacity, through command of the sea, to make any Continental opponent sick of the war and anxious to make peace on terms satisfactory to her."[32] In the interwar period, it was believed that air power could be used in a similar way. Like many other contemporaries who were scarred psychologically and physically by their experiences in the stalemated trench fighting of the 1914–18 Western Front, Liddell Hart assumed that a modern state, due to its complex economic and political structures, offered a target critically vulnerable to a sudden and overwhelming blow from the air. Thus, he argued in the 1920s that airplanes and gas would demoralize the enemy without the sheer physical destruction and death that would be necessary if land forces were deployed in a battle.[33]

After 1918, it seemed plausible to argue that "precision bombing" of the enemy's industrial bases would cause significantly less damage and casualties for both sides than the kind of warfare that had just been experienced. However, few had illusions that strategic bombing of industrial and population centers would not entail dreadful carnage. As Baldwin explained in his famous speech in Parliament in 1932, "any town which is within reach of an aerodrome can be bombed within the first five minutes of war from the air, to an extent which was inconceivable in the last war.... The only defense is in offence, which means that you have to kill more women and children more quickly than the enemy if you want to save yourselves."[34]

Here comes the moral paradox of the "British way of warfare" represented by the concept of strategic bombing in the interwar period. The liberal ethics of war is unequivocal in its condemnation of violence against non-combatants, insisting that civilians on both sides of the conflict are innocent victims.[35] However, in order to prevent war or at least to reduce the costs of life, decent liberal people, many of them enthusiastically, did support strategies based on foreseeable if not intentional killing of civilians.[36] Does it mean, then, that liberal ethics carries no weight in comparison with purely "rational" considerations?

An illustrative case is provided by the use of air power in colonial policing in Mesopotamia (present-day Iraq). Churchill, as Secretary of State both for war and air from 1919 to 1921, and as colonial secretary thereafter, promoted the idea of deploying the RAF for imperial policing.[37] The financial argument was overwhelming. Whereas the Army's counter-insurgency operations in Mesopotamia in 1920/21 cost annually £20 million, the RAF was able to manage successfully the territory from 1922 on for only £650,000 a year.[38]

However, the adverse side of the RAF's low cost was the use of terrorist methods, or "frightfulness," as was the term internally used by the RAF. The aircraft equipped with bombs, gas and machine-guns were supposed to strike fear into the tribesmen, and hence, to scatter, or better still, deter any rebellion. Nonetheless, the credibility of this threat required occasional demonstrations of the destructive power available to the RAF, including, as Air Marshal Sir John Salmond (1881–1968) put it, the "cruel necessity of killing not only non-combatants but people innocent of any complicity."[39]

The government realized that the practices of air policing were morally problematic. A huge uproar was created after aircraft were used to quell internal unrest during the Punjab disturbances of 1919, resulting in 36 casualties. The Hunter Committee, appointed to investigate the causes of the Punjab events and the measures taken to deal with them, came to the conclusion that there was no "immediate and manifest urgency" to justify the use of bombs and machine guns. The Committee then recommended that unless appropriate rules were formulated, aircraft should not be employed for internal security duties.[40] Also, the army representatives frequently questioned the practices of air policing in order to advocate traditional methods of imperial policing. To them, bombs and machine guns were incompatible with the intention "to keep order and gradually to reconcile hostile tribes to civilized rule."[41] In spite of these objections, air policing was extended to the North-West Frontier of India. However, the ethical considerations prevented the government from deploying the RAF into places where its effects could be reported by the media and thus provoke public outrage.[42] For the same reason, the Cabinet refused to deploy the air force, which proved its effectiveness in Mesopotamia and South Arabia, to quell insurgency in Palestine in the late

1930s. The majority view held that in this case, air policing should be avoided because as War Secretary Alfred Duff Cooper put it, "air bombing would merely mean the destruction of the homes of innocent people and the driving of moderate opinion into the arms of the extremists."[43]

Moreover, the deployed airmen themselves recognized the ethical challenge of their service, and hence, tried to work out methods in which killing would be avoided at all. Air Marshal Salmond reported as early as 1924 that it had already been "a commonplace here that aircraft achieve their result by their effect on morale, and by the material damage they do ... and not through the infliction of casualties."[44] To avoid casualties, warning notices that bombing was going to take place were delivered to the target place 24 hours in advance. The RAF manual instructed that these warning notices "must be phrased in the most careful manner":

> They must indicate clearly why the government feels it necessary to enforce its will; that the government pressure will take the form of a blockade that will be effected by making the villages and certain defined areas around them dangerous by bombing; that the village must be evacuated and the women and children removed to safety outside the areas to be blockaded; that no attempt is being made to kill anyone, in fact that the bombing will be rigorously restricted to the places specified in the bombing notices, and finally that the terms of submission are the following and that political authorities will be available at such and such a place to accept these terms.[45]

The RAF's punitive strikes were thus confined to, for example, attacking livestock, burning up stores of fuel prepared for winter, or destroying roofs of huts. The RAF came to call this method "air blockade" in an obvious attempt to draw a parallel with the traditional naval procedure, and thus, counter any allegations of inhumanity.[46]

In a similar vein, the moral conflict affected the policy of strategic bombing, too. Despite the prominence of the policy of strategic bombing between the wars, when the war at last broke out in September 1939, only few RAF bombers took off for targets in Germany, and even those few were loaded not with bombs, but with leaflets. "To enlighten the German people about the behavior of their rulers," wrote Kingsley Martin in the *New Statesman*, "is the most important of all tasks before us."[47] When it was suggested to Kingsley Wood (1881–1943), the Secretary of State for Air, during the first months of war to bomb ammunition stocks hidden in the Black Forest, he replied with abhorrence: "Are you aware it is private property? [...] Why, you will be asking me to bomb Essen next!"[48]

Such moral scruples had lasted only until Germany invaded and defeated Norway, Belgium, the Netherlands, Luxemburg and France in May and June 1940. At the time, the RAF, for the first time, tried to attack strategic targets on German soil. However, the British bombers were too vulnerable to German fighters in daylight, so night raids remained the only possibility. However, at night, the navigation, target identification and bomb aiming were too inefficient to hit specific military or industrial targets.[49] Although the original intention was to attack militarily important objects, the actual effect of the bombing was the completely indiscriminate killing of civilians. Despite this fact, the RAF went on with bombing industrial centers and cities because "the bombers alone" were seen to "provide the means of victory."[50]

By the spring of 1942, the War Cabinet had designed a bombing offensive against German cities with the explicit object of de-housing a huge portion of German workers.[51] A year later, it was agreed at the Anglo-American-French leaders' conference at Casablanca that the air attacks on Germany should intensify with the objectives of "the destruction and dislocation of the German military, industrial, and economic system and the undermining of the morale of the German people to the point where their capacity for armed resistance is fatally weakened."[52] In the midst of war, moral scruples were effectively overridden, and the peacetime strategy of massive strategic bombing materialized. As a direct consequence, about 300,000 Germans, most of them civilians, died, and another 780,000 were seriously injured.[53] However, the impact on the actual production of German war industry, as discovered after the war's end by the *United States Strategic Bombing Survey*, had been negligible, and the will of the Germans to fight had not been broken, either, by the destruction of German cities.[54]

The suppressed moral scruples reappeared at the end of the war. Despite the prominent place the bombing campaign occupied in the Anglo-American strategy, the ultimate sacrifice of 55,000 airmen from RAF Bomber Command was not adequately commemorated and honored for almost seven decades after the war's conclusion. Among the British service chiefs, it was only the head of Bomber Command, Marshal of the RAF, Sir Arthur "Bomber" Harris, who was not granted a peerage.[55] In addition, not till 2012 was the Bomber Command Memorial unveiled in London. As Michael Walzer notes, "there seems to have been a conscious decision not to celebrate the exploits of Bomber Command or to honor its leader [...] In such circumstances, not to honor was to dishonor." Although Churchill never admitted that "the bombing constituted a wrong," the refusal to ennoble Harris and honor the Bomber Command went some distance, says Walzer, towards "re-establishing a commitment to the rules of war and the rights they protect."[56]

Conclusion

To conclude, the British propensity to technological solutions was intimately related to antimilitarism. On the one hand, the modern technology was viewed as a barrier against militarism; on the other hand, owing to the liberal mistrust of the military, the civilians had confidence to pursue radical and revolutionary approaches to defense and military strategy without the expert recommendation of the armed forces.

However, the British case also shows how the liberal attraction to revolutionary technology can very easily produce a faulty strategy. The interwar attraction to the airplane is a case in point. The popular enthusiasm in the airplane confused the real potential of the contemporary air force with idealistic and futuristic dreams. This is an obvious instance of ideological "dissimulation." Through dissimulation, ideologies may justify situations by misidentifying them, often by equating particular conditions with an ideal.[57]

The British defense policy showed a tendency to utilize advanced technology to prevent war by deterring the aggressor. In the interwar period, it was believed that the air power either could act as such a deterrent or if unsuccessful in this capacity, could bring a war to a quick and, in terms of lives, inexpensive conclusion. As a consequence, Britain was not only inadequately prepared for the Second World War when it actually came but also felt it necessary to resort to bombing campaigns that, apart from hundreds of thousands of mostly civilian casualties, did result in only negligible, or even negative strategic effects.[58] Nevertheless, to reiterate, it was this misunderstanding of the real effects of the strategic bombing that resulted in this conflict between the liberal attraction to technological solution of war, on the one hand, and the ethical principle of discrimination in warfare, on the other.

NOTES

1. Michael Walzer, *Just and Unjust Wars: A Moral Argument with Historical Illustrations* (New York: Basic Books, 2000), 255.

2. See e.g., United States Strategic Bombing Survey, "United States Strategic Bombing Survey: [Reports]," (Washington, D.C.: The Survey, 1945); Patrick Maynard Stuart Blackett, *Military and Political Consequences of Atomic Energy* (London: Turnstile Press, 1948).

3. David Edgerton, "Liberal Militarism and the British State," *New Left Review*, 185 (1991); see also *England and the Aeroplane* (London: Macmillan, 1991); *Warfare State: Britain, 1920–1970* (Cambridge: Cambridge University Press, 2006).

4. Edgerton, *Liberal Militarism and the British State*, 148–49.

5. Walzer, *Just and Unjust Wars*, 296.

6. John Locke, *Two Treatises of Government* (Cambridge: Cambridge University Press, 1988), 181–82; see also Michael W. Doyle, *Ways of War and Peace: Realism, Liberalism, and Socialism* (London; New York: Norton, 1997), 221.

7. James T. Johnson, "The Meaning of Non-Combatant Immunity in the Just War/Limited War Tradition," *Journal of the American Academy of Religion* 39, no. 2 (1971): 167.

8. Immanuel Kant, "Metaphysics of Morals," in *Toward Perpetual Peace and Other Writings on Politics, Peace and History: Immanuel Kant*, ed. Pauline Kleingeld (New Haven and London: Yale University Press, 2006), 143.

148   II. The Age of the World Wars

9. "Idea for a Universal History from a Cosmopolitan Perspective," in *Toward Perpetual Peace and Other Writings on Politics, Peace and History: Immanuel Kant*, ed. Pauline Kleingeld (New Haven and London: Yale University Press, 2006), 5–6.

10. James Mill, *The History of British India* (London: Baldwin, Cradock, and Joy, 1817), 460.

11. Such a tendency to prevent innovation of military doctrine was observed e.g., by Elizabeth Kier, *Imagining War: French and British Military Doctrine between the Wars* (Princeton: Princeton University Press, 1997). According to Barry R. Posen, it is not so much institutional culture as parochialism that prevents innovations. Interventions of civilians are, hence, often necessary to force the military to adapt adequately to changing strategic needs. Barry R. Posen, *The Sources of Military Doctrine: France, Britain, and Germany between the World Wars* (London: Cornell University Press, 1984). The importance of an 'immense external pressure, [either] from an undeniable previous failure, or from above by a strong, authoritarian, and imaginative personality' is also stressed by Jonathan Shimshoni, "Technology, Military Advantage, and World War I: A Case for Military Entrepreneurship," *International Security* 15, no. 3 (1990): 215. Analyzing current transformation of the British military, Theo Farrell finds that, on the one hand, the military initiated this transformation on its own without any significant intervention of its civilian masters; on the other hand, this transformation is shaped so as to fit the established institutional culture. Theo Farrell, "The Dynamics of British Military Transformation," *International Affairs* 84, no. 4 (2008).

12. Shimshoni, *Technology, Military Advantage, and World War I*, 214. The natural conservatism of the military was accepted as an assumption also by Stephen P. Rosen, despite the fact that his analysis of successful cases of military innovation leads him to the conclusion that militaries can and do innovate on their own. Stephen Peter Rosen, *Winning the Next War: Innovation and the Modern Military* (Ithaca: Cornell University Press, 1991).

13. T.H.E. Travers, "Technology, Tactics, and Morale: Jean De Bloch, the Boer War, and British Military Theory, 1900–1914," *The Journal of Modern History* 51, no. 2 (1979): 276.

14. Ibid., 286.

15. Kier, *Imagining War*, 113.

16. Ibid., 89–91.

17. Colonel G.F.R. Henderson, quoted in Hew Strachan, *The Politics of the British Army* (Oxford: Clarendon Press, 1997), 5.

18. See David E. Omissi, *Air Power and Colonial Control: The Royal Air Force 1919–1939* (Manchester: Manchester University Press, 1990).

19. See George C Peden, *Arms, Economics and British Strategy: From Dreadnoughts to Hydrogen Bombs* (Cambridge: Cambridge University Press, 2007); John Ferris, "Treasury Control, the Ten Year Rule and British Service Policies, 1919–1924," *The Historical Journal* 30, no. 04 (1987): 859–83; C. I. Hamilton, "British Naval Policy, Policy-Makers and Financial Control, 1860–1945," *War in History* 12, no. 4 (2005): 371–95.

20. Hamilton, *British Naval Policy*, 386.

21. Peden, Arms, *Economics and British Strategy*, 104; Ferris, *Treasury Control*, 868.

22. Ferris, *Treasury Control*, 871.

23. John Baylis, *Ambiguity and Deterrence: British Nuclear Strategy, 1945–1964* (Oxford: Clarendon Press, 1995), 371; Colin McInnes, *Hot War, Cold War: The British Army's Way in Warfare, 1945–1995* (London: Brassey's, 1996), 11.

24. From the 1930s to the end of the 1960s, Liddell Hart was explicitly cited in the debates in the Parliament as many as 98 times. "Hansard," UK Parliament, http://hansard.millbanksystems.com/.
25. Brian Bond, "Leslie Hore-Belisha at the War Office," in *Politicians and Defence: Studies in the Formulation of British Defence Policy 1845–1970*, ed. I.F.W. Beckett and John Gooch (Manchester: Manchester University Press, 1981), 116–17.
26. "Hc Deb 10 November 1932: International Affairs," in *Hansard* (London: UK Parliament), vol. 270 c632.
27. The novel *Shape of Things to Come* was published in 1933 and the film *Things to Come*, directed by William Menzies, was released in 1936.
28. *Air Force for the Peace Front. A Plan Prepared by the Military Research Committee of the New Commonwealth Institute*, (London: Peace Book Co., 1939); David Davies, *The Problem of the Twentieth Century: A Study in International Relationships* (London: Ernest Benn, 1938), 475–87; see also Roger A. Beaumont, "Right Backed by Might the International Air Force Concept," (2001); Brett Holman, "World Police for World Peace: British Internationalism and the Threat of a Knock-out Blow from the Air, 1919–1945," *War in History* 17, no. 3 (2010).
29. Davies, *The Problem of the Twentieth Century*, 440.
30. Ibid., 427.
31. John Stuart Mill, "Public and Parliamentary Speeches Part I November 1850—November 1868," in *The Collected Works of John Stuart Mill*, ed. John M. Robson and Bruce L. Kinzer (London: Routledge and Kegan Paul, 1988). Ch.80: 'England's Danger through the Suppression of Her Maritime Power, 5 Aug, 1867'.
32. Basil Henry Liddell Hart, *The Revolution in Warfare* (London: Faber & Faber, 1946), 69; Cf. 'The British Way in Warfare: A Peappraisal, in Michael Howard, The Causes of Wars (London: Unwin Paperbacks, 1983), 189–207.
33. Brian Bond, Liddell Hart: *A Study of His Military Thought* (London: Cassell, 1977), 39–41.
34. "Hc Deb 10 November 1932: International Affairs," vol. 270 c632.
35. Walzer, *Just and Unjust Wars*, 296.
36. E.g., Neville Chamberlain spoke of his 'enthusiasm' for on air force. *George C. Peden, British Rearmament and the Treasury, 1932–1939* (Edinburgh: Scottish Academic Press, 1979), 121.
37. Peden, *Arms, Economics and British Strategy*, 105.
38. Roger Broad, *Conscription in Britain, 1939–1964: The Militarisation of a Generation* (London: Routledge, 2006), 21.
39. Charles Townshend, *Britain's Civil Wars: Counterinsurgency in the Twentieth Century* (London: Faber and Faber, 1986), 98.
40. Srinath Raghaven, "Protecting the Raj: The Army in India and Internal Security, C. 1919–39," *Small Wars & Insurgencies* 16, no. 3 (2005): 265–67.
41. Townshend, *Britain's Civil Wars*, 97.
42. Peden, *Arms, Economics and British Strategy*, 100.
43. Thomas Mockaitis, *British Counterinsurgency, 1919–1960* (London: Macmillan, 1990), 35.
44. Townshend, *Britain's Civil Wars*, 99.
45. Quoted in Mockaitis, *British Counterinsurgency, 1919–1960*, 30–31.
46. Townshend, *Britain's Civil Wars*, 99.
47. Quoted in Michael Eliot Howard, *War and the Liberal Conscience* (London: Hurst, 2008), 95.
48. Quoted in Broad, *Conscription in Britain*, 37.

150   II. The Age of the World Wars

49. Blackett, *Military and Political Consequences of Atomic Energy*, 14–15.
50. Winston Churchill in September 1940, quoted in Walzer, *Just and Unjust Wars*, 259.
51. Blackett, *Military and Political Consequences of Atomic Energy*, 18.
52. Quoted in Ibid., 19.
53. Walzer, *Just and Unjust Wars*, 255.
54. Blackett, *Military and Political Consequences of Atomic Energy*, 19.
55. See Max Hastings, *Bomber Command* (London: Pan, 2010); Robin Neillands, The Bomber War: Arthur Harris and the Allied Bomber Offensive, 1939–1945 (London: John Murray, 2001).
56. Walzer, *Just and Unjust Wars*, 324–25.
57. Mark Warren, "Liberal Constitutionalism as Ideology: Marx and Habermas," *Political Theory* 17, no. 4 (1989): 513–14.
58. See Richard J Overy, *The Bombing War: Europe 1939–1945* (London: Allen Lane, 2013).

Works Cited

Air Force for the Peace Front. A Plan Prepared by the Military Research Committee of the New Commonwealth Institute. London: Peace Book Co., 1939.
Baylis, John. *Ambiguity and Deterrence: British Nuclear Strategy, 1945–1964*. Oxford: Clarendon Press, 1995.
Beaumont, Roger A. "Right Backed by Might the International Air Force Concept" (2001).
Blackett, Patrick Maynard Stuart. *Military and Political Consequences of Atomic Energy*. London: Turnstile Press, 1948.
Bond, Brian. "Leslie Hore-Belisha at the War Office," in *Politicians and Defence: Studies in the Formulation of British Defence Policy 1845–1970*, ed. I.F.W. Beckett and John Gooch, 110–31. Manchester: Manchester University Press, 1981.
Bond, Brian. *Liddell Hart: A Study of His Military Thought*. London: Cassell, 1977.
Broad, Roger. *Conscription in Britain, 1939–1964: The Militarisation of a Generation*. London: Routledge, 2006.
Davies, David. *The Problem of the Twentieth Century: A Study in International Relationships*. London: Ernest Benn, 1938.
Doyle, Michael W. *Ways of War and Peace: Realism, Liberalism, and Socialism*. London; New York: Norton, 1997.
Edgerton, David. *England and the Aeroplane*. London: Macmillan, 1991.
Edgerton, David. "Liberal Militarism and the British State," *New Left Review* 185 (1991): 138–69.
Edgerton, David. *Warfare State: Britain, 1920–1970*. Cambridge: Cambridge University Press, 2006.
Farrell, Theo. "The Dynamics of British Military Transformation," *International Affairs* 84, no. 4 (2008): 777–807.
Ferris, John. "Treasury Control, the Ten Year Rule and British Service Policies, 1919–1924," *The Historical Journal* 30, no. 04 (1987): 859–83.
Hamilton, C.I. "British Naval Policy, Policy-Makers and Financial Control, 1860–1945," *War in History* 12, no. 4 (2005): 371–95.
"Hansard." UK Parliament, http://hansard.millbanksystems.com/.
Hastings, Max. *Bomber Command*. London: Pan, 2010.
"Hc Deb 10 November 1932: International Affairs," in *Hansard*. London: UK Parliament.

Holman, Brett. "World Police for World Peace: British Internationalism and the Threat of a Knock-out Blow from the Air, 1919–1945," *War in History* 17, no. 3 (Jul 2010): 313–32.
Howard, Michael. *The Causes of Wars*. London: Unwin Paperbacks, 1983.
Howard, Michael Eliot. *War and the Liberal Conscience*. London: Hurst, 2008.
Johnson, James T. "The Meaning of Non-Combatant Immunity in the Just War/Limited War Tradition," *Journal of the American Academy of Religion* 39, no. 2 (1971): 151–70.
Kant, Immanuel. "Idea for a Universal History from a Cosmopolitan Perspective," trans. David L. Colclasure, in *Toward Perpetual Peace and Other Writings on Politics, Peace and History: Immanuel Kant*, ed. Pauline Kleingeld, 3–16. New Haven and London: Yale University Press, 2006.
Kant, Immanuel. "Metaphysics of Morals," trans. David L. Colclasure, in *Toward Perpetual Peace and Other Writings on Politics, Peace and History: Immanuel Kant*, ed. Pauline Kleingeld, 110–49. New Haven and London: Yale University Press, 2006.
Kier, Elizabeth. *Imagining War: French and British Military Doctrine between the War* (Princeton: Princeton University Press, 1997).
Liddell Hart, Basil Henry. *The Revolution in Warfare*. London: Faber & Faber, 1946.
Locke, John. *Two Treatises of Government*. Cambridge: Cambridge University Press, 1988.
McInnes, Colin. *Hot War, Cold War: The British Army's Way in Warfare, 1945–1995*. London: Brassey's, 1996.
Mill, James. *The History of British India*. London: Baldwin, Cradock, and Joy, 1817.
Mill, John Stuart. "Public and Parliamentary Speeches Part I November 1850–November 1868," in *The Collected Works of John Stuart Mill*, ed. John M. Robson and Bruce L. Kinzer. London: Routledge and Kegan Paul, 1988.
Thomas Mockaitis, *British Counterinsurgency, 1919–1960*. London: Macmillan, 1990.
Neillands, Robin. *The Bomber War: Arthur Harris and the Allied Bomber Offensive, 1939–1945*. London: John Murray, 2001.
Omissi, David E. *Air Power and Colonial Control: The Royal Air Force 1919–1939*. Manchester: Manchester University Press, 1990.
Overy, Richard J. *The Bombing War: Europe 1939–1945*. London: Allen Lane, 2013.
Peden, George C. *Arms, Economics and British Strategy: From Dreadnoughts to Hydrogen Bombs*. Cambridge: Cambridge University Press, 2007.
Peden, George C. *British Rearmament and the Treasury, 1932–1939*. Edinburgh: Scottish Academic Press, 1979.
Posen, Barry R. *The Sources of Military Doctrine: France, Britain, and Germany between the World Wars*. London: Cornell University Press, 1984.
Raghaven, Srinath. "Protecting the Raj: The Army in India and Internal Security, C. 1919–39," *Small Wars & Insurgencies* 16, no. 3 (2005): 253–79.
Rosen, Stephen Peter. *Winning the Next War: Innovation and the Modern Military*. Ithaca: Cornell University Press, 1991.
Shimshoni, Johnathan. "Technology, Military Advantage, and World War I: A Case for Military Entrepreneurship," *International Security* 15, no. 3 (1990): 187–215.
Strachan, Hew. *The Politics of the British Army*. Oxford: Clarendon Press, 1997.
Townshend, Charles. *Britain's Civil Wars: Counterinsurgency in the Twentieth Century*. London: Faber and Faber, 1986.
Travers, T.H.E. "Technology, Tactics, and Morale: Jean De Bloch, the Boer War, and British Military Theory, 1900–1914," *The Journal of Modern History* 51, no. 2 (1979): 264–86.

United States Strategic Bombing Survey, "United States Strategic Bombing Survey: [Reports]." Washington, D.C.: The Survey, 1945.
Walzer, Michael. *Just and Unjust Wars: A Moral Argument with Historical Illustrations.* New York: Basic Books, 2000.
Warren, Mark. "Liberal Constitutionalism as Ideology: Marx and Habermas," *Political Theory* 17, no. 4 (1989): 511–534.

Resource Policy and Technical Understanding
Aspects of Hitler's Wartime Economy[1]

ECKEHARD DWOROK

Anyone who has visited the Mittelbau-Dora concentration camp in Nordhausen (Thuringia), whose main focus was armaments production, including V2 rockets, is shocked by the gigantic size and massive scale of the 20-kilometers-long, 30-meters-high tunnel system. Until the above-ground camp was completed in the spring of 1944, the laborers were forced to live and work in inhuman conditions in tunnels hewn out of rock, where they had to toil in twelve-hour shifts. Hunger, disease, dust and moisture ensured that some 20,000 prisoners did not survive.[2] Not only did Dora fulfill its function as a man-eating machine, it also forced the damned to create the weapons of murder that were to kill their liberators and enslave them forever.

The Problem of the Economy of Scarcity and Hitler's Political Conclusions

In 1939 it was not Hitler's intention to unleash a new world war. He had discussed the failed war policy of the Kaiserreich (German Empire) in World War I in his books and writings as early as the beginning of the 1920s. Never again was a long lasting, debilitating war to be fought on several fronts against a militarily and economically powerful alliance of France, Great Britain, the USA and Russia (later the Soviet Union). The problem of the German economy of scarcity in World War I as a consequence of inadequate national resources was not unknown territory for Hitler; neither did he forget that, during the Great War, national resources were available only from a single source, and that the long, drawn-out conflict with its previously unheard-of consumption of materials required an encouragement of research, particularly in coal, oil, ore and chemical technology, as well as the total transformation of the German economy into industrial and armaments production. The geographic, economic and political structural changes brought about by the blockade policy of the victorious powers, too, had caused a massive change in Germany's overall situation before World War I, a fact of which Hitler was also well aware.[3] Hitler's subjective attitudes, which can be discerned with amazing ease solely from his books and writings, can certainly be seen as a consistent structure of thought.[4]

The limited economic options available to the Empire had been discussed in Germany's extraordinarily wide-ranging specialist literature as the main reason for the defeat, particularly following the collapse of 1918. However, Hitler accepted this view only partially. He attributed the reasons for failure more to the political, cultural, ethical and moral and Jewish influences woven into the fabric of society.[5]

On the other hand, Hitler points to the enemy's superiority in terms of materials and population, writing "that [...] [the enemy's] numbers [...] were, from the very beginning, greater than those of the German army and it had the arsenals of the whole world at its disposal."[6] In *Hitler's Second Book* one can read: "That [...] considering all factors, particularly in view of the limitations of our own raw material and thereby threatening dependence on other countries, the future of Germany [can be considered] very bleak and sad."[7] Thus, in Hitler's opinion, the first states that were to be removed from the coalition of victors were Italy and Great Britain; the Soviet Union would be conquered and serve as the resource-rich basis for a Greater Germany. In order to afford Germany a free hand in the conquest of the *Ostraum*, France was to be excluded, both militarily and politically. Hitler responded to the possible objection that Britain would oppose Germany's ambitions to become a great power with the comment: "England has cared so little about European affairs for so long as there was no threat that a world competitor would arise from them, whereby such a threat was perceived only in a development that would, one day, threaten its maritime and colonial hegemony."[8]

Hitler's considerations saw spheres of interest that did not overlap. Due to its failure to observe this maxim, the Kaiserreich's (German Empire) colonial policy necessarily had to "cause a brutal confrontation with England, as a global German economic policy could never avoid a decisive struggle with England."[9] Hitler also described the path that he was willing to take, if his policy towards Great Britain failed. Hitler was of the view that, in such a case, Russia would provide the necessary support. Only then could Germany shift to a maritime policy and "most likely utilize the enormous resources necessary for the expansion of a fleet"[10] to force Great Britain to its knees. Similar considerations can be observed in Hitler's book *Mein Kampf* from 1924.[11] In this line of reasoning, also laid out in 1928, Hitler is already indicating the path that, from his subjective point of view, it would be necessary to take, were Great Britain to refuse. The idea of dividing the world into spheres of interest was based on Hitler's assumption that the area of Eastern Europe, extending to the Urals, controlled by Germany would not hinder England's interests overseas and Italy's expansion into the Mediterranean.[12] For ideological reasons Fascist Italy was, in Hitler's view, one of its first potential allies that could leave the camp of the old enemy coalition.[13]

With regard to the *Ostraum*, Hitler had already stated in *Mein Kampf*: "Today, when we talk in Europe of new land and new soil, we can, first and foremost, think only of Russia."[14] And: "The giant empire in the east is ripe for collapse, and the end of Jewish rule in Russia will also be the end of Russia as a state."[15]

War, Duration of the War, Image of the War and Use of Means

In addition to the political possibilities, Hitler saw war as a legitimate and natural means of implementing his objectives. He was of the opinion that politicians, who rejected these means for moral, humanitarian or other reasons, forsook an essential means of enforcing their own policies. The prerequisite for these considerations, however, was the availability of the corresponding economic and military capabilities to enable a victorious conclusion to war. The question of the ability to pursue a long or short war was one that was subject to constant discussion in Germany, both before and during World War I. For example, in the Kaiserreich (German Empire) in 1907, it was assumed that France, in cooperation with Russia, was pursuing a policy of containment towards the ever more powerful German Reich.[16] Discussions of the duration of a war assumed a war on two fronts with duration of 6 to 12 months, even though the American Civil War, for example, had lasted for almost four years and had taken the form of an economic war.[17] In the mind of the military, victory against numerically superior forces would require that the enemy be attacked through a successive series of quick, destructive strikes. However, World War I is also an example of how, despite many self-sacrificing, operational military successes, the war duration desired by the Kaiserreich could not be achieved due to a lack of resources. The last hope of the German Reich lay in the defeat of Russia. Negotiations in 1917/18 for the Treaty of Brest-Litovsk of 3 March 1918 once again presented the Reich leadership with the opportunity to compensate for its situation through troop

156   II. The Age of the World Wars

reinforcements in the west and land gains in the east, particularly in Ukraine. However, the active military intervention of American divisions on the Western Front in the summer of 1918 destroyed this last hope.

Hitler's Lebensraum ideology was focused on the East. With regard to this, Rolf-Dieter Müller, Chief Scientific Director of the Military History Research Institute (MGFA), wrote the following in his book *Der Feind steht im Osten*: "For the then corporal Adolf Hitler, working as a messenger on the Western Front and forced to hide from enemy barrages in trenches, the deep incursion into Russian territory in 1918 acted as the starting-point of his personal vision of world power."[18]

For Hitler, who thought in military terms, the necessity for a short war was of extraordinary importance. He was aware that Germany would be in a weaker position than the Allies with respect to resources if they again

- acted unanimously and on time,
- caught up with a possible German arms advantage within a short period of time through targeted rearming measures and
- take events out of the hands of the Germans, and thus determine the deployment of resources as well as the duration of the war.

The repetition shown here, and the situation in which Germany, further weakened both economically and militarily by the Versailles Treaty, was associated in specialist literature (particularly by economic and military historians) with a so-called blitzkrieg concept. The successful implementation of this would, so it seemed, free Germany from the necessity of a long war. Thus the economic historian A.S. Milward wrote that

> the blitzkrieg strategy was indeed extremely reasonable and appropriate for the German economic situation. It corresponded to the reduced capacity of the German economy following the Treaty of Versailles and the additional shortage of resources [...] It was an expedient economic answer to the Allied tactics of blockade and hindering of delivery [...] avoided most economic issues associated with the complete exhaustion of all production factors for the war effort.[19]

The disarmament enforced by the victorious powers led to the almost total liquidation of the remaining war material. The provisional Reichswehr was reduced from 300,000 men to 100,000 professional soldiers and the navy reduced to 15,000 men; all paramilitary organizations and volunteer corps were disbanded. The Reichswehr had to do without planes, tanks, heavy artillery and chemical weapons. Most munitions factories were closed, tens of thousands of machine tools were destroyed and the import of arms was prohibited.

However, from the beginning, the heads of the army and navy endeavored to rebuild a national army, free from all restrictions, despite the prohibition. One focus was the training of the military command staff in order to meet the need for a well-trained general staff, commissioned and noncommissioned officers in the event of a later expansion of the military. Also, the Treaty of Rapallo, concluded with Soviet Russia on 16 April 1922, which also included agreements on the military and armaments, facilitated both the testing and production of munitions and the development of new aircraft and armored vehicles on Russian soil. Correspondingly, Germany was provided with military training areas, allowing it to practice plane and tank warfare, as well as training in new heavy and chemical weapons systems. In return, the Reichswehr placed military technology and the knowledge of German troop commanders at the disposal of the Red Army.[20]

On 4 February 1933, only a few weeks after Hitler's appointment as Chancellor in 1933, he announced the following, multistage basic plan to Reichswehr commanders:

- Germany must first be consolidated and fortified domestically,
- eliminate its opponent, France, through a special alliance policy towards Great Britain and Italy and
- finally, conquer Lebensraum in the east.[21]

Up until 1935, Hitler had largely left the secret planning and concrete implementation of the restoration of Germany's military capability to his commanders and told them about his strategic objective of conquering the *Ostraum*[22] without "being taken too seriously" by the generals and without encountering opposition to or questioning of the idea.[23] As also noted by Rolf-Dieter Müller: "Hitler's declarations that he wished to energetically pursue the struggle against Versailles and the rearmament of Germany formed the consensus."[24]

One of Hitler's considerations of defense policy from 1929[25] gives an interesting insight into his assessment of the tanks that would later become the military's main weapon. Although the Allies had banned the Germans from operating tanks, Hitler pointed to the element of surprise and penetrating power of a concentration of tanks, aware as he was of Great Britain's massed tank attack on 20 November 1917 (which initially was quite successful but unable to convert its breakthrough at Cambrai into an operation that was decisive to the outcome of the war). During one of Hitler's visits to the military weapons test site in Kummersdorf, leading German tank theorist and later tank general Guderian conducted a tank training exercise, to which Hitler responded: "That's what I need!"[26] The fact that Guderian's ideas coincided with Hitler's expectations pointed to the conformity of the politician with the general. Hitler promoted Guderian and the construction of tank divisions despite considerable resistance on the part of supreme command. Hitler's demand of 5 November 1937 that the Wehrmacht be capable of striking at any time, as well as his comment of 23 May 1939 that the enemy should be overwhelmed, so to speak, from the barracks have, however, little to do with a blitzkrieg concept.

Poland was also to be quickly smashed by the Wehrmacht as, only two days after 1 September 1939, Britain and France had declared war on the Third Reich, the war that Hitler did not want at that time; an Allied advance into the Ruhr area would have represented a heavy blow to Germany—possibly one that would have decided the war. The Allies, who had hitherto responded to Hitler's violations of the Treaty of Versailles through a policy of appeasement, did not, this time, conform to the expectations of Hitler the gambler. The Anglo-French declaration of war meant that Hitler had himself committed the same mistake as the German leadership in 1914. The enclosure of the inferior Polish military between Germany, East Prussia and Slovakia was a predetermined geographical factor, and on 17 September 1939 the Red Army occupied the agreed parts of Poland in accordance with the secret agreement between Stalin and Hitler. German tank forces still fought tactically, as part of divisions, and not independently over an extended operational space.[27]

The Third Reich was not in a position to undertake *Tiefenrüstung* (armament based on abundant resources) and General Thomas, head of the German Defense Economy and Armament Office, had warned the chief of the Oberkommando der Wehrmacht (Supreme High Command of the German Armed Forces), Field Marshal Keitel, of Germany's actual war readiness on the Sunday before the beginning of the Poland campaign, submitting to him "visual documentation on the war economic capabilities of Germany and the rest of the world powers." Keitel had submitted these documents to Hitler, who declared that he "did not share [General Thomas'] anxiety over the danger of a world war, especially since he had now got the Soviet Union on his side."[28]

Blitzkrieg

The term *Blitzkrieg*, as described by Karl-Heinz Frieser in his standard work *Blitzkrieg-Legende*, was not part of the Wehrmacht's official military terminology[29]; nevertheless, it was on everyone's lips. For armored and motorized infantry divisions, the Wehrmacht used the term *Schnelle Truppen* (fast troops), which the non-motorized mass of the army had difficulty following. However, the combined deployment of air force and armored forces on narrow deployment strips during the Polish campaign had led to offensive procedures that facilitated long-range, operational advance and securing of gains during the France campaign. Yet, the prevailing opinion among generals was that there was little or no chance of the repetition in the West of the success of the tanks in the Polish campaign.[30] The Wehrmacht leadership, satisfied with having finally settled accounts with Poland without a real relief attack being launched in favor of the country by Franco-British forces, analyzed ammunition consumption over the eighteen-day period and the insufficient remainders of supplies, which would perhaps have been sufficient for one third of their divisions[31] for a month. Breakdown rates of vehicles in motorized units were up to 50 percent and would have seriously jeopardized a further immediate, successful campaign in the West, as Hitler initially intended.[32]

Hitler, who actually intended to build up his industrial base for *Tiefenrüstung* through a series of piece-by-piece conquests, particularly in the East, failed in the Russian campaign in 1941 due to the resistance of the Soviet army, the weather, shortages of material and the unlawful treatment of the populace. According to General Thomas, ill-defined, often overlapping responsibilities prevented the optimization of armament efforts from the start.

Hitler's early plans for an attack against the Allies in the West in late 1939 to June 1940 were met with stubborn resistance from many officers who had been shaped by World War I and who were now staff officers in leading posts, and repeatedly warned of the military superiority of the Allies, which would lead to a long war of attrition. Likewise, the constantly postponed attack date also paralyzed *Breitenrüstung* (broad armament). As a result, the experience of the German economy of scarcity from 1914–18 hindered plans to align the economy for a short, mobile, large-scale war of aggression in the West in 1939–40. Hitler's Directive no. 6 on warfare was part of General Halder's deployment order of 19 October 1939 and included the following orders:

- to strike as early as possible against strong sections of enemy units,
- to conquer as much territory as possible in order to
- then have a basis for the continuation of warfare.[33]

Hitler's later comment: "That's the old Schlieffen Plan with a strong right flank on the Atlantic coast; you can't conduct operations like that twice with impunity."[34] This comment provokes astonishment as it was Hitler himself who had determined the specifications.

The long war against France, Great Britain and, in the background, the United States, which had been feared by Hitler and many staff officers, prevented the necessary mass production of tanks and planes for a consistently planned, short *Blitzkrieg*.[35] Thus the comparison of forces as of 10 May 1940 shows the clear quantitative and qualitative superiority of the Allies at the start of the German offensive.

On the western front, the German Army possessed about 2,439 tanks, of which 1,478 Type I and II tanks were suitable for, at best, infantry support rather than tank battles due to inadequate armoring. This corresponded to almost two-thirds of the German tank force and was at odds with the need for superior concentrations of tanks to achieve a breakthrough against the enemy. Actual Type III (349 pieces) and Panzer IV (278) battle tanks, as well as 334 captured Czech, represented a total of *961* tanks suitable for combat. While the Panzer IV was equipped with a substantial 7.5cm gun, its short barrel meant that it was only effective in close combat. German losses: 714 tanks, 428 of which were Types I and II.

The number of combat-suitable French tanks alone was vastly superior to German numbers. The French military could (with the exception of the 450 AMR and AMC light armored vehicles as well as 315 Renault FT [mod.] tanks) draw on equivalent or superior armored vehicles, reckoned in armor and weaponry, of the models Renault 35 (900 pieces), Hotchkiss 39 (770), FCM (100), D1 and D2 (145), SOMUA (300) and 274 of the feared Char B2 vehicles, giving a total of 2,489 tanks suitable for tank combat. However, these forces did not have adequate radio technology, and were not, overall, intended, trained or deployed for major operations, but primarily for selective tactical infantry support.[36] The French General Georges, who was deployed as commander of the northeastern section of the front, commented on this issue. "I do not see why we should give a Panzer division the means to exploit a front breakthrough, when they, as a rule, will not have the opportunity to apply these means."[37]

Comparison of Air Forces as of 10 May 1940

The actual strength of the Allied air forces (France, Great Britain, Belgium and the Netherlands) was 4,469 bombers and fighters at the front and behind the lines, against 3,578 Luftwaffe combat aircraft. At the moment of the German attack on 10 May 1940, the balance of power in favor of the German Luftwaffe relativized with 2,589 fighters, bombers and dive bombers against the 1,453 combat-ready Allied aircraft available at that point of time, as the Germans, aware of attack data, had more machines in the air.[38] In qualitative terms, in 1940 the French bomber models were the most advanced. British bombers were mostly superior to the comparable German bombers, with the exception of the Ju 88. The German Ju 87 dive bomber was deployed with particular success against point targets in the armored combat following opportunities for real testing in the Spanish Civil War. It was a plane of a type that the Allies did not have, but due to its slowness it was easy for fighter planes to shoot down. The comparison of losses is surprising. Thus while the French air force lost 892 aircraft, only 316 of these were in aerial battles, while French fighters shot down 733 German aircraft. British losses amounted to 1,029 aircraft. In the western campaign the Luftwaffe lost 1,559 aircraft due to lack of training.[39]

Also, the next two deployment orders did not lead to any strategic, *Blitzkrieg*-like successes in two to three priority areas due to lack of armored forces. Moreover, Hitler, obviously not particularly satisfied with the deployment order of 30 January 1940, talked about a breakthrough at Sedan, to the horror of the army high command. However, three priorities at the same time would have entailed the deployment of the army's armored forces.

The Chief of Staff of Army Group A, Lieutenant-General von Manstein, had already developed similar ideas at this time. Strong armored forces were to make a surprise advance through the Ardennes, overcoming the Meuse area in the Sedan region, in order to first reach the Somme estuary at the rear of the Allied front with tank forces acting operatively with offensive flank protection. The strategically and operationally minded Manstein made an unusual team with the likewise very successful tank commander Guderian. A plan that was condemned as "crazy and reckless" by the high command, but was later endorsed by Army High Command (OKH) following the Mechelen Incident that led to the knowledge of Allied operational intentions.

Lieutenant-General von Manstein was able to convince Hitler at a meeting with him on 17 February 1940 at the Reich Chancellery in Berlin. His "Sickle Cut Plan" aimed at the rapid destruction of the Allied forces[40]; however, the question as to whether Hitler was aware of the risks of large-scale operational advances without adequate flank protection and continuous access to troops in the rear remains open. In crisis situations, Hitler tended to prohibit his commanders from exercising independent operational flexibility.

On 25 June 1940, the Armistice of Compiègne was concluded following the defeat of the Allies. Considered in detail: The OKH had only partially implemented Manstein's Sickle Cut Plan. For example, the leadership of Army Group A, as well as Hitler, attempted several times to slow the rapid attack speed of the leading armored units, redirect or even halt them, as the situation was such that, in exceptional circumstances, many officers in a variety of functions disregarded "any and all orders and regulations" from supreme command and invoked, if need be, German mission-type tactics.[41] It is probable that Hitler's order to stop before Dunkirk threw away the chance to defeat Great Britain, whose army, renewed and then victorious, could not have faced the Germans in the North African desert war. Hitler owed the victory in the West to his decisive officers, who led from the front, and whose courage and willingness to take risks, as well as their idiosyncrasies, eventually led to a quick victory through the surprising setting of priorities and flexibility.

However, Hitler was betrayed by contradictions and arbitrary actions. And was it not he who had repeatedly urged his military to launch the campaign in the West at the earliest possible opportunity? With his decision on

Dunkirk, the Führer's intention was to show his generals who made the final decision in the military/political sphere and that he (Hitler) should not be ignored.[42] The hubris can now be seen in the fact that the victory went to the heads of Hitler and parts of the high command in such a way that they now assumed that the Soviet Union, too, with its massive industrial capacities and its vast geographical space, could also be conquered in a real *Blitzkrieg*.

General Thomas, the head of the Defense Economy and Armaments Office, had in a memorandum of 20 February 1941 given the impression that the Soviet Union's resources and arms industry centers lying west of the Urals could become available to the German war effort.[43] However, this came with reservations: "if it succeeds" and "depends on the following conditions."[44] In relation to these considerations, on 11 February 1941 Hitler demanded that the High Command of the Wehrmacht (OKW) provide illustrative maps on production locations and their economic output. This was sent to Hitler on 20 February 1941.[45]

The "Barbarossa" campaign of conquest was launched on 22 June 1941 and was only planned to last for a few months, concluding with the defeat of the Soviet Union in the same year. However, despite initial major victories by the Wehrmacht, the war with the Soviet forces had also led to the high consumption of materials by the Germans, as well as considerable losses of crews and commanders. As early as 21 August 1941, Hitler ordered, before the onset of winter, not the capture of Moscow, but the capture of the Crimea, the industrial and coal area around Donetsk and the cutting-off of the Russian oil supply from the Caucasus. His response to his skeptical general staff and commanders was: "My generals know nothing about the war economy."[46]

The victorious campaigns of the first years of the war had not led to any drastic revisions of overlapping competences within the various organizations. The total concentration of the economy on the war did not seem necessary as problems with shortages and organizational weaknesses still appeared bearable. Following the euphoria of victory after the French campaign, Hitler even approved the deployment of considerable armament capacities for e.g., construction projects,[47] believing that he could also meet civilian needs. As formulated by Eichholtz, who thought in terms of government monopolies: "One of the most important causes was doubtless the fact that, following the lightning victories in the West, the monopolies were lukewarm in their support for and cooperation with the Todt plan as they saw substantial goals as having been already achieved and were already preparing for the peace."[48] With the failure of the Blitzkrieg in the East and the entry of the USA into the war, Hitler was faced with the situation that he had always wanted to prevent: armed conflict with opponents who, in economic terms alone, were superior to him and could not be matched.

Technology and Wonder Weapons

Hitler believed that true, war-secure self-sufficiency for Germany was possible only through his territorial policy in the East, as it was here that he hoped to find the resources that Germany lacked. According to him Russia was the area to provide the necessary strategic depth. Thus in his secret *Memorandum on the Tasks for a Four-year Plan* he demanded that "the Wehrmacht become the foremost army in the world [...] in its training, deployment of formations, in armament" and that this task be "unconditionally subordinated to all other requirements."

As a result, Hitler first demanded military and economical war capability for *Blitzkrieg* in order to implement his Lebensraum concept, namely the destruction of world Bolshevism and the Judaism behind it.[49]

In Hitler, technological affairs had an admirer and patron, attributed with a certain ability to estimate the future effectiveness of technology.[50] Thus, as early as 1927 Hitler supported rocket experiments by his acquaintance, Max Valier, and published several articles on his work in the *Illustrierter Beobachter*.[51] In 1936 Hitler ordered that the Army Ordnance Department set up a rocket construction facility where, at one time, over 2,000 scientists and engineers were working on Hitler's desired rocket weapon, which he hoped to use to knock the resource-rich USA out of the war with Germany.[52] On the other hand, argued Speer, "Hitler's technical horizon ended with World War I," i.e., his technological interest chiefly focused on traditional weapons systems. Thus he, for example, showed little interest in the construction of an atomic bomb[53] which would have been abruptly neutralized due to lack of time and the resource dependency of the Third Reich.[54] The testing of chemical weapons was heavily promoted in the Third Reich; nuclear development was halted due to disputes over areas of authority, erroneous scientific developments and lack of financial support. Interrogations of captured German scientists showed that Germany had at no time the opportunity to develop a nuclear bomb.[55] For the Allies, in the belief that they were in a race with Germany to develop a bomb, significant funds were available to implement research into and the production of an atomic bomb in particular. Hitler promoted chemical weapons with the large-scale industrial production of the nerve gases tabun and sarin, "which should guarantee Germany sufficient superiority in a gas war."[56] In the summer of 1942 the British had, however, constructed an anthrax weapon against animals for the purpose of producing a weapon of mass destruction, likewise with mostly fatal consequences for human targets.[57] While the German nerve gas was a deadly warfare agent, it was clearly inferior to the anthrax weapon.[58] Whereas tabun gas would have disappeared after a few days, anthrax pathogens would have made a city uninhabitable for a period of fifty years. "In the poker of deterrence and retribution," says Rolf-Dieter Müller, "the absence of bacterial weapons meant" that Hitler could not use his nerve gas.[59]

The surprise attack on the Soviet Union on 22 June 1941 was not really a surprise. Although Stalin had been receiving warnings for some time, he reacted passively. Historian Michael Salewski refers to Stalin's behavior after the Hitler-Stalin Pact[60] of 23 August 1939. Following the occupation of Poland on 17 September 1939, Stalin had achieved the following: 3 November 1939—attack on Finland; 15 June 1940—occupation of Lithuania; 28 June 1940—occupation of Bessarabia.[61] In order to better present himself to the world as a victim of National Socialist Germany, he had turned a blind eye to an attack that was judged inevitable.[62]

As the *Blitzkrieg* against the Soviet Union of 22 June 1941—this time planned—had, despite initially massive entrapment victories against the Red Army, already failed in the winter of 1941 due to the surprise Soviet counteroffensive at Moscow on 5 December 1941, Hitler had put himself in an economically hopeless situation no later than at the declaration of war on the United States of 11 December 1941—Japan had attacked Pearl Harbor on 7 December 1941. The powerful arming policy of the USA, with its massive shipments to the USSR and the significant increase in Soviet production of tanks, aircraft and artillery east of the Urals in the first quarter of 1942,[63] allowed no real improvement in the war situation, despite the reconfiguration of the German war economy to mass production and more effective technology.

Hitler's Final Deployment of Technology

When building the Luftwaffe, the Wehrmacht focused on operational army support at the expense of strategic bombers and was therefore unable to attack e.g., Soviet munitions factories east of the Urals. Out of the V1 "retaliation weapons" and flying bombs, approximately 10,500 of which were deployed against London, only 25 percent reached their targets. Rockets' launch pads in northern France were bombed.[64] Out of the total 5,797 V2 rockets, the precursor of ballistic missiles with a radius of 300 km, only about half were launched, most of them towards London and Antwerp. Rolf-Dieter Müller quotes a figure of approximately 10,000 deaths and injuries.[65] However, these were of no strategic importance as the rockets had a payload of only one ton.

At the end of February 1945, a high proportion of Me 262 aircraft, a jet aircraft of which 1,000 were produced, had been shot down. Some of these were fitted with an R4M air-to-air missile ("Hurricane"). Due to lack of fuel and poorly trained pilots, most of these stayed on the ground.[66]

The production process for the new Walter XXI submarines for underwater travel with snorkels was quite complicated. These boats had an underwater range of 340 nautical miles at a speed of 5 knots. They were produced in underground facilities in eight sub-segments and then delivered to shipyards for final assembly.[67] With the deployment of the first XXI boats, the Allies bombed ports and shipyards in late March/early April, sinking twenty-four boats and damaging twelve more.[68]

The German tank types Panther, Tiger and Tiger II (Königstiger) had nothing to fear from Allied tanks so long as the ground could support their weight and they were supported by air forces. In Russia, some Königstiger tanks sank into the ground, and on the western front the Luftwaffe was unable to provide the necessary support due to lack of air superiority. Allied fighter bombers thus mostly enjoyed considerable success when engaging German tanks during the day. In addition, fuel shortages also hindered the mobility of these combat vehicles in both the East and West.

Another striking factor that was of decisive importance in the development of the war was the decryption of German orders and messages at all military and political levels using Enigma technology during World War II. It were Polish, British and American analysts who unlocked the cryptically encoded German intentions for the Allies at an early stage and, in this manner, frustrated the German's plans.

Fortunately, the aforementioned, technically quite remarkable German developments could not change the outcome of the war; Germany at no time possessed weaponry of strategic significance that was superior to that possessed by the Allies—neither tanks, nor aircraft, nor rockets, nor submarines.

NOTES

1. This essays offers just a short survey and critical explanation of military terms and how Hitler as the Führer of the Third Reich tried to understand and implement them during the Second World War (1939-1945). Parts of the arguments have already been discussed in my Ph.D. thesis (Eckehard Dworok, *Konventionelle Kriegsführung und kriegswirtschaftliche Zwänge*, Kassel 1985), but for this chapter, I also considered new research with regard to this field of interest.
2. Cf. Yves Beón, *Planet Dora* (Gerlingen: Bleicher Verlag, 1999).
3. Adolf Hitler, *Mein Kampf* (München: Zentralverlag der NSDAP, 1942), 156.
4. Eberhard Jäckel, *Hitlers Weltanschauung* (Stuttgart: DVA, 1981), 27.
5. Hitler, *Mein Kampf*, 247-248.
6. Ibid., 249.
7. Gerhard L. Weinberg ed., *Hitlers zweites Buch* (Stuttgart: DVA, 1961), 123.
8. Ibid., 167. Hitler used to speak of "England" instead of "Great Britain."
9. Ibid., 100.
10. Ibid., 101.
11. Hitler, *Mein Kampf*, 156-160.
12. Jäckel, *Hitlers Weltanschauung*, 44.
13. Weinberg, *Hitlers zweites Buch*, 216.

II. The Age of the World Wars

14. Hitler, *Mein Kampf*, 742.
15. Ibid., 743.
16. Christopher Clark, *Die Schlafwandler* (München: DVA, 2012), 216.
17. Cf. Eckehard Dworok, "*Konventionelle Kriegsführung und kriegswirtschaftliche Zwänge*" (Ph.D. diss., University of Kassel, 1985), 67.
18. Rolf-Dieter Müller, *Der Feind steht im Osten* (Berlin: Links Verlag, 2011), 19.
19. Alan S. Milward, "Der Einfluß ökonomischer und nichtökonomischer Faktoren auf die Strategie des Blitzkrieges," in *Wirtschaft und Rüstung am Vorabend des Zweiten Weltkrieges*, edited by Friedrich Forstmeier and Hans-Erich Volkmann (Düsseldorf: Droste Verlag, 1975), 189. Yet, Karl-Heinz Frieser does not agree with this argument. Cf. Karl-Heinz Frieser, *Blitzkrieg-Legende* (München: DVA, 2012).
20. Philippe Masson, *Die deutsche Armee* (München: Herbig, 1996), 23; Müller, *Der Feind steht im Osten*, 31.
21. Karl-Heinz Ludwig, *Technik und Ingenieure im Dritten Reich* (Düsseldorf: Droste Verlag, 1974), 310.
22. Rolf-Dieter Müller, *Der letzte deutsche Krieg 1939–1945* (Stuttgart: Klett Kotta, 2005), 20.
23. Ludwig, *Technik und Ingenieure*, 310–311.
24. Müller, *Der Feind steht im Osten*, 39.
25. Adolf Hitler, "Tankrüstung im Zeichen der Abrüstung," *Illustrierter Beobachter* (1929).
26. Heinz Guderian, *Erinnerungen eines Soldaten* (Neckargemünd: Kurt Vowinkel Verlag, 1960), 18.
27. Frieser, *Blitzkrieg-Legende*, 22.
28. Georg Thomas, *Geschichte der deutschen Wehr- und Rüstungswirtschaft 1918–1943/45* (Boppard am Rhein: Boldt Verlag, 1966), 11.

Thomas defined *Breitenrüstung* (broad armament) as the establishment and equipping of the greatest possible number of military units within a short period. *Tiefenrüstung* (in-depth armament) encompassed the raw-materials basis and manufacturing potential, semi-finished and intermediate products, standby systems, strategic roads construction and the stockpiling of raw materials and military equipment. This was intended to secure the state's resilience for a years-long war. P. 8 f.

29. Frieser, *Blitzkrieg-Legende*, 6.
30. According to lieutenant general Georg von Sodenstern (5 May 1940). Cf. ibid., 23.
31. Franz Halder, *Kriegstagebuch des Chefs des Generalstabes des Heeres 1939*, vol. 1 (Stuttgart: Kohlhammer, 1962), 99.
32. Frieser, *Blitzkrieg-Legende*, 27.
33. Ibid., 74.
34. Ibid., 74.
35. Ibid., 31.
36. Ibid., 44–50.
37. William L. Shirer, *Der Zusammenbruch Frankreichs* (Zürich: Droemer/Knaur, 1969), 441.
38. Frieser, *Blitzkrieg-Legende*, 57.
39. Cf. for other data: Alfred Neubert et al., "Die Kriegsmittel. Wehrmacht, Technik und Waffen," in *Geschichte des Zweiten Weltkrieges*, ed. Ploetz Verlag, supervisor: Andraes Hillgruber (Würzburg: Ploetz Verlag, 1960), 158–159.
40. Frieser, *Blitzkrieg-Legende*, 94.
41. Ibid., 434.

42. Ibid., 368–195.
43. Rolf-Dieter Müller, "Von der Wirtschaftsallianz zum kolonialen Ausbeutungskrieg," in *Das Deutsche Reich und der Zweite Weltkrieg*, Bd.4, ed. Militärgeschichtliches Forschungsamt (Stuttgart: DVA, 1983), 126–127.
44. Thomas, *Geschichte der deutschen Wehr- und Kriegswirtschaft*, 531.
45. Müller, *Von der Wirtschaftsallianz zum kolonialen Ausbeutungskrieg*, 126. Also cf. Dworok, *Konventionelle Kriegsführung*. This book provides the copy of a historical map (USSR), on which Hitler's resource strategy was based on.
46. Werner Jochmann, *Adolf Hitler. Monologe* (Hamburg: Albrecht Knaus, 1980), 58, 62, 70, 76, 78.
47. Albert Speer, *Erinnerungen* (Berlin: Propyläen, 1970), 191–195.
48. Dietrich Eichholtz, *Geschichte der deutschen Kriegswirtschaft 1939–1945*, vol.1 (Berlin: Akademie Verlag), 131–135.
49. Michael Salewski, *Deutschland und der Zweite Weltkrieg* (Paderborn: Ferdinand Schöningh, 2005), 191.
50. Ludwig, *Technik und Ingenieure im Dritten Reich*, 89.
51. Henry Picker, *Hitlers Tischgespräche im Führerhauptquartier* (Stuttgart: Seewald, 1976), 476.
52. Ibid.
53. Speer, *Erinnerungen*, 246.
54. Rolf-Dieter Müller, "Albert Speer und die Rüstungspolitik im totalen Krieg," in *Das Deutsche Reich und der Zweite Weltkrieg*, vol. 5,2, ed. Bernhard R. Kroener, Rolf-Dieter Müller und Hans Umbreit. Militärgeschichtliches Forschungsamt (Stuttgart: DVA, 1999), 697–700.
55. Klaus Hoffmann, *J. Robert Oppenheimer* (Berlin: Springer Verlag, 1995), 137.
56. Müller, *Albert Speer und die Rüstungspolitik im totalen Krieg*, 705. The Allies didn't know about the existence of tabun throughout World War II.
57. Ibid., 719.
58. Müller, *Albert Speer und die Rüstungspolitik im totalen Krieg*, 724.
59. Ibid.
60. Salewski, *Deutschland und der Zweite Weltkrieg*, 194.
61. This had been determined in the secret protocol, which was appended to the Hitler-Stalin-Pact. The pact and the protocol were signed by Ribbentrop (Germany) und Molotow (USSR) on 23 August 1939.
62. Salewski, *Deutschland und der Zweite Weltkrieg*, 195.
63. Klaus Reinhardt, *Die Wende vor Moskau* (Stuttgart: DVA, 1972), 33.
64. Ludwig, *Technik und Ingenieure im Dritten Reich*, 448.
65. Müller, *Der letzte deutsche Krieg*, 143.
66. Ludwig, *Technik und Ingenieure im Dritten Reich*, 456.
67. Masson, *Die Deutsche Armee*, 344.
68. Ludwig, *Technik und Ingenieure im Dritten Reich*, 462.

WORKS CITED

Béon, Yves. *Planet Dora: Als Gefangener im Schatten der V2-Rakete*. Gerlingen: Bleicher, 1999.
Clark, Christopher. *Die Schlafwandler*. München: Beck, 2013.
Dworok, Eckehard. *Konventionelle Kriegsführung und kriegswirtschaftliche Zwänge*. Ph.D. Thesis, Kassel 1985.
Eichholtz, Dietrich. *Geschichte der deutschen Kriegswirtschaft 1939–1945*, Vol. 1: 1939–1941. Berlin: Akademie-Verlag, 1971.

Frieser, Karl-Heinz. *Blitzkrieg-Legende. Der Westfeldzug 1940*. Munich: Oldenbourg, 2012.
Guderian, Heinz. *Erinnerungen eines Soldaten*. Heidelberg: Vowinckel, 1951.
Hoffmann, Klaus. *J. Robert Oppenheimer: Schöpfer der ersten Atombombe*. Berlin: Springer, 1995.
Hitler, Adolf. *Mein Kampf*. Munich: Franz Eher Nachf., 1942.
Hitler, Adolf. "Tankrüstung im Zeichen der Abrüstung. Wehrpolitische Betrachtung," *Illustrierter Beobachter*, 28 September 1929.
Jäckel, Eberhard. *Hitlers Weltanschauung: Entwurf einer Herrschaft*. Stuttgart: Deutsche Verlagsanstalt, 1981.
Kriegstagebuch: Tägliche Aufzeichnungen des Chefs des Generalstabes des Heeres 1939-1942, ed. Franz Halder. Stuttgart: Kohlhammer, 1962.
Kroener, Bernhard R.; Müller, Rolf-Dieter and Umbreit, Hans. *Das Deutsche Reich und der Zweite Weltkrieg. Organisation und Mobilisierung des deutschen Machtbereichs. Kriegsverwaltung, Wirtschaft und personelle Ressourcen 1942-1944/45*. Stuttgart: Deutsche Verlagsanstalt, 1999.
Ludwig, Karl-Heinz. *Technik und Ingenieure im Dritten Reich*. Düsseldorf: Droste Verlag, 1974.
Masson, Philippe. *Die deutsche Armee: Geschichte der Wehrmacht, 1935-1945*. Munich: Herbig, 1996.
Milward, A. S. "Der Einfluß ökonomischer und nichtökonomischer Faktoren auf die Strategie des Blitz-Krieges," in *Wirtschaft und Rüstung am Vorabend des Zweiten Weltkrieges*, ed. Friedrich Forstmeier. Düsseldorf: Droste Verlag, 1975: 189-201.
Müller, Rolf-Dieter. *Der Feind steht im Osten: Hitlers geheime Pläne für einen Krieg gegen die Sowjetunion im Jahr 1939*. Berlin: Links Verlag, 2011.
Müller, Rolf-Dieter. *Der letzte deutsche Krieg 1939-1945*. Stuttgart: Klett-Cotta, 2005.
Müller, Rolf-Dieter. "Von der Wirtschaftsallianz zum kolonialen Ausbeutungskrieg," in *Der Angriff auf die Sowjetunion: Das Deutsche Reich und der Zweite Weltkrieg*, Vol. 4, ed. Horst Boog, et al. Frankfurt am Main: Fischer, 1996: 141-245.
Picker, Henry. *Hitlers Tischgespräche im Führerhauptquartier*. Stuttgart: Seewald, 1976.
Reinhardt, Klaus. *Die Wende vor Moskau: Das Scheitern der Strategie Hitlers im Winter 1941/42*. Stuttgart: Deutsche Verlagsanstalt, 1972.
Salewski, Michael. *Deutschland und der Zweite Weltkrieg*. Paderborn: Schöningh, 2005.
Shirer, Wiliam L. *Der Zusammenbruch Frankreichs: Aufstieg und Fall der 3. Republik*. Munich/Zurich: Droemer/Knaur, 1969.
Speer, Albert. *Erinnerungen*. Berlin: Propyläen, 1970.
Thomas, Georg. *Geschichte der deutschen Wehr- und Rüstungswirtschaft (1918-1943/45)*. Boppard am Rhein: Boldt, 1966.
Treue, Wilhelm. "Hitlers Denkschrift zum Vierjahresplan 1936," *Vierteljahrshefte für Zeitgeschichte* 3/2 (1955): 184-210.
Weinberg, Gerhard L. *Hitlers zweites Buch: Ein Dokument aus dem Jahr 1928*. Stuttgart: Deutsche Verlagsanstalt, 1961.

PART III.
THE COLD WAR

A Weapon Changed the World
The AK-47 and the Consequences for Asymmetric Warfare

FRANK JACOB

Introduction

> A world gone crazy gave its gun to a 12-year-old, an Ak-47 assault rifle, he fumbled with it and dropped down classmates in cold blood, there was anger and fun, the palace drunk has a loaded gun and he is fiddling with it at a nearby church premises, there is a pandemonium, anger and fun, a grenade is tucked in the mouth of the drunk too, passer-bys are shocked to the spine and no one dares get close ... this fun is dreadful, but the drunk knows no misery, he knows no pain, just like the child with his Ak-47 [...] this is the fate of all black Africans and their leaders.[1]

This is not only true for Africa because humans have always tried to kill each other in the most effective way.[2] Whether for territory, money, or power, war has been an essential part of our history since the beginning of our record keeping. Due to this course, people were always eager to invent better and more efficient methods to kill their antagonists. Rifles and pistols have been one of the most common killing instruments since the 17th century.[3] Nevertheless, the most famous one, the one that would change the art of war in a tremendous way, is the assault rifle AK-47 (*Awtomat Kalaschnikowa, obrasza 47*).[4] It has become famous because it is "so cheap and simple that it can be bought in many countries for less than the cost of a live chicken"[5] and is rightfully called the "weapon of the century."[6]

However, this modern but simple weapon, which "has all the aesthetical appeal of a toilet plunger"[7] not only proved to be successful during the last decades of war after its invention in 1947 by the former tank commander Mikhail Kalashnikov (1919–2013), but also changed warfare by stimulating the growth of asymmetric warfare in Asia, the Middle East, Africa, and Latin and South America.[8] It, furthermore, is a vivid expression of the fact that the modernization of weaponry is also responsible for a higher grade of human death.[9] With the use of the AK-47, killing was no longer a professional part of war; it became as easy as playing a game, and child soldiers in Africa and Latin America have used this assault rifle to kill their enemies in the name of goals they themselves could not understand.[10]

The following essay will outline the history of the invention of the AK-47 as a first step. After this, I will focus on the proxy wars between the United States and the Soviet Union, which were able to show the supremacy of the new weapon. In addition, it should be explained what factors were especially responsible for the success and the long period of existence of this weapon on several battlefields around the world. Furthermore, I will try to highlight the consequences of the use of the AK-47 during the so-called "new wars"[11] and its meaning for the theory of warfare, especially with regard to asymmetric warfare since the 1970s.

Inventing the AK-47

When Germany started its war against the Soviet Union in June 1941, the Wehrmacht was better equipped than the Russian soldiers.[12] This experience was also shared by tank commander Mikhail Kalashnikov, who had to face the German submachine guns during the Battle of Bryansk, where many of his comrades were slaughtered by a mass barrage of bullets.[13] Kalashnikov himself was wounded and from this moment onward, he could only think about inventing a better rifle for his comrades, which would make defending their motherland possible. The Russian soldiers needed something to counter the German *Maschinenpistole* MP40/MP41,[14] which was also known as the "Schmeisser," because Hugo Schmeisser (1884–1953)[15] had worked on a later version of the gun. Despite the good ideas for the new weapon's design by the former sergeant of the Soviet Army, they were not taken into consideration by established weapons designers like Alexey Sudayev (1912–1946) and Sergei Simonov (1894–1986)[16]; both of these individuals looked down on the uneducated Kalashnikov. Nevertheless, the Soviet authorities recognized a possible genius in the young man and sent him to a technical school. He would eventually design a weapon that could match the German Mkb42 or MP42 even though it was created too late to help his comrades since the war had already ended by 1947.

During the invention process, the question of suitable ammunition for the new weapon played a decisive role. While the classical rifles used by the infantry in World War II used single-shot rounds, which were powerful and could be used to fire long distances, an ammunition ranging between pistol and long-rifle was needed because the soldiers would have been able to carry more ammunition with them into battle, while the cartridges as a whole would have been cheaper as well.[17]

Regardless of the delay, this weapon was bound to make its inventor famous despite his lack of financial compensation for his invention, which was sent as a gift of friendship to several communist countries in the following decades and also copied in countries like China, North Korea, and Iran.[18] The final test for this new kind of assault rifle was conducted during the Hungarian Crisis in 1956, when Soviet soldiers, equipped with this new instrument of warfare, suppressed one of the first uprisings of the Cold War era.[19] The Mikoyan-Suslov Report on the situation in Budapest in October 1956 describes the AK-47's success very simply; it was a demonstration that was also visible to the entire world:

> On the streets together with the Soviet troops were Hungarian patrols. In contrast to Buda, where it was calm, there was continuous shooting in Pest between isolated groups of provocateurs and individuals and our machine-gunners, beginning at the bridge and extending to the ministry of Defense building, as well as toward the Central Committee building. Our men did more of the shooting; to solitary shots we replied with salvos.[20]

The advantages of the new Soviet assault rifle were obvious. The AK-47, with few moving parts, was a weapon that never jammed. It was also resistant against heat so it could be used in every environment no matter if it were a desert or a jungle.[21] Firing 600 rounds a minute, it could arouse a high grade of destruction even though the AK-47 did not always fire straight. Kalashnikov's invention proved to be a success; however, the inventor, as a consequence of the fact that his invention remained unpatented and was gifted to other communist states to support them during the emerging Cold War, never became rich.[22] He just became a figurehead who was used to show the world the potential of the proletarian hero who invented an incredibly successful assault rifle to save his comrades from the danger represented by the Germans and international fascism. Kalashnikov advanced through the military ranks, and in later years, the government used to send him on commercial trips to other countries, where his fame was used to sell the AK-47 and its follow-up models. Before he died in December 2013, Kalashnikov confessed that he was haunted by the fear of being responsible for the death of so many people.[23] With regard to this, one is able to state that an invention that was designed to end the war in Russia was used to wage wars in several other countries during the following decades. One cannot blame the inventor for his idea because he could not foresee the dimension of the killings that his creation would achieve. Still, one has to underline the fact that it was a weapon that was invented as well. That weapons do kill people was nothing new; however, the rate of "success" that was achieved by this simple weapon has not been seen before.

The Proxy Wars

While there were just a few AK-47s in the first proxy war between the United States and the Soviet Union, the Korean War (1950–1953)[24] and the second proxy war in Vietnam (1955–1975)[25] emphasized the supremacy of the new weapon. The United States had not been interested in providing submachine guns or assault rifles during the war. Due to that lack of foresight, the famous M1[26] remained in service for far too long, and later, U.S. army officials had no interest in the concurrent ideas of other weapons' producers aside from the Springfield Armory,[27] which would provide troops with the M16,[28] the American assault rifle in Vietnam. There, the U.S. soldiers met their new and deadly antagonist, the AK-47. The supremacy of the Soviet weapon was undeniable, and the GIs tried to get an enemy weapon as soon as possible during combat because the M16 jammed too often and was not made for the tropical climate of the Vietnamese jungle. This practice was prohibited by the army leadership because the sound of a shooting AK-47 produced friendly fire in the area. In the dense jungle, the soldiers often could not see very well, but they could hear the enemy, and the sound of a firing Soviet assault rifle determined the direction of their own gunfire.

Vietnam finally became a strike against American self-confidence and world power status, a fact that was described by Colonel Fitzgerald, the military attaché at the U.S. Embassy in the USSR in 1966: "I'm a soldier and am therefore obliged to maintain the policy of my government and follow the directions of my command, but as a man I may sometimes be ashamed for the undermined prestige of the USA."[29] The AK-47 was mostly responsible for the success of strikes in Vietnam and for the decline of America's image around the globe. The great power, with all its might, was beaten by Vietnamese rice farmers who were armed with Soviet weapons.

However, during the conflict between the Soviet Union and the mujahedeen in Afghanistan, the Americans had recognized the worth of the AK-47 and used it for their own targets by aiding the

> Afghan counterrevolutionaries. In order to coordinate the activity in this direction, a working group was created in Islamabad; it included officials from the general staff and military intelligence (ISI) of Pakistan and representatives of the U.S., British, and Egyptian embassies. At one of their meetings the group discussed its specific operations in order to conduct subversive tactics. They also

reviewed the participation of individual countries in organizing the rebel movement on D[emocratic] R[epublic] [of] A[fghanistan] territory. In particular, the training of saboteurs and terrorists would be done in the F[ederal] R[epublic] [of] G[ermany], where by the end of 1980, a number of centers operated to teach guerilla warfare methods to Pakistani servicemen and persons of Afghan nationality. The period of training was set at one and a half months. In the first half of September the next group of saboteurs flew to the FRG for training.[30]

The mujahedeen, trained in the aforementioned camps, were equipped with the Soviet weapons by the CIA, which had bought them in China and other bloc states and sent them to Afghanistan through the Pakistani borderland.[31] There, the soldiers of the Soviet Army had to face the destructive power of their own weapons. The Afghan fighters always used the cheap and easily used weapon to let their opponents know that although they might have been able to conquer some territory, they would never be able to hold it for a long time.[32] When the mujahedeen prepared ambushes for the Soviet troops, they could always rely on the firing strength of their weapons, which had been shipped from the battlefields of the last proxy war and China to provide the Afghan rebels with a mighty and cheap answer to Russian occupation.

Therefore, armed with MANPADs (Man-Portable Air-Defense Systems) and genuine Soviet assault rifles, the mujahedeen were able to counter the Northern threat. However, seen in retrospect, the war did not accomplish anything.[33] In 1992, the mujahedeen finally were able to take over the power in Kabul, followed by the Taliban four years later. Their rule finally created "a safe haven for al–Qaeda"[34] from where the terrorists were able to prepare their attacks against the World Trade Center and the Pentagon in 2011. Nonetheless, these were not the only problems that were created in Afghanistan. On the one hand, the Taliban might still use the same weapons they received from the Americans in the 1980s to kill the members of the international troops there, and on the other hand, the weapons left the country to be used in further violent battles all around the globe. Therefore, U.S. support due to the Afghan endeavor laid the ground for future problems with the weapon, which today is mainly used by terrorists and guerrillas that are also eager to kill U.S. soldiers. The current state of affairs is just a natural consequence of the way the AK-47s were distributed after the end of the Soviet engagement in Afghanistan.

The Global Perspective and Asymmetric Warfare

By the time the Soviet-Afghan War ended in 1989, the history of the AK-47 had just begun. The rifles were almost indestructible, and international traders took over the ground concerning the guns. Those weapons that did not remain in Afghan or Al-Qaeda hands went straight to the Middle East, Latin America, or Africa. There, the weapon became a symbol of guerrilla warfare, and many coups d'état were successful as a consequence of the use of the AK-47. The assault rifle ensured that Charles Taylor was able to raid Liberia, establish his rule, and bring war to his neighboring states.[35] However, it was not just Liberia that became a victim of this weapon in the 20th century; Sierra Leone,[36] Somalia,[37] the Congo,[38] and many other countries all had to face the cruelties that could be produced from its use.

The weapon had also been shipped to Nicaragua in the following decades, where it was used by the Sandinistas, who received it through Cuba, as well as by the Contras, who received it from the CIA.[39] Since the countries of the Soviet bloc were allowed to produce the famous weapon, it was shipped to several battlefields over the years. Finally, the trade was taken over by private traders who shipped the AK-47 to every possible frontier of war around the world. The weapon is cheap enough to produce that every militant force is able to use it in their plans. In some regions of the world, the AK-47 is so widespread that one could buy it for just a few dollars.

Far crueler is the fact that African and Latin American children have been used as soldiers in these conflicts, because the weapon that changed the world is as easy for children to learn how to use as is a toy. Lastly, it has also been used by drug dealers who are eager to possess these cheap assault rifles in order to secure drug routes from their enemies. Nevertheless, these assault rifles are an essential part of the "new wars" and asymmetric warfare. Asymmetric warfare is no modern phenomenon[40] because there are also examples for such a kind of war in the Greek and Roman antiquity. However, in the modern era, there seem to be more violent conflicts that used to be defined and still are defined as asymmetric. Basically, we are able to define five levels of asymmetry[41]:

1. a disequilibrium of power
2. an imbalance of the motivation of the two parties' soldiers
3. a differing legitimation or level of statehood
4. a discrepancy of the used methods
5. a difference of the quality of the used instruments of warfare

The impact of the AK-47 on this kind of warfare is visible especially when one is focusing on points one and five because it is able to change the disequilibrium of power, and there is a high grade of difference between superior weaponry and the Soviet assault rifle.

Due to the success story of this cheap and almost indestructible weapon, it is a logical consequence that warfare was changed by its introduction. There is no such thing as supreme warfare anymore because even farmers can use the assault rifle to kill U.S. GIs and many other soldiers all around the world. The discrepancy in the used methods is also intensified in such a way that guerrilla warfare becomes even more efficient when the guerrillas are equipped with the superior but cheaper weapon. Therefore, those who are eager to fight in an asymmetric war are also eager to have the AK-47, and as long as these rifles are accessible and cheap and are still being shipped around the globe after one conflict ends to open a new one, people will die as a consequence.

What changed as well was the fact that the Western world and its technology were no longer superior to the so-called "Third World." In asymmetric warfare, it was no longer the surplus of equipment that decided the battle, but motivation, tactics and in many cases, the superiority of the cheaper banana-rifle. The battles of conservative troops against revolutionary or anti–Western forces in several countries were no longer part of the traditional history of warfare; this is a fact that has been experienced by the many soldiers who have had to face the effects of the AK-47 and were surprised that their opponents were able to produce a high grade of damage with such simple methods. The U.S. campaigns in Afghanistan and Iraq must consequently be seen as a vivid effect of a shortsighted leadership that must have forgotten how many weapons had been sent to this country by the CIA. It seems impossible to count the lives that have been taken in these conflicts by the AK-47s of rebel troops, or will be taken by Isis fighters,[42] who are equipped with the same weaponry.

Conclusion

The AK-47 was invented to end a war, but its production started just after the war. Its superiority became visible during the Vietnam War when it made the American soldiers fear their invisible enemy even more. However, the story of the weapon did not end with the war in Southeast Asia. It was shipped to another battlefield, where it was used by the mujahedeen against the Soviet troops. With the defeat of the Red Army in this country, the AK-47s were again left to bring death and bloodshed to the so-called Third World. It has been shown that this weapon has been responsible for the change of warfare, highly stimulating a type of battlefield situation known as asymmetric warfare. As long as there are small groups aiming to destroy the existing order of a country or to fight a superior military power, the AK-47 will remain an icon of power in conflicts that are called "Low Intensity Conflicts" by Martin van Creveld.[43] It seems that the circular trip of the weapons will never end as long as there are possibilities for its use by guerrillas, gangsters or terrorists around the globe.

The AK-47, today ranked "as the deadliest, most prevalent and most game-changing individually wielded weapon in the history of military armament,"[44] will remain an almost perfect instrument of killing in the upcoming decades, and as long as there is bloodshed around the globe, this famous assault rifle will be part of modern warfare. This fact was recognized by Kalashnikov himself, who regretted his invention in later years: "I'm proud of my invention, but I'm sad that it is used by terrorists. I would prefer to have invented a machine that people could use and that would help farmers with their work—for example, a lawnmower."[45]

NOTES

1. Nijoku Saint Jerry A., *AK-47 in a Wild Why World: Contemporary African Issues—Humour—Poetry* (Bloomington: Author House, 2008).

2. Some basic accounts that give a broad survey of this violent part of human history are provided by Christon I. Archer, John R. Ferris, Holger H. Herwig, and Timothy H. E. Travers, *World History of Warfare* (Lincoln, NE: University of Nebraska Press, 2002), John Keegan, *A History of Warfare* (New York: Alfred A. Knopf, 1993), and Geoffrey Parker, *The Cambridge History of Warfare* (Cambridge: Cambridge University Press, 2005).

3. For detailed accounts see A.E. Hartink, *Gewehre Enzyklopädie: Büchsen aus aller Welt* (Eggolsheim: Nebel-Verlag, 2003), Udo Knispel, *Gewehre: Übersicht über die Entwicklung der einzelnen Waffentypen* (München: Heyne, 1975), and Günther Reinhold, *Allgemeine Geschichte der Handfeuerwaffen* (Holzminden: Reprint-Verlag, 2001—originally published in 1909).

4. The term AK-47 is used here as a substitute for the several types or follow-up models that were used since 1947. For a detailed survey of the different types and technical details see Nigel Bennett, *AK-47 Assault Rifle: The Real Weapon of Mass Destruction* (Stroud: Spellmont, 2010).

5. Larry Kahaner, *AK-47: The Weapon that Changed the Face of War* (Hoboken, NJ: Wiley, 2007), p. 2.

6. Stephan Wilkinson, "AK-47: Weapon of the Century," *Military History* 30/3 (2013), 29–35.

7. Ibid., 29.

8. On asymmetric warfare see Anthony H. Cordesman, *Terrorism, Asymmetric Warfare, and Weapons of Mass Destruction: Defending the U.S. Homeland* (Westport: Praeger, 2002), Larisa Deriglazova, *Great Powers, Small Wars: Asymmetric Conflict since 1945* (Washington: Woodrow Wilson Center Press, 2014), Adam Lowther, *Americans and Asymmetric Conflict: Lebanon, Somalia, and Afghanistan* (Wesport: Praeger, 2007), Max G. Manwaring, *The Complexity of Modern Asymmetric Warfare* (Norman: University of Oklahoma Press, 2012), and Paul Thaza, *Asymmetric Conflicts: War Initiation by Weaker Powers* (Cambridge: Cambridge University Press, 1994).

9. The most well-known example is the atomic bomb, which seems to be the nadir of the interrelationship between technology and a weapon explicitly invented for mass destruction. When Niels Bohr (1885–1962) was asked during a Soviet interrogation if there were a method of protection against this weapon he stated: 'I am sure that there is no real method of protection from atomic bomb. Tell me, how you can stop the fission process which has already begun in the bomb which has been dropped from a plane? It is possible, of course, to intercept the plane, thus not allowing

it to approach its destination—but this is a task of a doubtful character, because planes fly very high for this purpose and besides, with the creation of jet planes, you understand yourself, the combination of these two discoveries makes the task of fighting the atomic bomb insoluble." "The Interrogation of Niels Bohr," November 28, 1945, History and Public Policy Program Digital Archive, State Archive of the Russian Federation (GARF). CWIHP Bulletin No. 4, Fall 1994, "Soviet Espionage and the Bomb." http://digitalarchive.wilsoncenter.org/document/111839 (Last access, 15 March 2015).

10. The original model had just eight parts that could be moved at all. Also compare Frank Jacob, "Children and War," in *Encyclopedia of Human Services and Diversity*, ed. Linwood H. Cousins and Geoffrey J. Golson (Los Angeles: SAGE, 2014) and Frank Jacob, "Child Soldiers," in *The SAGE Encyclopedia of World Poverty*, 2nd edition, ed. Mehmet Odekon and Geoffrey J. Golson (Los Angeles: SAGE, 2015).

11. The term was coined by Mary Kaldor, *New and Old Wars* (Cambridge: Polity Press, 1998). One aspect of the so-called new wars is, that they are no longer wars between states, but are rather waged by local warlords, guerrilla groups or networks of international terrorism. See: Herfried Münkler, *Die neuen Kriege* (Hamburg: Rowohlt, 2010), 7.

12. Christian Hartmann, *Wehrmacht im Ostkrieg: Front und militärisches Hinterland 1941/42* (Munich: Oldenbourg, 2010), pp. 243–283 and Christan Hartmann, *Unternehmen Barbarossa: Der deutsche Krieg im Osten 1941–1945* (Munich: Beck, 2011), 37–48.

13. Kahaner, *AK-47*, 9–12. The Germans knew about the power of submachine guns. Even the Reichsführer-SS demanded the development and construction of a new type of submachine gun by the Brünner-Waffenwerke (Brünner Arms Factory). See National Archives Berlin, BArch NS 19/2476.

14. The German troops were equipped with the follow-up model MP42 in 1942, National Archives Berlin, BArch NS19/2088. On the development of the German submachine guns and assault rifles see Hans Dieter Götz, *German Military Rifles and Machine Pistols, 1871–1945* (Atglen: Schiffer Publishing, 1990).

15. Available is just a short biography of Schmeisser, published in the Suhler Kleine Reihe (Vol. 29): Norbert Moczarski, *Hugo Schmeisser. Zwischen Tabu und Legende: Der weltbekannte Suhler Waffenkonstrukteur 1884–1953* (Meiningen/Suhl, 2009). See also: http://www.schmeisser-germany.de/ger/portrait_hugoschmeisser_ger.html (Last access, 15 March 2015). The company is still producing and selling weapons today.

16. On Simonov's inventions see: Graham Priest, "Simonov's Automatic Rifles & Bayonets," http://www.infantry-weapons.org/docs/Priest_6.pdf (Last access, 15 March 2015).

17. Wilkinson, *AK-47*, 31–32.

18. The Soviet Union supported other communist countries, especially China during the years leading to the Korean War, with weapons, see: "Minutes of Conversation between I.V. Stalin and Zhou Enlai," August 20, 1952, History and Public Policy Program Digital Archive, APRF, f. 45, op. 1, d. 329, ll. 54–72. Translated for NKIDP by Danny Rozas. http://digitalarchive.wilsoncenter.org/document/111244 (Last access, 15 March 2015).

19. For a vivid description of the events during the Hungarian crisis, Michael Korda, *Journey to a Revolution: A Personal Memoir and History of the Hungarian Revolution of 1956* (New York: Harper Perennial, 2007) is highly recommended.

20. "Mikoyan-Suslov Report" October 24, 1956, History and Public Policy Program

Digital Archive, Archive of Foreign Policy, Russian Federation (AVP RF) F. 059a, Opis 4, Papka 6, Delo 5, Listy 1–7. http://digitalarchive.wilsoncenter.org/document/110981 (Last access, 15 March 2015).

21. Kahaner, *AK-47*, 3.
22. Wilkinson, *AK-47*, 30.
23. Luke Harding, "Kalashnikov inventor haunted by unbearable pain of dead millions," *The Guardian*, 13 January 2014, http://www.theguardian.com/world/2014/jan/13/kalashnikov-weapon-inventor-spiritual-pain-dead-millions (Last access, 15 March 2015).
24. Bruce Cumings, *The Korean War* (New York: Modern Library, 2011), is one of the best introductive accounts on this topic.
25. An extensive work on the Vietnam War is provided by Bernd Greiner, *Krieg ohne Fronten. Die USA in Vietnam* (Hamburg: Hamburger Edition, 2007).
26. Bruce N. Canfield, *The M1 Garand Rifle* (Woonsocket, RI: Mowbray Publishing, 2013) provides a comprehensive history of this famous U.S. rifle.
27. For the importance of this armory, see National Park Services, *Conservative Innovators and Military Small Arms: An Industrial History of the Springfield Armory, 1794–1968* (Washington: BiblioGov, 2012).
28. For a survey of the history of the M16 Gordon Rottman, *The M16* (London: Osprey, 2011) is recommended.
29. "Memorandum, P. Ivashutin to CC CPSU on U.S. Military Attaché Colonel Fitzgerald" August 23, 1966, History and Public Policy Program Digital Archive, SCCD, F. 5, Op. 58, D. 262, LI. 237–38. Translated for CWIHP by Mark H. Doctoroff. http://digitalarchive.wilsoncenter.org/document/114838 (Last access, 15 March 2015).
30. "A Report by Soviet Military Intelligence" September 01, 1981, History and Public Policy Program Digital Archive, A. A. Lyakhovskiy's "Plamya Afgana" ("Flame of the Afghanistan veteran"), Iskon, Moscow, 1999. Translated for CWIHP by Gary Goldberg. http://digitalarchive.wilsoncenter.org/document/111796 (Last access, 15 March 2015).
31. This connection was also depicted in the comedy-drama Charlie Wilson's War (2007).
32. Anthony Brandt, "Afghanistan Fiasco," *Military History* 30/5 (2014), 52.
33. Ibid., 53.
34. Ibid.
35. Colin M. Waugh, *Charles Taylor and Liberia: Ambition and Atrocity in Africa's Lone Star State* (London/New York: Zed Books, 2011), 123–152. In 1989 Charles Taylor started his invasion of Liberia with the support of only 168 armed men.
36. Lansana Gberie, *A Dirty War in West Africa: The RUF and the Destruction of Sierra Leone* (Bloomington: Indiana University Press, 2005).
37. Ken Menkhaus, *Somalia: State Collapse and the Threat of Terrorism* (New York: Routledge, 2004).
38. Thomas Turner, *Congo* (Cambridge: Polity Press, 2013).
39. For a description of the so called Iran-Contra Affair see: Jürgen Grafelmann, "The Swing State: U.S. Interest and Fickleness in the Face of Tyranny," in *Dictatorships without Violence? How Dictators Assert Their Power*, ed. Frank Jacob (Würzburg: Königshausen & Neumann, 2014).
40. Beatrice Heuser, *Rebellen. Partisanen. Guerilleros: Asymmetrische Kriege von der Antike bis heute* (Paderborn: Ferdinand Schöningh, 2013), 15–22.
41. Klaus-Peter Lohmann, "Zur Entwicklung der modernen Kriegführung. Grundlegende Asymmetrien und eine mögliche Strategie," in *Asymmetrische*

Kriegführung—ein neues Phänomen der Internationalen Politik, ed. Josef Schlröfl and Thomas Pankratz (Baden-Baden: Nomos, 2004), 62.

42. John Hall, "'Come and get your AK-47, your grenades and your vest pack : British ISIS fighter lures underage jihadist away from his parents with travel advice on reaching Middle East," Daily Mail, 24 June 2014, http://www.dailymail.co.uk/news/article-2667034/Come-AK-47-grenades-vest-pack-British-ISIS-fighter-lures-underage-jihadist-away-parents-travel-advice-reaching-Middle-East.html (Last access, 15 March 2015).

43. Martin van Creveld, *Die Zukunft des Krieges* (München: Gerling Akademie Verlag, 2001), 94–101.

44. Wilkinson, *AK-47*, 30.

45. Kate Conolly, "Kalashnikov: 'I wish I'd made a lawnmower,'" *The Guardian*, July 30, 2002, http://www.theguardian.com/world/2002/jul/30/russia.kateconnolly (Last access, 15 March 2015).

Works Cited

Primary Sources

"A Report by Soviet Military Intelligence" September 01, 1981, History and Public Policy Program Digital Archive, A.A. Lyakhovskiy's "Plamya Afgana" ("Flame of the Afghanistan veteran"), Iskon, Moscow, 1999. Translated for CWIHP by Gary Goldberg. http://digitalarchive.wilsoncenter.org/document/111796.

Federal Archive Berlin, BArch NS19/2088.

Federal Archive Berlin, BArch NS 19/2476.

"Memorandum, P. Ivashutin to CC CPSU on U.S. Military Attaché Colonel Fitzgerald" August 23, 1966, History and Public Policy Program Digital Archive, SCCD, F. 5, Op. 58, D. 262, LI. 237–38. Translated for CWIHP by Mark H. Doctoroff. http://digitalarchive.wilsoncenter.org/document/114838.

"Mikoyan-Suslov Report" October 24, 1956, History and Public Policy Program Digital Archive, Archive of Foreign Policy, Russian Federation (AVP RF) F. 059a, Opis 4, Papka 6, Delo 5, Listy 1–7. http://digitalarchive.wilsoncenter.org/document/110981.

"Minutes of Conversation between I.V. Stalin and Zhou Enlai," August 20, 1952, History and Public Policy Program Digital Archive, APRF, f. 45, op. 1, d. 329, ll. 54–72. Translated for NKIDP by Danny Rozas. http://digitalarchive.wilsoncenter.org/document/111244.

"The Interrogation of Niels Bohr," November 28, 1945, History and Public Policy Program Digital Archive, State Archive of the Russian Federation (GARF). CWIHP Bulletin No. 4, Fall 1994, "Soviet Espionage and the Bomb." http://digitalarchive.wilsoncenter.org/document/111839.

Secondary Sources

Archer, Christon I., et al. *World History of Warfare*. Lincoln: University of Nebraska Press, 2002.

Bennett, Nigel. *AK-47 Assault Rifle: The Real Weapon of Mass Destruction*. Stroud: Spellmont, 2010.

Brandt, Anthony. "Afghanistan Fiasco." *Military History* 30/5 (2014), 44–53.

Canfield, Bruce N. *The M1 Garand Rifle*. Woonsocket, RI: Mowbray Publishing, 2013.

Conolly, Kate. "Kalashnikov: 'I wish I'd made a lawnmower,'" *The Guardian*, July 30, 2002, http://www.theguardian.com/world/2002/jul/30/russia.kateconnolly.

Cordesman, Anthony H. *Terrorism, Asymmetric Warfare, and Weapons of Mass Destruction. Defending the U.S. Homeland.* Westport: Praeger, 2002.
Creveld, Martin van. *Die Zukunft des Krieges.* München: Gerling Akademie Verlag, 2001.
Cumings, Bruce. *The Korean War.* New York: Modern Library, 2011.
Deriglazova, Larisa. *Great Powers, Small Wars: Asymmetric Conflict since 1945.* Washington: Woodrow Wilson Center Press, 2014.
Gberie, Lansana. *A Dirty War in West Africa: The RUF and the Destruction of Sierra Leone.* Bloomington: Indiana University Press, 2005.
Götz, Hans Dieter. *German Military Rifles and Machine Pistols, 1871–1945.* Atglen: Schiffer Publishing, 1990.
Grafelmann, Jürgen "The Swing State: U.S. Interest and Fickleness in the Face of Tyranny," in *Dictatorships without Violence? How Dictators assert their Power,* ed. Frank Jacob. Würzburg: Königshausen & Neumann, 2014, 263–269.
Greiner, Bernd. *Krieg ohne Fronten: Die USA in Vietnam.* Hamburg: Hamburger Edition, 2007.
Hall, John. "'Come and get your AK-47, your grenades and your vest pack': British ISIS fighter lures underage jihadist away from his parents with travel advice on reaching Middle East," *Daily Mail,* 24 June 2014, http://www.dailymail.co.uk/news/article-2667034/Come-AK-47-grenades-vest-pack-British-ISIS-fighter-lures-underage-jihadist-away-parents-travel-advice-reaching-Middle-East.html.
Harding, Luke. "Kalashnikov inventor haunted by unbearable pain of dead millions," The Guardian, 13 January 2014, http://www.theguardian.com/world/2014/jan/13/kalashnikov-weapon-inventor-spiritual-pain-dead-millions.
Hartink, A.E. *Gewehre Enzyklopädie, Büchsen aus aller Welt.* Eggolsheim: Nebel-Verlag, 2003.
Hartmann, Christan. *Unternehmen Barbarossa: Der deutsche Krieg im Osten 1941–1945.* Munich: Beck, 2011.
Hartmann, Christian. *Wehrmacht im Ostkrieg. Front und militärisches Hinterland 1941/42.* Munich: Oldenbourg, 2010.
Heuser, Beatrice. *Rebellen. Partisanen. Guerilleros: Asymmetrische Kriege von der Antike bis heute.* Paderborn: Ferdinand Schöningh, 2013.
Jacob, Frank. "Children and War," in *Encyclopedia of Human Services and Diversity,* ed. Linwood H. Cousins and Geoffrey J. Golson. Los Angeles: SAGE, 2014.
Jacob, Frank. "Child Soldiers," in *The SAGE Encyclopedia of World Poverty,* 2nd edition, ed. Mehmet Odekon and Geoffrey J. Golson. Los Angeles: SAGE, 2015.
Jerry, Nijoku Saint A. *AK-47 in a Wild Why World: Contemporary African Issues—Humor—Poetry.* Bloomington: Author House, 2008.
Kahaner, Larry. *AK-47: The Weapon that Changed the Face of War.* Hoboken, NJ: Wiley, 2007.
Kaldor, Mary. *New and Old Wars.* Cambridge: Polity Press, 1998.
Keegan, John. *A History of Warfare.* New York: Alfred A. Knopf, 1993.
Knispel, Udo. *Gewehre: Übersicht über die Entwicklung der einzelnen Waffentypen.* München: Heyne, 1975.
Korda, Michael. *Journey to a Revolution: A Personal Memoir and History of the Hungarian Revolution of 1956.* New York: Harper Perennial, 2007.
Lohmann, Klaus-Peter. "Zur Entwicklung der modernen Kriegführung. Grundlegende Asymmetrien und eine mögliche Strategie," in *Asymmetrische Kriegführung—ein neues Phänomen der Internationalen Politik,* ed. Josef Schlröfl and Thomas Pankratz. Baden-Baden: Nomos, 2004, 57–68.

Lowther, Adam. *Americans and Asymmetric Conflict: Lebanon, Somalia, and Afghanistan.* Wesport: Praeger, 2007.
Manwaring, Max G. *The Complexity of Modern Asymmetric Warfare.* Norman: University of Oklahoma Press, 2012.
Menkhaus, Ken. *Somalia: State Collapse and the Threat of Terrorism.* New York: Routledge, 2004.
Moczarski, Norbert. *Hugo Schmeisser. Zwischen Tabu und Legende. Der weltbekannte Suhler Waffenkonstrukteur 1884–1953.* Meiningen/Suhl, 2009.
Münkler, Herfried. *Die neuen Kriege.* Hamburg: Rowohlt, 2010.
National Park Services, *Conservative Innovators and Military Small Arms: An Industrial History of the Springfield Armory, 1794–1968.* Washington: BiblioGov, 2012.
Parker, Geoffrey. *The Cambridge History of Warfare.* Cambridge: Cambridge University Press, 2005.
Priest, Graham. "Simonov's Automatic Rifles & Bayonets," http://www.infantryweapons.org/docs/Priest_6.pdf.
Reinhold, Günther. *Allgemeine Geschichte der Handfeuerwaffen.* Holzminden: Reprint-Verlag, 2001—originally published in 1909.
Rottman, Gordon. *The M16.* London: Osprey, 2011.
Thaza, Paul. *Asymmetric Conflicts: War Initiation by Weaker Powers.* Cambridge: Cambridge University Press, 1994.
Turner, Thomas. *Congo.* Cambridge: Polity Press, 2013.
Waugh, Colin M. *Charles Taylor and Liberia: Ambition and Atrocity in Africa's Lone Star State.* London/New York: Zed Books, 2011.
Wilkinson, Stephan. "AK-47. Weapon of the Century." *Military History* 30/3 (2013), 28–35.

Tous Azimuts
Yugoslavia's Defense Policy in the Cold War

James Horncastle

In terms of its population and economic might, Yugoslavia is a small country. Nevertheless, its prestige and political influence as well as its defence potentials are comparable with those of the big countries. An aggressor is highly unlikely to take part in a venture and commit aggression expecting to achieve immediate success against a country in which every able citizen is prepared and more importantly, motivated and determined to defend his freedom and independence. We are, therefore, right in stating that we may lose the first battle but never the war.[1]—Josip Broz Tito (1892–1980)

Josip Broz Tito, while delivering a speech to the 11th Congress of the League of Communists of Yugoslavia in 1978, outlined the main principle of Yugoslavia's defense policy of Total National Defense (TND): human power. Yugoslavia, due to its relatively small population and moderate economic development, could not hope to stand up to or defeat either NATO or the Warsaw Pact in a conventional battle. The superior development of the two alliances, which in communist parlance equated with industrial output, meant that they would be able to significantly outnumber the Yugoslavs in war materiel. Furthermore, the rapid pace at which technological developments were occurring and being combined for military purposes in the Cold War, such as the brisk developments in aircraft designs, meant that even if Yugoslavia established a strong conventional army capable of engaging an invading force in a set-piece battle, as it had organized in the early 1950s, it would quickly be rendered obsolete. As a result, Yugoslavia, in the 1970s, could only ensure its defense by making the cost of invasion for either bloc so great that it would deter them from engaging in hostilities in the first place.[2]

This essay will examine how Yugoslavia's development of TND in 1969, and its continued refinement until the state's collapse in 1991, were significantly influenced by the country being a small, non-aligned state in the Cold War. The Cold War combined the Industrial Revolution of the nineteenth century with the rapid technological developments of the twentieth century to produce an environment where small states could no longer produce a credible conventional deterrent to the Great Powers. Many small countries, whether through choice or coercion, were forced to adhere to the dominant military blocs of the era.[3] Initially, Yugoslavia followed this path, but by the 1960s, the political leadership, because it desired an independent foreign policy, had to develop a defense policy that did not rely on either the West or the East for military support. TND, which replaced the military emphasis on large conventional weapons derived from heavy industry with guerrilla warfare tactics waged by light armed forces, was Yugoslavia's answer to this dilemma.

An important issue one must take into consideration in any discussion of military hardware and its production is that the technology itself rarely, if ever, determines the course of action that a state will undertake. It is common when discussing military hardware to only focus on its material aspects. Instead, to properly assess the role of military hardware, one must engage with the social, cultural, and political dynamics around its use as well. Jeremy Black, in his most recent work on the role of technology and warfare, explains:

> Dethroning technology from the central position in the narrative and explanation of military capability and change does not, however, entail denying its importance or neglecting the degree to which warfare has autonomous characteristics. Instead, it is necessary to adopt a more nuanced approach to the different factors—material, political, cultural, social, and other—that play a role in military capability and change, considering them not as reified concepts that compete but rather in a manner that allows for the multiple character of their interaction.[4]

Thus, in considering the role that technology played in helping to shape Yugoslavia's defense policy, it must not be to the detriment of other factors. Instead, the role of technology and industry should be considered in relation to the additional factors Black identified. Specifically, with regards to this paper, Yugoslavia's foreign policy and military culture significantly influenced decisions that the country reached in terms of how and which military technologies to emphasize in its defense policy.

It is also important to consider that until the 1980s, the Cold War, from a military standpoint, was a relatively unique period in modern military history in which industrialization and technology were equally important in terms of developing and equipping a conventional army. During this period, new weapons systems came online in short intervals. The Cold War increased the difficulty of incorporating these technological leaps as both quantity and quality were equally important factors in projecting one's will upon the enemy. Jeremy Black explained that while technological developments are important, "there is also the issue of production. [...] it is [...] necessary to be able to manufacture large numbers of a new weapon, and at a consistent standard."[5] For the majority of the world's countries, including eventually the Soviet Union, it was simply impossible to keep up with demands in both of these fields. Marshal Nikolai Ogarkov (1917–1994), Chief of the Soviet General Staff, in 1983 stated, "We [the Soviet Union] will never be able to catch up with you [the United States] in modern arms until we have an economic revolution."[6] Ogarkov's comment demonstrates two important facts. First, military decisions rarely occur in a vacuum. Instead, military decisions are reached at the nexus of political, social, and cultural values and imperatives. Second, given that the Soviet Union eventually could not even meet the demands of this technological period, puts in perspective the challenge that smaller countries faced in meeting their defensive needs. Yugoslavia, which recognized this reality much sooner than the Soviet Union, confronted these implications while the two superpowers struggled for global hegemony.

Important to this discussion was that Yugoslavia, immediately after the Second World War, de-emphasized its irregular military culture in order to adopt a conventional army. Yugoslavia, during the Second World War, had been one of the few countries to wage a successful guerrilla war against the Axis occupation.[7] Nevertheless, Yugoslavia rejected this military tradition in the post–Cold War years for two reasons, the first of which was practical. Yugoslavia, in the immediate post–Second World War years, was an appendage of Soviet policy in the region.[8] For this purpose, a conventional force, with force projection capabilities, was of considerable greater utility than an irregular army, whose force projection capabilities would be minimal. The conventionalization of Yugoslavia, for lack of a better term, was successful to the point that it was considered by the United States intelligence to be the second strongest army in the Eastern Bloc, behind only the Soviets.[9] Given that the remainder of the Communist countries in the Balkans, because of their affiliation with Nazi Germany in the Second World War, had severely restricted armies, a conventionally strong Yugoslavia was of great utility to Soviet policy in the immediate postwar years.

The Soviets, to achieve this practical end, belittled the accomplishments of the Yugoslav partisans in order to hasten the military and political shift towards a conventional deterrent. Joseph Stalin (1878–1953), in an April 1945 meeting with Tito, compared the ineffectiveness of the Yugoslav partisan bands with the effectiveness of the Bulgarian army's conventional forces.[10] Because of the rivalry that existed between Yugoslavia and Bulgaria, this insult carried considerable weight.[11] Tito reached a breaking point, and according to Milovan Djilas (1911–1995), "shouted that the Yugoslav Army would quickly rid itself of its weaknesses," with weakness being associated with irregular warfare.[12] Tito's influence within the bureaucracy meant that this shift acquired significant institutional momentum, one that the Yugoslavs, over the next twenty years, would find difficult to alter.

Yugoslavia, however, was forced to develop an independent defense policy because of the Tito-Stalin Split, which occurred on 28 June 1948, when Yugoslavia was expelled from the Cominform.[13] The Tito-Stalin Split was a defining moment in the Cold War, as in time, it demonstrated to the outside world that international Communism was not a monolithic entity.[14] More consequential for Yugoslavia, however, was that it now faced the possibility of Soviet invasion with which it had to counter with relatively, sub-standard military equipment. As Tito was forced to later admit in a 1950 speech:

> It is true that we received some army equipment [from the Soviet Union], but this cost so much that if we had continued to buy from Russia our workers and peasants would have had to devote most of their work to paying for this brotherly aid. Of the 220 guns which the Soviet Union sent us, 85 were obsolete but repainted; some of the tanks were worn out; and 30 mobile tank-repair shops were incomplete. The field telephone units were and still are unworkable. Other supplies were equally worn, rusty, and useless.[15]

There is no way to confirm Tito's accusation that the poor quality of the equipment was the result of the Soviet Union's giving inferior equipment although the excessive cost of the equipment is at least confirmed by earlier Yugoslav reports regarding the fees associated with Soviet assistance.[16] Equally significant, however, was the question of quantity.

In the late 1940s and early 1950s, Yugoslavia's war industries were in a poor state of affairs. Tito, in the same speech where he described the low quality of Yugoslavia's military hardware, bluntly stated the status of the country's wartime industries: "Immediately after the last war Yugoslavia had no thought of intensive rearmament nor of building her own war industry, for at the time we relied on our alliance with the Soviet Union and the aid she promised us. Thus, Yugoslavia's few pre-war armament factories were turned over to producing machinery for agriculture and mining."[17]

Tito's apologetic purposes aside, he was being forthright when stating that Yugoslavia's military industries were underdeveloped. The Tito-Stalin Split had interrupted Yugoslavia's Five Year plan and thrown all segments of the economy, including military industries, into chaos.[18] According to Tito, Yugoslavia's solution to this dilemma in the early years of the Tito-Stalin Split was to "embark on [their] own rearmament program. The denunciation by the Cominform countries of their peace treaties forced us to speed up the construction of our war industry, since this was not included in the Five Year Plan which had just become law."[19] While this was a good start and provided

Yugoslavia with many small arms, Yugoslavia, in 1950, was incapable of designing, let alone producing, heavy conventional arms: tanks, jet-fighters, and other war materiel, which could compete with the Red Army.[20] A small, underdeveloped state like Yugoslavia lacked the internal means of defending itself, at least if its leadership insisted on undertaking the task by conventional means.

By 1951-2, the strategic situation had significantly shifted to the detriment of Yugoslavia, and as a result, it sought a significant material infusion from the United States. The Korean War demonstrated to the world that the Soviet Union could project its forces in an area that it deemed to be of strategic significance or where it believed it possessed a regional advantage.[21] The Balkans was one such region. A 1952 intelligence assessment by the CIA stated:

> If the adjacent Satellites, with Soviet logistic support, should attack before 1953, they could at least drive the Yugoslav forces from the plain area generally north and east of the Danube. The Yugoslav forces probably could not maintain effective organized resistance even in the mountainous area for an extended period unless adequately supported logistically from the outside.[22]

The report went on to elaborate the primary reason for this newfound vulnerability: its material decline relative to the Soviet satellite states. According to the report, "the numerical strength of the Yugoslav armed forces has remained relatively constant throughout the past two or three years, but Yugoslav materiel has deteriorated [relative to its opponents]."[23] Even this statement was an exaggeration, as it did not take into consideration the wear and tear associated with daily use. The Yugoslav People's Army needed modern weaponry if it were to defend itself against the Soviet Union's satellite states.

American military support to Yugoslavia was formalized in the "Military Assistance Agreement Between the United States and Yugoslavia" on 14 November 1951. The specific terms of the agreement are, admittedly, vague because of the nature of the agreement, but it provided the framework for American aid to Yugoslavia for the 1950s. According to Article I of the Military Assistance Agreement, the United States "will make or continue to make available to the Government of the Federal People's Republic of Yugoslavia equipment, materials, services, or other assistance" and in exchange, Yugoslavia committed to provide:

> the United States of America with reciprocal assistance by continuing to facilitate the production and transfer to the United States of America in such quantities and upon such terms and conditions as may be agreed on, of raw and semi-processed materials required by the United States of America as a result of deficiencies or potential deficiencies in its own resources, and which may be available in Yugoslavia.[24]

The Americans, in other words, would provide military hardware in exchange for Yugoslav raw materials for the American economy. For Yugoslavia in the 1950s, if it were to have a powerful conventional army in the age of heavy industry and rapid weapons development, it needed a powerful patron. Given the strategic realities of the Cold War, it was a mutually beneficial arrangement.

The results of American support for Yugoslavia's conventional army were dramatic. The Yugoslav armed forces, at the beginning of 1952, consisted of 325,000 men, organized into 32 divisions. Furthermore, Yugoslavia spent more on the military as a percentage of its national budget than any other state in the world.[25] Maintaining this rate of spending would have been impossible without causing severe social and cultural disorder, which would have only assisted the Soviet political offensive against Yugoslavia.[26] American military aid, however, stepped into this breach. Over the course of the 1950s, the United States committed three-fourths of a billion dollars in military aid to Yugoslavia.[27] In materiel terms, America's support in the 1950s worked out to 850 main battle tanks, mainly updated M4 Shermans; 1,580 anti-tank guns of various types; 100 Canadair Sabre jet interceptors; and 250 jet fighter bombers, of which were 200 Republic F84 Thunderjets and 50 North American F-86 Sabres.[28]

A major international development occurred just as American military aid was beginning to have its desired effect of increasing Yugoslavia's military capabilities: the death of Joseph Stalin on 5 March 1953. The Yugoslav government, with Stalin's death, was granted a temporary reprieve for two reasons. First, the internal struggle within the Communist Party of the Soviet Union leadership meant that the Soviet Union was unlikely to partake in any foreign adventures. In fact, the Soviet Union was likely to undertake less foreign adventures because of the internal instability that Stalin's death created.[29] Second, and more importantly, the new Soviet leadership, under General Secretary Nikita Khrushchev (1894–1971), recognized the mistakes of the Stalin period.[30] In particular, Khrushchev recognized the damage that the Tito-Stalin split had caused to the international socialist movement. This recognition culminated in Khrushchev's undertaking a visit to Yugoslavia on 2 June 1955, where he acknowledged the Yugoslav argument that there were different roads to communism.[31] Yugoslavia, at least temporarily, was safe from Soviet aggression.

It is important to note that while the Yugoslav government and armed forces emphasized a conventional defense between 1945–1955, they did not completely reject the idea, or implementation, of an irregular warfare option. In 1949, Svetozar Vukmanović-Tempo (1912–2000), one of Tito's most trusted aides, was made Chief Commander of Partisan Units. He described his activities as stockpiling "arms, mines, explosives—everything needed for action and which the army had at the time—were set apart for each area in which partisan and other groups were to operate. This material was well hidden in places known only to members of the units' headquarters."[32] To some degree, this was a practical recognition that even if Yugoslavia established a significant conventional force, it would be incapable of defeating the Soviet Union. In 1952, the Chief of Staff of the Yugoslav Army, Koča Popović (1908–1992), allegedly stated, "in one-week we will have a partisan movement, not a regular army."[33] While there is no way of confirming this statement, in the face of an overwhelming Soviet and Satellite attack, the reality of the situation would have been clear to Popović's military mind. Nevertheless, Yugoslavia continued to emphasize a conventional defense policy; until such a policy became untenable, institutional momentum would see that the conventional defense policy was emphasized.

Yugoslavia's new international environment also permitted the Belgrade regime to de-emphasize military spending and focus on its internal economic development. Yugoslavia's economic advancement during this period was nothing short of remarkable. The Yugoslav economy, from 1956 to 1964, had undergone rapid growth. Ljubomir Madžar, a Yugoslav economist, noted that the Yugoslav economy grew by 11.6 percent per annum between 1956–1960 and 8.6 percent per annum between 1960–1964.[34] This economic growth rate was greater than both that of the United States and the Soviet Union during this period.[35] While this growth, to a certain extent, was due to the underdeveloped nature of the Yugoslav economy, it still represented significant overall gains. Nevertheless, Yugoslavia still lagged behind the Great Powers from an absolute industrial and technological standpoint. In the "Conclusions of the Central Committee on Current Tasks of Communists in the Implementation of Reform" of 1966, the Central Committee of the LCY recognized that "the modernization of the economy on the basis of the latest scientific and technological achievements" was one of their vital tasks.[36] One area that the Yugoslav economy, in particular, was significantly behind Great Powers was in arms production.

Yugoslavia's newly reestablished relationship with the Soviet Union in the 1950s and '60s was the only factor that permitted it to develop an extensive domestic arms industry. While this relationship allowed Yugoslavia to develop in some areas, most notably small arms, Yugoslavia's small industrial base and economic limitations hindered its ability to create domestically complex weaponry. This issue is best demonstrated by examining the aeronautics industry. According to Marko Milivojević, "by 1961, a mixture of reverse-engineering (copying foreign designs), foreign licenses and the development of indigenous design/production capabilities had enabled Yugoslavia to produce a number of [...] weapons systems."[37] Specifically, Yugoslavia was able to produce several varieties of ground-attack aircraft, most notably the *Galeb* and *Jastreb*. While developing these planes was an accomplishment in itself, the *Galeb* and *Jastreb* would not ensure air superiority in case of war with either superpower.

The weakness of Yugoslavia's military industrial complex was that except for relatively simple weapons, like the *Galeb* and *Jastreb*, the country could not produce front line machinery needed for a conventional conflict. Yugoslavia's military industrial complex was still largely dependent upon the Soviet Union for technological development and licensing rights, which it had achieved during the rapprochement between the USSR and Yugoslavia that occurred in the aftermath of Khrushchev's 1955 visit. For example, between 1962 and 1968, Yugoslavia imported from the Soviet Union 760 T-54/55s, 200 BTR-40/50/60s, 1,000 various pieces of artillery, 15 *Shersen* torpedo boats, and 140 MiG-21s.[38] The only way that Yugoslavia was able to maintain a conventional defense policy, in other words, was through the external support of the Soviet Union, especially given the country's lack of a nuclear deterrent.[39] The inability to possess nuclear weapons further limited Yugoslavia's ability to possess a conventional deterrent. Nevertheless, only when it became impossible for Yugoslavia to receive the conventional support it needed would it be forced to re-evaluate its defense policy.

While Yugoslavia's military capabilities were declining, relative to what they had been at the start of the Tito-Stalin split, this was in part due to the country's pursuit of the policy of Non-Alignment. Officially founded in Belgrade in 1961, the policy, as Rinna Kullaa notes in *Non-Alignment and its Origins in Cold War Europe*, can actually be traced as far back as the Tito-Stalin split, when Yugoslavia committed itself to an independent course under Soviet pressure to conform.[40] By officially pursuing the policy in 1961, however, Yugoslavia formally committed itself to an independent course, and in the future, conflicts would not be able to appeal to one of the blocs to protect it from another powerful alliance. Committing itself to a foreign policy of non-alignment had major strategic ramifications, but only if relations with one of the blocs declined. During most of the 1960s when Yugoslavia maintained cordial relations with both blocs, this was not a significant issue.[41] Only when the international environment changed would Yugoslavia be forced to confront their newfound isolation.

Yugoslav fears of invasion and the evidence that their defense policy was unable to meet their foreign policy requirements became evident after the Warsaw Pact's invasion of Czechoslovakia in 1968. Warsaw Pact forces moved against Czechoslovakia in 1968 in order to halt the country's liberalization policies under Alexander Dubček (1921–1992). The Soviets belatedly legitimized their actions by proclaiming the Brezhnev Doctrine. The Brezhnev Doctrine stated that the measures taken by the Soviet Union, jointly with other socialist countries, in defending the socialist gains of the Czechoslovak people are of great significance for strengthening the socialist community, which is the main achievement of the international working class. [...] The sovereignty of each socialist country cannot be opposed to the interests of the world of socialism, of the world revolutionary movement. Lenin demanded that all Communists fight against small nation narrow-mindedness, seclusion and isolation, consider the whole and the general, subordinate the particular to the general interest.[42]

All socialist countries were supposed to submit to the international—in actual fact Soviet—interests. This policy statement directly threatened Yugoslavia, as the most deviant of Eastern Bloc countries. Yugoslavia's government, both publically and privately, condemned the invasion and what they saw as the Soviets' attempting to impose "limited sovereignty" upon the socialist world. While the Soviet Union would later try to allay these concerns, they were too late. Yugoslavia, responding to the Brezhnev Doctrine, passed the 1969 National Defense Law, which contained within it the essence of the defense policy that Yugoslavia would possess for the remainder of its existence: TND.

The Yugoslav People's Army of the 1950s, one that had proven capable, for the most part, of assuring Yugoslavia's independence, no longer existed. Furthermore, the rate at which military technology was developing had accelerated its decline even further. As Ljubomir Petrović explained in 1970, "Weapons and military equipment 'age' very rapidly. At the time of the First World War, they could be used for 20 years, while now, under present-day conditions, they become obsolete in a matter of five years. The development of armaments and equipment is now an expression of scientific and technological progress."[43]

While this statement is slightly hyperbolic, the fact that it was published in one of the official journals of the League of Communists of Yugoslavia is demonstrative of it at least being taken seriously within party circles. Yugoslav officials certainly would have liked to be at the forefront of this arms production, but the size of the country's economy, relative to the rest of the world, precluded it from participating.[44] In other words, Yugoslavia, if it wished to be nominally independent of super bloc politics, would have to develop a defense policy that allowed it to overcome its technological and industrial weaknesses.

The 1969 National Defense Law maintained a conventional deterrent yet primarily sought to overcome its technological and industrial weakness by developing a new body: the Territorial Defense Forces (TDF). The TDF was Yugoslavia's recognition, as General Nikola Ljubičić (1916–2005) later explained, "of the people as a military factor."[45] The TDF, at first glance, was similar to other reserve forces in other countries. Like most reserve forces, the TDF consisted of individuals who had served in the YPA as conscripts and were then required to serve part-time in the TDF until the age of 60. Periodic training would ensure that the soldier's individual skills, in theory, would not deteriorate. Furthermore, it would be able to launch a variety of military operations. As Tito explained:

> Territorial Defence, the most massive part of our armed forces, is distinguished by a wealth of organizational forms and ability to engage in fast, effective, elastic and varied forms of combat and all other forms of struggle and resistance. I specially wish to stress that Territorial Defence should retain and nurture the specific features of its internal organization and methods of most adequate use. In line with this, it is imperative further to create latitude for development of self-management initiative and responsibility of working people and citizens, young people and women, organization of associated labour, neighbourhood communities and organizations, in relation to Territorial Defence. Training and preparation for combat and all other forms of struggle and resistance should embrace a still larger number of people, both men and women, and young people as well.[46]

In order to fulfill the above principles, the TDF was broken down into two distinct branches. The first branch, the maneuvering brigades, can be described as an addition to the traditional reserve of the YPA. These units, Col. Mihajlo Čanović explained, would "depending on their equipment, fire power, and combat capacity and mobility, [...] operate as modern combat formations."[47] Evidently, while there was much desire to completely decentralize command functions, this was not completely the case, as Čanović noted that "if necessary, some of such units can be converted into YPA units."[48] This mixed approach to the maneuvering brigades, effectively YPA formations but organized at the republic level, shows the tension that existed within Yugoslav military between those who wished to maintain a conventional force and those who advocated the exploitation of Yugoslavia's manpower resources for greatest effect.

The second part of the TDF, the "Tactical Units of Territorial Defense," was much closer to the partisan roots of the YPA. Col. Čanović described these units as being "designed for operations in a narrow territory; they are made up of numerous units of varied kind, organized, outfitted, and trained for carrying out various missions within the territory which they cover."[49] What was meant in this context by the term "various missions" was that the units would conduct any armed resistance that forced an invading army to commit significant troops to maintain control of the region. As these units would be conducting irregular operations and needed every tactical advantage that they could obtain, they were "formed at the level of communes, local communities and organizations of associated labour" within the area that they would operate.[50] By emphasizing local roots, the tactical units, although not as well trained as a traditional army, would compensate through their specialization in local terrain. Furthermore, being decentralized entities, the Tactical TD units would not be vulnerable to a blitzkrieg offensive, thereby fulfilling one of the primary requirements of TND and further strengthening Yugoslavia's shift from a conventional to unconventional defense to cover up the weaknesses of its technological and industrial underdevelopment. Small, guerrilla bands operating on the periphery were fully able to exploit Yugoslavia's proficiency in small arms, and caches of them were positioned throughout the country, but particularly in the mountainous redoubt of Bosnia and Herzegovina, to ensure the country's continued resistance.

Despite being a military organizational success, Yugoslavia's development of Total National Defence also helped sow the seeds of its destruction. In its effort to ensure that Yugoslavia was safe from external threats, it overlooked the fact that devolution of powers made it easier for nationalist forces to destabilize the federation. Although unity was always emphasized in any publications on TND, the only organization that took the threat seriously, particularly after Tito's death in 1980, was the YPA. As a political force, however, the YPA was increasingly marginalized in the inter-republic political fighting that became increasingly prevalent throughout the 1980s.[51] When Yugoslavia proceeded down the path of civil war, the republics, despite the YPA's efforts to recentralize command functions and alter TND to be a more conventional army, found that the defense policy had provided them with ready-made armies with which to pursue their secessionist policies.[52]

Yugoslavia, in an effort to overcome their economic, technological, and industrial weaknesses, attempted several different means, eventually culminating in their development of TND in 1969. While initially Yugoslavia was able to overcome their developmental problems through external support, whether being from the Soviet Union or the United States, their desire to pursue an independent foreign policy meant that this was impossible. Instead, Yugoslavia would have to rely upon its internal strength to achieve the security of the states, which meant relying on the one resource— manpower instead of technology—that it had in abundance. In so doing, Yugoslavia created a comprehensive defense system that was capable of resisting outside aggression or at least making it so costly that attacking the country was not an option. While it succeeded in this objective, it was such an effective policy that it helped lay the grounds for the state's eventual dissolution.

NOTES

1. Josip Broz Tito, "The League of Communists of Yugoslavia and Total National Defence and Social Self-Protection" *Socialist Thought and Practice* 19 (1978) 36.

2. The relationship between Yugoslavia and the Western Bloc in the Cold War is complex. While some scholars have argued that Yugoslavia had little to fear from the West, it remained a potential threat within Yugoslav military thought for most of its existence. In fact, when the Yugoslav People's Army attempted to suppress the

Slovenian and Croatian independence movements, it was able to mobilize in an efficient manner in part due to the plan's congruence with troop positions for a feared invasion by NATO forces. See: Martin Špegelj, "The First Phase, 1990: the JNA prepares for aggression and Croatia for defence," in *The War in Croatia and Bosnia-Herzegovina, 1991-1995*, ed. Branka Magaš and Ivo Žanić (London: Frank Cass, 2001), 25.

3. Even France, which for both political and prestige purposes withdrew from NATO's integrated command structure in 1966, still remained a member of the alliance and, through the Lemnitzer-Ailleret Agreements in 1967, was accounted for in NATO grand strategy. See Sten Rynning, *Changing Military Doctrine: Presidents and Military Power in Fifth Republic France, 1958-2000* (Westport, CT: Greenwood Publishing Group, 2001), 54–55.

4. Jeremy Black, *War and Technology* (Bloomington: Indiana University Press, 2013), 54.

5. Black, *War and Technology*, 16.

6. General Nikolai Ogarkov, *Chief of the Soviet General Staff*, cited in L.H. Gelb, "Who Won the Cold War?" *New York Times*. 20 August 1992.

7. For a nuanced look at Second World War Yugoslavia see: Stevan K. Pavlowitch, *Hitler's New Disorder: The Second World War in Yugoslavia* (New York: Columbia University Press, 2008), passim.

8. For an examination of Yugoslavia's actions in the immediate post-war period see: Lorraine M. Lees, *Keeping Tito Afloat: The United States, Yugoslavia, and the Cold War* (University Park: Pennsylvania State University Press, 1997), 1–44.

9. Military Intelligence Division, cited in Lees, *Keeping Tito Afloat*, 9.

10. Milovan Djilas, *Conversations with Stalin* (New York: Harcourt Brace, 1963), 112.

11. Much of the Bulgarian-Serbian/Yugoslav rivalry was the result of their mutual competition for Ottoman Macedonia. For a clear analysis see: Evangelos Kofos, *Nationalism and Communism in Macedonia* (Thessaloniki, Institute for Balkan Studies, 1964), passim.

12. Djilas, *Conversations with Stalin*, 112.

13. The Cominform was the international communist coordinating body that succeeded the Third Communist International. For an analysis of Soviet intentions behind the Cominform see: Vojtech Mastny, *The Cold War and Soviet Insecurity: The Stalin Years* (New York: Oxford University Press, 1996), 30–47.

14. Wayne S. Vucinich, *At the Brink of War and Peace: The Tito-Stalin Split in a Historic Perspective* (New York: Brooklyn College Press, 1982) passim.

15. Josip Broz Tito, 'Speech on 28 December 1950,' *Documents on International Affairs, 1949-50*, ed. S. Everett Gleason et al., vol. IV (London: Oxford University Press, 1953), 505–6.

16. Djilas, *Conversations with Stalin*, 155.

17. Josip Broz Tito, "Speech on 28 December 1950," 505.

18. Lees, *Keeping Tito Afloat*, 60.

19. Josip Broz Tito, "Speech on 28 December 1950," 506.

20. Marko Milivojevic, *Yugoslavia's Military Industries* (Bradford, UK: University of Bradford, 1990), 1–4.

21. Mastny, *The Cold War and Soviet Insecurity*, 96–7.

22. "Probable Developments in Yugoslavia and the Liklihood of Attack Upon Yugoslavia, Through 1952," Central Intelligence Agency, http://www.foia.cia.gov/sites/default/files/document_conversions/89801/DOC_0000269266.pdf (Last access, 17 February 2014).

23. Ibid.

24. "Military Assistance Agreement Between the United States and Yugoslavia on 14 November 1951," in *American Foreign Policy 1950–1955, Basic Documents*, Vol. I (Washington, D.C.: U.S. Government Printing Office, 1957) 2160–63.

25. In 1952, Yugoslavia spent twenty-two percent of its national budget on defense. See A. Ross Johnson, *Total National Defense in Yugoslavia* (Santa Monica, CA: RAND Corporation, 1971), 2.

26. Ivo Banac, *With Stalin against Tito: Cominformist Splits in Yugoslav Communism* (Ithaca, NY: Cornell University Press, 1988), passim.

27. Calculations based off information in Stephen Broadberry and Alexander Klein's, "Aggregate and Per Capita GDP in Europe, 1870–2000: Continental, Regional, and National Data with Changing Boundaries" (Paper presented at European Commission's 7th Framework Programme for Research, Brussels, Belgium, 2011); and Ljubomir Madžar, "Economic Development, 1947–1968," *The Yugoslav Survey* 11 (1970): 26.

28. Ronald L. Tarnstrom, *Handbooks of Armed Forces: The Balkans*, Part II (Lindsberg, KS: Trogen Publications, 1981; 3rd Ed.: 1984) 104–5, 119–121.

29. This theory, however, is undergoing increased academic scrutiny. See Balázs Szalontai, *Kim Il Sung in the Khrushchev Era: Soviet-DPRK Relations and the Roots of Despotism, 1953–1964* (Stanford: Stanford University Press, 2006) 34.

30. Most symbolic of this shift was the 'Secret Speech' Khrushchev later delivered in 1956. See Nikita Khrushchev, *Speech to 20th Congress of the C.P.S.U.*, 24–25 February 1956. http://www.marxists.org/archive/khrushchev/1956/02/24.htm (Last access, 12 May 2014).

31. Albert S. Lindemann, *A History of European Socialism* (New Haven, CT: Yale University Press, 1984), 329.

32. Svetozar Vukmanović-Tempo, *Revolucija koja teče* (Belgrade: Kommunist, 1971), 106.

33. Popović, cited in Roberts 150.

34. Ljubomir Madžar, "Economic Development, 1947–1968," *The Yugoslav Survey* 11 (1970): 26.

35. American annual growth from 1945–1960 was 6.3% and the USSR's growth rate between -1958 was also 6.3%. See: Ross Gregory, *Cold War America, 1946 to 1990* (New York: Facts on File, 2002), 69.

36. "Conclusions of the Central Committee on Current Tasks of Communists in the Implementation of Reform," *Socialist Thought and Practice* 6 (1966): 130.

37. Milivojević, *Yugoslavia's Military Industries*, 5.

38. Ibid., 5–6.

39. Yugoslavia did launch a nuclear weapons program in 1950, but for mysterious reasons deactivated before the Prague Spring. See Stevan Dedijer, *Stevan Dedijer—My Life of Curiosity and Insights: A Chronicle of the 20th Century* (Lund, SE: Nordic Academic Press, 2009) 168 and Andrew Koch, "Yugoslavia's Nuclear Legacy," *The Nonproliferation Review* 4 (1997): 124.

40. Rinna Kullaa, *Non-Alignment and its Origins in Cold War Europe: Yugoslavia, Finland and the Soviet Challenge* (London: I.B. Tauris, 2012), 26–51.

41. For the Yugoslav perspective on relations during this time, see: "Relations between Yugoslavia and the U.S.S.R. (1955–1969)," *The Yugoslav Survey* 11 (1970): 121–156.

42. Pravda, cited in L. S. Stavrianos, *The Epic of Man* (Englewood Cliffs, N.J.: Prentice Hall, 1971), 465–466.

43. Ljubomir Petrović, "War Production and Social Reproduction," *Socialist Thought and Practice* 10 (1970): 53.
44. See footnote 1.
45. Nikola Ljubičić, "The Epoch-Making Significance of Tito's Military Achievement," *Socialist Thought and Practice* 17 (1977): 4.
46. Josip Broz Tito, "President Tito on Total National Defence," *Yugoslav Survey* 18 (1977): 3-24.
47. Ibid., 23.
48. Mihajlo Čanović, "Territorial Defence of the SFRY," *Yugoslav Survey* 21 (1980): 53-60.
49. Ibid., 56.
50. Ibid., 57.
51. For an analysis of the political role of the Yugoslav People's Army's in the country's collapse see: Miroslav Hadžić, *The Yugoslav People's Agony: The Role of the Yugoslav People's Army* (Farnham, Surrey, UK: Ashgate Publishing, 2002).
52. How the TDF's, and the Civilian Defence Forces, contributed to the collapse of Yugoslavia is fully explored in Jamie Horncastle, "A House of Cards: The Yugoslav Concept of Total National Defence and its Critical Weakness," *Macedonian Historical Review* 2 (2011): 285-302.

Works Cited

American Foreign Policy 1950-1955, Basic Documents, Vol. I. Washington, D.C.: U.S. Government Printing Office, 1957.

Banac, Ivo. *With Stalin against Tito: Cominformist Splits in Yugoslav Communism*. Ithaca, NY: Cornell University Press, 1988.

Black, Jeremy. *War and Technology*. Bloomington: Indiana University Press, 2013.

Broadberry, Stephen and Klein, Alexander. "Aggregate and Per Capita GDP in Europe, 1870-2000: Continental, Regional, and National Data with Changing Boundary," Paper presented at European Commission's 7th Framework Programme for Research. Brussels, Belgium, 2011.

Čanović, Mihajlo. "Territorial Defence of the SFRY," *Yugoslav Survey* 21 (1980): 53-60.

"Conclusions of the Central Committee on Current Tasks of Communists in the Implementation of Reform," *Socialist Thought and Practice* 6 (1966): 128-38.

Dedijer, Stevan. *Stevan Dedijer—My Life of Curiosity and Insights: A Chronicle of the 20th Century*. Lund, SE: Nordic Academic Press, 2009.

Djilas, Milovan. *Conversations with Stalin*. New York: Harcourt Brace, 1963.

Documents on International Affairs, 1949-50. Ed. S. Everett Gleason et al. Vol. IV. London: Oxford University Press, 1953.

Gelb, L.H. "Who Won the Cold War?" *New York Times*. 20 August 1992.

Gregory, Ross. *Cold War America, 1946 to 1990*. New York: Facts on File, 2002.

Hadžić, Miroslav. *The Yugoslav People's Agony: The Role of the Yugoslav People's Army*. Farnham, Surrey, UK: Ashgate Publishing, 2002.

Horncastle, Jamie. "A House of Cards: The Yugoslav Concept of Total National Defence and its Critical Weakness," *Macedonian Historical Review* 2 (2011): 285-302.

Johnson, Ross A. *Total National Defense in Yugoslavia*. Santa Monica, CA: RAND Corporation, 1971.

Khrushchev, Nikita. *Speech to 20th Congress of the C.P.S.U., 24-25 February 1956*. http://www.marxists.org/archive/khrushchev/1956/02/24.htm.

Koch, Andrew. "Yugoslavia's Nuclear Legacy," *The Nonproliferation Review* 4 (1997): 123–8.
Kofos, Evangelos. *Nationalism and Communism in Macedonia*. Thessaloniki: Institute for Balkan Studies, 1964.
Kullaa, Rinna. *Non-Alignment and its Origins in Cold War Europe: Yugoslavia, Finland and the Soviet Challenge*. London: I.B. Tauris, 2012.
Lees, Lorraine M. *Keeping Tito Afloat: The United States, Yugoslavia, and the Cold War*. University Park: Pennsylvania State University Press, 1997.
Ljubičić, Nikola. "The Epoch-Making Significance of Tito's Military Achievement," *Socialist Thought and Practice* 17 (1977): 3–30.
Lindemann, Albert S. *A History of European Socialism*. New Haven, CT: Yale University Press, 1984.
Madžar, Ljubomir. "Economic Development, 1947–1968," *The Yugoslav Survey* 11 (1970): 23–42.
Mastny, Vojtech. *The Cold War and Soviet Insecurity: The Stalin Years*. New York: Oxford University Press, 1996.
Milivojevic, Marko. *Yugoslavia's Military Industries*. Bradford, UK: University of Bradford, 1990.
Pavlowitch, Stevan K. *Hitler's New Disorder: The Second World War in Yugoslavia*. New York: Columbia University Press, 2008.
Petrović, Ljubomir. "War Production and Social Reproduction," *Socialist Thought and Practice* 10 (1970): 46–58.
"Probable Developments in Yugoslavia and the Liklihood of Attack Upon Yugoslavia, Through 1952," *Central Intelligence Agency*. http://www.foia.cia.gov/sites/default/files/document_conversions/89801/DOC_0000269266.pdf.
"Relations between Yugoslavia and the U.S.S.R. (1955–1969)," *The Yugoslav Survey* 11 (1970): 121–56.
Rynning, Sten. *Changing Military Doctrine: Presidents and Military Power in Fifth Republic France, 1958–2000*. Westport, CT: Greenwood Publishing Group, 2001.
Špegelj, Martin. "The First Phase, 1990: the JNA prepares for aggression and Croatia for defence," in *The War in Croatia and Bosnia-Herzegovina, 1991–1995*, ed. Branka Magaš and Ivo Žanić. London: Frank Cass, 2001, 14–40.
Stavrianos, L.S. *The Epic of Man*. Englewood Cliffs, N.J.: Prentice Hall, 1971.
Szalontai, Balázs. *Kim Il Sung in the Khrushchev Era: Soviet-DPRK Relations and the Roots of Despotism, 1953–1964*. Stanford: Stanford University Press, 2006.
Tarnstrom, Ronald L. *Handbooks of Armed Forces: The Balkans, Part II*. Lindsberg, KS: Trogen Publications, 1981; 3rd Ed.: 1984.
Tito, Josip Broz. "The League of Communists of Yugoslavia and Total National Defence and Social Self-Protection," *Socialist Thought and Practice* 19 (1978):
Tito, Josip Broz. "President Tito on Total National Defence," *Yugoslav Survey* 18 (1977): 3–24.
Vucinich, Wayne S. *At the Brink of War and Peace: The Tito-Stalin Split in a Historic Perspective*. New York: Brooklyn College Press, 1982.
Vukmanović-Tempo, Svetozar. *Revolucija koja teče*. Belgrade: Kommunist, 1971.

Technology, Warfare and Intra-Alliance Rivalry
The U.S.-West German Main Battle Tank Harmonization in the 1970s

BENEDICT VON BREMEN

The Cold War between the North Atlantic Treaty Organization (NATO) and the Warsaw Pact (WP) never turned into a "hot" conflict but resulted in an international arms race consuming billions of dollars in tax money whereby falling behind meant a disadvantage—and possible annihilation—in a potential war.[1] The latter's main battlefield would most likely be a divided Germany, the so-called Central Region[2] where 620,000 soldiers from seven NATO nations—the Federal Republic of Germany (FRG), the United States of America, the United Kingdom, the Netherlands, Belgium, Canada, and France[3]—were stationed west of the Intra-German Border.[4] Both military blocs were armed to the teeth with an ever-evolving arsenal ranging from small arms to nuclear weapons. While all NATO countries had a common goal—deterring a WP attack in the first place and successful defense in the case of war—the allies also had national security and economic interests that at times, turned friends into rivals.[5] This was especially obvious in defense cooperation, i.e., collaborating on researching, developing, producing, and fielding military materiel. While, theoretically, having the same—or standardized[6]—weapons in an alliance means streamlined and cheaper logistics and supply,[7] the latter two are mostly national responsibilities in NATO. Its military arsenals were and are, therefore, highly destandardized.[8] It was in the mid-1970s that questions about NATO's military capabilities, the economic means to achieve them, and intra-alliance economic rivalry often culminated in public discussions about multinational defense cooperation. A case example for this is the harmonization of the latest generation of main battle tanks (MBT) by the West German *Bundeswehr* and the United States Army which also functions as a lens to look at the Cold War context of changing transatlantic relations and NATO's evolving military strategy and tactics.

In the early years of NATO, much military materiel was provided by the United States to its Western European[9] allies, whose defense industries had been largely destroyed in World War II. In the late 1950s, a shift occurred from buying ready-made U.S. materiel to purchasing licenses. Western European defense industries became capable of manufacturing materiel themselves again, and licensing helped European NATO members to improve by gaining insight into modern—i.e. American—ways of production. In the 1960s, larger European NATO members such as France, the United Kingdom, and in part, also West Germany, could provide much of their armed forces' needs through domestic production again. While the 1950s had been a time of quasi-standardization based on American defense goods, the 1960s saw a destandardization of national arsenals in NATO.[10]

In almost all modern and sophisticated areas, though, the United States was leading, especially in air and space technology. An example is the widely licensed F-104 "Starfighter" jet fielded by about half of NATO's air forces. West Germany, with a barely existent air and space industry after World War II, especially profited highly from licensing. After a hesitant start in the 1950s, the following decade saw the resurgence of a West German defense industry base in certain areas such as small arms[11] and tracked vehicles, especially tanks,[12] for which Germany had built up an (in)famous reputation in World War II. In other areas in which West Germany lacked expertise such as in missile technology, the FRG began to heavily cooperate with France after the 1963 Elysée Treaty.[13] West Germany, therefore, was both dependent on and highly profiting from international arms cooperation.[14]

NATO itself devised only a short-lived program for multinational cooperation. These NATO Basic Military Requirements (NBRMs) were intended to improve standardization on the alliance level since problems of supply became more and more obvious with growing re-nationalization and destandardization. Only a few bi- or at most trinational projects, though, were successfully completed, making it from the research and development (R&D) phase to field service.[15] Several problems concerning multinational defense cooperation surfaced, most importantly differing national requirements, varying replacement cycles, and not least industry interests.[16]

Conspicuously absent in these collaborative efforts was the United States. Due to its industrial base, research capabilities, and financial means, it could afford to unilaterally upkeep all-spectrum armed forces on land, in the air, and on and below sea, providing them with American-made materiel from combat boots to intercontinental missiles.[17] In one field, though, the U.S. seemed to lag behind: main battle tanks (MBT).

The MBT concept of a relatively lightweight, agile standard tank with large firepower replaced tanks of different classes—light, medium, heavy— and their accompanying World War II era tactics from the 1950s to 1960s. Tanks were perhaps *the* symbol of land warfare, in which the alleged numerical superiority of the Red Army was especially conspicuous. At the Lisbon Conference in 1952, NATO members had agreed upon conventional (non-nuclear) force numbers of 96 army divisions but in reality, never reached more than about 30.[18] During the years of "massive retaliation,"[19] conventional forces served merely as a "tripwire" to set off nuclear exchange (or to deter armed conflict in the first place); manpower was substituted with kilotons. This changed with the Kennedy Administration's introduction of "flexible response." The new strategy entailed replying to different threats at varying levels of escalation instead of answering any type of aggression with a massive retaliatory nuclear strike. This necessitated an improvement of conventional forces throughout the alliance, and only after years of heated debate was flexibility of response adopted by NATO[20] in 1967.[21]

It was under the aegis of U.S. Secretary of Defense Robert McNamara, a prominent proponent of both "flexible response" and reliance on technological superiority, that a U.S.–West German MBT cooperation—at the time one of the few transatlantic collaborative projects—came into being: the MBT-70, or Panzer 70. In the 1960s, the development of the Leopard 1[22] showed the expertise of West German tank manufacturers, while the latest—and first—U.S. MBT, the M-60, proved unsatisfactory. West German–American cooperation on an MBT seemed logical; the Germans had the know-how to produce state-of-the-art tanks, while the Americans could provide latest-generation technology.[23] This common endeavor, therefore, suggested benefits for both sides. Research and development (R&D) started, but the problems of multi-, or in this case bi-, national cooperation soon surfaced. There was no common staff but rather two separate national ones that could not, when they met at all, even agree on simple but important questions such as whether to use either the imperial or the metric system. The main problems, as with many cooperative defense projects, were diverging national requirements. In its last (and still prototype stage) model, the MBT-70 was everything—and nothing. Everything, because as many requirements as possible from both sides had been incorporated into the design; nothing, because trying to please everyone made the Panzer 70 too big and conspicuous because of its size and most of all, too expensive. First, the West Germans in 1969 and then the Americans backed out in 1971 because of alleged fiscal constraints. The MBT-70 was history. Ideas for another West German MBT, the Leopard II, were already on the shelf, and its fielding was scheduled for the 1970s. The U.S. Army, though, was still lacking a capable MBT. The M-60 was quickly outdated with regards to the latest generation of Soviet tanks such as the T-62 and the T-72, while the Leopard II was designed to (out)match its possible eastern adversaries.[24]

The end of the Vietnam War meant a renewed American focus on Europe.[25] The next conflict was supposed to be fought in the Central Region, where the experience not of jungle and guerrilla warfare but of World War II and its tank battles seemed to count. Many military reformers of the post-Vietnam U.S. Army were veterans of that conflict. They wanted to win the next war, and their role model became Israel, which had, in 1973, defended itself against the numerical superiority of Egyptian and Syrian armed columns. The lessons of the October War, in which some of the latest designs of U.S. and Soviet arms manufacture had been pitted against each other, were, in the eyes of both U.S. and West German military men, applicable to a possible conflict in the Central Region. Here, numerically outmatched but technologically superior NATO troops, just like the Israeli Defense Forces, would wage a mobile defense based on counter-offensives. This was fully in tune with NATO's strategy of "flexible response," under which conventional warfare had become feasible again in order to resort to tactical nuclear battlefield weapons as late as possible.[26] One of the major weapons of the 1973 October War was the MBT, a proof for supporters of armored warfare that the advent of guided missiles—also heavily used in the Middle East—did not spell the end of the tank. This made it ever more pressing for the U.S. Armed Forces to introduce a capable MBT, and development of the XM-1 tank started frantically in 1973.[27]

The 1970s also saw a renewed interest and felt a need for NATO standardization, this time on both sides of the Atlantic. As mentioned earlier, the introduction of flexible response necessitated the improvement of the conventional part of the NATO triad of deterrence/defense next to tactical battlefield and strategic nuclear weapons—the latter two majorly, if not solely, supplied by the United States. The USSR's heavy investment in the modernization and build-up of its armed forces in all fields during the Brezhnev era made this all the more pressing.[28] The 1970s also saw the end of the post–World War II boom years and their economic growth.[29] Instead of investing in latest generation war materiel, some European NATO countries cut down their troop numbers and saved money by delaying the introduction of new materiel, thereby drawing criticism of not sharing the burden of the common defense.[30] The question, especially from 1974 on, was how to strengthen NATO in the face of such odds.

One solution seemed to be "RSI" (Rationalization, Standardization, Interoperability).[31] Interoperability meant using at least standardized ammunition,[32] fuel, and spare parts (while the actual weapons—whether assault rifles or airplanes—were still nationally developed and produced) to streamline logistics. While complete, alliance-wide standardization was deemed impossible, more multinational collaborative ventures would, at least, foster partial standardization. This all should have helped to rationalize NATO: spending available money for defense more economically and at the same time strengthening the alliance's military capabilities. The earlier mentioned destandardization of NATO arsenals remained a main focus of RSI (and multinational defense cooperation) proponents, with the prime example often promulgated at the time being the Warsaw Pact and its *de facto* standardization on Soviet materiel.[33]

Fueling the pleas for more cooperation, the 1974 "Callaghan Report"[34] called for a transatlantic "two-way street" of arms, technology, and cash flow. Callaghan's rationale was that America should purchase more European-made materiel. With U.S. dollars, European allies could then spend more on sophisticated American weaponry, thereby helping standardization, strengthening NATO's defenses, and easing economic competition between the military allies. Already in the mid-1960s, European complaints talked of a "technology gap" between America and its allies, urging for more transatlantic cooperation so that NATO Europe could benefit from the U.S. technological advances. America, though, was unwilling to freely provide its latest knowledge, as technological superiority was seen as an important advantage in the Cold War arms race with the Soviet Union, and instead promoted more European cooperation.[35] A successful outcome of the latter, at least according to proponents of defense collaboration who believed cooperation could work, was the West German-British-Italian Multi-Role Combat Aircraft (MRCA) "Tornado."[36]

In 1974, a Memorandum of Understanding (MoU) was signed between the West German Minister and U.S. Secretary of Defense, Georg Leber and James Schlesinger, respectively—both promoters of more intra-allied cooperation—pledging to work together on their respective current MBT programs.[37] West German print media, ranging from weekly news magazine *Der Spiegel*[38] to special interest defense industry outlets such as *Wehr & Technik*,[39] especially saw the "harmonization" of the American XM-1 and West German Leopard II programs as a test case for the two-way street—and particularly for American willingness to actually cooperate on such transatlantic endeavors. It seems, though, that West German commentators misinterpreted the "nebulous"[40] MoU. Many of them thought that should the Leopard II prove superior in American tests—and West German experts were more than sure about this—the U.S. Army would then adopt it as its new MBT (and West Germany would gain entrance into the lucrative U.S. defense market). This, though, was only an option for the United States.[41] When a Leopard II model was provided for testing in late 1976 and early 1977, the concept of the two-way street was severely strained.

Before this examination, the Leopard II had already had to pass a number of American hurdles: Congress, the U.S. military, and the American developers of XM-1 prototypes (General Motors and Chrysler). In his memoirs, then–Secretary of Defense Donald Rumsfeld talks of "the iron triangle" in the Pentagon: "a network of entrenched relationships among the military and civilian bureaucracies in the Defense Department, the Congress, and the defense industry."[42] According to its nature, Congress is made up of politicians representing different (and at times differing) interests, and especially representatives with defense factories in their constituency will press for "buying American."[43] Congressmen in the Armed Services Committees will search for the best—that is, quickest and most cost-effective—solutions for the U.S. Armed Forces. The military, of course, also has its interests: to provide its soldiers with the best materiel possible, fitting the specific requirements of the armed forces. The defense industry wants to gain national contracts and will argue its case for keeping jobs as well as promulgating the superiority of U.S. materiel geared specifically for U.S. forces. Thus, the circle of the "iron triangle" closes.

Donald Rumsfeld, who had been U.S. ambassador to NATO under Nixon before he became secretary of defense under Ford, must have been aware of the needs of America's European allies. According to Rumsfeld's memoirs, he personally had to interfere with the Army's 1976 decision to announce an American winner for the XM-1 prototype competition before actually testing the Leopard II.[44] The contrary would have surely upset the West German allies not only because of their high hopes but also because of the signal effect it would have had on the two-way street and, therefore, America's willingness to work with its NATO partners instead of continuing to go it alone. The internal peace of the alliance seemed to be in danger. To the chagrin of the "iron triangle," the XM-1 decision for an American model was delayed in favor of the two-way street.

Nevertheless, the results of the U.S. tests of the Leopard II, published in early 1977, must have been pleasing to the iron triangle. The Chrysler XM-1 prototype satisfied most U.S. Army requirements for a new MBT, while many features of the Leopard II deemed important by the *Bundeswehr* such as *Tiefwatfähigkeit*,[45] did not play a role. This shows an already mentioned problem of multinational defense cooperation: differing national requirements. Still, an uproar went through the German press. *Der Spiegel* titled "Orientalische Sitten," accused the U.S. of continuing to "Buy American."[46] *Wehr & Technik* commentaries opined that West German know-how had been leaked to the U.S. without any reciprocal benefits for Germany (a claim usually made by U.S. critics of transatlantic defense cooperation because of fears that U.S. technology could be leaked, via exports, to America's enemies).[47] The view of the U.S. as unwilling to embark on a genuine two-way street was affirmed for West German commentators. Instead of a *Zweibahnstraße*, this was apparently more of the old *Einbahnstraße*, or one-way street. Other transatlantic defense projects at the time confounded this feeling. In the "deal of the century," the U.S. won over France in a bid for replacing the aging F-104 fleet of several NATO countries with the F-16. In some eyes, the U.S. had not only underbid the French Mirage with its "Fighting Falcon" but also somewhat bullied Denmark, Norway, Belgium, and the Netherlands with the claim of enhanced standardization. The U.S. Air Force had adopted the F-16 itself, and using the same aircraft in different national air forces seemed to be the answer to pleas for more standardization and interoperability. However, it was standardization on American terms and with an American product from which mostly American corporations profited, while the exchange for making the two-way street happen was, for example, "only" buying licenses for the Belgian MAG-58 machine gun. Most vocal of all, the French were outraged; instead of strengthening Europe by buying European—which meant, of course, buying French—the smaller NATO allies had bowed down to U.S. interests and predominance again.[48] On the other side of the Atlantic, newspapers were not as acerbic as their European counterparts. On the contrary, U.S. writers seemed to be very much understanding of European concerns,[49] while American political proponents and enemies of transatlantic defense cooperation held an intra–U.S. debate.[50]

The discussions on transatlantic defense cooperation and especially the case example of the West German-American harmonization of their tank programs in the 1970s can, when put into a larger context, not only tell us something about how NATO tried to improve its conventional defense at this juncture in the Cold War but also provide a lens through which to look at transatlantic relations in general. Western Europeans, especially due to the post-war economic boom of the 1950s and 1960s, had become more assertive when confronting the U.S. on economic terms. Also, the 1960s had shown how the Europeans were more vocal in NATO matters and tried to leave their imprint on alliance politics.[51] Nonetheless, while the United States had been politically and economically weakened, not least through its involvement in Southeast Asia, it was still the most influential member of the alliance. At the same time, West Germany had become more important, not least after France's withdrawal from the military part of NATO in the mid–1960s, and the FRG was more self-assured in its dealings concerning its security and economic interests. However, West Germany also faced a dilemma; on the one hand, it became a champion for Europe, not least because of its role in European integration as part of the European Economic Community (EEC). The FRG had to negotiate transatlantically, with France out of NATO but in the EEC. On the other hand, West Germany needed the United States and its military potential, not only for the additional manpower and materiel but especially because of the nuclear security guarantee the USA could provide for deterrence—and, therefore, Germany's defense.[52] Additionally, there then were German economic interests in a defense base that had grown due to the buildup of the *Bundeswehr* and that, in the 1970s with its economic crises, put forward similar arguments as its American counterpart. These arguments were similar in terms of keeping jobs and profiting from the spin-off effects of military R&D for the civilian market as well as from the monetary gains through arms exports.[53] While debates about transatlantic defense cooperation continued throughout the 1980s—and actually do so up to this day[54]—Western Europeans, disappointed by America's unwillingness to establish a genuine two-way street on equal terms, enhanced intra–European defense collaboration.

The United States eventually did not introduce the Leopard II but the XM-1 (later called M-1 Abrams). The least common denominator—which interoperability, in my eyes, is—was that the U.S. adopted the German smoothbore 120 mm tank gun made by Rheinmetall (which was surrounded by other tests and conflicts, especially with regards to Great Britain).[55] Rumsfeld hailed this gun as a success, especially because the 120 mm proved superior to Iraq's (Soviet-supplied) tanks in 1991 and 2004.[56] I would also claim, although for other reasons, that the smallest common denominator, the standardized tank cannon (and its ammunition), was a success. In literature, whether contemporary news media or the few scholarly works dedicated to the topic of NATO defense cooperation, it is mostly high-profile projects—and especially their failures—that receive most of, if not all, the attention. However, standardizing a tank gun and accompanying ammunition, although seemingly only a "small" step, was better than having different guns and ammunition. This thereby actually did what proponents of multinational arms cooperation in NATO had hoped for: enhancing the capabilities of the alliance with advanced weaponry.

While World War III, as envisioned by (former) high-ranking NATO officers such as Belgian Robert Close[57] or British Sir John Hackett[58] in the mid- to late 1970s, and its accompanying violence never materialized, the preparations for this conflict continued on both sides of the Iron Curtain. War plans were devised, strategies and tactics were updated, and new defense materiel was fielded. Billions of dollars, pounds sterling, and Deutschmarks were spent on the deterrence of—or eventual defense during—a war. The West German–U.S. attempt at tank harmonization provides a lens through which to look at these preparations for World War III and at the same time, lays open to us some problems of transatlantic relations in NATO during the 1970s.

NOTES

1. Bernd Greiner, "Wirtschaft im Kalten Krieg. Bilanz und Ausblick," in *Ökonomie im Kalten Krieg*, ed. Bernd Greiner, Christian Th. Müller and Claudia Weber (Bonn: Bundeszentrale für politische Bildung, 2010), 7–28.

2. The part of (West) Germany south of Schleswig-Holstein (which was part of the Northern Region) to the West German-Austrian border.

3. Despite France's 1966 resignation from NATO's military organization, French forces were still stationed in southwestern Germany.

4. Frederick Zilian, Jr., "The Shifting Military Balance in Central Europe," in *The United States and Germany in the Era of the Cold War , 1945–1990: A Handbook*, Vol. 2: 1968–1990, ed. Detlef Junker (New York: Cambridge University Press, 2004), 155–162.

5. Cf. Wallace J. Thies, *Friendly Rivals: Bargaining and Burden-Shifting in NATO* (New York & London: M.E. Sharpe, 2003).

6. Cf. e.g., John L- Clarke, "NATO Standardization: Panacea or Plague?" *Military Review* 59:4 (April 1979): 59–65, here 59: "Standardization refers to the process of selection by more than one member nation of the alliance of the same major end item, such as the same fighter-bomber or armored vehicle." NATO's definition of standardization today talks of "the development and implementation of concepts, doctrines and procedures to achieve and maintain the required levels of compatibility, interchangeability or commonality needed to achieve interoperability." "Standardization," NATO, last access June 24, 2014, http://www.nato.int/cps/en/natolive/topics_69269.htm (Last access, 10 March 2015).

7. Keith Hartley, NATO Arms Co-Operation: A Study in Economics and Politics (London, et al.: George Allen & Unwin, 1983), 3–4.

8. Peter Schlotter, "Armaments Cooperation in Western Europe," *Bulletin of Peace Proposals* 10:1 (1979): 47–56.

9. In this article, European NATO members.

10. This short history of (de)standardization and defense cooperation is mostly based on Christoph Grams, *Transatlantische Rüstungskooperation: Bedinungsfaktoren und Strukturen im Wandel* (1990—2005) (Baden-Baden: Nomos, 2007).

11. E.g. Heckler & Koch.

12. E.g. Krauss-Maffei.

13. E.g. HOT, MILAN, ROLAND.

14. Cf. Grams, *Transatlantische Rüstungskooperation*.

15. E.g. the Breguet Atlantic reconnaissance plane.

16. Johannes Steinhoff, *Wohin treibt die NATO? Probleme der Verteidigung Westeuropas* (Hamburg: Hoffmann und Campe, 1976), 198.

17. U.S. Congress, Office of Technology Assessment, *Arming Our Allies: Cooperation and Competition in Defense Technology OTA-ISC-449* (Washington, D.C.: U.S. Government Printing Office, 1990).

18. Steinhoff, *Wohin treibt die NATO*, 20.

19. North Atlantic Military Committee, Decision on M.C. 48: A Report by the Military Committee on the Most Effective Pattern of NATO Military Strength for the Next Few Years (November 22, 1954), in *NATO Strategy Documents 1949–1969*, ed. Gregory W. Pedlow (NATO: 1997), 229–50, http://www.nato.int/archives/strategy.htm (Last access, 10 March 2015).

20. North Atlantic Military Committee, Final Decision on MC 14/3: A Report by the Military Committee to the Defence Planning Committee on Overall Strategic Concept for the Defense of the North Atlantic Treaty Organization Area (January 16, 1968), in Ibid., 345–70.

21. U.S. Secretary of Defense Robert McNamara first introduced the idea of flexible response to the NATO allies at the 1962 summit in Athens. It took another five years for the alliance to adopt the strategy. One criticism was that the United States

would remove its nuclear arsenal and decouple its own security from that of its European allies; moreover, it was feared that a war, albeit one fought without atomic arms, would become more feasible. Supporters claimed that flexibility, especially in light of Mutually Assured Destruction, was needed—only if threats on all levels, starting in the conventional field, were to be answered, with credible deterrence possible. Moreover, Americans always wanted the Europeans to do more for the common defense, while European critics stated that their countries could not do more. Cf. especially Robert de Wijk, "Flexibility in Response? Attemtps to Construct a Plausible Strategy for NATO 1959-1989" (Ph.D. diss., Rijksuniversiteit te Leiden, 1989).

22. Fielded by the Bundeswehr in 1965 and exported/licensed to many NATO partners (the Netherlands, Belgium, Denmark, Norway, Canada, Greece, Turkey), thereby quickly becoming a state-of-the-art MBT.

23. Among them a 155mm tank gun that could shoot both grenades and missiles.

24. Cf. especially Thomas L. McNaugher, *Collaborative Development of Main Battle Tanks: Lessons from the U.S.-German Experience, 1963–1978* (Santa Monica, CA: RAND, 1981).

25. Cf. e.g., Henry Kissinger, "Address before the Annual Meeting of the Associated Press Editors at New York," April 23, 1973, University of California, Los Angeles, http://www.sscnet.ucla.edu/polisci/faculty/trachtenberg/ffus/YearEur%28text%29.pdf (Last access, 24 June 2014).

26. Cf. Michael Schmid, "Nukleares Skalpell oder Damoklesschwert? Strategiediskussionen und Militärkonzepte der NATO und der USA in Zeiten von 'Flexible Response', Doppelbeschluss und PD-59" (1968–1980), Universität Augsburg, 2007, http://opus.bibliothek.uni-augsburg.de (Last access, 10 March 2015).

27. McNaugher, *Collaborative Development*, 38.

28. The question of conventional force balance and numbers still cannot satisfactorily be answered. A Soviet division differed from a NATO one e.g., in size. Other examples, at times unquantifiable, are training standards and the "modernity" of materiel; the dislocation of troops, etc. It should not be forgotten that at least half of NATO's personnel was for supply, logistics, and maintenance, while a WP division had more combat soldiers. Cf. e.g., Zilian, The United States and Germany.

29. Cf. e.g., Niall Ferguson, et al. (eds.), *The Shock of the Global: The 1970s in Perspective* (Cambridge, et al.: Belknap, 2010).

30. Cf. e.g., Steinhoff, *Wohin treibt die NATO*; Robert Close, *Europa ohne Verteidigung? 48 Stunden, die das Gesicht der Welt verändern*, trans. Pierre Seguy (Bad Honnef, et al.: Osang, 1977).

31. Cf. Phillip Taylor, "Weapons Standardization in NATO: Collaborative Security or Economic Competition?" *International Organization* 36:1 (Winter 1982): 95–112.

32. The introduction of standardized rifle ammunition, as well as a standardized rifle, for all NATO forces had already been hotly debated in the 1950s. The USA got its preferred ammunition, the 7.62x51 mm. The big loser was Great Britain and its revolutionary rifle in a smaller caliber. Belgium was a partial winner—while its rifle design, the FN FAL, was not introduced by the U.S. Armed Forces, many NATO members (as well as other countries) adopted it, earning the FAL the nickname of "the strong arm of the free world." The 7.62 "NATO" remained the standard ammunition for assault rifles and light/medium machine guns until after the advent of the 5.56x45mm during the Vietnam War. Cf. Edward C. Ezell, "Cracks in the Post-War Anglo-American Alliance: The Great Rifle Controversy, 1947–1957," *Military Affairs* 38:4 (December 1974), 138–141.

33. This claim, though, was not completely true. Despite widespread standardization throughout the WP on Soviet materiel, there were some exceptions—Czechoslovakia, for example, did not use the (in)famous AK-47 assault rifle but a nationally developed rifle.

34. Thomas Callaghan Jr., *U.S./European Economic Cooperation in Military and Civil Technology: An Issues-Oriented Report* (Washington, D.C.: Department of Commerce, 1974).

35. Cf. Office of Technology Assessment, *Arming Our Allies*.

36. The research, development, and production of the MRCA of course faced the typical problems inherent in multinational defense cooperation, but the project proceeded from the 1960s until eventual fielding in the late 1970s and 1980s. Cf. e.g., Steinhoff, *Wohin treibt die NATO*, 253.

37. McNaugher, *Collaborative Development*, 41.

38. E.g. "Noch nie näher," *Der Spiegel* 29 (1976): 69–70.

39. E.g. Carl Damm, "Grünes Licht für die atlantische Zwei-Bahn-Straße?" *Wehr & Technik* 3 (1976): 9–10, 36.

40. McNaugher, *Collaborative Development*, 39.

41. Ibid., 41.

42. Donald Rumsfeld, *Known and Unknown: A Memoir* (London: Penguin, 2011), 219.

43. The "Buy American" clause dating back to the Great Depression actually hindered European arms sales to the U.S. Cf. e.g., Eliot Cohen, "NATO Standardization: The Perils of Common Sense," *Foreign Policy* 31 (Summer 1978): 72–90, here 72.

44. Rumsfeld, *Known and Unknown*, 220–221. Cf. also The Rumsfeld Papers, 2011, http://papers.rumsfeld.com/ (Last access, 10 March 2015).

45. The ability of a tank to drive, with the help of a tube, submerged in water for some time—an important feature for the Bundeswehr, as (West) Germany is full of small rivers and canals.

46. "Orientalische Sitten," *Der Spiegel* 12 (1977): 107–10.

47. Wolfgang Flume, "Panzerstandardisierung: Know-how nach USA?" *Wehr & Technik* 9 (1976): 48–50.

48. Cf. e.g., Clarke, *NATO Standardization*, 59–65; Hella Pick, "Wie ein Wirbelwind durch Europa—Der Präsident der Neuen in der Alten Welt," *Die Zeit* 24 (1976): 4–5.

49. Cf. e.g., David Binder, "U.S. and Bonn Gaining on Tank Components," *The New York Times*, Mar. 17, 1977.

50. Cohen, *Foreign Policy*, 72–90; John C. Culver, "The Argument for Standardization," *Foreign Policy* 31 (Summer 1978): 91–94.

51. Cf. e.g., Giles Scott-Smith, and Valerie Aubourg (eds.), *Atlantic, Euratlantic, or Europe-America?* (Paris: Editions Soleb, 2013).

52. Some Congressmen consistently threatened to remove U.S. troops from Europe if the Europeans did not do their part in burden-sharing. Cf. e.g., Junker, *The United States and Germany*.

53. Cf. Schlotter, *Bulletin of Peace Proposals*.

54. "Smart Defence," NATO, 2014, http://www.nato.int/cps/en/natolive/78125.htm (Last access, 10 March 2015).

55. Cf. e.g., John W. Finney, "NATO Allies Divided over Tank Gun," *The New York Times*, Apr. 18, 1976.

56. Rumsfeld, *Known and Unknown*, 221.

57. Close, *Europa ohne Verteidigung*.

58. Sir John Hackett, and others, *The Third World War: A Future History* (New York: Macmillan, 1979).

Works Cited

Binder, David. "U.S. and Bonn Gaining on Tank Components," *The New York Times*, Mar. 17, 1977.
John L. Clarke, "NATO Standardization: Panacea or Plague?" *Military Review* LIX, 4 (April 1979): 59–65.
Callaghan, Thomas, Jr. *U.S. / European Economic Cooperation in Military and Civil Technology: An Issues-Oriented Report*. Washington, D.C.: Department of Commerce, 1974.
Close, Robert. *Europa ohne Verteidigung? 48 Stunden, die das Gesicht der Welt verändern*, trans. Pierre Seguy. Bad Honnef: Osang, 1977.
Cohen, Eliot. "NATO Standardization: The Perils of Common Sense," *Foreign Policy* 31 (Summer 1978): 72–90.
Culver, John C. "The Argument for Standardization," *Foreign Policy* 31 (Summer 1978): 91–94.
Damm, Carl. "Grünes Licht für die atlantische Zwei-Bahn-Straße?" *Wehr & Technik* 3 (1976).
Ezell, Edward C. "Cracks in the Post-War Anglo-American Alliance: The Great Rifle Controversy, 1947–1957," *Military Affairs* 38, 4 (December 1974), 138–141.
Ferguson, Niall et al., eds. *The Shock of the Global: The 1970s in Perspective*. Cambridge: Belknap, 2010.
Finney, John W. "NATO Allies Divided over Tank Gun," *The New York Times*, Apr. 18, 1976.
Flume, Wolfgang. "Panzerstandardisierung: Know-how nach USA?" *Wehr & Technik* 9 (1976).
Grams, Christoph. *Transatlantische Rüstungskooperation: Bedinungsfaktoren und Strukturen im Wandel (1990–2005)*. Baden-Baden: Nomos, 2007.
Greiner, Bernd. "Wirtschaft im Kalten Krieg. Bilanz und Ausblick," in *Ökonomie im Kalten Krieg*, ed. Bernd Greiner, Christian Th. Müller and Claudia Weber. Bonn: Bundeszentrale für politische Bildung, 2010, 7–28.
Hackett, Sir John et al. *The Third World War: A Future History*. New York: Macmillan, 1979.
Hartley, Keith. *NATO Arms Co-Operation: A Study in Economics and Politics*. London: George Allen & Unwin, 1983.
Kissinger, Henry. "Address before the Annual Meeting of the Associated Press Editors at New York," April 23, 1973, *University of California, Los Angeles*, http://www.sscnet.ucla.edu/polisci/faculty/trachtenberg/ffus/YearEur%28text%29.pdf.
McNaugher, Thomas L. *Collaborative Development of Main Battle Tanks: Lessons from the U.S.-German Experience, 1963–1978*. Santa Monica, CA: RAND, 1981.
"Noch nie näher," *Der Spiegel* 29 (1976): 69–70.
North Atlantic Military Committee, *Decision on M.C. 48: A Report by the Military Committee on the Most Effective Pattern of NATO Military Strength for the Next Few Years* (November 22, 1954), in *NATO Strategy Documents 1949–1969*, ed. Gregory W. Pedlow (NATO: 1997), 229–250, http://www.nato.int/archives/strategy.htm.
North Atlantic Military Committee, *Final Decision on MC 14/3: A Report by the Military Committee to the Defence Planning Committee on Overall Strategic Concept for the Defense of the North Atlantic Treaty Organization Area* (January 16, 1968), in ibid., 345–70.

"Orientalische Sitten," *Der Spiegel* 12 (1977): 107–10.
Pick, Hella. "Wie ein Wirbelwind durch Europa—Der Präsident der Neuen in der Alten Welt," *Die Zeit* 24 (1976): 4–5.
Rumsfeld, Donald. *Known and Unknown: A Memoir.* London: Penguin, 2011.
Schlotter, Peter. "Armaments Cooperation in Western Europe," *Bulletin of Peace Proposals* 10, no. 1 (1979): 47–56.
Schmid, Michael. "Nukleares Skalpell oder Damoklesschwert? Strategiediskussionen und Militärkonzepte der NATO und der USA in Zeiten von 'Flexible Response,' Doppelbeschluss und PD-59" (1968–1980), *Universität Augsburg*, 2007, http://opus.bibliothek.uni-augsburg.de.
Scott-Smith, Giles and Aubourg, Valerie, eds. *Atlantic, Euratlantic, or Europe-America?* Paris: Editions Soleb, 2013.
"Standardization," *NATO*, http://www.nato.int/cps/en/natolive/topics_69269.htm.
Steinhoff, Johannes. *Wohin treibt die NATO? Probleme der Verteidigung Westeuropas.* Hamburg: Hoffmann und Campe, 1976.
Taylor, Phillip. "Weapons Standardization in NATO: Collaborative Security or Economic Competition?" *International Organization* 36, 1 (Winter 1982): 95–112.
Thies, Wallace J. *Friendly Rivals: Bargaining and Burden-Shifting in NATO.* New York & London: M.E. Sharpe, 2003.
U.S. Congress, Office of Technology Assessment, *Arming Our Allies: Cooperation and Competition in Defense Technology OTA-ISC-449.* Washington, D.C.: U.S. Government Printing Office, 1990.
Wijk, Robert de. "Flexibility in Response? Attemtps to Construct a Plausible Strategy for NATO 1959–1989." Ph.D. diss., Rijksuniversiteit te Leiden, 1989.
Zilian, Frederick Jr. "The Shifting Military Balance in Central Europe," in *The United States and Germany in the Era of the Cold War, 1945–1990: A Handbook, Vol. 2: 1968–1990*, ed. Detlef Junker. New York: Cambridge University Press, 2004, 155–62.

Equipping the Marine Corps for the 21st Century, 1975–1990

NATHAN R. PACKARD

"...we are in the best condition we have ever been in. When you compare the Corps of the mid-to-late 70's with the Corps of today, it is similar to comparing apples to oranges."[1]—Commandant Paul X. Kelly, 1986

"With the possible exception of the opening years of World War II, never had the Marine Corps changed so much gear so fast for so many."[2]—Colonel Allan Millett, 1991

The U.S. Marine Corps was in disarray in the aftermath of the Vietnam War. Indiscipline was widespread, morale was low, and the service's equipment was worn and outdated. Critics referred to it as a dinosaur; a military service that had outlived its usefulness. In response, the Marine Corps made fundamental changes to how it was organized, trained, and equipped. This essay focuses on the force modernization aspect of the Marine Corps' post–Vietnam reforms. After years spent chasing guerrillas in the jungles of Southeast Asia, the Marine Corps was not prepared to fight modern militaries. In the 1980s, however, the service transformed itself from a foot-mobile, light-infantry force to one capable of mechanized operations.

This essay begins with a discussion of the Marine Corps' relationship with technology. Next, it examines the precursors for technological innovation as evidenced by this case. It then offers a detailed description of the two employment concepts—maritime prepositioning and over-the-horizon assault—that drove the Marine Corps' efforts. Focusing on concepts of employment shows how leaders envisioned a set of capabilities being used to achieve desired objectives. The essay concludes with a discussion of the long-term implications of the Marine Corps' modernization program.

The argument that follows is four-fold. First, the Marine Corps' strategic mobility increased exponentially in the 1980s as did its combat effectiveness. By the end of the decade, the Marine Corps could get to more places faster than ever before and defeat mechanized adversaries. Second, these improvements were technology dependent. However, they were due more to the innovative employment of existing technologies than the development of new weapon systems. Third, sophisticated weapons were not a panacea. During the period in question, the service's inability to bring its top aviation and ground vehicle programs to fruition was a major source of frustration. Finally, most of the equipment used in the recent wars in Afghanistan and Iraq was procured during this period. Thus, an appreciation of the post–Vietnam modernization program is essential to understanding the 21st century Marine Corps.

The Marine Corps and Technology

Technology is defined as the application of knowledge to solve a problem or perform a function. In a strictly military sense, technology denotes the collection of equipment, vehicles, and systems used in warfare. In his study of the interrelationship between war and technology, military historian Martin van Creveld concluded, "war is completely permeated by technology and governed by it." However, he warned against technological determinism. Technology plays an important role, but it alone does not decide the conduct or outcome of a war.[3] Similarly, historian Jeremy Black stressed that technology is a necessary factor, but one that is in a dynamic relationship with force structure, doctrine, organization, and morale.[4]

An examination of the Marine Corp's modernization program supports the work of van Creveld and Black. Historically, the Marine Corps has had a love-hate relationship with technology. In *First to Fight*, a passionate treatise on Marine Corps history and values published in 1984, General Victor Krulak argued that an innovative streak was one of the service's defining features. He held that Marines "thought up or caused to come into being some of the most exciting—and useful—developments in modern operational concepts, weaponry, and equipment."[5] Most advances were related to amphibious assaults, the Marine Corps primary focus since the 1920s. Fearing they would be absorbed into the Army, Marines mastered a specialized form of warfare and developed the equipment needed to execute it.

On the other hand, technological innovation ran counter to other defining characteristics. The first was the institution's emphasis on the human dimension in war. Krulak considered the Marine Corps a "mystical brotherhood" and stressed intangible factors such as initiative, courage, and bravery as being decisive in battle. Post-Vietnam, this belief was evident in the Marine Corps' capstone doctrinal publication, *Warfighting*, which stated that "war is a clash between opposing human wills" in which "the human dimension is central." Refined over the course of the 1980s, less than four of *Warfighting*'s 100 pages were devoted to material considerations.[6]

General Krulak also highlighted thrift and readiness as central to the Marine Corps' worldview. He observed, "Frugality was, in short, the Corps's way of life."[7] The service's penchant for doing less with more stemmed from its desire to differentiate itself within the defense establishment. The Marine Corps had long held that it provided more fight for the defense dollar. Senior Marines believed the survival of their institution depended on Congress viewing it as a reliable investment. In addition, the Marine Corps' expeditionary mind-set contributed to its cautious approach to modernization. Marines prided themselves on being able to pack-up and ship-out on short notice. Sophisticated weapon systems tended to be expensive and heavy. Many Marines feared that modernization would come at the expense of the service's reputation for frugality and readiness.

Ultimately, the Marine Corps' post–Vietnam modernization program would bring each of these competing strands to the fore. A key question would be how to introduce new technologies while maintaining the primacy of the human element. The service would also have to balance its penchant for innovation with its expeditionary nature. How could it increase its firepower and lethality while sustaining a high state of readiness? At the same time, the Marine Corps would need to maintain its image as a good steward of the taxpayer's dollar. For the service's senior leaders, addressing these challenges would be a primary concern throughout the 1980s.

Preconditions

Why did the Marine Corps undertake a comprehensive modernization program in the 1980s and not in the immediate aftermath of the Vietnam War? The answer is rather straightforward. It was not until nearly a decade after Vietnam that the service finally had the key ingredients—the men, a mission, and the money—required to do so. Modernization depended upon quality personnel and innovative thinkers. The service also needed a strategic purpose to guide its efforts. Finally, modernization required funding. Leaders had to convince policymakers that replacing gear and equipment would be money well spent.

The Marine Corps' initial focus post–Vietnam was personnel reform.

By the end of the war, racial violence and other forms of indiscipline were widespread. Headquarters Marine Corps addressed these issues by reforming recruiting and recruit training, rigorously enforcing standards, and sacrificing end strength to preserve quality. By the early 1980s, disciplinary incidents had been reduced to manageable levels, and quality standards had increased dramatically. The number of recruits with a high school diploma, for example, increased from roughly 50 percent in 1972 to 90 percent by 1982.[8] Personnel reform was essential to force modernization. Commanders would have been hard-pressed to introduce sophisticated technologies in the absence of good order and discipline.

The importance of leaders who recognized the need for change cannot be overstated. The Arab-Israeli War occurred just as U.S. involvement in Vietnam was coming to a close. The conflict, fought from October 6 to 25, 1973, pitted a coalition of Arab states against Israel. It involved thousands of state-of the-art tanks and fighter aircraft maneuvering rapidly on and above the battlefield. During a little more than two weeks of fighting, the two sides lost somewhere in the neighborhood of 3,000 tanks, nearly six times more than the Marine Corps had in its entire inventory.[9] Marines and policymakers interpreted the war as a sign of things to come and feared the service was headed towards "comparative impotence." According to one analysis, "[t]he brutal truth is that ... the Marine Corps is an under-gunned, slow-moving monument to a bygone era in warfare."[10]

Institutional recognition that change was needed came in 1976. In 1975, Commandant Louis Wilson formed a commission to study the service's force structure and employment concepts. Completed in 1976, the commission's final report concluded, "today's Fleet Marine Forces should be organized, trained, and equipped to engage an armor-heavy enemy." Among other things, it called for using tanks as "a ground-gaining maneuver element" and a dedicated infantry fighting vehicle. The report's findings stood in sharp contrast to those of the previous force structure review. Conducted in 1969 at the height of the Vietnam War, the Armstrong Board recommended that the service remain a light infantry force oriented toward mid and low intensity conflict.[11] With the Haynes Report, Headquarters Marine Corps signaled a shift in course.

In terms of mission, the Marine Corps' two primary functions—amphibious assault and crisis response—were called into question in the aftermath of the Vietnam War. The war presented no opportunity for massed amphibious assaults. By the early 1970s, it had been more than two decades since such an operation was last conducted. Critics offered that if amphibious operations were an anachronism, then the Marine Corps was as well. The public reaction against the war discredited the idea of a crisis response force to be used at the President's discretion.

In 1979, however, the fall of the Iranian Shah and the Soviet invasion of Afghanistan led to a shift in national strategy producing what Commandant Robert Barrow referred to as a "golden era" for the Marine Corps.[12] Following the British withdrawal from the Middle East in 1971, the United States had relied on Iran to maintain stability in the region. The takeover of that country by revolutionary forces necessitated a strategic reassessment. When the Soviet Union invaded Afghanistan in December of 1979, it appeared that the situation in the Middle East, a region whose oil supplies were vital to the West's economy, was spinning out of control.

In response, President Carter promulgated the Carter Doctrine, which made it clear that the United States was prepared to use military force to ensure stability in the region. Thus, the United States became what one historian referred to as the "guardian of the gulf."[13] The Carter administration's strategic pivot and the resulting strategy-capability gap opened new opportunities for the Marine Corps. Senior Marines presented the service as the solution to the administration's most vexing foreign policy challenge—how to project military force into the Third World. In so doing, the Marine Corps secured a place of prominence for itself within the national security establishment. Secretary of Defense Harold Brown, who was known to joke about not needing a Marine Corps in 1977, asked Congress to increases the service's budget in late 1979.[14]

The administration of President Ronald Reagan endorsed its predecessor's policies, thereby solidifying the Marine Corps' place in national strategy. The administration's National Security Strategy, known as NSDD-32, held that seaborne expeditionary operations were essential to the execution of national policy; a view reinforced in other high-level guidance such as the Maritime Strategy and Amphibious Warfare Strategy.[15] In the opinion of Secretary of the Navy John Lehman, "the strategic requirements of the decade cry out for amphibious capability—forces with the flexibility and combat power embodied in the Marine air ground task forces."[16]

During his first five years in office, Reagan spent well over $1 trillion on defense, an amount that nearly equaled what was spent on defense during the Nixon, Ford and Carter administrations.[17] The Marine Corps' newfound strategic purpose was reflected in its budget, which grew by 10 percent in Fiscal Year (FY) 1981 and another 30 percent in FY 1982.[18] Marines used the additional funding to implement a comprehensive modernization program. In 1986, Commandant P.X. Kelley reported that the Marine Corps had either replaced or had a plan to replace its entire arsenal, everything from pistols to fighter aircraft. In General Kelley's estimate, "we are in the best condition we have ever been in. When you compare the Corps of the mid-to-late 70's with the Corps of today, it is similar to comparing apples to oranges."[19]

Maritime Prepositioning

Two overarching concepts—maritime prepositioning and over-the-horizon assault—drove the modernization program. Both centered on rapidly projecting military force beyond U.S. borders. Historically, Marine detachments have always been forward deployed with the fleet. Post-World War II, this typically took the form of Marine Amphibious Units (MAUs), small air-ground task forces made up of approximately 2,200 Marines. A MAU, renamed Marine Expeditionary Units (MEUs) in 1988, contains infantry and aviation elements as well as support personnel. Forward-deployed on specially designed ships, these units are prepared to respond quickly to any crisis, typically in a matter of days.

The question in the early 1980s was how to reinforce MAUs in the event of major combat operations. Traditionally, the Marine Corps gradually introduced forces in a process known as compositing. Post–1979, the message from the White House was to get there faster with more. Should war occur in the Persian Gulf, there would be no time for an incremental build-up. Massive combat power had to be introduced in the initial stages of a crisis.

To accomplish this objective, Headquarters Marine Corps worked with civilian officials to bring the Maritime Prepositioning Program to fruition. The concept, initiated in late 1979, involved loading military equipment on civilian cargo ships and prepositioning them in the Atlantic, Indian, and Pacific Oceans. In the event of a crisis, Marines would be airlifted to the region, marry up with their gear at a friendly port, and then serve as the advance party for a Marine Amphibious Force of up to 50,000 Marines. The process was designed to take less than 10 days. In support of the concept, the Carter administration's FY 1981 budget request included $300 million for new transport aircraft and cargo ships. By June of 1980, less than six months after the announcement of the Carter Doctrine, the Marine Corps had prepositioned the equipment and supplies for the 12,500-man 7th Marine Amphibious Brigade on ships home-ported on the island of Diego Garcia. The brigade itself was stationed at 29 Palms, California, where it conducted planning and training for desert warfare. By early 1982, the Marine Corps was conducting 25,000-man exercises to simulate an offload followed by combat in a desert environment. Less than three years later, the Maritime Prepositioning Force consisted of three squadrons capable of supporting three 16,000-man brigades for 30 days of combat operations.[20] Prepositioned forces were capable of landing anywhere port facilities were present. That they could move 200 miles inland meant roughly seventy-five percent of the world's population and access to the majority of major cities.

In terms of technology, the prepositioning concept was relatively simple. By purchasing or contracting for planes and cargo ships, the Marine Corps combined the speed of airlift with the hauling power of sealift. It was also cost-effective and relatively unobtrusive since permanent bases were not required. Furthermore, the additional lift capacity facilitated mechanization. To extend the operational reach of the brigades, the Marine Corps procured hundreds of armored personnel carriers, larger artillery pieces and new M1A1 tanks. Amphibious assault ships lacked the space needed to embark all these vehicles. Prepositioning ships, however, could follow in trace of the assault element with the bulk of the heavy equipment. Through prepositioning, the service was able to mechanize without sacrificing its expeditionary nature. It is also worth noting that the equipment associated with prepositioning was bought off-the-shelf. Other military services, mainly the U.S. Army or civilian industry, had been responsible for funding research and development. Ultimately, the Marine Corps relied on prepositioning to remain responsive and strategically relevant in a cost-effective manner.[21]

Over the Horizon Assault

A major limitation of prepositioning was that it required a permissive environment. Friendly ports and airfields had to be present in the vicinity of a crisis. For those situations where forcible entry was required, the Marine Corps advanced the concept of over-the-horizon assault. Bringing this concept to fruition would prove a far more difficult challenge.

Most of the evidence cited by General Krulak to support his thesis of Marines as innovators was drawn from the "golden age of amphibious warfare."[22] Prior to World War II, the Marine Corps staked its future on the amphibious mission. At the time, the means to safely transport men and equipment from large vessels to shore in the face of enemy fire did not exist. In a process that began in the 1930s, the Marine Corps took the lead in developing the specialized vehicles needed to prosecute amphibious landings. These vehicles included Higgins boats, amphibious tractors known as amtracks, and later, the helicopter. The service's achievements in this regard led to victory over Japan and wide acclaim. By the end of the war, the amphibious assault, a form of warfare very much dependent on emergent technologies, was central to the Marine Corps' institutional identity.

Following the introduction of the helicopter in the 1950s, the equipment and doctrine for attacking a defended coastline changed little. The landing force would assemble a few miles offshore, often within sight of the defenders. Following a preparatory bombardment, waves of slow-moving assault vehicles would advance on-line with the intent of overwhelming opponents with firepower. By the 1970s, however, the proliferation of anti-access weapons in the form of anti-ship missiles and precision-guided munitions led analysts to predict the demise of amphibious warfare. The general consensus was that "modern weaponry has made the conventional amphibious assault a potential killing zone for ships, landing craft, and troops."[23] It was no longer possible to get close enough to shore to launch an assault.

In response to threats posed by new technologies, Headquarters Marine Corps turned to technology for a solution. The concept of over-the-horizon assault was premised on using cutting-edge systems to launch assaults from 25 to 50 nautical miles offshore. Attackers would use the sea to maneuver and force defenders to spread their resources. The increased stand-off reduced the risk to ships and generated uncertainty as to the location of the assault.[24] Turning over-the-horizon assault from concept to reality depended on a trio of futuristic vehicles for ship-to-shore movement.

To replace traditional landing craft, the Navy developed the Landing Craft, Air Cushion (LCAC), a hovercraft that skimmed over the ocean on a cushion of air. The LCAC was capable of carrying 180 Marines or 60 to 75 tons of equipment. The vessels it replaced had top speeds of only eight knots and could access a mere 17 percent of the world's coastlines. By comparison, the LCAC traveled at upwards of 40 knots and could access 80 percent of the world's coastlines. In addition, floating on a cushion of air allowed it to safely travel over underwater mines and obstacles.[25] The LCAC represented a revolutionary advance in ship-to-shore movement. During the 1980s and 1990s, the Navy purchased a total of 91 LCACs.

While some proponents argued that a combination of LCACs and helicopters was sufficient to make over-the-horizon assault a reality, senior Marines were not satisfied with the state of the helicopter fleet. They sought a replacement for the CH-46 Sea Knight, the service's medium lift helicopter, which had been in service since 1961. Rather than refine helicopter technology, Headquarters Marine Corps turned to vertical and/or short take-off and landing (V/STOL) technology to dramatically improve performance capabilities.

In theory, V/STOL aircraft incorporated the best characteristics of rotary-wing and fixed-wing flight. They could take off and land vertically, thereby eliminating the need for built-up airfields. Once aloft, they could achieve speeds similar to airplanes. The Sea Knight's replacement, V-22 Osprey, was a tiltrotor aircraft. Prototypes had two large rotatable nacelles, one on each wing, which housed an engine and a three-bladed proprotor. For takeoff and landing, the Osprey operated like a helicopter with the nacelles vertical and rotors horizontal. Once airborne, the nacelles rotated forward 90 degrees to convert the Osprey to a more fuel efficient, higher speed turboprop aircraft. In 1985, the head of Marine Corps Aviation described tiltrotor technology as "the single most significant development in aviation since the jet engine."[26] The Osprey's capabilities greatly exceeded those of the Sea Knight. It could carry 20,000 pounds of cargo, reach speeds of 350 mph and had an operating radius of 426 miles. By comparison, the Sea Knight could carry 5,000 pounds at 166 mph and had a radius of only 151 miles.

Initially, the Osprey was a joint program, and each of the four services had acquisition plans for their own variants. Over time, however, the other services, citing budgetary constraints, either dropped out or greatly reduced the number of aircraft they intended to buy. The lack of institutional support from the other services resulted in the Marine Corps' being the sole advocate for the program on Capitol Hill. It is also left the Marine Corps on its own to solve the challenges associated with the first military use of tiltrotor technology. Perhaps the greatest challenge was designing an Osprey large enough to meet requirements in terms of airspeed and payload that could fit aboard existing amphibious shipping. To ensure proper stowage, elaborate mechanisms were developed to fold the rotors and wings. Rotors capable of folding, however, had to be shorter than optimal for vertical flight, thereby necessitating modifications to the engines. Other challenges involving weight and avionics further delayed development.

Over time, solving the technical problems proved costly and time-consuming. Although the program was initiated in 1981, the first Osprey did not fly until 1989. As the smallest of the services, the Marine Corps struggled to manage a major aviation program. The aircraft was eventually fielded in 2007, but the project took nearly a decade longer than expected. Sadly, thirty Marines and civilians were killed during the testing phase. The program was also plagued by cost overruns. In 1986, initial estimates were that 1000 aircraft would be produced within 10 years at a cost of $37.7 million per unit. By 2009, it was estimated less than 500 aircraft would be delivered at a cost of $93.4 million each. In addition, the costs associated with operating and maintaining the Osprey were more than double what was originally estimated.[27]

The Advanced Amphibious Assault Vehicle (AAAV), also known as the Expeditionary Fighting Vehicle (EFV), was the third leg of the over-the-horizon triad. Amtracks provided armored protection to the assault force during ship-to-shore movement and mobility once ashore. In the mid-1980s, it was the state of the amtrack fleet more than any other factor that hindered the implementation of over-the-horizon assault. At the time, the Marine Corps relied on the Assault Amphibious Vehicle (AAV) as its principle troop carrier. The AAV, however, did not travel much faster than its World War II-era predecessors. If an attack had been launched from 20 miles offshore, it would have taken nearly five hours for an AAV to make the round trip. Helicopters and LCACS could traverse the same distance in minutes.

It was imperative that the Marine Corps possess an amtrack capable of achieving the water speeds necessary to keep pace with the other elements of the assault force. According to the Marine Corps' head of research and development, producing such a vehicle was the service's "most ambitious endeavor" and one that was essential to the over-the-horizon concept.[28] In 1985, Commandant Paul X. Kelley decided to stop developing amtracks along the lines of AAVs in favor of a new series of vehicles with far greater speed and range.[29] Like its predecessor, the EFV would carry troops from ship to shore and serve as an armored personnel carrier on land. The EFV, however, represented a quantum leap in terms of performance capabilities. Prototypes carried 17 fully equipped Marines and traveled at speeds of 23 to 29 mph at sea and 30 mph on land. AAVs moved at a comparatively glacial 6 to 8 mph at sea and 15 to 20 mph on land. In addition, prototypes mounted a 30mm cannon and possessed the speed and armor needed to operate with tanks on land.[30]

As early as 1990, critics charged that procuring such a sophisticated vehicle would consume a disproportionate share of the service's budget.[31] A vehicle capable of travelling at high speeds over water needed to be light. Fighting on land required armor, which tended to be heavy. These contradictory capabilities could be combined in a single vehicle but not at an acceptable cost. The original plan was to buy 1,025 vehicles at roughly $8 million each. By 2010, no vehicles were operational, and it was estimated that the Marine Corps would only be able to afford 573 vehicles at $24 million apiece. According to a 2011 Congressional Research Service Report, the costs were so high that purchasing the vehicle would consume 90 percent of the service's ground equipment budget. That year, the program was cancelled due to cost overruns.[32]

Of the three vehicles associated with over-the-horizon assault, only the LCAC, a Navy led initiative, was fielded on schedule in 1987. As the Marine Corps' top aviation and ground acquisition priorities from the mid–1980s onward, the Osprey and EFV collectively consumed the vast majority of research and development funds and considerable institutional energy. However, not a single Osprey or EFV reached the operating forces until 2007. Even then, it was only the Osprey that did so. Perhaps the service overreached in seeking a set of capabilities that simply could not be achieved economically. With over-the-horizon assault, the Marine Corps tied the future of amphibious warfare to a trio of sophisticated vehicles. In so doing, the service seemed to have forgotten that one of the most appealing features of World War II era vehicles was that they could be procured in sufficient quantities in a timely manner and at an acceptable cost.

Over time, the Osprey and the EFV came to define the Marine Corps in the halls of Congress. As a result, the service sacrificed its hard-won reputation for thrift. According to analyst William Lind, these programs represented the emergence of a "second Marine Corps" whose "highest goal is programs, money and bureaucratic success 'inside the Beltway.'" Historically, the service's message to Congress and the American people had been, "We're not like the other services. We aren't about money and stuff. We're about war." The new message coming from Headquarters Marine Corps in the form of glossy handouts and its testimony before Congress was "We are just like the other services. We too are now about money and programs." In Lind's opinion, the service was trading its warrior ethos and reputation for frugality—the very sources of its political support—for costly programs.[33]

In the final analysis, Reagan era defense spending provided the Marine Corps with the resources needed to modernize the force. Without the buildup, the service would have fallen even further behind potential adversaries. It is difficult to imagine the Marine Corps remaining strategically relevant had it continued to use weapon systems that predated the Vietnam War. On the other hand, Headquarters Marine Corps became overly focused on procurement. Over time, the service grew accustomed to levels of spending that were not sustainable over the long-term. When the defense budget started to contract in 1987, the Marine Corps was saddled with expensive programs that it could not bring to fruition.

Conclusion

The true test of any piece of equipment or employment concept is combat effectiveness. Does the technology help to achieve the desired strategic outcomes? In 1990, Operation Desert Shield validated the prepositioning concept. It took less than 10 days for the 7th Marine Brigade to get to Saudi Arabia and unload its equipment. With their 28 LAVs, 58 M60A1 tanks, and 100 amphibious tractors, the Marines provided the first combat-ready armored formation in theater. U.S. Army armored units did not arrive until weeks later.[34] Eventually, all three prepositioning squadrons deployed. According to one after-action report, "It was the prepositioned ships of the Marine Corps and Army that saved the day during the early stages of Desert Shield."[35] The Marine Corps' contribution to the war effort eventually totaled 92,000 Marines, 1101 fighting vehicles, and 372 aircraft, much of it transported via the prepositioning construct.[36] In less than 15 years, maritime prepositioning went from concept to combat-tested capability.

The over-the-horizon assault concept, on the other hand, proved infeasible. Leaders had an overarching vision, but the capabilities required were too expensive. The use of helicopters in combination with LCACs increased the reach of amphibious forces; however, the absence of a high-speed, armored personnel carrier meant the concept could never be executed as originally intended. The limitations of conventional amphibious operations were evident during Desert Shield/Desert Storm. The Navy and Marine Corps rapidly assembled a sizable amphibious force off the heavily defended Kuwaiti Coast. Theater commander General Norman Schwarzkopf, however, declined to order an amphibious assault out of fear of excessive casualties.

The Marine Corps' post–Vietnam modernization program supports the work of historian David Edgerton, who argued that technology is too often associated with new inventions rather than what has been most useful. Since World War II, the U.S. military has been preoccupied with producing the next best machine or missile. The answer to emerging strategic challenges, however, is more likely to be found in combining and organizing existing resources in novel ways. As evidenced by this case, it was new concepts for employing existing technologies, not high-tech weapon systems, that enabled the Marine Corps to accomplish its mission. The Osprey and EFV were largely irrelevant. Both programs were a drain on funds, time, and intellectual energy. In this case, new inventions were economically and militarily irrational.[37] Low-cost, logistics based solutions proved the most rewarding. Thus, it is important to take a holistic approach to military technology. It should be considered in the context of its use. The best vehicles or systems may not be the ones that are superior in all categories but rather the ones that can be fielded in sufficient numbers when needed.

To explain why the Marine Corps was so wedded to the over-the-horizon concept and its trio of high-tech vehicles, one must go back to World War II. General Krulak described a "stubborn faith" in the amphibious assault as being part of the fabric of the institution. The Marines had to keep it viable or risk irrelevance. In this way, the Osprey and the EFV shed light on the symbolic value of technology and the meaning behind it. The decision to proceed with these programs was not just the product of rational analysis—history, pride, and service culture also played a role.[38]

Ultimately, the Marine Corps used technology to reaffirm its strategic relevance. By the mid-1980s, the service's firepower and mobility were exponentially greater than it had been during Vietnam. On the other hand, materiel limitations prevented the Marine Corps from realizing its goal of conducting a true over-the-horizon assault. The end result was an incongruous mix of old and new. Commanders had to integrate slow-moving displacement-type landing craft and AAVs into their landing plans without comprising the advantages gained by faster LCAC and heliborne elements. The principle of combined arms called for the integration of different weapons to achieve mutually complementary effects; however, compatibility issues among the different elements of the assault force detracted from its overall effectiveness. It was left to commanders to creatively employ their forces to maximize advantages and mask weaknesses.

For the Marine Corps, the failure of the over-the-horizon concept reinforced its traditional ambivalence towards technology. Marines resisted the

III. The Cold War

technological triumphalism that followed the First Gulf War. Unlike the other services, they did not subscribe to the notion that a technology driven revolution in military affairs had taken place, a conclusion derived in part from the problem-plagued Osprey and EFV programs. In the 1990s, the Marine Corps placed a renewed emphasis on the human dimension and devoted more attention to low-intensity conflicts and counterinsurgency operations. Power projection remained the focus, but in a low-tech, more personal form.[39]

NOTES

1. P.X. Kelley, "Statement on Posture, Plans, and Programs for Fiscal Years 1987 through 1991," reprinted in *Marine Corps Gazette* (April 1986): 27.
2. Allan R. Millet, *Semper Fidelis: The History of the United States Marine Corps* (New York: Macmillan, 1991), 619.
3. Martin van Creveld, *Technology and War: From 2000 BC to the Present* (New York: The Free Press, 1989), 1–6.
4. Jeremy Black, *War and Technology* (Bloomington, IN: Indiana University Press, 2013), 33.
5. Victor H. Krulak, *First to Fight: An Inside View of the U.S. Marine Corps* (Annapolis, MD: Naval Institute Press, 1984), 67.
6. Ibid., 156 and *Fleet Marine Force Manual* (FMFM)—1, Warfighting (Washington, D.C.: Headquarters, United States Marine Corps, 1989).
7. Krulak, *First to Fight*, 143.
8. Aline D. Quester, *Marine Corps Recruits: A Historical Look at Accessions and Boot Camp Performance* (Center for Naval Analysis, September 2010) and Robert Alan Packard, Jr. "Premature Attrition in the U.S. Marine Corps," Master's Thesis, Naval Postgraduate School, Monterey, CA, December 1976, 8. For a contemporary account of what came to be known as "The Great Personnel Campaign" see BGen Bernard E. Trainor, "The personnel campaign issue is no longer in doubt," *Marine Corps Gazette* (January 1978).
9. Estimates place Israeli losses at 400 tanks destroyed, 600 damaged, and 102 planes lost; the Arabs lost 2,300 tanks and between 300 and 500 aircraft. By comparison, the Marine Corps had 450 tanks in its entire inventory as of 1975, and many of these were outdated or in long-term storage. See Martin Binkin and Jeffrey Record, *Where Does the Marine Corps Go from Here?* (Washington, D.C.: The Brookings Institution, 1976), 83. For more on the Arab-Israeli War see Edgar O'Ballance, *No Victor, No Vanguished: The Arab-Israeli War, 1973* (Novato, CA: Presidio Press, 1997).
10. William S. Lind and Jeffrey Record, "Twilight for the Corps?" *Proceedings of the U.S. Naval Institute* (July 1978): 39.
11. United States Marine Corps, *Mission and Force Structure Study* (Haynes Board Report) (Washington: Headquarters Marine Corps, 1976). Copy available in Marine Corps Archives and Special Collections, Quantico, VA.
12. "CMC, General Robert H. Barrow, Speech, Retired Officers' Luncheon," 18 March 1980, Speeches and Talks, Barrow Papers, Marine Corps Archives and Special Collections, Quantico, VA.
13. Michael A. Palmer, *Guardians of the Gulf: A History of America's Expanding Role in the Persian Gulf, 1833–1992* (New York: The Free Press, 1992).
14. Lt. Col. Kenneth R. Burns, USMC, "Mobilization Studies Program Report— Marine Corps Warfighting Capability: A Comparison Between the Periods 1977–1980

and 1981–1984," *Research Report for the College of the Armed Forces*, March 1985, 30. For more on the Carter administration's strategic pivot see Olav Njolstad, "Shifting Priorities: The Persian Gulf in U.S. Strategic Planning in the Carter Years," *Cold War History*, Vol. 4, No. 3 (April 2004): 21–55.

15. National Security Decision Directive-32 (NSDD-32), "U.S. National Security Strategy," May 20, 1982, http://www.reagan.utexas.edu/archives/reference/Scanned%20NSDDS/NSDD32.pdf (Last access, 20 June 2013) and John B. Hattendorf and Captain Peter M. Schwarz, eds., *U.S. Naval Strategy in the 1980s: Selected Documents* (Newport, R.I.: Naval War College Press, 2008).

16. J.F. Lehman, Jr., "Amphibious Capability and Maritime Strategy," *Marine Corps Gazette* (October 1981): 39.

17. Daniel Wirls, Buildup: *The Politics of Defense in the Reagan Administration* (Ithaca, NY: Cornell University Press, 1992), 36.

18. Burns, "Mobilization Studies Program Report," 60.

19. P.X. Kelley, "Statement on Posture, Plans, and Programs for Fiscal Years 1987 through 1991," reprinted in *Marine Corps Gazette* (April 1986): 27. See Dov S. Zakheim, "The Role of Amphibious Operations in National Military Strategy," *Marine Corps Gazette* (March 1984): 37–39 for an itemized list of specific procurements.

20. George C. Wilson, "Carter Budget Envisions a Force for Quick, Long-Distance Reaction," *Washington Post*, November 27, 1979 and "Marines to Form Rapid Reaction Force," *Washington Post*, December 6, 1979. See also Gen. Robert H. Barrow, U.S. Marine Corps (Retired), *Oral History Transcript* (Sessions 14 and 15), Brigadier General Edwin H. Simmons Interviewer, *History and Museums Division*, Headquarters, U.S. Marine Corps, Washington, D.C., 1978–1994 and White Letter No. 2–81, Amphibious Operations and Maritime/Near Term Prepositioning Ships, 17 February 1981, Robert H. Barrow Collection, "Speeches and Letters, 1981–1983," *Special Archives and Collections, Library of the Marine Corps*, Quantico, VA.

21. For more on the MPF concept see General Accounting Office, *National Security and International Affairs Division, Military Afloat Prepositioning: Wartime Use and Issues for the Future* (Washington, D.C., 1992); Major Bernard T. Burchell, "Maritime Prepositioning Forces: A Historical Analysis," *Command and Staff College Paper* (1993), Marine Corps Archives and Special Collections, Quantico, Virginia; and Scott W. Conrad, *Moving The Force Desert Storm and Beyond* (Washington, D.C.: U.S. Government Printing Office, 1994).

22. John Gordon, "General Thomas Holcomb and 'The Golden Age of Amphibious Warfare,'" *Delaware History* 21 (1985): 256–270. For our purposes here, the "golden age" refers to the period from 1942 through 1952, which encompassed the island-hoping campaigns in the Pacific, the Allied landings in Italy and France, and the Inchon landing and other amphibious operations during the Korean War.

23. Stephen L. Goertzen, "The Feasibility of Over-the-Horizon Assault for U.S. Navy and Marine Corps Forces" (Master's Thesis, U.S. Army Command and General Staff College, 1993), 3.

24. For one of the first calls for updated doctrine see Colonel R.B. Rothwell, "Toward A New Amphibious Tactical Concept," *Marine Corps Gazette* (July 1983). For a more developed, in-depth description of the over-the-horizon concept from one of its main proponents see Thomas C. Linn, "Blitzing the Beach: Over-the-Horizon Assault," *Armed Forces Journal International* (August 1988): 84–89. See also Lt. Col. Douglas E. Humston, "Over the Horizon–2000: A Futuristic Concept for the Conduct of Amphibious Operations," *Amphibious Warfare Review* (Winter 1989): 14–18. For a critique see Jon T. Hoffman, "The High Cost of Reaching the Beach," *Proceedings*

116 (November 1990): 67–71. For a balanced overview see Goertzen, "The Feasibility of Over-the-Horizon Assault for U.S. Navy and Marine Corps Forces."

25. Rothwell, "Toward A New Amphibious Tactical Concept"; U.S. Navy Fact File, Landing Craft, Air Cushion—LCAC, http://www.navy.mil/navydata/fact_display. asp?cid=4200&tid=1500&ct=4 (accessed 05 April 2014); GlobalSecurity.org, Landing Craft, Air Cushion (LCAC), http://www.globalsecurity.org/military/systems/ship/lcac.htm (Last access, 10 May 2014).

26. Lt. Gen. Keith A. Smith, "Marine Aviation FY 86 Posture Statement," *Marine Corps Gazette* (May 1985).

27. For a comprehensive account of the Osprey see Richard Whittle, *The Dream Machine: The Untold Story of the Notorious V-22 Osprey* (New York: Simon and Schuster, 2010). For specific costs see U.S. Government Accountability Office, Report to Congressional Requesters, "Assessments Needed to Address V-22 Aircraft Operational and Cost Concerns to Define Future Investments" (May 2009), http://www.gao.gov/new.items/d09482.pdf. Accessed on 10.5.2014.

28. Major General Ray Franklin, "A Ready Corps, A Steadfast Tradition: The USMC's 'Disciplined Approach' to Acquisition Management," *Sea Power* (April 1989): 62.

29. Gen. Paul X. Kelly, USMC, "Assault Amphibious Vehicle Development," *Memorandum for the Secretary of the Navy from the Commandant of the Marine Corps*, Headquarters, United States Marine Corps, Washington, D.C., 8 April 1985.

30. Andrew Feickert, "The Marines' Expeditionary Fighting Vehicle (EFV): Background and Issues for Congress," *Congressional Research Service*, March 14, 2011, http://assets.opencrs.com/rpts/RS22947_20110314.pdf (Last access, 10 March 2014).

31. Hoffman, "The High Cost of Reaching the Beach," 69.

32. Feickert, "The Marines' Expeditionary Fighting Vehicle."

33. William S. Lind, "Two Marine Corps," undated, http://www.dnipogo.org/lind/lind_6_4_04.htm. Accessed on 12.5.2014.

34. Kenneth Estes, *Marines Under Armor: The Marine Corps and the Armored Fighting Vehicle, 1916–2000* (Annapolis: Naval Institute Press, 2000), 185.

35. Scott W. Conrad, *Moving The Force Desert Storm and Beyond* (Washington, D.C.: U.S. Government Printing Office, 1994); BGen Edwin H. Simmons, "Breaching the So-Called Impenetrable Barrier," *Marine Corps Gazette* (November 1998): 89.

36. BGen. Edwin H. Simmons, "Breaching the So-Called Impenetrable Barrier," *Marine Corps Gazette* (November 1998): 89.

37. David Edgerton, *The Shock of the Old: Technology and Global History Since 1900* (Oxford: Oxford University Press, 2007), xi, 17 and 143. Edgerton uses the phrase militarily irrational to describe Nazi Germany's V-2 rocket project. He defines it as an effort to develop a wonder weapon that, in the end, sapped resources from more productive programs.

38. Krulak, 110.

39. Interview with Lt Gen Paul Van Riper, "The Immutable Nature of War," NOVA/PBS, http://www.pbs.org/wgbh/nova/military/immutable-nature-war.html (Last access, 29 December 2011). See also Charles Krulak, "The Three Block War: Fighting in Urban Areas," in *Vital Speeches of the Day*, Vol. 64, Iss. 5 (15 December 1997): 139–141; Charles Krulak, "The Strategic Corporal: Leadership in the Three Block War," *Marine Corps Gazette* (January 1999): 18–23; and Counterinsurgency, U.S. Army Field Manual FM 3-24 / Marine Corps Warfighting Publication No. 3-33.5 (December 2006), http://usacac.army.mil/cac2/Repository/Materials/COIN-FM3-24.pdf (Last access, 1 March 2013).

Works Cited

Barrow, Robert H. U.S. Marine Corps (Retired), Oral History Transcript (Sessions 14 and 15), Brigadier General Edwin H. Simmons, Interviewer, History and Museums Division, Headquarters, U.S. Marine Corps, Washington, D.C., 1978–1994.
Binkin, Martin, and Jeffrey Record. *Where Does the Marine Corps Go from Here?* Washington, D.C.: The Brookings Institution, 1976.
Black, Jeremy. *War and Technology.* Bloomington, IN: Indiana University Press, 2013.
Burchell, Bernard T. "Maritime Prepositioning Forces: A Historical Analysis," Command and Staff College Paper (1993), Marine Corps Archives and Special Collections, Quantico, Virginia.
Burns, Kenneth R. USMC, "Mobilization Studies Program Report—Marine Corps Warfighting Capability: A Comparison Between the Periods 1977–1980 and 1981–1984," *Research Report for the College of the Armed Forces*, March 1985, 30.
"CMC, General Robert H. Barrow, Speech, Retired Officers' Luncheon," 18 March 1980, Speeches and Talks, Barrow Papers, Marine Corps Archives and Special Collections, Quantico, VA.
Conrad, Scott W. *Moving The Force Desert Storm and Beyond.* Washington, D.C.: U.S. Government Printing Office, 1994.
Counterinsurgency, U.S. Army Field Manual FM 3-24 / Marine Corps Warfighting Publication No. 3-33.5 (December 2006), http://usacac.army.mil/cac2/Repository/Materials/COIN-FM3-24.pdf.
Creveld, Martin van. *Technology and War: From 2000 BC to the Present.* New York: The Free Press, 1989.
Edgerton, David. *The Shock of the Old: Technology and Global History Since 1900.* Oxford: Oxford University Press, 2007.
Estes, Kenneth. *Marines Under Armor: The Marine Corps and the Armored Fighting Vehicle, 1916–2000.* Annapolis: Naval Institute Press, 2000.
Feickert, Andrew. "The Marines' Expeditionary Fighting Vehicle (EFV): Background and Issues for Congress," *Congressional Research Service*, March 14, 2011, http://assets.opencrs.com/rpts/RS22947_20110314.pdf (accessed March 10, 2014).
Fleet Marine Force Manual (FMFM)—1, *Warfighting.* Washington, D.C.: Headquarters, United States Marine Corps, 1989.
Franklin, Ray. "A Ready Corps, A Steadfast Tradition: The USMC's 'Disciplined Approach' to Acquisition Management," *Sea Power* (April 1989).
General Accounting Office, National Security and International Affairs Division, *Military Afloat Prepositioning: Wartime Use and Issues for the Future.* Washington, D.C., 1992.
Goertzen, Stephen L. "The Feasibility of Over-the-Horizon Assault for U.S. Navy and Marine Corps Forces." Master's Thesis, U.S. Army Command and General Staff College, 1993.
Gordon, John. "General Thomas Holcomb and 'The Golden Age of Amphibious Warfare,'" *Delaware History* 21 (1985): 256–270.
Hattendorf, John B., and Captain Peter M. Schwarz, eds. *U.S. Naval Strategy in the 1980s: Selected Documents.* Newport, R.I.: Naval War College Press, 2008.
Hoffman, Jon T. "The High Cost of Reaching the Beach," *Proceedings* 116 (November 1990): 67–71.
Humston, Douglas E. "Over the Horizon–2000: A Futuristic Concept for the Conduct of Amphibious Operations," *Amphibious Warfare Review* (Winter 1989): 14–18.

Interview with Lt. Gen. Paul Van Riper, "The Immutable Nature of War," NOVA/PBS, http://www.pbs.org/wgbh/nova/military/immutable-nature-war.html.

Kelley, Paul X. "Statement on Posture, Plans, and Programs for Fiscal Years 1987 through 1991," reprinted in *Marine Corps Gazette* (April 1986).

Kelly, Paul X. USMC, "Assault Amphibious Vehicle Development," Memorandum for the Secretary of the Navy from the Commandant of the Marine Corps, Headquarters, United States Marine Corps, Washington, D.C., 8 April 1985.

Krulak, Charles. "The Strategic Corporal: Leadership in the Three Block War," *Marine Corps Gazette* (January 1999): 18–23.

Krulak, Charles. "The Three Block War: Fighting in Urban Areas," in *Vital Speeches of the Day*, Vol. 64, Iss. 5 (15 December 1997).

Krulak, Victor H. *First to Fight: An Inside View of the U.S. Marine Corps*. Annapolis, MD: Naval Institute Press, 1984.

Lehman, J.F. Jr. "Amphibious Capability and Maritime Strategy," *Marine Corps Gazette* (October 1981).

Lind, William S. and Record, Jeffrey. "Twilight for the Corps?" *Proceedings of the U.S. Naval Institute* (July 1978).

Lind, William S. "Two Marine Corps," undated, http://www.dnipogo.org/lind/lind_6_4_04.htm.

Linn, Thomas C. "Blitzing the Beach: Over-the-Horizon Assault," *Armed Forces Journal International* (August 1988): 84–89.

"Marines to Form Rapid Reaction Force," *Washington Post*, December 6, 1979.

Millet, Allan R. *Semper Fidelis: The History of the United States Marine Corps*. New York: Macmillan, 1991.

National Security Decision Directive -32 (NSDD-32), "U.S. National Security Strategy," May 20, 1982, http://www.reagan.utexas.edu/archives/reference/Scanned%20NSDDS/NSDD32.pdf.

Njolstad, Olav. "Shifting Priorities: The Persian Gulf in U.S. Strategic Planning in the Carter Years," *Cold War History*, Vol. 4, No. 3 (April 2004): 21–55.

O'Ballance, Edgar. *No Victor, No Vanguished: The Arab-Israeli War, 1973*. Novato, CA: Presidio Press, 1997.

Packard, Robert Alan, Jr. "Premature Attrition in the U.S. Marine Corps," Master's Thesis, Naval Postgraduate School, Monterey, CA, December 1976.

Palmer, Michael A. *Guardians of the Gulf: A History of America's Expanding Role in the Persian Gulf, 1833–1992*. New York: The Free Press, 1992.

Quester, Aline D. *Marine Corps Recruits: A Historical Look at Accessions and Boot Camp Performance*. Center for Naval Analysis, September 2010.

Rothwell, R.B. "Toward A New Amphibious Tactical Concept," *Marine Corps Gazette* (July 1983).

Simmons, Edwin H. "Breaching the So-Called Impenetrable Barrier," *Marine Corps Gazette* (November 1998).

Smith, Keith A. "Marine Aviation FY 86 Posture Statement," *Marine Corps Gazette* (May 1985).

Trainor, Bernard E. "The personnel campaign issue is no longer in doubt," *Marine Corps Gazette* (January 1978).

United States Marine Corps, Mission and Force Structure Study (Haynes Board Report). Washington: Headquarters Marine Corps, 1976.

U.S. Government Accountability Office, Report to Congressional Requesters, "Assessments Needed to Address V-22 Aircraft Operational and Cost Concerns to Define Future Investments" (May 2009), http://www.gao.gov/new.items/d09482.pdf.

White Letter No. 2-81, Amphibious Operations and Maritime/Near Term Prepositioning Ships, 17 February 1981, Robert H. Barrow Collection, "Speeches and Letters, 1981–1983," Special Archives and Collections, Library of the Marine Corps, Quantico, VA.

Whittle, Richard. *The Dream Machine: The Untold Story of the Notorious V-22 Osprey.* New York: Simon and Schuster, 2010.

Wilson, George C. "Carter Budget Envisions a Force for Quick, Long-Distance Reaction," *Washington Post*, November 27, 1979.

Wirls, Daniel. *Buildup: The Politics of Defense in the Reagan Administration.* Ithaca, NY: Cornell University Press, 1992.

Zakheim, Dov S. "The Role of Amphibious Operations in National Military Strategy," *Marine Corps Gazette* (March 1984).

From AirLand Battle to Effects-Based Operations
United States Air Force and Army Doctrine Development from 1980 to 2001

DANIEL FUHRER

Introduction

After the Vietnam War, the Army dominated doctrine development[1] in the United States as general officers such as William E. DePuy and Don A. Starry promoted the ultimate (conventional) land war in the 1980s to be fought against the forces of the Warsaw Pact in Europe. This latter action was promoted by institutionalizing their concept *AirLand Battle*. On the other hand, thanks to its quite decisive effort in Operation Desert Storm, the Air Force seemed to take over the lead in the debate on modern warfare or the "image of war" respectively in the early 1990s, culminating in the idea of Effects-Based Operations.[2] On both occasions, modern technology was either planned to be the decisive element to gain victory or was conceived to be.

The analysis of the argumentation of critics and supporters of both these concepts is necessary to understand today's U.S.-dominated western view on modern war. Apart from scientific military publications (e.g. journals, studies, diploma projects), the official military regulations (often called manuals[3]) are the second major starting point for this evaluation. The concepts of AirLand Battle as well as Effects-Based Operations both gained a foothold in official publications. It is, therefore, necessary to survey as well, within the scope of this study, to what extent these concepts shaped the language use in general and terminology in particular.

According to the historical background presented, it seems appropriate to restrict the evaluation period to the timeframe between 1980 and 2000. The research presented is based on the contents of a master's thesis that is also part of an ongoing Ph.D. project (*From AirLand Battle to AirSea Battle*) at the University of Zurich in 2012.

After Vietnam: Active Defense

When General William E. DePuy took over the U.S. Army's Training and Doctrine Command (TRADOC) in 1973, he wanted, after the U.S. Vietnam experience, to adjust the Army and its doctrine again to a big conventional land war in Europe. To gain this effect, the Field Manual (FM) 100-5 Operations[4] had to be rewritten. However, it was not only the Vietnam War, but the Arab-Israeli war in 1973 as well, which influenced the new doctrine. Modern land war was imagined to be fast, intensive, brutal and deadlier than ever. Tanks, mechanized infantry and tactical aircraft would meet each other in gigantic battles, supported by artillery and air forces, fighting around the clock. According to analysis done by TRADOC, the Warsaw Pact's weapons were numerous and excellent, as was its armed forces doctrine; this would allow the Pact to go against NATO defenses with mass and speed. In General DePuy's eyes, NATO defense lines in Europe would not stand against a Soviet attack. The deployment of nuclear weapons on the tactical level would, on the political level, be considered too late, and as a result, large areas of Western Europe would be harmed.

The basic idea of the concept developed to counter this enemy, Active Defense, was to drill on modern weapons and their employment in combat. This would help the U.S. forces to stand against a Warsaw Pact onslaught despite numerical inferiority and throw back enemy forces thanks to the technological superiority of U.S. weapons.[5] However, soon critics said DePuy's doctrine was suited primarily to a conventional war in Europe and not necessarily to other types of conflicts. Sample application of the new doctrine in exercises in Europe unveiled Active Defense's faults: a battle which was, because of the necessary lateral movements, difficult to coordinate; predictable tactics; and piecemeal destruction by follow-on enemy forces. Consequently, in a minimum amount of time, there was a renewed need for another doctrine in which the fight at the front line was coordinately and simultaneously fought against follow-on enemy forces.

General Don A. Starry,[6] successor to DePuy, took over TRADOC in 1977. He had experienced possible problems with Active Defense in exercises in

Europe as commander of Vth Corps. Under Starry's guidance, FM 100–5 was rewritten again.[7] In contrast to the earlier version, soldiers were not solely the operators of their machines; factors such as training, morale and adaptability were added to the manual. *AirLand Battle*, as this edition of the manual was also called, differed in principle not decisively from Active Defense. The distinction could mainly be found in the principle of synchronization, on which AirLand Battle rested. Synchronization in this context meant more than only coordinated action—it should result "from an all-pervading unity of effort throughout the force."[8] The added concept of Deep Battle or Deep Attack[9] should help the U.S. Army to destroy follow-on echelons of Warsaw Pact forces in collaboration with the Air Force; the whole battle should be coordinated on the newly introduced operational level.

"Symphony of Destruction"

Maneuver and firepower should prevent Warsaw Pact reinforcements from flowing to the frontlines. Both of these terms would dominate the discourse on "what war should look like" for the time being, especially regarding the ground battle, as they are the counter argument opposite the Warsaw Pact's rushing masses. As early as 1981, a preliminary concept of the new doctrine, which had been drawn under the guidance of Starry, was published. The concept dubbed the AirLand Battle and Corps 86 proposed the Deep Attack: striking follow-on enemy forces with firepower to isolate the first wave of attackers at the frontlines. This should enable one's own maneuver. Enemy strongpoints or key systems should also be targeted with fire.[10] Under the axiom Extending the Battlefield, the foremost enemy wave should be destroyed at the first encounter. At the same time, a second wave had to be attacked in the depth of the battlefield, so to be prevented from intervening at the FLOT (Forward Line of Troops). These actions would allow U.S. forces to take the initiative from the enemy and make him collapse in the end.

To be successful on this battlefield, longstanding German concepts such as *Auftragstaktik* were incorporated. The concept of the *Schwerpunkt* was adopted as well in the scope of renewed works such as *Center of Gravity* about Carl von Clausewitz, translated into termini. The basic idea underlying the new Field Manual should be to locate enemy vulnerabilities and concentration of the own point of main effort in exactly the same location.[11] The study "AirLand Battle and Corps 86[qm] put the Corps, and thereby the operational level, forward as the implementing element for AirLand Battle. The Corps should coordinate its own battle into the depth with the Numbered Air Force[12] in the same Area of Operations (AO).[13] AirLand Battle and Corps 86 propagated the absolute necessity of the battle into the depth of the area as well as the absoluteness of a synchronization with the battles at the FLOT and in one's own backyard (Rear Battle), taking place in parallel:

> Deep attack is [...] an absolute necessity to winning. [...] deep attack particularly in an environment of scarce acquisition and strike assets must be tightly coordinated over time with the decisive close-in battle. Without this coordination, many expensive and scarce resources may be wasted on apparently attractive targets whose destruction actually has little payoff in the close-in battle. [...] It's all one battle.[14]

In a downright "Symphony of Destruction,"[15] advances of armored and/or mechanized forces, Cruise Missiles into the rear, air interdiction to isolate the battlefield and air assaults should impede the arrival of further enemy waves on the battlefield, whereas firepower had to be decisive. With AirLand Battle, the weaknesses of Soviet doctrine, as propagated by U.S. analysts, had to be exploited: the rigid leadership system, which apparently tolerated only few initiatives on lower levels, the general tendency to hold precisely onto battle plans at higher command, the education system, which let only little creativity take place and the more scientific Approach to the battle.[16] Western analysts also attested a growing technological inferiority of the Warsaw Pact's forces, as Skinner describes.[17]

Therefore, they would mainly rely on their numerical superiority as well as surprise:

> mass, momentum, and continuous combat are the operative tactics. Breakthrough (somewhere) is sought as the initiator of collapse in the defender's system of defense. [...] In the alternative, surprise is substituted for mass in the daring thrust tactic. [...] What is important is that superiority in numbers permits him to keep a significant portion of his force out of the fight [...] follow-on echelons gives the enemy a strong grip on the initiative which we must wrest from him, then retain in order to win.[18]

When General Starry and his team had finished circulating the concept AirLand Battle and Corps 86 within the Army, the basic ideas were incorporated into the new 1982 edition of the FM 100–5 Operations. Another edition was published in 1986, once NATO members voiced critique towards the 1982 edition, which proposed the deployment of tactical nuclear weapons without restrictions. In 1986, this guideline was relativized, and it determined that the deployment of nuclear weapons was only to be done with agreement by the other member states.

Both Field Manual editions showed the imagination of a battle taking place that could take days instead of weeks to unfold. Front and rear on the battlefield would become blurred as well.[19] Blue (U.S. or NATO) operations had to be quick, unpredictable and disorienting. Improvisation, initiative and aggressiveness were asked for.[20] According to the Fundamentals of AirLand Battle Doctrine, as described in the 1986 edition, "The object of all operations is to impose our will upon the enemy—to achieve our purposes. To do this we must throw the enemy off balance with a powerful blow from an unexpected direction, follow up rapidly to prevent his recovery and continue operations aggressively to achieve the higher commander's goals."[21] Terms such as balance and will brought to mind a boxing match in which the enemy would be brought off balance[22] by targeted blows and then beaten into unconsciousness. On the one hand, the doctrine showed the image of chaos on the battlefield; on the other hand, the military wanted to regulate it through synchronization:

> Synchronization includes but is not limited to the actual concentration of forces and fires at the point of decision. Some of the activities that must be synchronized in an operation—interdiction with maneuver, for example, or the shifting of reserves with the rearrangement of air defense—must occur before the decisive moment and may take place at locations far distant from each other.[23]

Synchronization was, therefore, a topic in military publications as well. Here, Lieutenant Colonel Donald L. Mercer, Assistant Army Attaché to Moscow, in the May 1984 edition of *Military Review* states: "By synchronizing the attack, [meaning] to strike at specified points and times, a synergistic effect can be obtained. That is to say, the results of such an attack will be far more catastrophic than separate attacks on the same elements over a longer period of time."[24]

Hence, the sum of all attacks should have a devastating effect on the enemy. Follow-on echelons should be attacked by artillery and fighter planes in the depth of the area. Charles J. Dick similarly explained in *Military Review* in September 1985: "Each will seek to disrupt the enemy and force him onto the defensive in a disadvantageous position. This will be done at first by air and long-range artillery strikes and the use of forward and raiding detachments, and then by the attacks of advanced guards."[25]

New Weapons for the Army

To facilitate this "way of war," new weapons should be deployed. A network of sensors and weapons systems should locate the second and third waves of the Soviet armies as well as the Operational Maneuver Groups (OMG)[26] and destroy them before they could reach the FLOT.[27] Among the new sensors was the Joint Surveillance Target Attack Radar System (JSTARS), a flying radar platform that was engineered to scan the ground for vehicles. The AH-64 attack helicopter as well as the Pershing II, a precision guided ballistic missile, the Multiple-launch Rocket System (MLRS) and the Copperhead Projectile to be employed by the field artillery were to bring the firepower to the battlefield. In addition, TACFIRE (Tactical Fire Direction), a command and control system, should help to guide the "symphony of destruction." The recourse to technical means to destroy the enemy in masses is obvious when looking at AirLand Battle, especially the faith towards weapons that would be mature only in the decades to come. The mentioned modern weapons were, at that time, not named explicitly, but they occupied the professional audience. In August 1984, the commanding general of the2nd Armored Division,[28] Major General John W. Woodmansee Jr., described the implications of the microchip in *Military Review*: "The chip is the technological key to the new doctrine—the counterpart to the blitzkrieg's use of the gasoline engine. [...] The chip is also the basic technology for turning 'dumb' munitions into precision-guided munitions and for developing advanced night vision devices that will allow us to fight at night almost as we do in the daytime."[29] The technological foundations were therewith acknowledged already: modern sensors as well as precise weapons systems should enable more firepower. The understanding was that Deep Attack would be fought primarily with firepower. Leonhard, therefore, accuses AirLand Battle of being too technology-based and having neglected the dynamics of leadership, morals, deception, fatigue and other factors.[30] And this even as "initiative," mental agility and *Auftragstaktik* were presumed to be decisive for the conduct of the "chaotic" battle.

As the term "AirLand Battle" indicates, the concept depended on cooperation with the Air Force. The manual from 1982 indicated: "The Air Force is an equal partner in the air-land battle. It supports the battle with counter-air and air interdiction operations [...] Air interdiction operations destroy, isolate, neutralize, or delay the enemy's military potential before it can influence friendly operations."[31] The Commission on Integrated Long-Term Strategy in 1988 pointed out that Precision Guided Munitions (PGM) could substitute tactical nuclear weapons in their spectrum of operations in the future. That comprised (at least in the heads of some planners) even the deployment in the Deep Battle.[32] In 1988, Major Robert M. Chapman, Chief, Air Warfare and Simulation Branch at the Air Command and Staff College, wrote in the *Airpower Journal* about the role of technology: "The battlefield was never a safe place, but technology has increased the danger. [...] One advantage of precision guidance is that fewer weapons are needed to destroy a target."[33] Hence, the so-called Smart Bombs[34] would increase destructive power in a more effective way. The advantages of PGM had been discussed as early as in 1985 by James P. Coyne in the October edition of the *Air Force Magazine*:

> Key to the employment of these weapons on the modern battlefield is minimum exposure time for the aircraft employing them. In the Vietnam era, ground support aircraft operated in flights of four, staying over the target area for periods of several minutes to deliver ordnance. This would be suicide today because of the

deadly ground-to-air defenses. [...] Weapons coming into the inventory in the future will enable pilots to reduce exposure time even more, perhaps to as little as five seconds.[35]

The general consensus was that technological possibilities would facilitate the precise destruction of important targets and enable pilots to stay out of the dangerous surface-to-air missile (SAM) umbrellas. Thus, theoretically, in the very near future, not every enemy vehicle will have to be targeted singularly, but the possibility exists to single out bridges or road junctions to stop whole formations at once.

Apart from the fighter plane (for example the new F-15E Strike Eagle attacker) and MLRS, the attack helicopter with its anti-tank missiles was planned to attack into the "depth" as well. In 1988, Lieutenant General Crosbie E. Saint, commanding general, III Corps and Colonel Walter H. Yates Jr., commanding officer, 6th Cavalry Brigade (Air Combat), discussed the role of the AH-64 Apache in different editions of *Military Review*. First, the advantages in the Close Operations were mentioned: "Attack helicopter units [...] have the ability to focus combat power and influence the tempo of battle with awesome speed, flexibility and versatility. [...] That is, they are not committed to battle pending full development of the scheme of maneuver and the appropriate moment to strike at a created or recently discovered vulnerability."[36] Then the Deep Operations: "It becomes clear that air maneuver with attack helicopters is the most responsive and sustainable operation available to a corps commander for influencing the deep operation."[37] Both authors seemed to be strong supporters of the attack helicopter. Indeed, the combination of the Apache and its Hellfire missile represented a quantum leap over the Cobra with its wire-guided missiles (TOW). It has to be said, though, that attack helicopters normally would be vulnerable to enemy aircraft and even moderate air defenses. After successes against Iraqi armor in 1991 as well as effective sneak attacks at the beginning of Desert Storm, the attack helicopter idea was somehow demystified during the conventional phase of Operation Iraqi Freedoms' in 2003.[38]

Operation Desert Storm as a Template for Airpower

AirLand Battle was developed further towards the end of the 1980s, resulting in the concept of AirLand Battle Future that was being worked on as Operation Desert Storm already was taking place. After the dissolution of the USSR, the United States became the sole remaining superpower and demonstrated its conventional superiority in 1991. Operation Desert Storm showed the effectiveness of PGM and Stealth[39]; moreover, the Army could have beaten the Iraqi Army possibly even by using fewer troops, which the

Air Force liked to point out repeatedly. On the one hand, this victory strengthened the self-confidence of the military and its political influence; on the other hand, it enlarged the already enormous belief in technology.[40]

After experiences in Operation Desert Storm, the concept of Revolution in Military Affairs (RMA),[41] which was coined by military reformers, favored the Air Force increasingly. The aerial campaign against Iraq in 1991 had shown facets of a new "type of war": the Iraqi Army had been attrited, and its Command and Control capabilities (C2) had been hampered at the very same time. Despite that, the ideas of airpower proponents such as General Buster C. Glosson or Colonel John A. Warden III, who would have preferred to have no ground war at all, were not entirely implemented.[42] It was Warden, then, who conceived the idea of the enemy as a system in an article in *Airpower Journal*, and therewith, he carried his modern vision of aerial warfare to extremes. In the 1995 article, Warden wrote about a Five Ring model, which he meant to be suited for any type of enemy: "If we are going to think strategically, we must think of the enemy as a system composed of numerous subsystems. Thinking of the enemy in terms of a system gives us a much better chance of forcing or inducing him to make our objectives his objectives and doing so with minimum effort and the maximum chance of success."[43] Warden named leadership, organic essentials, infrastructure, population and fielded military forces to be the five parts of this system. The problem would be the identification of the Centers of Gravity: "Every state and every military organization will have a unique set of centers of gravity or vulnerabilities. [...] The most important requirement of strategic attack is understanding the enemy's system. The system understood, the next problem becomes one of how to reduce it to the desired level or to paralyze it if required."[44]

It now ultimately seemed possible to attack the enemy parallel on different levels. General Ronald R. Fogleman, then chief of staff of the United States Air Force, described a very similar concept in the April 1996 edition of the *Air Force Magazine*: "While these may vary as a function of the enemy, these centers generally include things like the leadership elite, command and control, internal security mechanisms, war production capability, and one, some, or all branches of the armed forces—in short, it's the enemy's ability to effectively wage war."[45] The idea was not new. General "Billy" Mitchell, one of the dominant advocates of airpower in the U.S. in the interwar period, envisioned aircraft attacking the enemy deep in its own territory with huge weapons, especially war-relevant industry and population centers. The Italian Gulio Douhet had even proposed attacks with chemical or biological weapons.[46]

Ultimately, the terms and *termini* used were, in the essence, the same as Warden's. The editor-in-chief of the *Air Force Magazine*, John T. Correl, wrote about the Deep Strike (Deep Attack as from the concept of AirLand Battle) in 1996 and adopted terms from Warden such as parallel attack on centers of gravity: "The dominant requirement for deep attack in a major regional conflict is to strike the enemy's centers of gravity and to do it rapidly, accurately, and with intensity. [...] The objective is to attack these centers of gravity 'in parallel'—all of them at once—rather than serially."[47]

However, the new language that the Air Force was using, did not please everyone. In the summer 1996 edition of the *Airpower Journal*, Colonel Richard Szafranksi, Chair of National Military Strategy at the Air War College, discussed the problems the Air Force faced when it had to demonstrate the worth of its means considering the budget cuts hitting all branches: "The Air Force can talk of the 'enemy as a system' or of striking plural strategic 'centers of gravity,' but few people in the Air Force know precisely what those phrases mean."[48] Szafranski hereby points to the problem of targeting, which even Warden had not been able to clarify properly. Despite all the available new technology, there existed no instrument to discern the most important target from other, lesser ones. This seems to be even more fitting to the counterinsurgency environment in today's Afghanistan. The Air Force paper, "Global Engagement," which represented an Air Force answer to the Joint Vision 2010 published by the Defense Department, nonetheless did again mention, in 1996, the center of gravity in a passage about "modern war."

The Air Force also recognizes the emerging reality that in the 21st century, it will be possible to find, fix or track and target anything that moves on the surface of the earth. "Global Engagement: A Vision for the 21st Century Air Force" is based on a new understanding of what air and space power mean to the nation—the ability to hit an adversary's strategic center of gravity directly as well as prevail at the operational and tactical levels of warfare.[49]

"Global Engagement" holds a lot of confident statements and visions regarding the future of war although not all can be cited here. The Air Force did, by all means, want to present the advantages of its technological capabilities (against the backdrop of the mentioned budget cuts). More than a few of these arguments and terms and termini, which came with them in 1997, got into the new Air Force Doctrine Document (AFDD). In the second chapter in this AFDD 1 about the "Airman's Perspective," the authors emphasized the special capabilities of air forces:

Generally, surface forces must mass combat power before launching an attack, whereas airpower is singularly able to launch an attack from widely dispersed locations and mass combat power at the objective. Moreover, from an airman's perspective, mass is not based only on the quantity of forces and materiel committed. [...] Mass is an effect that air and space forces achieve through efficiency of attack. Today's air and space forces have altered the concept of massed forces. [...] Today, a single precision weapon that is targeted using superior battlespace awareness can often cause the destructive effect that in the past took hundreds of bombs.[50]

The claim that one smart bomb could do the work of hundreds of dumb bombs was to be a constant in Air Force "promotions." The Army, too, pointed as early as in its concept Force XXI to the future deployment of smaller, more effective units, and not masses of tanks.[51] In general, Operation Desert Storm is, within the Air Force, rehashed again and again (until today) as the ideal "image of war." Nevertheless, its unique circumstances (long build-up phase, coalition partners with infrastructure in the theater, enemy without far-going ambitions) are seldom put into perspective. An enemy could be stopped and beaten by only using airpower in the so-called Halt Phase even before another phase to build up forces and gain the initiative would follow. Therefore, the enemy would be forced beyond the culminating point "through the early and sustained overwhelming application of air and space power"; the culminating point seems to be similarly taken from Clausewitz as the center of gravity.[52]

Army proponents on the other side, in this case Dr. Earl H. Tilford, Jr., of the Strategic Studies Institute at the U.S. Army War College, questioned if a future enemy could be beaten by only using air strikes: "Perhaps, if all our enemies confront us with large mechanized forces in open terrain, [...] Halt will probably work. But just because the last enemy we fought was so obliging is no indication that the next one will be."[53] Tilford, therewith, criticized the ideal image coming from the Air Force, which was based on the experiences of Operation Desert Storm (and therefore related to advanced technology compared to the enemy). Frank Finelli argued similarly in the 1999 summer edition of the *Airpower Journal*: "If an adversary chooses to mass his military formations deep in the battle space and segregate them from his populace, then aerospace power may work wonders. However, an adversary is likely to disperse his force to make us employ our aircraft and precision munitions at uneconomic rates."[54]

Nonetheless, Air Force proponents during the 1990s, in general, came to the conviction that thanks to airpower, a ground offensive had become unnecessary. This discussion has to be looked at against the backdrop of hot budget debates and quarreling during these years.[55] In this period, the U.S. intervened, as mentioned before, mainly using air strikes or peacekeepers (prominently in the Balkans, but for example in Haiti, too).

Effects-Based Operations

The airpower idea was even further refined and pushed forward when Lieutenant General Deptula promoted the Effects-based Operations (EBO). Deptula, in 2001, served as Commander of the Combined Air Operations Center for Operation Enduring Freedom. He wrote not only about a revolution in warfare but also about monumental changes. He based his ideas on

Warden's concept: "The capacity for a simultaneous attack on the entire array of high value objectives with little or no need to suppress enemy air defenses opens the door to monumental changes in the conduct of war—enables surprise at the tactical level, a larger span of influence, fewer casualties, paralyzing effects, and shorter time to impose effective control over the enemy."[56] Deptula wanted physical destruction to be only an effect: "In this approach, destruction is used to achieve effects on each of the systems the enemy organization relies on to conduct operations or exert influence—not to destroy the systems, but to prevent them from being used as the adversary desires."[57]

Deptula similarly emphasized how the enemy system could be hit simultaneously at different points. According to Deptula, it was no longer necessary to roll back enemy ground forces and air forces in advance. Deptula wrote about the usefulness of ground forces: "Surface forces will always be an essential part of the military, but massing surface forces to overwhelm an enemy is no longer an absolute prerequisite to impose control over the enemy."[58] Deptula, thereby, escalated the idea of the decisive airstrike (against the backdrop of the budget discussion) further.[59] It is indeed possible to argue that the deployment of a mechanized unit does imply much more effort necessary than an attack by stealth aircraft. The effect would be very different, nevertheless: an attack from the air does not, in any case, create the same impression on enemy soldiers as a ground force occupying territory. A similar image of airpower was presented by the editor-in-chief of the *Air Force Magazine* in June 2001: "In theater conflict, the first substantial force to engage the enemy will be advanced stealth aircraft that open the door for other land, sea, and air forces to follow."[60] This description seems to be a derivative of the Halt Phase concept and shows the Hype about the stealth bomber being still persistent. In a position paper, Army Colonel Gary H. Cheek contradictorily held the opinion that airpower would, in the future, not be able to end a conflict: "Thus, while air power is alluring because it does not require American soldiers on the ground, by itself it lacks the compelling force that ensures decision in conflict."[61] He blamed the airpower proponents for underestimating the enemy: "Advocates of effects-based operations misread this trend in lethality, as if enemies will not be able to react to the use stealth and precision weapons."[62] Both officers in the Army and the Air Force were convinced they could achieve specific effects—their argument was whether airplanes or troops were better calculated to achieve these effects.

Conclusion

Adrian R. Lewis argues that technology only makes killing more efficient, but this would never deter a determined enemy.[63] Perhaps this would be a fitting concluding statement for this research. This circumstance is evident when regarding the language use describing the "image of war": since Operation Desert Storm in 1991, the United States Air Force has pointed out increasingly how airstrikes with stealth planes deploying PGMs are more efficient compared to the deployment of ground forces. Nonetheless, at the same time, the idea of killing by itself seems only to have been made more agreeable by the concept of the effect (instead of destruction or annihilation). Christopher Tuck further sees the tendency towards a post-heroic American culture of strategy that imagines a war fought through wide distances with minimal casualties.[64]

In the 1980s, on the other side, AirLand Battle was conceived unmistakably to be the gigantic symphony of destruction of the Warsaw Pact's mass armies. Technology back then played an important role, as it was the means for the defense against a seemingly superior enemy even though factors such as initiative or morality were postulated at the same time. Mass and speed stood representative for the technological gigantism that was propagated. In the scope of the AirLand Battle, the Army proposed the image of a boxing match (balance, will, blow) against the numerically superior enemy Warsaw Pact. On the other side, the Air Force coined the idea of the surgical strike and paralysis of the enemy in the scope of EBO.

The American scientific and technological approach to war dominates the discussion heavily in the period analyzed. Efficiency coined the discourse on warfare, especially in the scope of EBO; PGMs were thought to be more precise, and therefore, more efficient than ground forces. Moreover, the thought of efficiency reflects the difficult financial state of the armed forces in the 1990s as well. However, the wars in the Balkans and the intervention in Somalia were harbingers of a war reality that did not fit as well to ideas such as Effects-based Operations. What began at the onset of the 21st century was a decade-long battle that seemed to be more similar to the Vietnam War than to all that which was propagated until then. Robert M. Gates, secretary of defense under George W. Bush and Barack Obama, is cited as follows: "In my opinion, any future defense secretary who advises the president to again send a big American land army into Asia or into the Middle East or Africa should 'have his head examined,' as General MacArthur so delicately put it."[65]

NOTES

1. Doctrine is hereby understood to be the institutionalized view on "war" and "warfare," refer to Headquarters, *Department of the Army: Field Manual 3-0, Operations* (Washington, D.C., 2008), D-1: "Army doctrine is a body of thought on how Army forces intend to operate as an integral part of a joint force. Doctrine focuses on how to think—not what to think. It establishes [...] how the Army views the nature of operations."
2. Adrian R. Lewis, *The American Culture of War: The History of U.S. Military*

III. The Cold War

Force from World War II to Operation Iraqi Freedom and Omaha Beach (New York: Routledge Chapman & Hall, 2007); Thomas G. Mahnken, *Technology and the American Way of War since 1945* (New York: Columbia University Press, 2008).

3. For example "instructions," "guideline" or even "guide" to "war" or "warfighting."

4. *Field Manual 100-5*, later on 3-0, is one of the Army's two basic documents apart from Field Manual 1, and it is on top of the structure of regulations and manuals.

5. The Big Five were part of this range of weapons: the M1 Abrams main battle tank (MBT), the medium transport helicopter UH-60 Blackhawk, the attack helicopter AH-64 Apache, the infantry fighting vehicle (IFV) M2/3 Bradley, and the ground-based surface-to-air missile system Patriot.

6. Starry had been Commander, V Corps in Europe and commander, Armor Center and School; after his tenure at TRADOC, he became Commander, Readiness Command, which prepared overseas deployments of U.S. troops.

7. Headquarters, *Department of the Army: Field Manual 100-5, Operations* (Washington, D.C., 1982).

8. Ibid., 2-3.

9. According to U.S. comprehension: effect primarily through fire into the depth of the battlefield; Robert R. Leonhard, *The Art of Maneuver: Maneuver-Warfare Theory and AirLand Battle* (Novato: Presidio Press, 1991), 144.

10. Headquarters, "U.S. Army Training & Doctrine Command: U.S. Army Operational Concepts," TRADOC *Pamphlet 525- 5 The AirLand Battle and Corps 86* (25 March 1981), 11-15.

11. John L. Romjue, *From Active Defense to AirLand Battle: The Development of Army Doctrine 1973-1982* (United States Army Training and Doctrine Command, Fort Monroe, Virginia, June 1984), 59.

12. A Numbered Air Force owns Wings and Squadrons in a certain Area of Operations.

13. Headquarters, "U.S. Army Training & Doctrine Command: U.S. Army Operational Concepts," TRADOC *Pamphlet 525-5 The AirLand Battle and Corps 86* (25 March 1981), 40-41.

14. Ibid., 3.

15. Robert M. Citino, *Blitzkrieg to Desert Storm: The Evolution of Operational Warfare* (Lawrence: University of Kansas, 2004), 262.

16. Robert R. Tomes, *U.S. Defense Strategy from Vietnam to Operation Iraqi Freedom: Military Innovation and the New American Way of War, 1973-2003* (London: Routledge, 2007), 112.

17. Douglas W. Skinner, *AirLand Battle Doctrine, Professional Paper 463 / September 1988* (Alexandria, Virginia: Center for Naval Analyses, 1988), 6-8.

18. Headquarters, "U.S. Army Training & Doctrine Command: U.S. Army Operational Concepts," TRADOC *Pamphlet 525- 5 The AirLand Battle and Corps 86* (25 March 1981), 5.

19. Ibid., 67.

20. Ibid., 68.

21. Headquarters, *Department of the Army: Field Manual 100-5, Operations* (Washington, D.C., 1986), 14.

22. Hereto the so-called OODA loop (observe, orient, decide, act) or Boyd Cycle has to be named, proposed by Air Force Colonel John Boyd in 1976. This approach should help to guide reactions up to the strategic level to bring the enemy off balance;

John R. Boyd, *Destruction and Creation* (U.S. Army Command and General Staff College, September 3, 1976).
   23. Ibid., 17.
   24. Donald L. Mercer, "Targeting Soviet Forces," *Military Review* (Mai 1984), 24.
   25. Charles J. Dick, "Soviet Operational Concepts," *Military Review* (September 1985), 33.
   26. Consisting of an armored division or even a Corps, the OMG should comprise one or multiple Independent Maneuver Element(s) to probe for gaps or weaknesses in the enemy's lines and open breaches, into which up-moving forces could advance at once; see David M. Glantz, *Soviet Military Operational Art: In Pursuit of Deep Battle* (London: Routledge, 1991), 228–234.
   27. Mahnken, *Technology*, 128–129.
   28. During the Cold War, the primary mission of the 2nd Armored Division was to prepare to conduct heavy armored combat against Warsaw Pact forces in defense of NATO. The division was part of the U.S. Army's plan to move divisions to Europe in the event of a Warsaw Pact attack on NATO. One of its Brigades was permanently forward deployed to Germany (2nd Armored Division [Forward]). Its missions were either to secure airfields and staging areas for the deployment of III Corps from the United States or to deploy directly to the Inter-German Border (IGB) to establish a blocking position.
   29. John W. Woodmansee Jr., "Blitzkrieg and the AirLand Battle," *Military Review* (August 1984), 27.
   30. Leonhard, *Maneuver-warfare*, 139–141.
   31. Headquarters, *Department of the Army: Field Manual 100-5, Operations* (Washington, D.C., 1982), 7-6–7-7.
   32. Tomes, *U.S. Defense Strategy*, 104.
   33. Robert M. Chapman, "Technology, Air Power, and the Modern Theater Battlefield," *Airpower Journal* (Summer 1988).
   34. The term Smart is mentioned mainly together with the smart bombs or other modern PGM, which are able to pursue their target after acquisition by themselves and can even distinguish their target from others.
   35. James P. Coyne, "Coordinating the Air-Ground Battle," *Air Force Magazine* (October 1985), 68.
   36. Crosbie E. Saint, and Walter H. Yates, Jr., "Attack helicopter operations in the AirLand battle: CLOSE OPERATIONS," *Military Review* (June 1988), 4.
   37. Ibid., 3–5.
   38. Richard J. Newman, "Ambush at Najaf," *Air Force Magazine* (October 2003), 60–63.
   39. Stealth comprises different measures taken to reduce the radar cross section (RCS) of a plane (today vehicles or ships as well); Mahnken, *Technology*, 160–167.
   40. Lewis, *The American Culture of War*, 378–383.
   41. A Revolution in Military Affairs includes changes of technological, organizational as well as doctrinal scope. The herein specifically addressed RMA was linked by U.S. analysts to the increasing digitalization and interconnection on the battlefield beginning with Operation Desert Storm in 1991. James Kievit and Steven Metz, *Strategy and the Revolution in Military Affairs: From Theory to Policy* (U.S. Army War College, Strategic Studies Institute, June 27, 1995). Additional literature: MacGregor Knox and Williamson Murray, *The Dynamics of Military Revolution 1300-2050* (Cambridge: Cambridge University Press, 2001); Alvin and Heidi Toffler, *War and Anti-War: Survival*

242　III. The Cold War

at the Dawn of the 21st Century (London: Grand Central Publishing, 1994); Robert J. Bunker, "Generations, Waves, and Epochs—Modes of Warfare and the RMPA," *Airpower Journal* (Spring 1996); Martin van Creveld, *Technology and War—From 2000 BC to the Present* (London: Touchstone, 1989); J.F.C. Fuller, *Armament and History: A Study of the Influence of Armament on History from the Dawn of Classical Warfare to the Second World War* (London: Da Capo Press, 1946) and Andrew F. Krepinevich, "Cavalry to Computer—The Pattern of Military Revolutions," *The National Interest* (Fall 1994).

42. Benjamin Buley, *The New American Way of War. Military Culture and the Political Utility of Force* (London: Routledge, 2008), 79.

43. John A. Warden III, "The Enemy as a System," *Airpower Journal* (Spring 1995).

44. Ibid.

45. Cited in John T. Correll, "The New American Way of War," *Air Force Magazine* (April 1996).

46. Martin van Creveld, *The Age of Airpower* (New York: Public Affairs, 2011), 55–57.

47. John T. Correll, "Deep Strike," *Air Force Magazine* (April 1996).

48. John T. Correll, "Deep Strike," *Air Force Magazine* (April 1996), 56.

49. Department of the Air Force, "Global Engagement: A Vision for the 21st Century Air Force" (Washington, D.C., 1996).

50. United States Air Force, "Air Force Doctrine Document 1[qm] (September 1997), 16.

51. Headquarters, "U.S. Army Training & Doctrine Command: Force XXI Operations," TRADOC *Pamphlet 525 5: A Concept for the Evolution of Full-Dimensional Operations for the Strategic Army of the Early Twenty-First Century* (1 August 1994), 2–9: "Looking at conventional and high-intensity warfare, recent military-technical developments point toward an increase in the depth, breadth, and height of the battlefield. This extension of the battlespace with fewer soldiers in it is an evolutionary trend in the conduct of war."

52. The culminating point (Kulminationspunkt) describes the climax (Höhepunkt) after which the defender (the coalition forces in Operation Desert Storm) can go on the offensive.

53. Earl H. Tilford Jr., *Halt Phase Strategy: New Wine in Old Skins* (Strategic Studies Institute, U.S. Army War College, Carlisle, 1998), 13–14.

54. Frank Finelli, "Transforming Aerospace Power," *Airpower Journal* (Summer 1999), 9.

55. After the Quadrennial Defense Review in 1997, the proposition was made to have the Air Force reduce 26,900 personnel versus 15,000 in the Army and 18,000 in the Navy. The F-22 program should be slashed also, as well the B-2 and JSTARS; Tilford, *Halt Phase Strategy*, 3–4.

56. David A. Deptula, *Effects-Based Operations: Change in the Nature of Warfare* (Arlington: Aerospace Education Foundation, 2001), 4–5.

57. Ibid., 11.

58. Ibid, 18. In April 2001 Deptula as well published an article about EBO in the Air Force Magazine: David A. Deptula, "Firing for Effects," *Air Force Magazine* (April 2001), 46–48.

59. After the Quadrennial Defense Review in 1997, the proposition was made to have the Air Force reduce 26,900 personnel versus 15,000 in the Army and 18,000 in the Navy. The F-22 program should be slashed also, as well the B-2 and JSTARS. Confer Tilford, *Halt Phase Strategy*, 3–4.

60. John T. Correll, "Evolution of the Aerospace Force," *Air Force Magazine* (June 2001), 2.
61. Gary Cheek, "Effects-Based Operations: The End of Dominant Maneuver?" in *Transformation Concepts for National Security in the 21st Century*, ed. Williamson Murray (Strategic Studies Institute of the U.S. Army War College, Carlisle, 2002), 86.
62. Ibid, 88.
63. Lewis, *The American Culture of War*, 388.
64. Christopher Tuck, "Land Warfare," in *Understanding Modern Warfare*, ed. David Jordan et al. (Cambridge: Routledge Chapman & Hall, 2008), 114–115.
65. Tom Shanker, "Warning against Wars like Iraq and Afghanistan" *New York Times*, February 26, 2011, A7.

Works Cited

Boyd, John R. *Destruction and Creation*. U.S. Army Command and General Staff College, September 3, 1976.
Buley, Benjamin. *The New American Way of War: Military Culture and the Political Utility of Force*. London: Routledge, 2008.
Bunker, Robert J. "Generations, Waves, and Epochs: Modes of Warfare and the RMPA." *Airpower Journal* (Spring 1996).
Chapman, Robert M. "Technology, Air Power, and the Modern Theater Battlefield." *Airpower Journal* (Summer 1988).
Cheek, Gary. "Effects-Based Operations: The End of Dominant Maneuver?" in *Transformation Concepts for National Security in the 21st Century*, ed. Williamson Murray. Strategic Studies Institute of the U.S. Army War College, Carlisle, 2002.
Citino, Robert M. *Blitzkrieg to Desert Storm: The Evolution of Operational Warfare*. Lawrence: University of Kansas, 2004.
Correll, John T. "Deep Strike." *Air Force Magazine* (April 1996).
Correll, John T. "Evolution of the Aerospace Force." *Air Force Magazine* (June 2001).
Correll, John T. "The New American Way of War." *Air Force Magazine* (April 1996).
Coyne, James P. "Coordinating the Air-Ground Battle," *Air Force Magazine* (October 1985).
Creveld, Martin van. *Technology and War: From 2000 BC to the Present*. London: Touchstone, 1989.
Creveld, Martin van. *The Age of Airpower*. New York: Public Affairs, 2011.
Department of the Air Force, *Global Engagement: A Vision for the 21st Century Air Force*. Washington, D.C., 1996.
Deptula, David A. *Effects-Based Operations: Change in the Nature of Warfare*. Arlington: Aerospace Education Foundation, 2001.
Deptula, David A. "Firing for Effects." *Air Force Magazine* (April 2001), 46–48.
Dick, Charles J. "Soviet Operational Concepts." *Military Review* (September 1985).
Finelli, Frank. "Transforming Aerospace Power." *Airpower Journal* (Summer 1999).
Fuller, J.F.C. *Armament and History: A Study of the Influence of Armament on History from the Dawn of Classical Warfare to the Second World War*. London: Da Capo Press, 1946.
Glantz, David M. *Soviet Military Operational Art: In Pursuit of Deep Battle*. London: Routledge, 1991.
Headquarters, *Department of the Army: Field Manual 100–5, Operations*. Washington, D.C., 1982.
Headquarters, *Department of the Army: Field Manual 100–5, Operations*. Washington, D.C., 1986.

Headquarters, *Department of the Army: Field Manual 3-0, Operations.* Washington, D.C., 2008.
Headquarters, "U.S. Army Training & Doctrine Command: Force XXI Operations," *TRADOC Pamphlet 525 5A Concept for the Evolution of Full-Dimensional Operations for the Strategic Army of the Early Twenty-First Century* (1 August 1994).
Headquarters, "U.S. Army Training & Doctrine Command: U.S. Army Operational Concepts," *TRADOC Pamphlet 525-5 The AirLand Battle and Corps* 86 (25 March 1981).
Kievit, James, and Steven Metz. *Strategy and the Revolution in Military Affairs: From Theory to Policy.* U.S. Army War College, Strategic Studies Institute, June 27, 1995.
Knox, MacGregor, and Williamson Murray. *The Dynamics of Military Revolution 1300-2050.* Cambridge: Cambridge University Press, 2001.
Krepinevich, Andrew F. "Cavalry to Computer—The Pattern of Military Revolutions." *The National Interest* (Fall 1994).
Leonhard, Robert R. *The Art of Maneuver: Maneuver-Warfare Theory and AirLand Battle.* Novato: Presidio Press, 1991.
Lewis, Adrian R. *The American Culture of War: The History of U.S. Military Force from World War II to Operation Iraqi Freedom and Omaha Beach.* New York: Routledge Chapman & Hall, 2007.
Linn, Brian M. *Echo of Battle: The Army's Way of War.* Cambridge: Harvard University Press, 2007.
Mahnken, Thomas G. *Technology and the American Way of War Since 1945.* New York: Columbia University Press, 2008.
Mercer, Donald L. "Targeting Soviet Forces." *Military Review* (Mai 1984).
Newman, Richard J. "Ambush at Najaf." *Air Force Magazine* (October 2003).
Romjue, John L. *From Active Defense to AirLand Battle: The Development of Army Doctrine 1973-1982 (United States Army Training and Doctrine Command).* Fort Monroe, Virginia, June 1984.
Saint, Crosbie E., and Walter H. Yates, Jr. "Attack Helicopter Operations in the AirLand Battle: CLOSE OPERATIONS." *Military Review* (June 1988).
Shanker, Tom. "Warning Against Wars Like Iraq and Afghanistan." *New York Times* (February 26, 2011).
Skinner, Douglas W. *AirLand Battle Doctrine, Professional Paper 463 / September 1988.* Alexandria, Virginia: Center for Naval Analyses, 1988.
Szafranski, Richard. "Interservice Rivalry in Action." *Airpower Journal* (Summer 1996).
Tilford, Earl H., Jr. *Halt Phase Strategy: New Wine in Old Skins.* Strategic Studies Institute, U.S. Army War College, Carlisle, 1998.
Toffler, Alvin, and Heidi Toffler. *War and Anti-War—Survival at the Dawn of the 21st Century.* London: Grand Central Publishing, 1994.
Tomes, Robert R. *U.S. Defense Strategy from Vietnam to Operation Iraqi Freedom: Military Innovation and the New American Way of War, 1973-2003.* London: Routledge, 2007.
Tuck, Christopher. "Land Warfare," in *Understanding Modern Warfare*, ed. David Jordan, et al. Cambridge: Routledge Chapman & Hall, 2008.
United States Air Force: *Air Force Doctrine Document 1* (September 1997).
Warden III, John A. "The Enemy as a System." *Airpower Journal* (Spring 1995).
Woodmansee, John W., Jr. "Blitzkrieg and the AirLand Battle." *Military Review* (August 1984).

PART IV.
THE AGE OF "NEW WARS"

Technology and War
Nanotechnology, Precision and Globalization

JEFFREY M. SHAW

"By far the most important insight it is possible to gather from knowing and understanding the past is that what is should not be construed as what has always been, nor as what necessarily must be, nor as what can be."[1]

Throughout history, technological advances and new inventions have often led to increased lethality on the battlefield. As technological advances have led to more accurate and more powerful weapons as well as to more efficient means for organizing, sustaining, and supplying large armies, military casualties and collateral damage to civilian populations have generally increased. However, it is worth noting that "advances in lethality have not been exclusively caused by weapons."[2] In many cases, inventions, tools, and artifacts have been adopted by armed forces even when their intended use was not necessarily related to the military. Ever since the Bronze Age gave way to the Iron Age, various technologies of many different types have contributed to the inexorable increase in the destructive nature of warfare. However, it might be the case that advances in nanotechnology, precision weaponry, and information and communication technology have the potential to reverse this trend. This chapter suggests that advances in these three areas may have the potential to reduce the lethality of warfare, with a commensurate reduction in casualties on both the battlefield as well as within civilian populations.

One important question that must be addressed is, "what do we mean when we use the term 'technology'?" Are we referring to specific products or to specific machines, gadgets, or weapons? Or is it rather a manifestation of some human drive to seek new methods of efficiency that the word "technology" refers? Various philosophers have provided definitions of technology that are useful in this particular argument. French philosopher Jacques Ellul (1912–1994), when writing about technology, used the term *technique* to describe the largely autonomous movement towards maximum efficiency in every human endeavor. He wrote, "*Technique* refers to any complex of standardized means for attaining a predetermined result. Thus, it converts spontaneous and unreflective behavior into behavior that is deliberate and rationalized. The Technical Man is [...] committed to the never-ending search for "the one best way" to achieve any designated objective."[3] However, a more precise definition of technology may be required for our purposes. The contemporary American philosopher Carl Mitcham proposes that "technology, or the making and using of artifacts, is a largely unthinking activity," and that "the need to think about technology is nevertheless increasingly manifest," especially since "the inherent complexity and practical efficacy of modern technologies call forth diverse kinds of thinking—scientific and technical, of course, but also economic, psychological, political, and so forth."[4] Mitcham's plea to think about technology in its many manifestations and Ellul's assertion that technology (*technique*) is a self-perpetuating process that constantly seeks maximum efficiency in every human endeavor provide the intellectual framework through which three visible manifestations of the technological process—nanotechnology, precision weaponry, and information/communication technology—will be examined.

Technological advances should not be considered only in light of changes in the types of weapons deployed by various antagonists on the battlefield or even in terms of specific products or devices. In fact, as Israeli military historian and theorist Martin Van Creveld has observed, "the common habit of referring to technology in terms of its capabilities may, when applied within the context of war, do more harm than good."[5] He goes on to explain that "even the very conceptual frameworks employed by our brains in order to think about war and its conduct."[6] These ideas lead us to the supposition that technology is about more than simply the visible manifestations of the technological process. In fact, technology refers to ideas such as language, writing, and even patterns of thought that are influenced and reinforced by the never-ending quest for efficiency. As such, when discussing the impact and influence of technology on warfare, we can include a number of different concepts, from the individual weapons and their employment, to the overall technical milieu within which they are employed.

In keeping with this theme, the American sociologist and historian Lewis Mumford (1895–1990) has proposed that history can be roughly divided into three phases based on the dominant forces of technology that characterized each age. His general outline conforms to the notions that efficiency is a driving force behind technology's continual advance, as Ellul described, and that for the most part; this continued advance is largely "an unthinking activity," as Mitcham explained. The first phase that Mumford described was the Eotechnic, followed by the Paleotechnic, and most recently, the Neotechnic. The clock characterizes the Eotechnic phase, providing a new regimentation to time and to the tasks that were now made possible based on the division of time throughout the day. Monasteries were the social manifestations that resulted from the technology of the clock, but the impact of the clock can also be seen in the military sphere. Here is an example of a technology clearly not designed with any specific military application in mind, but one that had a major impact on the intellectual constructs that would regiment much of society, starting with the monastery, and moving into the factory and the barracks. About the clock and the tremendous impact that the clock had on not only medieval society but our own as well, Mumford observed, "it is with the collective organization and regimentation of the army that the conflicts between men have reached heights of bestiality and terrorism."[7] Regimentation is a direct corollary of the basic practice of time-keeping that the clock made possible. Technology and warfare continued to advance in tandem, the one influencing the other, throughout the early modern period. Referring primarily to the Western world, Mumford observed, "finding the instruments of warfare more effective, men sought new occasions for their use."[8] He stated:

> The general indoctrination of soldierly habits of thought in the seventeenth century was, it seems probable, a great psychological aid to the spread of machine industrialism. In terms of the barracks, the routine of the factory seemed tolerable and natural. The spread of conscription and volunteer militia forces throughout the Western World after the French Revolution made army and factory, so far as their social effects went, almost interchangeable terms. And the complacent characterizations of the First World War, namely that it was a large-scale industrial operation, has also a meaning in reverse: modern industrialism may equally well be termed a large-scale military operation.[9]

Here we see an indirect linkage between the prevailing technical milieu and warfare. Industrialism has, according to Mumford, been the handmaiden of the large-scale military operation, a phenomenon especially evident in the carnage of the First World War. Hew Strachan, the world's leading First World War historian, seconds this notion with the statement that "the extension of the battlefield [...] was a direct result of Europe's industrialisation."[10] The intellectual stultification of the factory could be seen in many sectors of society, to include the military, which was a near mirror-image of the factory. Perhaps though, it is possible that the information age of the twenty first century, so different in kind from the industrial age of assembly lines and hierarchical social structure, might usher in a different relationship between technology and warfare, one that reverses the trend of ever-increasing casualty rates and destruction. If the factory and industrialization shaped the character of warfare to such an extent in the eighteenth and nineteenth century, then we can propose that globalization and the information and communication revolution of the twenty-first century may also have an impact on the character of warfare, although as will be seen in the final section of this chapter, the overall impact of these types of technologies may actually reduce the lethality of warfare. In Mumford's writing, we see that technology and warfare have advanced towards greater degrees of efficiency together, largely resulting in an increase in the destructive nature of warfare up until now. Also, we see that the systems that provide order and stability for society at large can have a tremendous influence over the conduct and character of warfare.

Martin van Creveld outlines a somewhat similar progression of historical eras in *Technology and War*. Briefly, he presents the age of tools, from earliest times up to about 1500; the age of machines, from 1500–1830; the age of systems, from 1830–1945; and the age of automation, from 1945 to the present day. It is not our purpose to examine how van Creveld proposes that technology influenced the conduct of warfare in these eras, but his general thesis is that over time, technology has become increasingly linked to the practice of war, and that "war is completely permeated by technology and governed by it."[11] van Creveld's observations lead us to a conclusion similar to that which one would reach having studied Mumford. Not only does warfare become more destructive as technology continues to advance and increase in efficiency, but the employment of military force and the development of military efficiency is often shadowed by the prevailing social structures which are also conditioned by technology.

However, as technological advancement has continued at an accelerated pace in the last few decades, perhaps the time will come when the lethality of warfare is actually brought under control or even reversed. Advances in nanotechnology, precision, and information/communication technology may potentially render warfare somewhat less lethal in the long run to both combatants and civilians.

The first technological advance that could have the potential to reduce the destructive potential of warfare is nanotechnology. Of all the new technologies prevalent in the twenty first century, these "new technologies, of which nanotechnology leads the way, make the craft of war and violence easier and less costly to participate in from an offensive point of view."[12] While this might lead one to conclude that nations might be more willing to engage in offensive warfare, potentially more destructive, it is also likely that "on the whole, nanotechnology will likely be transformative in its nature and will bring about a more highly enabled military."[13] The military application of nanotechnology, as well as its potential to change the fundamental nature of many other aspects of contemporary life, deserves further examination. "In international relations, the specter of all-out nuclear war led to tense relations between the major nations of the world. However it also probably kept the

Cold War cold, instead of the situation resulting in a third world war."[14] Others have noted that employing nanotechnologically-based weaponry has the potential to "help reduce, or even completely avoid, civilian casualties" with the resulting implication that "future warfare may well be expected to become more humane."[15]

A dissenting argument must be taken into account when addressing the idea that nanotechnology could potentially usher in an era of *less* destructive warfare. Going beyond the Cold War paradigm of mutually assured destruction as the prevailing intellectual construct in international affairs, Mark Gubrud has argued that the potentially devastating possibilities inherent in nanotechnological development would require an unprecedented level of international cooperation and oversight. His general thesis is that nanotechnologically-enabled military forces will not be constrained by the traditional international system, composed as it is of treaties and precedent for how, when and why armed force should be deployed. He states:

> A race to develop early military applications of molecular manufacturing could yield sudden breakthroughs, leading to the abrupt emergence of new and unfamiliar threats, and provoking political and military reactions which further reinforce a cycle of competition and confrontation. A very rapid pace of technological change destabilizes the political-military balance.[16]

While similar statements could have been made at the beginning of the Cold War, a fact which Gubrud acknowledges in his argument, it obviously remains to be seen if nanotechnology can be integrated peacefully or not into the existing international order. The possibilities for chaos on an unimaginable scale could be predicted with ease if one assumes that the potential for new weaponry, new uses of nanotechnology and specifically for molecular manufacturing fall into the wrong hands or into the right hands that do not yet understand the full ramifications of these new weapons. While it is likely that nanotechnology will change some aspects of society, economically, politically and perhaps in other ways as well, it is also highly likely that "the sudden, complete overturning of the current world system of states (with several non-state actors) is unlikely."[17]

Philosopher Hans Lenk provides a counterargument to the idea that nanotechnology "run amok" might herald an age of chaos and destruction. He has proposed that the globalization of technology "and the technicalization of almost everything leads to a new unity of the world, engenders a new 'technogenic world'" that is "technological, informational, interactive, [and] integrated," such that "we seem to live in a media-electronic global village."[18] The contrasting visions offered by both Gubrud and Lenk offer contemporary observers a choice between two extremes. However, the verdict on nanotechnology's impact on future warfare is still out. It is safe, at this point, to assume that:

Nanotechnology may thus serve as a potential "game changer" in the military landscape. One of the major factors that are currently hindering military applications of nanotechnology is the pre-existing military mindset. Weapons development is driven, in large part, by the current operational needs, rather than future operational possibilities. Nanotechnology is like a transistor—it in itself does not do any good or harm, but the application of nanotechnology and their integration into a larger system produce novel functions and effects.[19]

Nanotechnology has yet to make an appreciable impact on military technology, but the implications could clearly be that the nature of warfare is changed. It remains to be seen what this impact will be, but an optimistic projection might be that the destructive nature of warfare could be brought into check, or at least, nations may be deterred from plunging headlong into the abyss that Mark Gubrud proposes.

Perhaps the many technological advances in precision weaponry could also act to reverse the increasingly destructive nature of contemporary warfare. With the increases in precision guidance and accuracy that have taken place over the last decade, "there appears to be no downward side" to the "potential to minimize collateral and civilian casualties" as precision capabilities continue to be advanced and refined.[20] Precision is a broad category, and within it, one finds primarily targeting systems rather than actual kinetic weapons. The U.S. preponderance of technologically advanced capabilities during Operation Iraqi Freedom in 2003 included "pervasive GPS capabilities, new sensor systems, near-real time 'sensor to shooter' intelligence, and computer-networked communications," all of which "allowed U.S. forces to leverage the four key elements of the modern battlespace—knowledge, speed precision, and lethality—and to prevail quickly at minimal cost."[21] In a conventional conflict in which armed forces are arrayed against each other, such as the opening stages of Operation Iraqi Freedom, "commanders can then use massed and/or precision firepower and maneuver their forces to avoid fratricide and collateral damage," and these technologies might also allow antagonists to "reduce civilian casualties and unintended damage."[22]

One might notice a paradox in the examples presented here. Operation Iraqi Freedom did, in fact, demonstrate that certain technologies, when applied with a specific operational objective in mind, could lead to a quick, decisive conventional military victory. However, once the conventional phase of the operation ended, Iraq was plagued by years of deadly violence. According to van Creveld, "the effect of the vast majority of weapons has been limited mainly to tactics."[23] This statement applies especially to the categories of nanotechnology and precision technology, which generally have the potential to influence the development and employment of certain specific types of weapons that will be of utility on the battlefield and will most likely be under the control of a tactical commander at some level. Referring to the technological advantage that European powers enjoyed over Asian nations in the sixteenth and seventeenth centuries, historian Adam Clulow observed:

> As a recent conflict in Iraq or Afghanistan tells us, even the most potent technological advantage requires the presence of specific conditions in order to be used effectively. In early modern Asia these prerequisites were only rarely met and there was a significant gap between potential and actual application. For every instance of a successful campaign, there are numerous examples in which their capacity to make effective use of superior technology was partially curtailed, largely contained, or entirely suppressed.[24]

Whether or not advanced weapon systems can help the U.S. or any other nation achieve their national political objectives is worthy of further study in some other venue.

Another example of the potential of precision weaponry to lower the body count on the battlefield can be found by examining the continued United States campaign that has employed unmanned aerial vehicles (UAVs) along the Afghan-Pakistani border. The *Economist* [news magazine] found that "residents of the tribal areas confirmed that many see individual drone strikes as preferable to the artillery barrages of the Pakistani military."[25] This view demonstrates that a technological advance such as the stealth and precision offered by the Predator drone might be preferable to the largely random artillery barrages that would otherwise be unleashed if the Pakistani military chose to deploy traditional military force in pursuit of particular national security objectives. This interview by the *Economist* cannot be considered in any way conclusive or representative of a larger trend throughout the tribal areas, but the notion that the strikes might be seen in a positive light challenges preconceptions that have been put forth from this region and from the Pakistani government. The idea could be proposed that the technology afforded by these platforms might change the calculus of warfare to the point that casualties could be reduced at the same time that military objectives are met on the "battlefield." However, also demonstrated in this case is the idea that there is a message inherent in the use of predator drones over Pakistan, and the message that is conveyed through official channels congruent with Pakistan's strategic objectives may not match the actual situation on the ground. The battle for messaging is as important as the effects that the drones are having and potentially will have in the future against selected Al Qaeda targets whether in Pakistan or wherever else they are targeted.

Our discussion so far has examined nanotechnology and precision weaponry. The third technological advance that has the potential to impact the lethality of warfare is information and communication technology. Taking another look at the meaning of technology itself and adding to the idea proposed by Carl Mitcham that technology is largely an "unthinking activity," Martin van Creveld explains that "technology is perhaps best understood as an abstract system of knowledge, an attitude towards life and a method for solving its problems."[26] As this "abstract system" permeates more and more of our everyday existence to include the unparalleled growth of social media and information technology in general, perhaps we can say that the decision to employ the military instrument of power will be impacted by the changed nature of the globalized international landscape of the twenty-first century global community.

Many U.S. officers have expressed the opinion that information-age technology will likely give nations that employ such technologies in militarily innovative ways substantial advantages against adversaries that do not.[27] Perhaps this might be the case if information technologies could be neatly stove piped into the military domain and not also employed by nearly every other human being on the planet in the form of cell phones, smart phones, iPads, and the multitude of other hand held devices that have proliferated in the wake of the inexorable advance of information and communication technology. British author Emile Simpson has recently argued in *War From the Ground Up: Twenty-first Century Combat as Politics* that increased globalization and the proliferation of information and communication technology has the potential to radically alter the contemporary battlefield, and not in ways that U.S. officers (or officers from any other professional armed force) will find advantageous. Military force may increasingly be used in a non-violent manner, designed to influence an enemy and to persuade or compel various actors rather than seek their outright destruction or defeat. Simpson stated, "armed forces conduct many actions through non-violent means, often termed 'non-kinetic' in military jargon. These have significantly expanded in the first decade of this century, not least due to the possibilities of the internet and the proliferation of mobile phones, but also any number of other information media."[28] Clearly, Simpson is suggesting that information technology and the ability to rapidly transmit photos and stories around the world at light speed have the potential to influence armed forces, and more importantly, the political decision makers who are ultimately responsible for deploying those armed forces in pursuit of various political objectives. A similar idea has been proposed by British General Rupert Smith, whose *The Utility of Force* opens with the statement that "war no longer exists."[29] He refers here to the idea that in the contemporary world, warfare is no longer the clash of armed forces on the battlefield, as has been the case since the dawn of history. Simpson and Smith together present the idea that globalization and information technology are partly responsible for the transformation of warfare from a violent confrontation between massed armies to the contemporary wars that feature amorphous enemies and non-state actors. In this hazy environment within which information is often distorted and confused, stated strategic and political objectives of one side or the other (or both) may not be fully understood, as the very creation and promulgation of strategic messaging is impacted by the kaleidoscope of information and the technological devices available to distribute these messages around the globe.

Both Simpson and Smith are practitioners of warfare as well as commentators on its changed nature; Simpson served as an infantry officer in the Gurkha Rifles in Afghanistan, and Smith was one of Britain's most experienced senior officers on his retirement in 2002. They both have concluded that contemporary conflicts will differ fundamentally from those that occurred even as little as twenty years ago. It is due to technological advances primarily in the field of information and communication technology that contemporary armed forces are often employed for less-than-lethal effect or for the pursuit of distinctly political as opposed to military objectives. Many of the impacts of technology are "somewhat esoteric," and not quantifiable by analyzing the "cost effectiveness or bang divided by buck" that they provide to the battlefield commander.[30] This is especially so in regards to the continued development and proliferation of information and communications technologies, which together contribute to the diffusion of the environment within which strategic messaging and "information campaigns" must take place. This environment also seems to lend itself to the continued deployment of precision weapons technologies since it has become more common for analysts to assert that "obliterating or annihilating the enemy is not a meaningful choice in today's security environment."[31] As already discussed, precision weapons tend to produce fewer casualties, and so the advance in information and communication technology may be indirectly furthering research in the field of precision weaponry in order to allow for the most effective means for nation states to still be able to at least locate and hopefully defeat an enemy in the contemporary international arena.

Information technology and the rapid transmission of images and messages are parts of the globalization process. The effects and implications of this process on the international system has been a topic of debate among scholars for the last few decades. The impact of globalization can be seen economically, politically, and socially. The bottom line for national security matters is that "globalization means that the definition of security and the fight for it will occur not on battlefields but in unconventional places against non-traditional security adversaries."[32] This idea may not portend a change in the intensity of warfare, as non-traditional adversaries could still have the means to cause widespread destruction. However, a nation's decision on whether or not to deploy armed force in a given situation might be changed under the rubric of the globalized, interconnected system in which we live today.

Ours is not the first era in which the prevailing technologies influenced strategists in their determination of when and how to use military force. For example, "Clausewitz wrote about war shortly after its transformation by Napoleon; war today is again being transformed by the information revolution, which forces liberal powers to reconsider strategic thought in relation to their use of armed force."[33] The implications here might consist in the utility of the military instrument being perceived differently as a result of the information revolution. Social forces have impacted warfare before, and the irony is that "just as Clausewitz emphasized that social forces were primarily what transformed war after the French Revolution, so too does globalization in its contemporary form, as a social force, change war again."[34] More than one recent scholar has made the parallel between the changed nature of warfare in the nineteenth century with that of the twenty first. Noting that "Napoleon's astonishing run of victorious battles was achieved through innovative use of existing technologies combined with new tactics and military organizational forms," David Betz adds to the idea that it is not only in the realm of actual weaponry that changes in the efficacy of the military instrument are likely to occur but changes also in organization are also partly responsible.[35] It is globalization in the twenty first century that provides the "organizational" change that may, in fact, alter the utility of employing the military instrument. Reflecting on "the history of military technological introduction, it is clear that it has actually been a process that gradually changes the international system, and is itself changed by the system in gradual ways."[36] Based on this proposition, we can surmise that the characteristics of globalization might be such that the international system within which nation states employ the military instrument might have changed enough to compel states to use the military instrument differently than in the past. With this possibility in mind, perhaps it is fair to conclude that the system itself might put the brakes on the application of lethal armed force, even in cases when armed forces have the capability to use violence in order to meet political objectives.

Globalization and the information revolution, which propels it further along, has altered not just the nature of the international stage, but also the prevailing conceptions and norms that govern the behavior of states and other actors on the world stage. An example of norms and behaviors that have been shaped by the information revolution is the idea of "gender mainstreaming" as a military strategy for achieving operational objectives through the employment of armed force. If, in fact, both Emile Simpson and Rupert Smith's assertion that contemporary war will be characterized largely by armed forces acting in non-kinetic capacities, gender mainstreaming, or the "holistic reshaping of personnel assignment policies, doctrine, education and training" may need to become the norm in NATO militaries "because it might well become crucial to the effective promotion of general [NATO] values in a world increasingly afflicted by scarcity and unpredictability."[37] This proposal that asserting NATO "values" may lead to operational advantage on the battlefield is consistent with the idea that military force may increasingly be called upon to achieve effects other than simply subduing an enemy armed force. Thus, it is also consistent with both Simpson and Smith's assertion that strategic messaging and the interpretation of military action by various actors may be as important as traditional measures of battlefield success to include territory captured and enemy troops defeated or killed. Gender mainstreaming is not simply a proposal to continue to open positions within the armed forces to women, but is a sophisticated explanation for how liberal democracies can continue to achieve operational objectives through the employment of military force on the contemporary battlefield.

Observers have noted that the in the wake of the Cold War, the Western world is today less likely to become involved in a major war against a peer competitor. What is new is the suggestion from authors such as Emile Simpson that the rapid spread of information and communication technology may have a part to play in this phenomenon. While violent acts are still with us, they are mostly "sad but negligible occurrences compared quantitatively with the casualties suffered in any war."[38] However, not all observers are as optimistic about the possibility that major wars, and increasingly destructive wars, may be on the wane. Noted Yale professor Donald Kagan once wrote:

> It is a special characteristic of the modern Western world, as opposed to other civilizations and the premodern Western world, to believe that human beings can change and control the physical and social environment and even human nature to improve the condition of life. The revolution in science and technology since the sixteenth century [...] and the intellectual revolution it produced in the eighteenth century encouraged the idea that human society [...] can be manipulated to produce peace, progress, and prosperity.[39]

Taking Kagan's thinking into account, we can conclude that there are dangers inherent in the idea that technology may have the potential to reduce the destructive nature of warfare. If globalization and the rise of information and communication technology change the "playing field" on which military forces have traditionally sought to set the conditions for political settlements to be reached, and if precision technologies and nanotechnology enable a more efficient yet less destructive armed force, then there may be a reaction among entities, whether state or non-state actors. It was India's former Army Chief of Staff who once said, "the lesson of Desert Storm is, 'Don't fight with the United States without a nuclear weapon.'"[40] Likewise, we can expect adversaries in the future who have no hope of achieving a political solution on the battlefield through employment of the military instrument, even in a radically asymmetric fashion, to resort to measures that include terrorism and possibly the use of WMD if and when they can acquire them. Witness Bashar Assad's use of chemicals against the Syrian opposition as an example of just such a possibility. Other actors on the world stage might try to act in a similar fashion to achieve their intended security objectives.

However, there is a distinct likelihood that continued advancements in the field of information technology and social media could significantly alter the "strategic environment" within which military force has traditionally been employed. If this phenomenon continues apace, it is quite likely that even the advanced weaponry of modern armies and forces of both state and non-state actors might be rendered somewhat less lethal. The danger also exists that the opposite will hold true—that actors will not seek to deploy traditional force, but would rather gamble on the use of non-traditional weapons such as nuclear-biological or chemical weapons in order to gain some advantage, hoping to be able to manipulate their own strategic message in the wake of such a catastrophe to their own advantage.

In summary, armed forces around the world have benefited from the many technological advances over the centuries. Technological advances have generally led to increased lethality and more casualties on the battlefield. Throughout history, technology has been a determining factor in the way that societies are shaped and how they operate, as outlined by historians such as Lewis Mumford and Martin van Creveld. Greater technological efficiency has often led to greater military capability, and thus, increased casualties in warfare. However, technology also may hold the key to decreased battlefield casualties as advances in areas not necessarily directly related to warfare and the armed forces continue to proliferate into the military realm. Nanotechnology, advances in precision capabilities, and information technology may hold the promise of making the military instrument less lethal in the long term.

NOTES

1. Martin Van Creveld, *Technology and War* (New York: The Free Press, 1991), 6.
2. Trevor Dupuy, *The Evolution of Weapons and Warfare* (New York: Bobbs-Merrill, 1980), 294.
3. Jacques Ellul, *The Technological Society*, trans. John Wilkerson (New York: Vintage Books, 1964), vi. A more thorough review of Ellul's concept of technique can be found in The Technological Society, pages vi–viii, x, xviii, xxv–xxvi, xxxvi, 13–18 and 19.
4. Carl Mitcham, *Thinking through Technology* (Chicago: University of Chicago Press, 1994), 1.
5. Van Creveld, *Technology*, 320.
6. Ibid., 1.
7. Lewis Mumford, *Technics and Civilization* (New York: Harcourt, Brace & Co., 1934), 83.
8. Ibid.
9. Ibid, 84.
10. Hew Strachan, *The First World War* (New York: Penguin, 2004), 42–43.
11. Van Creveld, *Technology*, 1.

12. Fritz Allhof, Patrick Lin and Daniel Moore, *What is Nanotechnology and Why Does it Matter?* (Chichester, West Sussex: Wiley-Blackwell, 2010), 181.
13. Ibid, 184.
14. Ibid, 172.
15. Hitoshi Nasu, "The Future of Nanotechnology in Warfare," *The Global Journal* (July 4, 2013). Available at: http://theglobaljournal.net/group/digital-news/article/1132/ (Last access, 20 November 2014).
16. Mark Gubrud, "Nanotechnology and International Security," presented at Fifth Foresight Conference on Molecular Nanotechnology, Palo Alto, CA. Available at: http://www.foresight.org/Conferences/MNT05/Papers/Gubrud/ (Last access, 20 November 2014).
17. Allhof, Lin and Moore, *Nanotechnology*, 181.
18. Hans Lenk, "Advances in the Philosophy of Technology: New Structural Characteristics of Technologies," *Society for Philosophy and Technology* 4 (fall 1998). Available at: http://scholar.lib.vt.edu/ejournals/SPT/v4n1/LENK.html (Last access, 20 November 2014). See also Hans Lenk, *Technokrate als Ideologie* (Stuttgart: Kohlhammer, 1973) for Lenk's explanation of technology as ideology, which is a notion similar to Ellul's technique.
19. Nasu, *Future*, n.p.
20. Robert Mandel, *Security, Strategy, and the Quest for Bloodless War* (Boulder, CO: Lynne Reimer Publishers, 2004), 67.
21. Robert L. Paarlberg, "Knowledge as Power: Science, Military Dominance, and U.S. Security," *International Security* 29 (summer 2004): 125.
22. Eugene J. Palka, Francis A. Galgano and Mark W. Corson, "Operation Iraqi Freedom: A Military Geographical Perspective," *Geographical Review* 95 (July 2005): 395.
23. Van Creveld, *Technology*, 312.
24. Adam Clulow, *The Company and the Shogun: The Dutch Encounter with Tokugawa Japan* (New York: Columbia University Press, 2014), 136–137.
25. "Drop the pilot: A surprising number of Pakistanis are in favour of drone strikes" *The Economist*, Oct. 19th 2013.
26. Van Creveld, *Technology*, 312.
27. Thomas G. Mahnken, *Technology and the American Way of War Since 1945* (New York: Columbia University Press, 2008), 226.
28. Emile Simpson, *War From the Ground Up: Twenty-First-Century Combat as Politics* (New York: Oxford University Press, 2013), 6. Simpson's innovative examination of the impact of information technology on the strategic landscape should be read as a counterpoint to Beatrice Heuser's *The Evolution of Strategy*. Heuser brings her account of strategic thinking up to the beginning of the twenty-first century, while Simpson provides a convincing "part 2[qm] to the discussion.
29. Rupert Smith, *The Use of Force* (New York: Random House, 2005), 3.
30. Van Creveld, *Technology*, 312.
31. Mandel, *Security*, 71.
32. Victor D. Cha, "Globalization and the Study of International Security," *Journal of Peace Research* 37 (May 2000): 400.
33. Simpson, *War*, 388–89.
34. Ibid., 74.
35. David Betz, "Clausewitz and Connectivity," *Infinity Journal* 3/1 https://www.infinityjournal.com/article/84/Clausewitz_and_Connectivity/ (Last access, 20 November 2014).

36. Allhof, Lin and Moore, *Nanotechnology*, 180.

37. Jody M. Prescott, "NATO Gender Mainstreaming: A New Approach to War Amongst the people?" *The RUSI Journal* 158 (Oct/Nov 2013): 61.

38. Beatrice Heuser, *The Evolution of Strategy: Thinking War from Antiquity to the Present* (Cambridge, UK: Cambridge University Press, 2010), 451.

39. Donald Kagan, *On the Origins of War* (New York: Doubleday, 1995), 3.

40. Charles A. Horner, "What We Should Have Learned in Desert Storm, But Didn't," *Air Force Magazine* 79 (December 1996). http://www.airforcemag.com/MagazineArchive/Pages/1996/December%201996/1296horner.aspx (Last access, 20 November 2014).

Works Cited

Allhof, Fritz, Patrick Lin, and Daniel Moore. *What is Nanotechnology and Why Does it Matter?* Chichester, West Sussex: Wiley-Blackwell, 2010.

Betz, David. "Clausewitz and Connectivity," *Infinity Journal* 3/1. Available at: https://www.infinityjournal.com/article/84/Clausewitz_and_Connectivity/.

Cha, Victor D. "Globalization and the Study of International Security," *Journal of Peace Research* 37 (May 2000): 391–403.

Clulow, Adam. *The Company and the Shogun: The Dutch Encounter with Tokugawa Japan*. New York: Columbia University Press, 2014.

Creveld, Martin van. *Technology and War*. New York: The Free Press, 1991.

"Drop the pilot: A surprising number of Pakistanis are in favour of drone strikes," *The Economist*, Oct. 19th 2013.

Dupuy, T.N. *The Evolution of Weapons and Warfare*. New York: Bobbs-Merrill, 1980.

Ellul, Jacques. *The Technological Society*, trans. John Wilkerson. New York: Vintage, 1964.

Gray, Colin S. "Does Theory Lead Technology?" *International Journal* 33 (Summer 1978): 506–523.

Gubrud, Mark A. "Nanotechnology and International Security," presented at Fifth Foresight Conference on Molecular Nanotechnology, Palo Alto, CA. Available at: http://www.foresight.org/Conferences/MNT05/Papers/Gubrud/.

Heuser, Beatrice. *The Evolution of Strategy: Thinking War from Antiquity to the Present*. Cambridge, UK: Cambridge University Press, 2010.

Horner, Charles A. "What We Should Have Learned in Desert Storm, But Didn't," *Air Force Magazine* 79 (December 1996). http://www.airforcemag.com/MagazineArchive/Pages/1996/December%201996/1296horner.aspx.

Kagan, Donald. *On the Origins of War*. New York: Doubleday, 1995.

Lenk, Hans. "Advances in the Philosophy of Technology: New Structural Characteristics of Technologies," *Society for Philosophy and Technology* 4 (Fall 1998). http://scholar.lib.vt.edu/ejournals/SPT/v4n1/LENK.html.

Mahnken, Thomas G. *Technology and the American Way of War Since 1945*. New York: Columbia University Press, 2008.

Mandel, Robert. *Security, Strategy, and the Quest for Bloodless War*. Boulder, CO: Lynne Reimer Publishers, 2004.

Mitcham, Carl. *Thinking through Technology: The Path between Engineering and Philosophy*. Chicago: University of Chicago Press, 1994.

Mumford, Lewis. *Technics and Civilization*. New York: Harcourt, Brace & Co., 1934.

Nasu, Hitoshi. "The Future of Nanotechnology in Warfare," *The Global Journal* (July 4, 2013). Available at: http://theglobaljournal.net/group/digital-news/article/1132/.

Paarlberg, Robert L. "Knowledge as Power: Science, Military Dominance, and U.S. Security," *International Security* 29 (Summer 2004): 122–151.
Palka, Eugene J., Francis A.Galgano, and Mark W. Corson. "Operation Iraqi Freedom: A Military Geographical Perspective," *Geographical Review* 95 (July 2005): 373–399.
Prescott, Jody M. "NATO Gender Mainstreaming: A New Approach to War Amongst the People?" *The RUSI Journal* 158 (Oct/Nov 2013): 56–61.
Simpson, Emile. *War From the Ground Up: Twenty-First-Century Combat as Politics*. New York: Oxford University Press, 2013.
Smith, Rupert. *The Utility of War*. New York: Random House, 2005.
Strachan, Hew. *The First World War*. New York: Penguin, 2004.

The Fallacy of Humane Killing
Interwar Debates About Air Power and Twenty-First Century "Killer Robots"

ADAM PAGE

Influential air power advocate and theorist Giulio Douhet wrote in his landmark book *The Command of the Air* that there is "what might be called the mysterious aspect of war." However hard an individual attempts to "think of it as something improbable and far away," he argued, it "presses upon everyone, and is shrouded by a heavy veil of mystery." Within this "mysterious aspect," hidden amongst a cloud of uncertainty, is borne "an eventuality of the future."[1] What seems "improbable and far away" has an impact even before it eventuates. It is contingent on the future, but as it "presses upon everyone," its significance develops in anticipation of its realization. Douhet was writing in a context when the development of mechanized armor and air power were rapidly transforming the conduct of war. His comments reflect simultaneously the unknowability of the future and the assumed logic of technological progress that promised to penetrate the mystery and make the improbable real. Douhet's sentiments can be reframed in the twenty-first century as advocates and critics alike highlight how new technologies of war, and in particular, the development of unmanned weapons systems, could transform how wars are fought. A major critical contribution to debates about new military technologies came in December 2012, when Human Rights Watch (HRW) published a report entitled "Losing Humanity: The Case against Killer Robots."

The research detailed numerous legal ethical concerns about the potential development and deployment of automated weapons systems.[2] The HRW report is part of the growing criticism and debate about the dangers of new technologies of warfare, and in particular, unmanned machines, or "killer robots."[3] In May 2014, the United Nations hosted the first multilateral talks of their kind on questions raised by the development of autonomous weapons systems. The growth in criticism and debate about such new technologies comes as unmanned aerial vehicles (UAVs) have become a central element in military operations, and unpiloted flying machines are increasingly being cited as solutions to problems that range from delivering mail to tackling poaching.[4] The main driving force for unmanned technologies historically has, however, been their potential military applications.

The arguments in favor of the development of such weapons systems generally focus around the claimed inevitability of automated weapons systems; the reduced risk to soldiers in war; and the imagination of a "machine morality" that would prevent human emotions like hate and anger influencing actors in war. Advocates argue that the development of new military technologies will bring about a more peaceful world by enabling a more humane and less bloody version of war. Here, there is a striking parallel between the arguments in favor of unmanned weapons systems and those made by advocates of air power between the First and Second World Wars.[5]

Priya Satia's work on the British bombing of Afghanistan in 1919, and Iraq in 1922, has cast new light on this period in the development of the theory and practice of air power.[6] In colonial contexts, air power was explained as a method of "air control" or "air policing" that was not limited to a specific period of conflict, but was presented as an ongoing solution to colonial control. Satia has drawn clear links between the air policing over Iraq and Afghanistan in the early 1920s and its twenty-first century reiteration through the use of drones above those countries and others.[7] Satia makes a convincing and compelling argument about the importance of understanding how historical memory and experience continue to shape responses to and representations of drone attacks. While drawing on Satia's work, this chapter loosens the focus from colonial air policing to discuss the development of air power theory more broadly.

Building on Satia's work, this essay analyzes the echoes of interwar debates about air power in contemporary discussions about "killer robots" in order to provide an opportunity to critically engage with current debates from an historical perspective. Michael Sherry argues that air power can be historically situated among "a host of other weapons invented or imagined in the nineteenth-century and celebrated for, their capacity to 'diminish the evils of war.'"[8] Twenty-first century debates are still framed by this assumption, and Douhet's "mysterious aspect of war" continues to press down upon everyone. However, by removing the veil of uncertainty historical, lessons can be learnt. The arguments made during the 1920s and 30s in favor of air power were proven wrong when air war on a global scale occurred and the theories culminated in the strategic bombing practices and mass destruction of the Second World War. Perhaps by understanding the cultural and political conditions that fed into beliefs that air raids would shorten war and save lives, the thinking supporting the development of unmanned weapons systems can be more effectively challenged.

Imagining Humane War

The bloody stasis of trench warfare and the arrival of air raids against cities had a profound impact on the development of military theory after 1918. Influential writers in the period such as Basil Liddell Hart and J.F.C. Fuller emphasized the importance of mobility and speed in warfare.[9] Liddell Hart championed tanks and armored warfare but cited air power as the truly revolutionary technology of modern war. He argued that in modern war, attacks from the air would be less destructive than what he described as the "mechanical butchery" of the First World War.[10] Specifically, he wrote that the toll felt by *armies* would be greatly reduced by air power that took the advantage away from the defensive. While doing this, however, he cast aerial attacks on cities as a more humane alternative to the military strategies of 1914–1918. He feared that a repeat of a conflict that followed the model of the First World War would "mean the breakdown of Western civilization," and air raids presented an alternative to this.[11]

This section discusses the echoes of arguments such as Liddell Hart's that new technologies would facilitate a less bloody and more humane version of war in twenty-first century ideas about unmanned weapons systems. What writers and military theorists between the wars called the "moral effect" of bombing can be re-situated amongst current debates about the disciplinary effects of drones. These ideas are framed within a broader argument that the focus on lowering the human, political and financial costs of waging war by imagining a more humane and version of conflict obscures questions about the legitimacy of going to war and makes the decision to use lethal violence easier and less accountable. The suggestion that air raids against cities would shorten war, and thus, save lives was a recurrent argument in the interwar period, but it was one which privileged the lives of soldiers over those of civilians even while effectively cancelling the distinction. Above all, it relied on the notion of the "moral effect" of bombing.

After the First World War, assessments of the effects of air raids on Britain and those carried out against Germany contributed some of the founding ideas and assumptions about air power. Theories of the "moral effect" and the power of air raids to inspire terror and social upheaval and disrupt production, together with the image of air power as a marker of national prestige, were articulated in the context of First World War air attacks. However, as Tami Biddle has shown, claims about the paralyzing effects of air raids were overstated and referred to cultural assumptions about urban populations that were not borne out by the reality.[12] The development of air power theory and practice after 1918 was shaped by the experience of the First World War both in the trenches and the perceived impact of air raids on cities.

The mass conscription of the First World War severely troubled distinctions between soldier and civilian, but the air power theories that followed it served to further fix the bomb-sights over civilians. The crucial difference was that conscription was a temporary emergency measure, whereas the definition of urban civilians as targets was a more lasting change. Air power advocates argued that attacks on cities and civilians were justified both by the industrialization of war, which had mobilized factories as armies, and by the belief that air raids would dramatically shorten war. Air power theorist, lawyer, writer, and civil servant in the Air Ministry James M. Spaight, wrote, in 1930, that attacks on cities would reduce the length of wars because, unlike trained soldiers, urban civilians did not possess the fortitude to endure air raids. He argued:

> Nothing even remotely approaching the casualties necessary to destroy the moral of an army should be required to demoralise the undisciplined civilian workers, of all ages and sexes, in a war factory. In the nature of these things, their breaking-point should be low. It is not to disparage their spirit to recognise this. Obviously they cannot be compared with the steel-hardened mass into which fighting troops are forged.[13]

The focus on the war factory and its "undisciplined civilian workers of all ages and sexes" reflected the broader dissolution of the boundaries between civilian and military that new technologies of war fed into. Air power theories were developed in dialogue with a redefinition of war that cast "civilian workers" as a primary target which, in turn, encouraged renewed focus on air power. Spaight wrote that "machine-power" and not "man-power" had become the crucial factor in warfare and that the production of weapons of war meant that the civilian workers, or the "machines behind the machines," were the most important target.[14]

The idea that attacks on factories and cities could paralyze a war economy and dramatically shorten war was an important element in the speculations that air power would lessen the death tolls of conflict. Liddell Hart argued that air power opened up the possibility "not only of war without bloodshed, but war without hostilities."[15] Spaight claimed, in 1938, that air power might have already brought the world to "the threshold of an era in which wars will be won *before* they are fought."[16] The idea that wars could be won without fighting was, in large part, a consequence of the multifaceted potential of air power. A key element in the interwar imaginaries of air power as a pacifying force was its close connection with gas and chemical warfare.

Images of planes dropping sleep-inducing gas onto cities, resulting in wars won in moments as a temporarily incapacitated population was overrun, proliferated in science fiction novels.[17] Such depictions of future wars were echoed in contemporary strategic debates. J.F.C. Fuller wrote that gas could be the most "humane" weapon of war, and he argued that gas need not be lethal but could force "an enemy to change his policy by bloodlessly defeating his army."[18] Fuller's argument was echoed outside of the military by biologist J.B.S. Haldane, who wrote that gas was a more humane weapon than conventional armaments.[19] Despite the claims that non-lethal gas could bloodlessly win wars, fears about poisonous gas resonated strongly across societies and governments before 1939, and much of the air raid precautions taken in Britain were focused around gas and the distribution of gas masks.[20]

The potential of non-lethal weapons to incapacitate rather than kill in war continues to be debated. Major General Peter Chiarelli of the U.S. Army has more recently stressed the importance of so-called "non-lethal effects" in modern counterinsurgency,[21] while Col. George Fenton, Director of the Joint Non-Lethal Weapons Directorate, U.S. Department of Defense, has said he would like "some magic dust to put everyone to sleep—combatant and non-combatant alike."[22] As Fuller envisaged, planes flying high over columns of troops and spraying an anesthetic gas that knocked the soldiers unconsciousness, so did dreams of bloodless war persist and continue to inform the dynamics behind military technological innovation.[23] Concealed within these imaginations of humane war, however, is the possibility that such theoretically non-lethal weapons will serve only to lower the requirements to be met before the political decision to go to war is taken. The argument that air power might function as a pacifying force that lowered casualties in war was reiterated in debates about the ability of aircraft to terrify an enemy population into defeat without the necessity of actually bombing them.

Spaight's assertion about the relatively weak moral fortitude of untrained civilians was reflected again in his argument that the fear of attack would be more damaging than the actual destruction caused by air raids. He argued that loss of output in factories would be a result of "abstention from work rather than actual destruction," and he stressed that "workers will be terrified rather than killed."[24] These assumptions also drew on the bombing reports from the First World War, in which speculations about the "moral effect" were placed above the material damage.[25] Spaight was explaining the theory of the "moral effect" of air power, a central tenet of the theory of air war. There were echoes of the cultural assumptions about colonial subjects documented by Satia in Spaight's analysis of the vulnerability and indiscipline of civilian subjects. Terror was considered more humane than killing, and as Satia has shown, the disciplinary effect of air power was a vital component of "air control" in imperial policy.[26] Aviation promised a technology of panoptic observation and "constant surveillance" that would "simply awe tribes into submission without the loss of life."[27] This notion had its equivalent in the "moral effect" argument put forward by Spaight about urban populations. Although the cultural imaginings were different from those identified by Satia about Arabian populations, the terrorizing power of the air was assured. The argument that air power can be effective through its potential rather than actual exercise of power, and thus, can lessen violence, persists in the twenty-first century.

The supposed economy of air power was tied closely to arguments about more humane methods of war after the trenches. Similarly, as the dual economic and political costs of large troop deployments appear less and less tenable in the twenty-first century, unmanned weapons systems are framed as increasing soldier safety and reducing the military footprint. As Satia highlights, when the British faced numerous colonial uprisings in the 1920s, they turned to the young Royal Air Force to patrol and bomb rather than a troop deployment that would have been more expensive, both economically and politically.[28] The place where new theories were tested and analyzed between the wars was far away from Europe, where the practice of air attacks was still highly disputed. While European nations attempted to build up their air forces in anticipation of future war, the practice of air power was recast as a method of colonial policing.[29] It is in the context of insurgency and unpopular wars with mounting casualties that the use of drones, or unmanned aerial vehicles (UAVs), has become an increasingly central aspect of military strategy and practice in the twenty-first century.[30] The removal of troops from front-line combat duties suggests that a conflict has ended, when, in fact, the continued deployment of remotely piloted UAVs maintains military observation and engagement in an area.[31] The ability to retain some military capacity in an area with a minimal commitment of actual soldiers reflects both political and economic imperatives.

In a period when the recruitment pool for soldiers in technologically advanced nations is shrinking, the cost of training, equipping and deploying large forces are high, and the public attitude towards foreign wars is skeptical, unmanned weapons systems offer an alternative.[32] The machines replace the soldiers and enable military operations to continue less visibly to domestic audiences whose media reports often focus on soldier deaths and injuries. The apparent potential for military operations to be carried out with little or no risk to soldiers through the use of tele-operated systems is a key driving force behind the development of military technology.[33] However, as the HRW report argues, a consequence of machines taking an increasingly large part of the risk, which soldiers would previously have been required to do, could be that politicians feel less anxiety about making the decision to go to war. It could become easier for governments to decide to go to war, whilst the cost of conflict is increasingly transferred from combatants to civilians in the affected areas.[34]

As Liddell Hart saw air power as an escape from the "mausoleums of mud built by Clausewitz and his successors," so did supporters present UAVs as an alternative to the intractable occupations and insurgencies that have characterized modern war from Vietnam to Afghanistan.[35] The operation of drones over Afghanistan and Pakistan from the Nevada desert follows the logic of distancing that was articulated with aerial bombing and intercontinental missiles. If supporters argue that drones and, potentially, armed autonomous robots could supplant soldiers in battlefields, such arguments are based not only on removing soldiers from danger, but also on improving the efficiency of military operations. New robotic technologies may just not replace human soldiers, the argument goes, but they might improve on them.

More Than Human, Less Than Human

Unmanned systems, in the words of Gordon Johnson of the Pentagon's Joint Force Command, "don't get hungry. They're not afraid. They don't forget their orders. They don't care if the guy next to them has just been shot." By escaping the biological and psychological limits of humanity, he argues, such technologies would function more effectively in a battlefield. "Will they do a better job than humans? Yes."[36] Johnson presents the physical and psychological costs of war as limits to the effective prosecution of orders. In the words of an unnamed Defense Advanced Research Projects Agency (DARPA) official, "the human is becoming the weakest link in defense systems."[37]

This section discusses how new weapons technologies and unmanned weapons systems are presented as being "more than human" in a way that sets them against the limits of human biology and psychology. It traces some of these arguments back to interwar debates about air power, which cast airplanes as powerfully transforming notions of time and space, and revolutionizing war. In both cases, these new weapons are designed to return the advantage to the attacking force after the experience of intractable and bloody conflicts. It then goes on to highlight how an assumed inevitability of progress and technical development obscures political and historical questions while imagery from science fiction feeds into cultural imaginings of the future that make such distant, often fanciful, weapons seem almost commonplace.

As P.W. Singer has written, unmanned systems can carry out complicated tasks for hour after hour without the need to pause or re-gather concentration or focus. Asking people to work on such intensely demanding tasks for extended periods may lead to potentially dangerous or, in the context of war, fatal mistakes.[38] The "removal of human limitations" was one of the chief strengths attributed to unmanned systems in the United Kingdom's Ministry of Defence 2011 report on current use and future potential of such systems.[39] As well as the ability to function for longer periods of time, supporters of unmanned systems stress their ability to work at "digital speed," detecting and responding in a temporal scale well beyond anything a human could emulate.[40] The limiting factor of human biology is also felt in relation to new aviation technologies. A clear example of how new weapons seem to move beyond human capacities is the creation of aircraft able to fly at hypersonic speed. Such aircraft can travel at velocities well beyond anything a human pilot could endure.[41] By dramatically increasing the speed of movement, hypersonic flight simultaneously increases the reach of aircraft. Similarly, air power advocates argued that the revolutionary potential of aviation heralded a new era not bound by the previous rules of time and space.

In 1925, Liddell Hart wrote admiringly that "aircraft enables us *to jump over* the army which shields the enemy government, industry, and people, and *so strike direct and immediately at the seat of the opposing will and policy.*"[42] With aviation, the world became a much smaller place, and the geographical boundaries of sea and land were transformed and flattened, just as ideas about fortification and defensive structures both of armies and architecture were suddenly outdated. It was the ability of the airplane to move at unprecedented speed and in three dimensions that air power advocates argued truly set it apart from other weapons and technologies.

Twenty-first century debates about hypersonic flight and UAVs and the visions of the air in the interwar period were both set against the limitations of older technologies and of human soldiers. Fuller argued that as technology progressed, older techniques of war became redundant, and he cited the transformation from reliance on muscular power to that of the petrol engine. "In the past," he wrote, "in order to increase the speed of the soldier the only means available was to mount him on an animal of greater muscular energy." Muscle, human and animal limited the potential for new technologies of war to be adopted. He continued, "if it were possible for an infantryman to carry a machine gun and several thousand rounds of ammunition, the rifle would long ago have been scrapped."[43] New technologies of mobilization broke through this barrier, but it was only with air power that movement could proceed in three dimensions, not bound to lines of advance, backwards and forwards, but able to leap up and over armies and cities.

Descriptions of the potential for enhanced speed and movement, within a broader reconfiguration of understandings of the potentialities of new weapons technologies, are echoed in twenty-first century discussions of new nanotechnologies and their military applications. Nanotechnology is cited as a potentially revolutionary science that could "fundamentally alter how societies function" as well as how wars are fought.[44] The strong military funding for such technologies reflects their role at the heart of visions of future warfare. The most immediate potential use of nanotechnologies is the miniaturization of weapons systems and sensors and the potential development of "super-fast quantum computers."[45] Miniaturization, in particular, is framed as enabling military intervention to reach into areas that have previously been hard to reach. The U.S. Air Force Research Lab released a video in which Micro Aerial Vehicles (MAVs) are graphically simulated. The small robotic devices, designed to look like birds or insects to hide in plain sight, purport to show a future in which small surveillance devices can penetrate previously closed off spaces. One insect-like machine hovers over a door until it is opened and then flies in. The video is subtitled "Unobtrusive, Pervasive, Lethal."[46] The scale becomes even smaller with the ongoing research on so-called "bionanobots," which military analysts envision could penetrate the human body through respiration before detonating inside the target.[47] Despite the radical nature of these technological visions, they are operated under similar principles to air power between the wars. The science fiction of tiny robots entering human bodies on their breath and killing them from the inside out is essentially what poison gas did a century earlier. The imperative to overcome all defensive barriers and bring every city, building, room and person within the striking potential of a technologically advanced military-informed aviation, and it informs nanobots.

Theorists of air power between the wars were often preoccupied with the potential uses of air power in the future, and similarly, twenty-first century military scientists working on nanotechnology operate and speak in terms of speculative potentialities. This conception is named in an Australian Department of Defence document as "Enabling Technology" for the "Army After Next."[48] In this document and in the numerous interviews conducted by Singer with relevant protagonists in the field for his book *Wired for War*, there is a clear sense of the self-image amongst technologists and scientists in the field of enterprise, innovation, and history-making. Singer highlights how ideas about the exponential development of technological change inform debates and imaginings about the future of robotics and artificial intelligence in the military in the twenty-first century. Citing Ray Kurzweil, a high-profile American scientist and inventor, Singer demonstrates the grip of the so-called "Law of Accelerating Returns" on the popular culture of innovative technologists.[49] Kurzweil says that if current trends continue, "the pace of technological change will be so rapid, its impact so deep that life will be irreversibly transformed."[50] This is not a value-free assertion, and the U.S. military plays a major role in the development of the technologies Kurzweil celebrates through funding and support.[51] The interconnectedness of the development of advanced technologies with militaries was also an important feature in the interwar creation of large bomber air forces.[52] In both cases, new innovations exhibited the scientific and technological strengths of a nation. It is then, perhaps, not surprising that the functionality of nascent technologies was, and continues to be, exaggerated. The hyperbolic utterances about future potential are not, however, just speculation that diminishes in significance as its fallacies are exposed.

The bombing surveys after the First World War referred to projections about what might have happened if the war had continued and new technological and strategic innovations progressed as evidence of the effectiveness of air attacks. One report from 1919 claimed that "with the progress in air science that seems likely to continue, it will be possible in a few years [...] for a powerful military nation [...] to obliterate cities in a night and produce the stunning moral effect necessary to victory."[53] The subsequent development of bombing technologies, a contingent process that depended on political support and funding was thus framed by this earlier assumption which had cast such advances as inevitable and already underway.

An interest in predicting the future and exponential dynamics of change presents technological development as existing in a temporal register that runs outside of the people responsible for the development and operates closer to an image of evolution than history. Fundamentally, it denies the agency behind the decisions to progress the technology. Singer quotes Eric Drexler, a leading figure in nanotechnology, as saying that "our machines are evolving faster than we are. Within a few decades they seem likely to surpass us. Unless we learn to live with them in safety, our future will likely be both exciting and short."[54] Such pronouncements, which explicitly place technology development outside the realm of human influence, have been countered by other experts in the field. The debate about the inevitability of such technologies has reached into the mainstream media.[55] The most prominent critic is the roboticist Noel Sharkey, who has written about the "evitability" of autonomous warfare and "killer robots."

Sharkey argues that the futurist visions of robot intelligence are muddied by loose language, vague conceptualizations, the preponderance of cultural imagery from science fiction, and the tendency to anthropomorphism in discussions about machines.[56] The claims by Ronald Arkin, roboticist at the Georgia Institute of Technology, are a particular focus of his criticism. Arkin is leading research on a U.S. Army funded project on "governing lethal behavior in autonomous systems," and he believes that autonomous battlefield robots could, potentially, operate in a war "more ethically than human soldiers are capable of." He describes the thesis of this research, which is ongoing, as being "that robots not only can be better in conducting warfare in certain circumstances, but they can also be more humane than humans in the battlefield."[57] For Sharkey, this is highly questionable and relies more on anthropomorphism than developments in artificial intelligence. The anthropomorphic rendering of robots into operators more akin to humans is itself a trope in science fiction writing and film. The important connections between science fiction and the development of new weapons technologies are revealed in both the discussions about air power between the wars and contemporary "killer robots."

There is a history of military interactions with science fiction writers that travels from H.G. Wells to Orson Scott Card, from *The War in the Air* (1908) to *Ender's Game* (1985), but extends both before and after these defining texts of the genre.[58] Cultural contexts frame the development of new technologies, and in the realm of new military technologies, science fiction is a common point of reference both explicitly and implicitly. In an industry that relies on military contracts, the way to make unreal technologies real is to situate them within a familiar cultural context. Hence, the Personnel Halting and Stimulation Response weapon became known as PHaSR, or "phaser," a deliberate and explicit reference to *Star Trek* designed to appeal to potential buyers.[59] However, such word play is more than a marketing tool. By attaching fictional imagery to the material development of new technologies, the processes of their development are placed on a temporal plane that excludes the possibility of deviation from the path to progress, as it imagined in these texts. They proclaim inevitability, where informed critics such as Sharkey stress "evitability."

The saturation of new military technologies within well-known cultural discourses of science fiction places unknown devices, the building of which would bring about unknown consequences, into a realm of knowledge that is based on fictional extrapolation. When the Zeppelin raids against Britain began in January 1915, they were framed by centuries of speculation about the power of an imagined flying machine to appear in the skies and drop bombs and explosives on those newly exposed below. Such a machine, made invulnerable by its altitude, was a staple of cultural imaginings of the future.[60] Air raids promised a future of unimaginable destruction, while writers such as H.G. Wells simultaneously heralded them as offering a unique chance to secure lasting world peace. In the interwar period, works of fiction were created and consumed in an ongoing dialogue with government declarations about the possible effects of future war.[61] The influence of air power can be measured in the economic and political commitment to aviation for military and civilian uses, as well as the proliferation of air raid science fiction, and public discussions about the value of being "air-minded." The interdependence of culture and politics is demonstrated in interwar debates about air war, in which, as Martin Ceadel has argued, popular fiction dramatized "ideas that were being currently put forward by Britain's leading military theorists."[62]

The apocalyptic images of mass destruction in novels and film were reflected in the developing theory of the "knock-out blow," through which, air power advocates argued, a city could be destroyed in an instant. Uri Bialer argues that the fear of a "knock-out blow" was a major motivating factor behind failed attempts to agree to international air disarmament in Europe in the 1930s.[63] These speculations, however, were closer to the depictions of future war drawn by Wells and his contemporaries than to the reality of air power and the practice of air attacks on surface targets in the 1920s.

In the twenty-first century, far off possibilities are translated into coming eventualities partly through reference to science fiction. Singer quotes an unnamed developer of robots for the U.S. military as saying that the imagery of robotics in science fiction makes "possibilities seem real, but also inevitable."[64] The telling and retelling of such stories brings, what Douhet described as the "vaguely felt eventuality" of future war, closer to realization by influencing concrete war preparations in peacetime. For Douhet, the preparation for war demands the "exercise of the imagination" and compels "a mental excursion into the future."[65] It is the contingency of this excursion and the uncertainty of the image of the future it describes that is relegated by the fantasies of humane war, or perfect machines.

Conclusion

The escalatory logic of military technological development was, and continues to be, masked by the dissemination of the notion of humane killing in war. The prospect of future war hung heavy in the 1920s and 1930s, and the threat of air raids, in particular, infected public political and cultural imaginings of the future. The repetition in military texts such as those by Spaight, Liddell Hart and Fuller of the image of aerial war as being quick, clean, and humane, yet devastating, were notions that were developed in culture and politics as well as technology and science. Such contingencies and interdependencies mean that new technological developments do not exist in isolation from the historical context of their conception and production. The fears of the potential of air power did not, however, cause governments to pursue a pacifist or disarmament policy. While attempts to limit the deployment of air power in Europe were discussed, practices and techniques were being developed by European nations away from Europe.

The "air control" strategies over colonial countries were predicated on surveillance and terror with the permanent threat of air attack as a powerful disciplinary tool and economic way of "policing" vast landscapes with scattered populations. Similar cultural assumptions about the targets of attacks and their responses to living under the shadow of air raids were echoed in theories of air power in which planes were repositioned over major European cities. Cultural assumptions about the targets of bombing informed the development of theories of air power that were set against the mud-bound trench warfare of 1914–1918. Air power could potentially lower the cost of war in terms of soldiers' lives, as unmanned weapons systems are framed by their ability to remove soldiers from the firing line.

New technologies that claim to remove soldiers from battlefields ignore the fact that the battlefield is increasingly an ostensibly civilian space. The emphasis on breaching boundaries and reaching further, faster and deeper into enemy territory that was so important in imaginations of the air between the wars continues to inform weapons technologies. Research is focused on the creation of increasingly small and mobile machines that can penetrate defensive spaces without the need for soldiers. Such visions are fed by cultural visions from science fiction and presented as an inevitable part of the progress of science and technology. Nevertheless, as the strategic bombing campaigns of the Second World War illustrates, speculations about humane killing and humane war are likely to dissipate quickly when the shooting begins. Just as the development of air power theory and technology was contingent on political and cultural factors, which are by definition shifting and negotiable, so too are twenty-first century unmanned weapons systems being conceived and constructed within a constellation of similar factors and influences. Despite the evidence from history, claims that new weapons can reduce the violence of war continue in the twenty-first century. By highlighting the fallacies of interwar air power theories, perhaps an important critical perspective can be brought to bear on contemporary debates.

Notes

1. Giulio Douhet, *The Command of The Air*, trans. Dino Ferarri (Washington, D.C.: U.S. Air Force History and Museums Program, 1998, first published 1921, this edition first published 1942), 145.

2. Human Rights Watch and the International Human Rights Clinic, *Losing Humanity: The Case Against Killer Robots* (2012).

3. The most prominent group is the Campaign to Stop Killer Robots, see www.stopkillerrobots.org. For a collection of critical voices from a variety of disciplines see the recent special issue of the International Review of the Red Cross, "New Technologies and Warfare," *International Review of the Red Cross* 94.886 (Summer 2012), 454–876.

4. Brian Handwerk, "Five Surprising Drone Uses (Besides Amazon Delivery)," National Geographic Website. URL: http://news.nationalgeographic.com/news/2013/12/131202-drone-uav-uas-amazon-octocopter-bezos-science-aircraft-unmanned-robot/. Accessed on 19.6.2014.

5. For a discussion of the development of theories of strategic bombing see Tami Davis Biddle, *Rhetoric and Reality in Air Warfare: The Evolution of British and American Ideas about Strategic Bombing, 1914–1945* (Princeton; Oxford: Princeton University Press, 2002).

6. Priya Satia, "The Defense of Inhumanity: Air Control and the British Idea of Arabia," *The American Historical Review* 111, no. 1 (February 2006): 16–51.

The Fallacy of Humane Killing (Page) 273

7. Priya Satia, "Drones: A History from the British Middle East," *Humanity: An International Journal of Human Rights, Humanitarianism, and Development* 5, no. 1 (Spring 2014): 1–31.
8. Michael Sherry, *The Rise of American Air Power: The Creation of Armageddon* (New Haven; London: Yale University Press), 5.
9. B.H. Liddell Hart, *Paris, or the Future of War* (London: Kegan Paul, 1925); J.F.C. Fuller, Reformation of War (London: Hutchinson & Co., 1923).
10. Liddell Hart, *The Memoirs of Captain Liddell Hart*. Volume I (London: Cassel, 1965), 140.
11. Liddell Hart, *Paris*, 10.
12. Ibid., 23.
13. J.M. Spaight, *Air Power and the Cities* (London: Longmans, 1930), 160.
14. Ibid., 137–139.
15. Liddell Hart, *Paris*, 20–21.
16. J.M. Spaight, *Air Power and the Next War* (London: Bles, 1938), 129.
17. A discussion of "gas novels" is included in Sven Lindqvist, *A History of Bombing* (London: Granta, 2001).
18. Fuller, *Reformation of War*, xiii, 111.
19. J.B.S. Haldane, *Callinicus: A Defence of Chemical Warfare* (London: Kegan Paul, 1925); Michele Haapamäki, *The Coming of the Aerial War: Culture and the Fear of Airborne Attack in Interwar Britain* (London: I.B. Tauris, 2014), 55–56.
20. This was evidenced by the distribution of 38 million gas masks in Britain around the period of the 1938 Munich crisis, Joseph S. Meisel, "Air Raid Shelter Policy and its Critics in Britain before the Second World War," *Twentieth Century British History* 5 (1994): 306.
21. Maj. Gen. Peter Chiarelli, quoted in Eve Massingham, "Conflict Without Casualties … A Note of Caution: Non-Lethal Weapons and International Humanitarian Law," *International Review of the Red Cross* 94:886 (Summer 2012): 684.
22. Massingham, "Conflict Without Casualties," 684.
23. Fuller, *The Reformation of War*, 143.
24. Spaight, *Air Power*, 160.
25. Biddle, *Rhetoric and Reality in Air Warfare*, 57.
26. Satia, "The Defense of Inhumanity," 33.
27. Priya Satia, "Drones: A History from the British Middle East," 6.
28. Ibid., 2.
29. For European rivalries in interwar air power programs see Andrew Barros, "Razing Babel and the Problems of Constructing Peace: France, Great Britain, and Air Power, 1916–1928," *English Historical Review* 126 (2011): 75–115.
30. Jeffrey A. Sluka, "Virtual War in the Tribal Zone: Air Strikes, Drones, Civilian Casualties, and Losing Hearts and Minds in Afghanistan and Pakistan," in Neil Whitehead and Sverker Finnström, eds. Virtual War and Magical Death: *Technologies and Imaginaries for Terror and Killing* (Durham, NC; London: Duke University Press, 2013), 181; Satia, "Drones," 7.
31. Satia, "Drones," 7.
32. Armin Krishnan, *Killer Robots: Legality and Ethicality of Autonomous Weapons* (Farnham: Ashgate, 2009), 2.
33. Sluka, "Virtual War," 182
34. "Losing Humanity," 4.
35. Liddell Hart, *Paris*, 89.
36. Gordon Johnson, quoted in Tim Weiner, "New Model Army Soldier Rolls

274   IV. The Age of "New Wars"

Closer to Battle," *New York Times*, Feb. 16, 2005. http://www.nytimes.com/2005/02/16/technology/16robots.html?_r=0. Accessed on 29.5.2014; Singer, *Wired for War: The Robotics Revolution and Conflict in the 21st Century* (New York: Penguin, 2009), 63.

37. Defense Advanced Research Projects Agency (DARPA) official, quoted in Singer, *Wired for War*, 64.

38. Ibid., 63.

39. Ministry of Defence, *Joint Doctrine Note 2/11: The UK Approach to Unmanned Aircraft Systems* (2011), 84.

40. Singer, *Wired for War*, 64.

41. Krishnan, *Killer Robots*, 62.

42. Liddell Hart, *Paris*, 43.

43. Fuller, *Reformation of War*, 137–138.

44. Jun Wang and Peter J. Dortmans, "A New Review of Selected Nanotechnology Topics and their Potential Military Applications," *Defence Science and Technology Organisation, Australian Government Department of Defence*, 2004, 1. Available at http://www.dsto.defence.gov.au/publications/2610/DSTO-TN-0537.pdf (Last access, 30 May 2014); Hitoshi Nasu, "Nanotechnology and Challenges to International Humanitarian Law: A Preliminary Legal Assessment," *International Review of the Red Cross* 94, no. 886 (Summer 2012): 653–672.

45. Krishnan, *Killer Robots*, 83–84.

46. US Air Force Research Lab, Air Vehicles Directorate, "Micro Aerial Vehicles." URL: http://videos.mediaite.com/video/Terrifying-Video-Demonstrates-B (Last access, 18 June 2014).

47. Krishnan, *Killer Robots*, 85. For an interesting and provocative discussion of gas war in this context see Peter Sloterdijk, *Terror From the Air*, trans. Amy Patton and Steve Corcoran (Los Angeles: Semiotext(e), 2009).

48. Wang and Dortmans, "A New Review," 1.

49. P.W. Singer, *Wired for War*, 94–108.

50. Ray Kurzweil, quoted in Singer, *Wired for War*, 104.

51. Singer, *Wired for War*, 106–7.

52. For aviation in Britain see David Edgerton, *England and the Aeroplane: An Essay on a Militant and Technological Nation* (Basingstoke: Macmillan, 1991).

53. Major E. Childers and E.N.G. Morris, 12 March 1919, in the National Archives, London: AIR 1/2115/207/56/1, quoted in Biddel, *Rhetoric and Reality*, 60.

54. Eric Drexler, quoted in Singer, *Wired for War*, 415.

55. See for example Tim Bowler, "'Killer Robots': Are They Really Inevitable?," *BBC News Website*, 21 May 2014. URL: http://www.bbc.co.uk/news/business-27332130 (Last access, 1 June 2014); Noel Sharkey, "America's Mindless Killer Robots Must be Stopped," *Guardian Newspaper Website*, 3 December 2012. URL: http://www.theguardian.com/commentisfree/2012/dec/03/mindless-killer-robots (Last access, 18 June 2014).

56. Sharkey, "The Evitability of Autonomous Robot Warfare," *International Review of the Red Cross* 94, no. 886 (Summer 2012): 787–799.

57. Ronald C. Arkin, quoted in Noel E. Sharkey, "The Evitability of Autonomous Robot Warfare," 789, 793.

58. For a brief overview see Singer, *Wired for War*, 150–169.

59. Ibid., 164.

60. Biddle, *Rhetoric and Reality*, 12, 21.

61. A key figure in the dialogue between fiction and military theory was H.G. Wells, see T.H.E. Travers, "Future Warfare: H.G. Wells and British Military Theory, 1895–1916," in *War and Society: A Yearbook of Military History*, eds. Brian Bond and

Ian Roy (London: Croom Helm, 1976), 67–87. For air war and literature in general see Martin Ceadel, "Popular Fiction and the Next War, 1918–1939," in *Class, Culture and Social Change: A New View of the 1930s*, ed. F. Gloversmith (Brighton: Harvester Press, 1980), 161–184; Susan Grayzel, "'A Promise of Terror to Come': Air Power and the Destruction of Cities in British Imagination and Experience, 1908–1939," in *Cities into Battlefields: Metropolitan Scenarios, Experiences and Commemorations of Total War*, Stefan Goebel and Derek Keene eds. (Farnham: Ashgate, 2011), 47–62.

62. Martin Ceadel, "Popular Fiction and the Next War, 1918–1939," 167.
63. Uri Bialer, *The Shadow of the Bomber: The Fear of Air Attack and British Politics, 1932–1939* (London: Royal Historical Society, 1980), 2.
64. Quoted in Singer, *Wired for War*, 164.
65. Douhet, *Command of the Air*, 145.

Works Cited

Barros, Andrew. "Razing Babel and the Problems of Constructing Peace: France, Great Britain, and Air Power, 1916–1928," *English Historical Review* 126 (2011): 75–115.

Bialer, Uri. *The Shadow of the Bomber: The Fear of Air Attack and British Politics, 1932–1939*. London: Royal Historical Society, 1980.

Biddle, Tami Davis. *Rhetoric and Reality in Air Warfare: The Evolution of British and American Ideas about Strategic Bombing, 1914–1945*. Princeton; Oxford: Princeton University Press, 2002.

Bowler, Tim. "'Killer Robots': Are They Really Inevitable?," BBC News Website, 21 May 2014. URL: http://www.bbc.co.uk/news/business-27332130.

Ceadel, Martin. "Popular Fiction and the Next War, 1918–1939," in *Class, Culture and Social Change: A New View of the 1930s*, ed. F. Gloversmith. Brighton: Harvester Press, 1980, 161–184.

Chiarelli, Maj. Gen. Peter quoted in Eve Massingham, "Conflict Without Casualties ... A Note of Caution: Non-Lethal Weapons and International Humanitarian Law," *International Review of the Red Cross* 94.886 (Summer 2012).

Childers, Major E., and E.N.G. Morris. 12 March 1919, in The National Archives, London: AIR 1/2115/207/56/1, quoted in Biddel, *Rhetoric and Reality*.

Douhet, Giulio. *The Command of The Air*, trans. Dino Ferarri. Washington, D.C.: U.S. Air Force History and Museums Program, 1998, first published 1921, this edition first published 1942.

Edgerton, David. *England and the Aeroplane: An Essay on a Militant and Technological Nation*. Basingstoke: Macmillan, 1991.

Grayzel, Susan. "'A Promise of Terror to Come': Air Power and the Destruction of Cities in British Imagination and Experience, 1908–1939," in *Cities into Battlefields: Metropolitan Scenarios, Experiences and Commemorations of Total War*, Stefan Goebel and Derek Keene eds. Farnham: Ashgate, 2011, 47–62.

Haldane, J.B.S. *Callinicus: A Defence of Chemical Warfare*. London: Kegan Paul, 1925.

Handwerk, Brian. "Five Surprising Drone Uses (Besides Amazon Delivery)," National Geographic Website. URL: http://news.nationalgeographic.com/news/2013/12/131202-drone-uav-uas-amazon-octocopter-bezos-science-aircraft-unmanned-robot/.

Haapamäki, Michele. *The Coming of the Aerial War: Culture and the Fear of Airborne Attack in Interwar Britain*. London: I.B. Tauris, 2014.

Hart, Liddell. *The Memoirs of Captain Liddell Hart. Volume I*. London: Cassel, 1965.

IV. The Age of "New Wars"

Hart, Liddell. *Paris, or the Future of War*. London: Kegan Paul, 1925; J.F.C. Fuller, *Reformation of War*. London: Hutchinson & Co., 1923.
Human Rights Watch, and the International Human Rights Clinic, *Losing Humanity: The Case Against Killer Robots* (2012).
International Review of the Red Cross, "New Technologies and Warfare," *International Review of the Red Cross* 94.886 (Summer 2012), 454–876.
Krishnan, Armin. *Killer Robots: Legality and Ethicality of Autonomous Weapons*. Farnham: Ashgate, 2009.
Lindqvist, Sven. *A History of Bombing*. London: Granta, 2001.
Meisel, Joseph S. "Air Raid Shelter Policy and its Critics in Britain before the Second World War," *Twentieth Century British History* 5 (1994).
Nasu, Hitoshi. "Nanotechnology and Challenges to International Humanitarian Law: A Preliminary Legal Assessment," *International Review of the Red Cross* 94:886 (Summer 2012): 653–672.
Ministry of Defence, *Joint Doctrine Note 2/11: The UK Approach to Unmanned Aircraft Systems* (2011).
Satia, Priya. "The Defense of Inhumanity: Air Control and the British Idea of Arabia," *The American Historical Review* 111:1 (February 2006): 16–51.
Satia, Priya. "Drones: A History from the British Middle East," *Humanity: An International Journal of Human Rights, Humanitarianism, and Development* 5, no. 1 (Spring 2014): 1–31.
Sharkey, Noel. "America's Mindless Killer Robots Must be Stopped," Guardian Newspaper Website, 3 December 2012. URL: http://www.theguardian.com/comment isfree/2012/dec/03/mindless-killer-robots.
Sharkey, Noel. "The Evitability of Autonomous Robot Warfare," *International Review of the Red Cross* 94, no. 886 (Summer 2012): 787–799.
Singer, N.N. *Wired for War: The Robotics Revolution and Conflict in the 21st Century*. New York: Penguin, 2009.
Sherry, Michael. *The Rise of American Air Power: The Creation of* Armageddon. New Haven; London: Yale University Press.
Sloterdijk, Peter. *Terror From the Air*, trans. Amy Patton and Steve Corcoran. Los Angeles: Semiotext(e), 2009.
Sluka, Jeffrey A. "Virtual War in the Tribal Zone: Air Strikes, Drones, Civilian Casualties, and Losing Hearts and Minds in Afghanistan and Pakistan," in *Virtual War and Magical Death: Technologies and Imaginaries for Terror and Killing*, ed. Neil Whitehead and Sverker Finnström. Durham, NC; London: Duke University Press: 2013.
Spaight, J.M. *Air Power and the Cities*. London: Longmans, 1930.
Spaight, J.M. *Air Power and the Next War*. London: Bles, 1938.
Travers, T.H.E. "Future Warfare: H.G. Wells and British Military Theory, 1895–1916," in *War and Society: A Yearbook of Military History*, eds. Brian Bond and Ian Roy. London: Croom Helm, 1976, 67–87.
U.S. Air Force Research Lab, Air Vehicles Directorate, "Micro Aerial Vehicles." URL: http://videos.mediaite.com/video/Terrifying-Video-Demonstrates-B.
Wang, Jun and Dortmans, Peter J. "A New Review of Selected Nanotechnology Topics and their Potential Military Applications," Defence Science and Technology Organisation, Australian Government Department of Defence, 2004. Available at http://www.dsto.defence.gov.au/publications/2610/DSTO-TN-0537.pdf.
Weiner, Tim. "New Model Army Soldier Rolls Closer to Battle," *New York Times*, Feb. 16, 2005. http://www.nytimes.com/2005/02/16/technology/16robots.html?_r=0.

Death from the Skies
A Just-War Perspective on the Rise of Unmanned Weapons Systems and the Reduction of Combatant and Noncombatant Casualties

TIMOTHY J. DEMY

Have the technologies of weapons, especially automated unmanned weapons systems that have arisen in the twenty-first century, fundamentally changed warfare? There has certainly been an exponential increase in the use of automated weapons and the drive toward robotic weapons. Enhanced capabilities of strike and surveillance potentially are giving users of those systems enormous advantages.

Nonetheless, what is to be thought of the ethics of those systems and the larger questions of the interface of humans and technology in the realm of warfare? Beyond the tactical, operational, and strategic levels of war is the ethical framework for war challenged? What follows is more descriptive and reflective than prescriptive, and hopefully, it will provide some background and information for consideration with respect to unmanned automated aerial weapons.

In June 1943, after almost four years of devastating conflict on the European Continent and with the end of hostilities not yet in sight, British Prime Minister Winston S. Churchill watched film footage of the Allied air campaign against the highly populated industrial area of the Ruhr. At one point, he sat up straight and exclaimed to another member of the war cabinet: "Are we beasts? Are we taking this too far?"[1] Ethical debates have yet to provide consensus answers to his questions.[2]

Something Old, Something New

Ethical concerns about aerial bombing are not new. The weapons and technology change, but the ethical concerns remain. There may be new dimensions of the ethical questions and new technologies such as the rise of UAVs (unmanned automated vehicles), especially "drones," but the basic questions have not altered much from the era of the Zeppelin raids over London during the First World War or the massive bombing campaigns of the Second World War.[3] Similarly, standoff military technologies are not new to warfare. For example, while the air war of the Second World War raised its own set of ethical questions, so too, did the submarine warfare, especially in the case of German torpedoes that left little or no wake so that defenders could not see them and take evasive action.[4]

Whether the weapon is one used in the air, on land, or in the sea, the ethical dimensions do not vary much beyond central questions. Thus, Chris Enemark writes:

> Likewise, long-range artillery, missiles, and inhabited aircraft enable the waging of war over great physical distances and, potentially, beyond the range of retaliation. A question that frequently arises with respect to drones is whether the advent of this technology signals change or continuity. Throughout history, new military technologies—the crossbow, gunpowder, the machine gun, the tank and the submarine, to take just a few examples—have occasioned debate over the changing character of war. Each innovation has prompted a mixture of outrage, awe and soul-searching on the part of users and victims alike.[5]

Thus, when one comes to the present-day debates about drones, there should be careful articulation and distinction of and among the concerns and responses as well consideration of what is new and what is not new at the core of the understanding of the nature of the weapon. Here again, Enemark's words are helpful:

> In one sense, therefore, the present degree of scholarly and journalistic attention to the rise of armed drones is nothing new, and there is a strong resonance with reactions to the initial introduction of older and now-familiar military technologies. In another sense, however, the advent of drones really is an unprecedented development because it has achieved the complete surmounting of physical limits of time and space in military affairs.[6]

One must consider whether the advent of drones is more evolutionary than revolutionary or whether there are aspects of both. What is at issue for the purposes of this essay is the relationship of UAVs—especially drones—to the principles of the just war tradition. Are drones compatible with the just war tradition, a tradition that is deeply embedded both legally and ethically in the Western way of war? The exponential rise of UAV technology and the use of it for both military and civilians have generated many headlines, much discussion, and editorials, articles, and books, and the literature in the field continues to grow.[7] It must also be remembered that not all drone usage by the military is from armed UAVs. The delivering of lethal force is only one use with another major one being surveillance. This essay does not look at the legal questions surrounding drones, the use of drones by civilian intelligence agencies, or the wisdom of using drones with respect to strategic and political decision-making.[8]

Drone technology combines the airplane and the missile in a reusable platform with the ability to strike as well as observe—it can be a strike weapon and a surveillance weapon in one platform, and one that is unmanned. This is in part why it is both evolutionary and revolutionary, and some believe that there has not been enough debate over the "embrace of something that might be regarded as politically desirable and yet morally worrisome: risk-free killing."[9] Specifically, Enemark writes that "the fact that drones are uninhabited injects a sufficient degree of newness into airpower as to require fresh ethical consideration. Specifically, if drones cross a line between a mode of killing that entails reduced risk to the killer and a mode of killing that is risk-free, it is worth asking whether war is going on at all."[10] On this point, one is reminded of French Field Marshal Pierre Bosquet's comment on observing the fateful charge of the British Light Brigade against the Russian cannon on 25 October 1854, during the Crimean War: *"C'est magnifique, mais ce n'est pas la guerre: c'est de la folie"* ("It is magnificent, but it is not war: it is madness").[11]

Just War and Jus in Bello

The just-war tradition is a broad framework that has served as a guide for centuries. The central tenets of the tradition have been developed and refined in response to both unique and persistent issues of war.[12] As the political contexts in which wars have been waged have changed along with developments in the technology and weapons of warfare, the tradition has accommodated such changes. Indeed, there is a moral obligation to wrestle with new issues and problems. Part of the strength of the just-war tradition is that it is an ongoing moral, legal, ethical, and religious dialogue that is centuries old. Just as the tradition responded to the nuclear age and wrestled with issues of weapons of mass destruction during the Cold War, so too, there has been more recently specific thought about the just war tradition and terrorism. More recently and specifically, the use of unmanned weapons systems has created a new need to look at the just war tradition.

In the just-war tradition, the questions Churchill is cited as having asked during the Second World War pertain to *jus in bello*—justice in war. The tradition looks at three separate categories—*jus ad bellum*, *jus in bello*, and *jus post bellum*. Each of these has separate components or principles.

The two principles of the *jus in bello* aspect of the just-war tradition are proportionality and noncombatant immunity (also called discrimination). The principle of proportionality dictates that combatant forces may not be subjected to greater harm than is necessary to secure victory and peace. The type of weapons and amount of force used must be limited to only what is needed to accomplish the mission. The principle of noncombatant immunity states that military forces must respect individuals and groups not participating in the conflict and must abstain from attacking them. Prisoners of war, civilians, and casualties are immune from intentional attacks and have a privileged status under international law.

The interpretation and application of these principles and indeed, all principles of the just-war tradition are not easy in contemporary warfare, nor is there any assurance that they will always receive strict adherence or even attempts at it, though the latter should be the case. Warfare is not clean or nice; it is horrible. It is in part, because of that, that the principles of the just-war tradition are used, not to promulgate war, but to contain it. They are principles of containment, not principles of conflagration. They are moral and ethical guidelines for attempting to minimize the death and devastation that always accompany war, and yet the number of civilian and noncombatant deaths in the twentieth century was staggering. At the beginning of the twentieth century, most of the war casualties (85 to 90 percent) were military. By the end of the Second World War, more than half the deaths were noncombatants. At the end of the twentieth century, the percentage had risen to more than seventy-five percent noncombatants.[13] The trend was rising rather than declining, yet the increase in noncombatant casualties post–Second World War was not directly because of weapons technology. Indeed, advances in weapons technology, specifically precision-guided-munitions (PGMs), have enabled users to decrease levels of violence and suffering.[14]

UAVs and Jus in Bello

With the rise of UAVs, the possibility of reversing the trend of increasing noncombatant deaths exists, and implementation of each of the principles of *jus in bello* has improved. Whereas in the Second World War precision bombing was desired and even acclaimed, it was rarely a reality, and the majority of bombs missed the target, frequently by more than four miles, and also significantly increased noncombatant deaths.[15]

While the use of UAVs raises important political, legal, and strategic concerns, as a weapons system, they have significantly improved the ability for precision targeting. Additionally, the non-military use of UAVs has grown much faster than other technologies of war that have been adapted for civilian use. As such, there is reason to believe that from a technological vantage point, UAVs may have the opposite effect of many technologies of war and quickly benefit those who use them in a non-military capacity.

Consideration of the use of drones with respect to *jus in bello* is contingent upon the use of them being legal in a specific circumstance. If they are not legal, then any discussion of proportionality is moot. For example, Avery Plaw argues that their use in Pakistan by the United States is legal, but on the opposite side of the argument, Mary E. O'Connell dissents.[16] The legality of recent and current usage by the United States under the Obama administration is contested, but for purposes of this essay, there is an assumption of legal usage in a *jus in bello* context.

The ability of PGMs, and specifically missiles fired from drones, to hit an intended target with extreme accuracy of inches to feet is uncontested. Precision targeting capability is a reality. Thus, the issue is not weapons accuracy but target certainty. The missile from the drone will hit that at which it is aimed. The ethical imperative is to aim at legitimate targets. Beyond the option of using drones, some ethicists such as Bradley Strawser argue that there is a moral obligation to use them. Summarizing his position, Strawser contends:

> any new technology that better protects the just warfighter is at least a prima facie ethical improvement and is morally required to be used unless there are strong countervailing reasons to give up that protection. I have argued that if using UAVs (as a particular kind of remote weapon) does not incur a significant loss of capability—particularly the operators' ability to engage in warfare in accordance with jus in bello principles—then there is an ethical obligation to use them and, indeed, transition entire military inventories to UAVs anywhere it is possible to do so.[17]

This is more than defending the option to use such weapons. It is arguing the moral necessity of using them in a just war context. To not use them is wrong.

Part of the argument for using drones goes beyond noncombatant casualties and pertains to reducing the risk of combatant casualties. There is a moral obligation not to risk lives in combat unnecessarily. To be sure, there is a moral decision to be made as to when such risks are necessary and not necessary. However, why send a pilot into harm's way if it is not required by the mission after all considerations are made? This is what Stawser terms "the principle of unnecessary risk."[18] Strawser understands well the opposition to drones and the arguments against them but believes that the criticisms are not valid with respect to the ethics of usage. He writes:

> All of the concerns regarding UAVs presently on offer do not negate this ethical obligation to use uninhabited weapon systems and should be properly viewed

instead as indictments against mistaken policy decisions and specific instances of force application—not as principled objections against UAVs themselves for none of the concerns are endemic to UAVs in any significant way.[19]

There are also those who argue against the position that favor the use of drones. As noted below, sometimes this is because of current policy and practice (concerns that Strawser does not counter), and sometimes it is opposition to the proportionality argument.

UAVs and Jus ad Bellum *(or* Jus ad Vim*)*

For some critics of drones, the issue and the greater question is one that is about *jus ad bellum* rather than *jus in bello*—do drones lower the threshold for going to war? In the just-war tradition, war is something that one enters as a last reasonable resort once an injustice occurs. Do drones make it easy to jump to war because of their one-sided technological advantage? Thus, Daniel R. Brunstetter writes:

> My fear is that the Obama administration has become so seduced by the advantages of drones—to keep U.S. soldiers out of harm's way, to limit (but not eliminate) non-combatant casualties, to deny Al-Qaeda safe havens—such that, *de facto*, the administration now acts as if the threshold of last resort no longer applies to drone strikes. The current drone policy thus challenges the notion of a "just war" President Obama outlined in his 2009 Nobel Prize Speech.[20]

Michael Walzer, whose work *Just and Unjust War: A Moral Argument with Historical Illustrations* on the just war tradition became a standard expression of the tradition after its release in the turbulent wake of the Vietnam War, echoes this view. He writes, "What is missing is for the Obama administration to recognize that drones, as they are currently used in anticipatory attacks against Al-Qaeda and similar organizations, run counter to the just war standards privileging the notion of last resort embraced in Obama's rhetoric and in official documents."[21] If Walzer's position is correct, then the question of drones and *jus in bello* is never reached in current drone usage. That does not mean that discussions of drones with respect unnecessary for that is not the case. Ethical considerations are essential. It does mean, however, that the considerations must be much broader and are more complex.

On the matter of drones and *jus ad bellum* and *jus in bello*, there is a third category of just war thought that can be brought to bear—jus ad vim (just use of force) in circumstances short of war. For much of the current use of military drones, perhaps that is where discussions should occur. Braun and Brunstetter believe so:

> *Jus ad vim* is an ethical category that has gained increased prominence in recent years due to the ambiguity of the war on terror, where much of the military

activity, such as drone strikes and special forces raids, fall short of the level of hostilities that would traditionally be associated with war, and yet are clearly beyond the bounds of law enforcement. While some scholars are critical of *jus ad vim* because of its perceived permissiveness and others contend that drones can be evaluated to jus ad bellum and *jus in bello* standards, we believe that differentiating between war and these acts short of war by conceptualizing the moral requirements of limited force within the category of *jus ad vim* provides both analytical clarity and a more nuanced appreciation of the potential ethical pitfalls of drone strikes.[22]

Why *jus ad vim* rather than *jus in bello*? They believe it gives opportunity to consider things that are not usually part of *jus in bello* proportionality decision making and because some of the decision making with respect to proportionality is misguided. They write:

> In addition, we assert that human rights concerns of civilians not usually considered in the proportionality calculus need to be taken into account. Such ethical constraints severely restrict the scope of proportionality balancing—the conscious decision that anticipated military advantage outweighs collateral damage—that can be employed.[23]

Braun and Brunstetter argue that proponents of drones and proportionality confuse technological precision with ethical proportionality and use a metric for proportionality that is either false or misunderstood. They contend:

> drones in fact deepen the proportionality dilemma. While drone pilots are immune from harm, civilians in the zones patrolled by drones most certainly are not. In an asymmetric struggle, it is not always easy to distinguish between combatants and noncombatants, and thus satisfy the *jus in bello* criterion of distinction. Moreover, once the precision of the weapons system is assumed to universally satisfy the requirements of proportionality, the door is opened for drones to be used against a problematically wide range of targets while making the use of non-lethal measures, such as capture, appear unfeasible.[24]

They argue further that proportionality proponents are misguided in their analysis at times because "proportionality is not comparable across historical eras."[25] Similarly, Henry Shue has argued that comparing death counts with numbers from civilian casualties in the Second World War is inappropriate because killing civilians was part of the bombing strategy.[26]

Beyond their arguments that proportionality is different from precision and proportionality is not comparable across historical eras, Braun and Brunstetter argue "proportionality is not comparable across tactics."[27] For them, the central point of drones, proportionality, and *jus in bello* "is not the meaning of the principle, but how it is to be assessed."[28] They believe: "Despite challenges in defining and measuring key terms such as 'civilian,' 'military advantage' and 'excessive,' it remains imperative to attempt to assess the proportionality of drone strikes."[29]

After studying drone strikes in Pakistan by the U.S. Military and the separate program of the CIA, Braun and Brunsetter believe that the disparity in collateral damage (unintended civilian deaths) is too great and highlights the need for stronger principles and policies:

> The disparity between CIA and military drones points to what one might call the proportionality spectrum: at the one end, the ability of drones to be very accurate (the less than 1 per cent of military strikes that caused collateral damage); in the middle, the 10 per cent military threshold; at the other end, the CIA strike rate that government officials claim are proportionate, but represent 23 per cent of strikes that caused collateral damage as well as other on-the-ground concerns. The range on this spectrum points to one of the inherent challenges of *jus in bello* proportionality, namely that proportionality can mean one thing here and another thing there, all under the umbrella of the same term, thus not really helping those not privy to classified information to adequately assess the morality of the strikes themselves.
>
> We contend that while it is unreasonable that CIA drones attain the 1 per cent level met by the military because of different strategic concerns, the actual 23 per cent level is too high for drones to be considered, as proponents claim, proportional.[30]

If they are correct, what then might be the ethical way forward? For them, it is an emphasis not on *jus in bello* but on *jus ad vim*.

> We have suggested employing an ethical framework calibrated to the use of force short of war—*jus ad vim*. The ambiguity of international law in light of the rising threat of non-state actors, combined with the dramatic increase in the use of limited force facilitated by drone technology, points to the need of a recalibrated ethical framework to evaluate acts of limited force, such as drone strikes in Pakistan. Such a framework would place greater scrutiny on the current proportionality balancing calculus of the CIA, while also bringing to the fore additional factors, such as human rights concerns, that are beyond the scope of traditional *jus in bello* proportionality. Creating an ethical framework for drone use based on *jus ad vim* would require working through a host of challenging questions that are beyond the scope of this argument, but we hope our initial analysis shows that the common refrain that drone use is proportionate leaves much to be desired, and that achieving ethical drone operations requires a more calibrated moral framework.[31]

Such a shift to studying drones and *jus ad vim* moves away from jus in bello in current operations and broadens the ethical considerations with respect to drones. It does not ethically prohibit their legitimate use in war. It seems to this author to say "maybe" with respect to *jus in bello*, but add that there is a fuller discussion and additional ethical considerations that must be undertaken. Such a perspective is partially what just-war advocate Michael Walzer speaks of with respect to the slippery slope of drone usage. Walzer writes:

> Now, does it make any difference if the actual killing is the work of a drone, operated by a technician sitting in an office 3,000 miles away? Surely the same

criteria apply to the drone as to any more closely manned machine. Why should we think it different from the sniper's rifle? The difference is that killing-by-drone is so much easier than other forms of targeted killing. The easiness should make us uneasy. This is a dangerously tempting technology. It makes our enemies more vulnerable than ever before, and we can get at them without any risk to our own soldiers.[32]

While this is good for the forces using the technology, there is a danger. Walzer notes, "But here is the difficulty: the technology is so good that the criteria for using it are likely to be steadily relaxed."[33]

Thus, the true challenge of using the technology of the drones or any other unmanned automated system may not be found in the act of using them, but in the temptation to use them. If so, then the issue is truly ethical and not technological, and it shows that regardless of whether the weapons of war are evolutionary or revolutionary, it are the humans who use them that deserve the greatest attention.

On this point of humans using weapons, there is always the possibility of a slippery slope on which we slide too far and achieve nothing. With respect to drones, Walzer reminds us:

> drones have been called "the only game in town." But we should think very carefully before relaxing the targeting rules and turning drones into a weapon like all the others. Their moral and political advantage is their precision, which depends on using them only against individuals whose critical importance we have established and about whom we have learned a great deal. Using them like an advanced form of artillery or like "smart" bombs isn't morally right or politically wise.
>
> This last point can be driven home very simply: imagine a world, which we will soon be living in, where everybody has drones.[34]

It is possible from the author's perspective that, as Strawser argues, there is a moral obligation to use drones when appropriate, but an ethically dangerous label of "use appropriately and handle with care" is also an ever-present reminder.

Conclusion

The answers to the many questions of UAVs and the ethics of war are not simple, and they should not be thought simple. Perhaps the words of twentieth-century American journalist H.L. Mencken are appropriate: "For every complex problem there is an answer that is clear, simple, and wrong."[35]

The use of drones, like any weapon, should not be without deep thought and firm commitment. It is not a clear-cut matter of "use them every time."

Deliberations must be thorough and conclusions and courses of action unambiguous. For present application of them, it may be that *jus ad vim* offers a *via media* and a better framework. Nevertheless, that does not negate their use or desirability for *jus in bello*.

The traumas and tragedies of war must never be forgotten or minimized. War is something that must never be considered casually. Because it is literally a matter of life and death, there must always be intense ethical scrutiny of it. Technology will not diminish that requirement. It will increase it. Also, on this matter, the lessons of history are appropriate. At the end of the Second World War, the United States government sought to study the bombing campaigns of the war in great detail in order to learn operational and strategic lessons for the future. The United States Strategic Bombing Survey board of civilian and military experts compiled a 208-volume study of the European theater and a 108-volume study of the Pacific theater. For this essay, two pertinent statements stand out. With respect to the bombing war in Europe, the summary volume states in the conclusion: "The great lesson to be learned in the battered towns of England and the ruined cities of Germany is that the best way to win a war is to prevent it from occurring. This must be the ultimate end to which our best efforts are devoted."[36] Looking to the unknown but anticipated future, the board declared: "The combination of the atomic bomb with remote-control with projectiles of ocean-spanning range stands as a possibility which is awesome and frightful to contemplate."[37] While this statement was not about drones, it was about complex weapons technologies that required somber reflection. As such, they do not differ from drones. While some might argue that the just-war tradition is no longer valid, that is not true. It remains a valid construct capable of addressing new technology.[38] However, the work is not easy.

In his seminal treatise *On War (Vom Kriege)*, the noted Prussian military theorist Carl von Clausewitz observed that war and conflict are multidimensional, with such events moving far beyond the technological, touching the psychological, intellectual, and spiritual dimensions of the human experience. "Theory becomes infinitely more difficult as soon as it touches the realm of moral values," he noted.[39]

So what then are we to make of Churchill's opening statement if we ask the same question with respect to the use of drones? "Are we beasts?" That is the question every military leader, every political leader, and indeed every citizen must answer. Ethicists, philosophers, theologians, strategists, political scientists, and military advisers can all weigh in, but the individual moral responsibility can never legitimately be abrogated or abandoned. It is not only the burden of command or the burden of leadership—it is the burden of being human.

Notes

1. Winston S. Churchill quoted in Martin Gilbert, *The Second World War: A Complete History* (New York: Henry Holt, 1989), 441. For a fuller study of the incident and ethical concerns behind it, see Christopher C. Harmon, "'Are We Beasts?' Churchill and the Moral Question of World War II Area Bombing," *Newport Paper* No. 1, December 1991, Naval War College, Newport, RI. On the overall bombing war, see Richard Overy, *The Bombing War: Europe 1939–1945* (London: Allen Lane, 2013) (published in the United States in 2014 as *The Bombers and the Bombed: Allied Air War Over Europe 1940–1945*). For an excellent overview of the ethics of the air war during the Second World War with respect to the British bombing, see Stephen A. Garrett, *Ethics and Airpower in World War II: The British Bombing of German Cities* (New York: St. Martin's Press, 1993). On American bombing and ethics, see Ronald Schaffer, "American Military Ethics in World War II: The Bombing of German Civilians," *The Journal of American History* 67:2 (Sept. 1980), 318–334.

2. Cf. Robin Neillands, *The Bomber War: The Allied Air Offensive against Nazi Germany* (New York: The Overlook Press, 2001), 382–406; Randall Hansen, *Fire and Fury: The Allied Bombing of Germany, 1942–1945* (New York: New American Library, 2009), 279–298; and A. C. Grayling, *Among the Dead Cities: The History and Moral Legacy of the WWII Bombing of Civilians in Germany and Japan* (New York: Walker & Co., 2006), 271–83. For an exceptional work on the development and application of strategic bombing, see Tami Davis Biddle, *Rhetoric and Reality in Air Warfare: The Evolution of British and American Ideas About Strategic Bombing, 1914–1945* (Princeton, N.J.: Princeton University Press, 2002).

3. Terminology varies with respect to UAVs. The spectrum of automated systems is termed unmanned automated vehicles, but one also sees the aerial components as unmanned aerial vehicles as also remotely piloted vehicles (RPAs) to distinguish them from aircraft with pilots in a cockpit. The colloquial term "drones" is well established in literature and used throughout this essay.

4. Christian Enemark, *Armed Drones and the Ethics of War: Military Virtue in a Post-Heroic Age* (London: Routledge, 2014), 3.

5. Ibid. On technological innovations and war see Max Boot, *War Made New: Technology, Warfare, and the Course of History, 1500 to Today* (New York: Gotham Books, 2006).

6. Ibid., 3.

7. For an introduction and overview of the UAVs and warfare see P. W. Singer, *Wired for War: The Robotics Revolution and Conflict in the 21st Century* (New York: Penguin Press, 2009). On airborne UAVs specifically, see, Bill Yenne, *Birds of Prey: Predators, Reapers and America's Newest UAVs* (North Branch, MN: Specialty Press, 2010). For a more technical perspective, see Norman Friedman, *Unmanned Combat Air Systems: A New Kind of Carrier Aviation* (Annapolis, MD: Naval Institute Press, 2010).

8. On the legal debates and issues, see Michael N. Schmitt, "Drone Attacks Under the Jus ad Bellum and Jus in Bello: Clearing the 'Fog of Law,'" *Yearbook of International Humanitarian Law* 13 (Dec. 2010): 311–26. On policy, see Micah Zenko, Reforming U.S. Drone Strike Policies. Council Special Report No. 65 January 2013 (New York: Council on Foreign Relations, 2013). See also essays by Daniel Byman and Audrey Kurth Cronin respectively "Why Drones Work: The Case for Washington's Weapon of Choice," *Foreign Affairs* 92:4 (July/August 2013): 32–43 and "Why Drones Fail: When Tactics Drive Strategy," *Foreign Affairs* 92:4 (July/August 2013): 44–54.

9. Enemark, *Armed Drones and the Ethics of War*, 2.
10. Ibid., 4.
11. Cited in Harold E. Raugh, *The Victorians at War, 1815–1914: An Encyclopedia of British Military History* (Santa Barbara, CA: ABC-CLIO Publishers, 2004), 93.
12. For recent consideration of the just-war tradition see James Turner Johnson, *Morality and Contemporary Warfare* (New Haven: Yale University Press, 1999); Steven P. Lee, *Ethics and War: An Introduction* (Cambridge, UK: Cambridge University Press, 2012); and Brian Orend, *The Morality of War* (Peterborough, Ontario: Broadview Press, 2006).
13. Dan Smith, *The State of War and Peace Atlas* (New York: The Penguin Group, 1997), 13–14.
14. James E. Hickey, *Precision-Guided Munitions and Human Suffering in War* (Burlington, VT: Ashgate Publishing, 2012), 2. Hickey's study specifically looks at the usage of PGMs by the United States from the Vietnam War through the Balkans conflict. It does not address the rise of UAV technology in the twenty-first century although the conclusions of his study are directly applicable to drone warfare.
15. Kenneth P. Werrell, *Death from the Heavens: A History of Strategic Bombing* (Annapolis, MD: Naval Institute Press, 2009), 122.
16. Avery Plaw, "Counting the Dead: The Proportionality of Predation in Pakistan," *Killing by Remote Control: The Ethics of an Unmanned Military*, ed. Bradley J. Strawser (Oxford: Oxford University Press, 2013), 126–53 and Mary E. O'Connell, "Rise of the Drones II: Examining the Legality of Unmanned Targeting," Hearing before the Subcommittee on National Security and Foreign Affairs, 111th Congress, 2nd session, 2010 accessed 1 December 2013, available at Internet: http://www.fas.org/irp/congress/2010_hr/drones2.pdf (Last access, 7 March 2014). See also Amitai Etzioni, "The Great Drone Debate," *Military Review* (March–April 2013): 2–13 and Scott Shaw, "The Moral Case for Dones," *The New York Times* (July 14, 2012), available on the Internet at http://www.nytimes.com/2012/07/15/sunday-review/the-moral-case-for-drones.html?_r=0 (Last access, 7 March 2014).
17. Bradley Jay Strawser, "Moral Predators: The Duty to Employ Uninhabited Aerial Vehicles," *Journal of Military Ethics* 9/4 (December 2010), 361–62.
18. Ibid., 344.
19. Ibid., 362.
20. Daniel R. Brunstetter, "Can We Wage a Just Drone War?" *The Atlantic* (19 July 2012), available at: http://www.theatlantic.com/technology/archive/2012/07/can-we-wage-a-just-drone-war/260055 (Last access, 10 November 2013). For an expansion of this see also Daniel R. Brunstetter and Megan Braun, "The Implications of Drones on the Just War Tradition," *Ethics & International Affairs* 25/3 (2011): 337–358 and Daniel R. Brunstetter and Megan Braun, "From Jus ad Bellum to Jus ad Vim: Recalibrating Our Understanding of the Moral Use of Force," *Ethics & International Affairs* 26/1 (2013): 87–106.
21. Michael W. Walzer, "Targeted Killing and Drone Warfare," *Dissent Magazine: A Quarterly of Politics and Culture* (Jan. 11, 2013), Internet at: http://www.dissentmagazine.org/online_articles/targeted-killing-and-drone-warfare (Last access, 7 March 2014).
22. Megan Braun and Daniel R. Brunstetter, "Rethinking the Criterion for Assessing CIA-Targeted Killings: Drones, Proportionality and Jus ad Vim," *Journal of Military Ethics*, 12/4 (December 2013), 306.
23. Ibid.
24. Ibid., 307–308.

25. Ibid., 308.
26. Henry Shue, "Concept Wars, Survival," *Global Politics and Strategy*, 50/2 (2008): 185–192.
27. Braun and Brunsetter, *Rethinking*, 309–310.
28. Ibid., 310.
29. Ibid.
30. Ibid., 316.
31. Ibid., 320.
32. Walzer, *Targeted Killing*. Walzer also writes of "force-short-of-war" (*jus ad vim*) in the Preface to the 4th edition of *Just and Unjust Wars: A Moral Argument with Historical Illustration* (New York: Basic Books, 2006), xvi–xvii.
33. Walzer, *Targeted Killing*.
34. Ibid.
35. Cited in Singer, *Wired for War*, 428.
36. The United States Strategic Bombing Survey. *The United States Strategic Bombing Survey Overall Report* (European War) September 30, 1945 (Washington, D.C.: Government Printing Office), 109.
37. Ibid.
38. Cf. J. Daryl Charles and Timothy J. Demy, *War, Peace, and Christianity: Questions and Answers from a Just-War Perspective* (Wheaton, IL: Crossway Publications, 2010), 247–248 and 342–343.
39. Carl von Clausewitz, *On War*, ed., trans. Michael Howard and Peter Paret (1832; repr., Princeton, NJ: Princeton University Press, 1976), 136.

Works Cited

Biddle, Tami Davis. *Rhetoric and Reality in Air Warfare: The Evolution of British and American Ideas About Strategic Bombing, 1914–1945*. Princeton, NJ: Princeton University Press, 2002.
Boot, Max. *War Made New: Technology, Warfare, and the Course of History, 1500 to Today*. New York: Gotham Books, 2006.
Braun, Megan, and Daniel R. Brunstetter. "Rethinking the Criterion for Assessing CIA-Targeted Killings: Drones, Proportionality and *Jus ad Vim*," *Journal of Military Ethics*, 12/4 (December 2013).
Brunstetter, Daniel R. "Can We Wage a Just Drone War?" *The Atlantic* (19 July 2012), Internet, available at: http://www.theatlantic.com/technology/archive/2012/07/can-we-wage-a-just-drone-war/260055.
Brunstetter, Daniel R., and Megan Braun. "From Jus ad Bellum to *Jus ad Vim*: Recalibrating Our Understanding of the Moral Use of Force," *Ethics & International Affairs*, 26/1 (2013): 87–106.
Brunstetter, Daniel R., and Megan Braun. "The Implications of Drones on the Just War Tradition," *Ethics & International Affairs* 25/3 (2011): 337–358.
Byman, Daniel, and Audrey Kurth Cronin. "Why Drones Fail: When Tactics Drive Strategy," *Foreign Affairs* 92:4 (July/August 2013): 44–54.
Byman, Daniel, and Audrey Kurth Cronin. "Why Drones Work: The Case for Washington's Weapon of Choice," *Foreign Affairs* 92:4 (July/August 2013): 32–43.
Charles, Daryl, and Timothy J. Demy. *War, Peace, and Christianity: Questions and Answers from a Just-War Perspective*. Wheaton, IL: Crossway Publications, 2010.
Clausewitz, Carl von. *On War*, ed., trans. Michael Howard and Peter Paret (1832; repr.). Princeton, NJ: Princeton University Press, 1976.

Enemark, Christian. *Armed Drones and the Ethics of War: Military Virtue in a Post-Heroic Age.* London: Routledge, 2014.
Etzioni, Amitai. "The Great Drone Debate," *Military Review,* (March–April 2013): 2–13.
Friedman, Norman. *Unmanned Combat Air Systems: A New Kind of Carrier Aviation.* Annapolis, MD: Naval Institute Press, 2010.
Garrett, Stephen A. *Ethics and Airpower in World War II: The British Bombing of German Cities.* New York: St. Martin's Press, 1993.
Gilbert, Martin. *The Second World War: A Complete History.* New York: Henry Holt, 1989.
Grayling, A.C. *Among the Dead Cities: The History and Moral Legacy of the WWII Bombing of Civilians in Germany and Japan.* New York: Walker & Co., 2006.
Hansen, Randall. *Fire and Fury: The Allied Bombing of Germany, 1942–1945.* New York: New American Library, 2009.
Harmon, Christopher C. "'Are We Beasts?' Churchill and the Moral Question of World War II Area Bombing," *Newport Paper No. 1,* December 1991, Naval War College, Newport, RI.
Hickey, James E. *Precision-Guided Munitions and Human Suffering in War.* Burlington, VT: Ashgate Publishing, 2012.
Johnson, James Turner. *Morality and Contemporary Warfare.* New Haven: Yale University Press, 1999.
Lee, Steven P. *Ethics and War: An Introduction.* Cambridge, UK: Cambridge University Press, 2012.
Neillands, Robin. *The Bomber War: The Allied Air Offensive against Nazi Germany.* New York: The Overlook Press, 2001.
O'Connell, Mary E. "Rise of the Drones II: Examining the Legality of Unmanned Targeting," *Hearing before the Subcommittee on National Security and Foreign Affairs, 111th Congress, 2nd session, 2010 accessed 1 December 2013,* available at Internet: http://www.fas.org/irp/congress/2010_hr/drones2.pdf.
Orend, Brian. *The Morality of War.* Peterborough, Ontario: Broadview Press, 2006.
Overy, Richard. *The Bombing War: Europe 1939–1945.* London: Allen Lane, 2013. (Published in the United States in 2014 as *The Bombers and the Bombed: Allied Air War Over Europe 1940–1945).*
Plaw, Avery. "Counting the Dead: The Proportionality of Predation in Pakistan," *Killing by Remote Control: The Ethics of an Unmanned Military,* ed. Bradley J. Strawser. Oxford: Oxford University Press, 2013, 126–53.
Raugh, Harold E. *The Victorians at War, 1815–1914: An Encyclopedia of British Military History.* Santa Barbara, CA: ABC-CLIO Publishers, 2004.
Schaffer, Ronald. "American Military Ethics in World War II: The Bombing of German Civilians," *The Journal of American History* 67:2 (Sept. 1980), 318–334.
Schmitt, Michael N. "Drone Attacks Under the Jus ad Bellum and Jus in Bello: Clearing the 'Fog of Law,'" *Yearbook of International Humanitarian Law* 13 (Dec. 2010): 311–326.
Shaw, Scott. "The Moral Case for Dones," *The New York Times* (July 14, 2012), available on the Internet at http://www.nytimes.com/2012/07/15/sunday-review/the-moral-case-for-drones.html?_r=0.
Shue, Henry. "Concept Wars, Survival" *Global Politics and Strategy,* 50/2 (2008): 185–192.
Singer, P.W. *Wired for War: The Robotics Revolution and Conflict in the 21st Century.* New York: Penguin Press, 2009.
Smith, Dan. *The State of War and Peace Atlas.* New York: The Penguin Group, 1997.

Strawser, Bradley Jay. "Moral Predators: The Duty to Employ Uninhabited Aerial Vehicles," *Journal of Military Ethics* 9/4 (December 2010).
The United States Strategic Bombing Survey Overall Report (European War) September 30, 1945. Washington, D.C.: Government Printing Office.
Walzer, Michael W. *Just and Unjust Wars: A Moral Argument with Historical Illustration.* New York: Basic Books, 2006.
Walzer, Michael W. "Targeted Killing and Drone Warfare," *Dissent Magazine: A Quarterly of Politics and Culture* (Jan. 11th 2013), Internet at: http://www.dissent magazine.org/online_articles/targeted-killing-and-drone-warfare.
Werrell, Kenneth P. *Death from the Heavens: A History of Strategic Bombing.* Annapolis, MD: Naval Institute Press, 2009.
Yenne, Bill. *Birds of Prey: Predators, Reapers and America's Newest UAVs.* North Branch, MN: Specialty Press, 2010.
Zenko, Micah. *Reforming U.S. Drone Strike Policies. Council Special Report No. 65 January 2013.* New York: Council on Foreign Relations, 2013.

About the Contributors

Roderick **Bailey** is a Wellcome Trust Research Fellow in the history of medicine at the University of Oxford. A graduate of the universities of Edinburgh and Cambridge, he specializes in the study of irregular warfare and resistance during the Second World War. He is the author of *The Wildest Province: SOE in the Land of the Eagle*, a study of SOE operations in Axis-occupied Albania and Kosovo, and *Target: Italy—The Secret War Against Mussolini* which was commissioned by the UK Government and is the official history of SOE's war on Fascist Italy.

Timothy J. **Demy** is a professor of military ethics at the U.S. Naval War College in Newport, Rhode Island. Prior to his appointment, he served as a Navy chaplain for 27 years. He received a B.A. at Texas Christian University, a Th.M. and Th.D. in historical theology from Dallas Theological Seminary and a Ph.D. in humanities and technology from Salve Regina University. He also has degrees in international relations, European history, national security and strategic studies. He has authored or edited more than twenty books.

Sebastian **Diziol** works at the Solivagus publishing company in Kiel. He received a B.A. in modern history and journalism from Karlsruhe University, an M.A. in history from the University of Nottingham and a Ph.D. from the University of Hamburg. He is at work on an edition of the correspondence of "common" people from World War II.

Eckehard **Dworok** was an officer in the Bundeswehr and studied economics, education studies and political science at the universities of Darmstadt and Kassel. In 1986, he received a Ph.D. with a focus on the economic warfare of Nazi Germany. He has taught economics and politics at the Professional School of Bebra as well as at the Hessian College of Economics and Administration in Rotenburg an der Fulda.

Gerrit **Dworok** is a high school teacher in Bavaria and lecturer in the Department of Modern History at the University of Würzburg. His research interests are the history of totalitarianism, the history of nationalism and the history of the former FRG (1949–1990). His doctoral thesis deals with the West German "Historikerstreit" of 1986.

About the Contributors

Daniel **Fuhrer** is a project manager in armed forces development at the Swiss Armed Forces Staff in Berne, Switzerland. He is working on a dissertation covering doctrine and the image of war development in the United States Army and Air Force. He is especially interested in technological and doctrinal concept development from a historical perspective and publishes regularly about armed forces transformation.

James **Horncastle** is a Ph.D. candidate at Simon Fraser University and a research affiliate of the Stavros Niarchos Foundation Centre for Hellenic Studies. He received an M.A. from the University of New Brunswick in 2011. His research interests include modern Southeast Europe, modern warfare, civil war, insurgency campaigns, and the modern Middle East. His dissertation examines the role that ethnic minorities played in the Greek Civil War, 1946–49.

Frank **Jacob** is an assistant professor of world history at the City University of New York, QCC. He received an M.A. from Würzburg University and a Ph.D. from Erlangen University. He previously taught modern history at Würzburg University and lectured in modern history and Japanese studies at Düsseldorf and Erlangen universities. The editor of the journals *Global Humanities* and the *Journal of East Asian History*, and the series *Comparative Studies from a Global Perspective*, he has published widely on Japanese, German, and global history.

Marc-André **Karpienski** is a trainee teacher at the Ernst-Barlach-Gymnasium Unna. He received an M.A. in medieval history and a Staatsexamen (equivalent to Master of Education) from the Westfälische Wilhelms-Universität Münster. He has worked as a lecturer in medieval studies at Münster University and at the Leuphana Universität Lüneburg. His most recent articles are on the presentation of medieval warfare in fantasy stories, and on the academic construction of Europe as a historical phenomenon.

Tomáš **Kučera** received a Ph.D. from Aberystwyth University, with a focus on liberalism and societal civil-military relations. His articles have been internationally published in several journals, including the *Czech Military Review*.

Kurt **Möser** is a professor of new history and the history of technology at the Karlsruhe Institute of Technology (KIT). He earned doctorate and master degrees from Konstanz University, studying history and literature. He was curator at the State Museum of Technology and Labour in Mannheim, taught at the universities of Erlangen and St. Gallen and lectured at the University of Oxford and Jawaharlal Nehru University, New Delhi. He is the author of numerous studies on the cultural history of technology, mobility history and military history.

Nathan R. **Packard** is a professor at the Naval War College and a Ph.D. candidate at Georgetown University. He received an M.A. in American studies from Georgetown University, and an M.A. in national security and strategic studies from the Naval War College. He is completing a dissertation on the U.S. Marine Corps' post–Vietnam reform efforts. A Marine Corps officer, he spent 2007 conducting counterinsurgency operations in Al Anbar Province, Iraq. His research interests include the role of force in foreign relations, and the reintegration of veterans.

About the Contributors

Adam **Page** is a postdoctoral fellow at the University of Lüneburg. He received a Ph.D. from the University of Sheffield for his dissertation "The Architecture of Survival: Planning the Future of Cities in the Shadow of Air War, Britain 1935–52," and is working on a research project called "Envisioning a Global Equilibrium as an Answer to World War in the Mid-Twentieth Century."

Christian **Scholl** is an assistant professor of medieval history at the University of Münster. He studied at the University of Trier and University College Dublin; his doctoral thesis was about the Jewish community of Ulm in the Later Middle Ages. He has published widely on the history of the Jews and Christian-Jewish relations in Medieval Europe and is working on a book about the Romans and Barbarians in the early Middle Ages.

Thomas **Schuetz** studied history and the history of science and technology in Stuttgart. His doctoral thesis dealt with the transfer of technology between the Orient and Occident. He is the foundation chair for the history of the impact of technology at the University of Stuttgart. His research interests include the industrialization of south-west Germany, environmental history, medieval technology and the history of winemaking.

Jeffrey M. **Shaw** is an associate professor of strategy and policy in the College of Distance Education at the U.S. Naval War College. He received an M.A. in military history from the American Military University, an M.A. in national security studies from the USAF Air Command and Staff College, and a Ph.D. in humanities from Salve Regina University. The author of *Illusions of Freedom: Thomas Merton and Jacques Ellul on Technology and the Human Condition* (Wipf and Stock), he has published in the fields of ethics, philosophy, and national security studies.

Benedict **von Bremen** is a research fellow in the American Studies department at Eberhard Karls Universität Tübingen, teaching history classes on U.S. foreign policy and America's wars. He received an M.A. in modern history and American studies from Tübingen University and is working on his dissertation, "Two-Way Streets and *Einbahnstraßen*: U.S. and West German Debates about NATO Defense Cooperation in the 1970s."

Olaf **Wagener** works at the Institute of European Art History at Heidelberg University. He received a B.A. from Siegen University and an M.A. from Heidelberg University. He is working on his Ph.D. about castles as centers of visual communication in the landscape in the Middle Ages. He is the editor of eleven books about castle sciences, with his most recent book dealing with toilets in the Middle Ages. He is the author of numerous works on castles and landscapes, wooden fortifications throughout the world, and siege warfare.

Jorit **Wintjes** works as a senior lecturer in ancient history at Julius-Maximilians-Universität Würzburg. His research interests include ancient naval history, women's military history in antiquity, political rhetoric in the Roman empire and naval history of the 1850–1914 period.

Index

Abbasid Revolution 47
Abdallah ibn az-Zubair 51
Advanced Amphibious Assault Vehicle 218
aerial camera 10, 119–120, 122–123
Afghanistan 172–173, 175–176, 178–179, 211, 214, 236, 243–244, 251, 253, 261, 266, 273, 276
age of extremes 99, 106, 109
agitation 100, 103, 107, 109
agitprop 100–101
agitpunkty 100
Air Force Magazine 233, 235, 238, 241–244, 258
air power 11, 142–144, 147, 238, 260–268, 270–273
aircraft 7, 121, 144–145, 157, 160, 164–165, 182, 188, 203, 213–215, 217–218, 220, 222, 229, 233–235, 237–238, 264, 267, 272, 275, 278, 287
AirLand Battle 228–231, 233–235, 239, 240–241, 244
Airpower Journal 233, 235–237, 241–244
AK-47 10–11, 169, 176–181, 207
Albania 133, 136, 293
Albarrana 50, 52
Alexander Nevski (movie) 103
al-Qaeda 174, 282
Alsace 72, 80, 83
Alt-Windstein 73
American Civil War 76, 155
ammunition 18–19, 22–23, 105, 145, 159, 170–171, 204, 206, 267
Amphibious Warfare Strategy 214
anthrax 163

Antwerp 164
Apache 234, 240
Appadurai, Arjun 125
Armstrong Board 213
Army Group A (Wehrmacht) 161
army spade 10
artillery 6, 9–10, 17–28, 37, 41–42, 58–61, 76, 111, 116, 119, 156, 164, 189, 216, 229, 232, 251, 278, 285
Asia 30, 37, 48, 55, 170, 175, 203, 210, 239, 251
Assad, Bashar 255
asymmetric warfare 7, 170, 174–176
atomic bomb 163, 176–177, 286
Auftragstaktik 230, 233
Australia 124–125
Austria 78
avant-garde 103, 107
Avars 30, 35, 37–38

Bachrach, Bernhard 31, 39, 42
ballistarii 20, 27
Banzai 4
Barbarossa Campaign 162, 177, 180
Barrow, Robert 225
Battleship Potemkin (movie) 10, 98, 102–104, 106, 108–110
Bavaria 1, 35, 293
Bayeux Tapestry 32, 47
Belgium 126, 145, 194–195, 197, 203, 206
Berwartstein 73, 80, 83
Betz, David 258
Bialer, Uri 275
Biddle, Tami 275, 289
Bijker, Wibe 125
Birdcage III 77

297

298 Index

Black, Jeremy 195, 225
Black Sea 104
Blitzkrieg 158–159, 161–164, 166, 168, 240–241, 243–244
Bloch, Ivan 14
bolt-thrower 22
bombing 137–138, 141, 143–147, 261–262, 264, 266, 269, 271–272, 278, 283, 286, 287
Boot, Max 125, 289
Borneo 127
Bosnia 192–193, 196
Bosquet, Pierre 279
bourgeois 86, 99, 101, 103, 105–106
Braun, Megan 289
Breitenrüstung 159, 166
Brest-Litovsk 155
Brezhnev Doctrine 189–190
British Isles 74
Bronze Age 245
Brunstetter, Daniel R. 289
Budapest 171
Buddha 134
Bundeswehr 198, 202, 204, 206–207, 293
Bürgertum 85–87, 91
Burma 127
Bush, George W., Jr. 239
Byzantine 34–35, 38–39, 41–42

C3I 121
Caesar, Julius 17, 72
caesarism 89
Caetani, Gelasio 78
Callaghan Report 201
Cambrai 157
camera 10, 120–121
Canada 197, 206
Canakkale 119
Candia 75
Capitol Hill 218
Card, Orson Scott 270
Carolingian 31, 35–36, 41
Carter, Jimmy 214–215, 223, 226–227
Carter Doctrine 214–215
Casablanca 146
Caucasus 162
cavalry 6, 58, 118
centurion 20
CH-46 Sea Knight 217
Chapman, Robert M. 243
Cheek, Gary H. 238, 243

chemical weapons 4, 156–157, 163, 256
Chiarelli, Peter 264, 273, 275
China 37, 48, 51, 58, 171, 173, 177
Christendom 45–46, 50, 75
Christianity 289
Chrysler 202
Churchill, Winston 119, 141, 144, 146, 150, 277, 279, 286–287, 290
CIA 127, 173–175, 186, 284, 288–289
cinema 100–103, 105, 107
civilians 47, 137–138, 144, 146–148, 218, 248, 262–264, 266, 278, 280, 283
civilization 54, 262
Clausewitz, Carl von 13, 14, 67, 69, 230, 237, 254, 257–258, 266, 286, 289
Close, Robert 208
Clulow, Adam 251, 257–258
Cobra 234
Col di Lana 78, 83
Cold War 8, 10–11, 148, 151, 169, 171, 182–185, 187, 189, 192–198, 201, 203, 205, 209, 223, 226, 241, 249, 255, 279
Colmar 72
Cominform 185, 193
communism 103, 106, 187
Compiègne 161
Congo 174, 178, 181
Conservative party 142
Cooper, Alfred 145
Corps 86 230–231, 240, 244
Correl, John T. 235
Cossacks 104
Council of the Lateran 47
Coyne, James P. 233, 241, 243
Crac de Chevaliers 49–50
Crete 75
Creveld, Martin van 8, 12–14, 114, 124–125, 175, 179–180, 211, 222, 225, 242–243, 246, 248, 250–251, 256–258
Crimean War 279
Cu Chi 78, 81, 83
culture 5, 63, 67, 85, 108, 115, 121, 140, 148, 183, 184, 221, 239, 268, 270

D-Day 17
Dalton, Hughes 127
Denmark 63, 126, 129, 206
Department for Agitation and Propaganda 100
De Puy, William E. 228–229
Desenberg 72, 79–80, 83

Dick, Charles J. 243
Dien Bien Phu 78, 81, 83
Djilas, Milovan 185, 193, 195
Doering-Manteuffel, Anselm 14, 109
Donetsk 162
Douhet, Giulio 235, 260–261, 271–272, 275
Dover 74
drones 251, 261–262, 265–266, 278–279, 281–288, 290
Dubček, Alexander 189
dummy fog signals 131
Dunkirk 161–162
Dura Europos 72

The Economist 251, 257–258
Edgerton, David 123, 137, 141, 147, 150, 221, 224–225, 274, 275
effects-based operations 238
Egypt 49, 172, 200
Eichholtz, Dietrich 162, 167
Eisenstein, Sergey 10, 98, 101–110
Ellul, Jacques 246, 256–258, 295
emotio 100
Enemark, Chris 278–279, 287–288, 290
Enigma 165
Essen 107, 109, 145
Euclid 48
Eurasia 50
Europe 9, 12, 14, 21, 28, 30, 32–39, 42–43, 48–49, 55, 57–58, 59, 64–66, 68–70, 88–89, 107–108, 126–127, 135, 150–151, 155, 189, 194–196, 200–201, 203, 205, 207, 209, 228–230, 240–241, 247, 265, 271, 286–287, 290, 294–295
European Economic Community 203
explosive coal 130, 133

F-15E Strike Eagle 234
F-16 Fighting Falcon 203
F-84 Thunderjet 187
F-86 Sabre 187
F-104 198, 203
fascism 106, 171
Federal Republic of Germany 197
Fenton, George 264
Feuerle, Mark 43, 54
film 10, 79, 87, 92, 94, 97–101, 103, 105–110, 128–129, 135, 142, 149, 270, 277
Finelli, Frank 243
Fitzgerald, Chr. G. 172, 178–179
Flag Song 91

Flavian 25
Fleet Marine Forces 213
FM 100-5 229–231
Fogleman, Ronald R. 235
Foot, M.R.D. 136
four-year plan 163
Freikorps 117
French Revolution 247, 254
Frieser, Karl-Heinz 168
frontier 174
Führer 162, 165
Fuller, J.F.C. 242–243, 262, 264, 267, 271, 273–274, 276
Fussel, Paul 116, 124–125
futuūah 46

Galeb 188–189
Garrison 74
gas war 163, 274
Gat, Azar 45, 52
Gates, Robert M. 239
gāzī 47, 201, 233, 235, 238, 241–244, 251, 258, 288, 291
gender mainstreaming 254
General Motors 202
Geneva Convention 133–134
Georgia Institute of Technology 269
German Navy League 9, 85–89, 93–94, 96
German Reich 85, 89–91, 155
Germanicus 17–18, 25, 28
Germany 9, 11, 13, 15, 17, 25, 72, 85–86, 88–90, 93, 97, 107–108, 110–111, 120, 123, 137–138, 145–146, 148, 151, 154–158, 163–165, 170, 184, 197–198, 201–207, 209, 224, 241, 262, 286–287, 290, 293, 295
ghulam 47
global civil war of ideologies 98, 101, 105–106
globalization 248–249, 252–255
Goebbels, Joseph 106
Goslar 72
Goths 35
Great Britain 85, 93–94, 153–155, 157, 159–161, 165, 204, 206, 273, 275
The Great Escape 79
Great War (World War I) 1, 3, 12, 15, 99, 111, 113–115, 119, 122–125, 154
Greece 36, 130, 206
grenade 132, 169
Griffith, David Wark 101

Gubrud, Mark 249–250, 257–258
Guderian, Heinz 157, 161, 166, 168
guerilla 173
Guirsberg 72
Gulf War 222
Gurkha Rifles 253

Haber-Bosch method 4
Hackett, John (Sir) 204, 208
Haiti 237
Halder, Franz 159, 166, 168
Hamburg 13–15, 67, 70, 87, 94, 96, 107, 109, 167, 177–178, 180–181, 205, 209, 293
Hamilton, C. I. 94, 97, 141, 148, 150
Hanse 85
hegemony 154, 184
Heinrich der Löwe 72
helix of death 8
Herzegovina 192, 193, 196
Higgins boats 216
Hitler, Adolf 10, 123, 153–159, 161–168, 193, 196
Hohenzollern 90
Holland 53, 55, 126
Hollywood 101, 103
Honnecourt, Villard de 48, 53–54
Hore-Belisha, Leslie 142, 149–150
House of Commons 142
Höxter 72, 80, 83
Human Rights Watch 260, 272, 276
humane killing 271–272
Hunnic bow 34
Huns 34–35, 40, 43
Hunter Committee 144

Iberian peninsula 45, 49–50
ideology 7, 45, 98–100, 102, 141, 156, 257
Illustrierter Beobachter 163, 166, 168
immunes 20
Imperial War Museum 130, 132, 135–136
index fossils 114
Industrial Age 4
industrialization 3, 7, 183, 247, 263
infantry 4, 6, 9, 17, 20, 24, 26, 34, 77, 114, 116, 141, 158–160, 171, 177, 181, 210, 213, 215, 229, 240, 253
Intolerance (movie) 101
Iran 171, 178, 214
Iraq 144, 175, 204, 211, 235, 243–244, 250–251, 261, 294
Ireland 74

Iron Age 245
Iron Curtain 204
Islam 45, 47, 50, 52–56
Islamic Empire 48
Israel 200, 213, 222, 226, 229, 246
Italy 30, 78, 120, 154–155, 157, 223, 293

Jastreb 189
Jerusalem 36, 49, 55
jihad 47
Johnson, Gordon 266, 273
Joint Force Command 266
Ju 87 160
Judaism 163
Jus ad Bellum 282, 287–290
Jus ad Vim 282, 288–289
Jus in Bello 279–280, 287, 290
Just War 147, 151, 279, 288–289

Kaempffert, Waldemar 5, 6, 12–13, 15
Kagan, Donald 255, 258
Kaiser 83, 86–87, 89, 90–92, 95, 97
Kaiserreich 94, 96, 153–155
Kalashnikov, Mikhail 170–171, 176, 178–180
Kant, Immanuel 139, 147–148, 151
Keegan, John 113, 124–125, 176, 180
Keim, August 86
Kelley, Paul X. 214, 219, 222–223, 226
Kennedy, John F. 199
Kerenski, Alexander 105
Khrushchev, Nikita 187, 194–195
Kiel 87, 119, 293
Kier, Elizabeth 151
killer robots 260–261, 269–270
Königstiger 165
Korea 78, 171
Korean War 81–82, 172, 177–178, 180, 186, 223
Koselleck, Reinhart 50, 54–55
Krulak, Victor 211–212, 216, 221–222, 224, 226
Krupp, Friedrich Alfred 86
Kuleschov, Lev 101, 107, 110
Kurzweil, Ray 268, 274
KZ (concentration camps) 117, 153

Labour Party 127
Lebensraum 156–157, 163
Leber, Georg 201
Leiden Maccabee manuscript 36
Lenin, Vladimir Ilyitsch 99–100, 107, 190

Leningrad 100
Lenk, Hans 258
Leopard II 199–202, 204
lethality 5, 7–11, 118, 212, 238, 245, 248, 250–251, 256
Lewis, Adrian R. 244
liberal ethics 137–138, 144
Liberia 174, 178, 181
Liddell Hart, Basil 142–143, 149–151, 262–263, 266–267, 271, 273–275
Limerick 74, 80, 84
Ljubićić, Nikola 190
Löbelbastei 75
Locke, John 151
London 15, 28, 39–43, 52–55, 64–66, 68–70, 77, 80–82, 94, 96, 97, 106–110, 123–125, 128, 130, 132, 135–136, 146–151, 164, 178, 181, 193–196, 205, 207–209, 240–244, 273–276, 287, 290
longbow 49
low intensity conflicts 8, 11, 175, 213, 222
Löwenstein 73, 80, 82
Luftwaffe 160, 164–165
Luxembourg 126

M-1 Abrams 204
M1A1 216
M4 Sherman 187
M16 172, 178, 181
Madžar, Ljubomir 188, 194, 196
MAG-58 203
magistri 20
Malaya 127
mamlūk 47
MANPADs 173
Manstein, Erich von 161
Marcellinus, Ammianus 34, 40, 42
Marine Amphibious Units 215
Marine Corps 11, 210–227, 294
Marine Expeditory Units 215
Marxism-Leninism 106
material turn 10, 111
Materialschlacht 111, 116
MBlink16 122–123
MBT-70 199
McNamara, Robert 199, 205
Me 262 164
Mein Kampf 155–166, 168
Menges, Wilhelm 86
Mercer, Donald L. 232, 241, 244
Mesopotamia 144

Metz, Karl-Heinz 5, 12–13, 15, 27
MI6 134
Micro Aerial Vehicles 268, 274, 276
Middle East 170, 174, 179–180, 200, 214, 239, 273, 276, 294
Middlebrook, Martin 124–125
militarism 85, 93, 137, 141, 147
Military History Research Institute 156
Military Review 208, 232–234, 241, 243–244, 288, 290, 294
militis christiani 47
Milivojević, Marko 188, 194
Mill, James 151
Mill, John Stuart 151
Milward, A.S. 156–166, 168
mining 9, 71–72, 74–76, 78–79, 118–119, 185
Mirage 203
Mitcham, Carl 246–247, 251, 256, 258
Mitterauer, Michael 48, 53, 55
Moltke, Bernhard Graf von 6
monarchy 120
montage style 101–103, 106
morality 111, 239, 261
Moscow 162, 164, 178–179
Mosfilm 101
MP 40 170
MP 41 170
mujahedeen 173, 175
Müller, Rolf-Dieter 168
Mumford, Lewis 246–248, 256, 258
Munster 74

nanotechnology 245–246, 248–251, 255, 268–269
Napoleon I 7, 88, 254
nationalism 8, 88, 293
NATO 122, 182–193, 197–209, 229, 231, 241, 254–255, 258–259, 295
naval operations 9
navy 85–94, 141, 156, 224
Nazi 13, 15, 107, 110, 129, 184, 224, 287, 290, 293
Nevada 266
New Statesman 145
new wars 7, 8, 170, 174, 177
New Zealand 77
Nicholas II 100
Nixon, Richard 202, 214
Nordhausen 153
Normans 32
North America 48

302 Index

North Rhine–Westphalia 72
Norton Griffiths, John 76
Norway 126, 145, 203, 206
nuclear bomb 163
Nuremberg 114
Nusret 119

Obama, Barack 239, 281, 282
occident 45–46, 48, 50, 52, 56, 295
O'Conell, Mary E. 281, 288, 290
October (movie) 10, 98–101, 103–106, 108–109
October Revolution 100, 101, 105
Odessa 103–104
Ogarkov, Nikolai 184, 193
OKH 161
OKW 162
Omaha Beach 17, 240, 244
Omdurman 5
Operation Desert Storm 228, 234–235, 237, 239, 241–242
Operation Enduring Freedom 237
orient 240
OSS 134
Ostraum 154–155
Ostrogoths 34
Ottoman Empire 52, 56, 60, 75, 193

Pacific Ocean 215, 223, 286
Palestine 45, 144
Panther 165
pars pro toto 102–103, 105–106
partisans 127, 184
Paternus, Tarrutienus 20
Pax Dei 46
peace 10, 142–143, 162, 185, 202, 255, 270, 280
Pennsylvania 39, 42, 76, 193, 196
Pentagon 173, 202, 266
Persians 34
Personnel Halting and Stimulation Response 270
Petrović, Ljubomir 190, 195–196
pilgrims 50
Plaw, Avery 290
pogrom 99
Polish campaign 158
Popović, Koca 188, 194
Port Arthur 3, 12, 15
precision-guided-munitions 280
precision weaponry 245–246, 250–251, 253

prisoners of war 79
Procopius of Caesarea 34
propaganda 7, 9–10, 86–92, 98–100, 102–103, 105, 107
proxy wars 170
Prussia 158
Pudovkin, Vsevolod 101, 107, 110
Punjab 144

R4M 164
radio 122, 127, 130–131, 160
Rapallo, treaty of 157
rat grenade 10
ratio 100
Reagan, Ronald 214, 220, 223, 227
Reconquista 9, 45, 46
Red Army 10, 100, 102, 157–158, 164, 175, 186, 199
Reichstag 86, 89, 94, 97
Reichswehr 156–157
Renault 160
revolution in military affairs 114–115, 120
Richer of Reims 32, 36
Riello, Giorgio 125
Roman Empire 8, 9, 40, 42–43, 61, 81, 82
Royal Air Force 137, 148, 151, 265
Ruhr 158, 277
Rumsfeld, Donald 202, 207, 209
Russia 100, 102, 104, 107, 110, 153–155, 157, 163, 165, 171, 185
Russian Civil War 99, 100, 102, 104
Russo-Japanese War 3, 12

St. Eloi 77
St. Gilles 49
St. Petersburg 105
Sakurai, Tadayoshi 3, 4, 12, 15
Salewski, Michael 164, 167–168
Salm-Horstmar, Otto Fürst zu 86
Salmond, John (Sir) 144–145
Sarajevo 79
Sarmatians 34
Sassanids 34, 72
Satia, Priya 276
Schlesinger, James 201
Schlieffen Plan 159
Schmeisser, Hugo 170, 177, 181
Schramm, Erwin 29
Schwarte, Max 111, 123, 125
Scotland 25, 61, 66, 70, 74, 81, 83

Secret Intelligence Service 127
Shah 214
Sharkey, Noel 269–270, 274, 276
Sherry, Michael 276
Shue, Henry 290
Sicily 45
Sickle Cut Plan 161
Sierra Leone 174, 178, 180
signaling apparatus 10, 123
Simonov, Sergej 170, 177, 181
Simpson, Emile 259
Singer, P.W. 290
Skythian bow 33–34
Smith, Rupert 259
Smith, Steve A. 103, 108
Somalia 174, 176, 178, 181, 239
South America 170
South Arabia 144
Soviet 10, 98–103, 105, 107–108, 110, 153–154, 157–159, 162, 164, 170–179, 184–190, 192–194, 196, 199–201, 204, 206–207, 214, 229, 231–232, 241, 243–244
Soviet-Afghan War 173
Soviet Union 100, 153–154, 158, 162, 164, 170, 172, 177, 184–190, 192, 201, 214
Spaight, James M. 263–265, 271, 273, 276
Spandau 113
Spanish Civil War 160
Special Operations Executive 10, 126, 135, 136
Der Spiegel 13, 15, 202, 207–209
Stalag Luft III 79, 81–82
Stalin, Joseph 101, 103, 106, 108, 158, 164, 167, 177, 179, 184–185, 187, 189, 193–196
Star Trek 270
Starry, Don A. 228–231, 240
Station XV 128–129, 131–132, 134–135
steps scene (*Battleship Potemkin*) 104
stirrup 9, 30–33, 36, 38–39
stone-thrower 20–22, 26–27
Strachan, Hew 81, 83, 148, 151, 247, 256, 259
Strasbourg 73–74
Strawser, Bradley 281–282, 285, 288, 290–291
submarine 278
Sudayev, Alexey 170
Sunni Muslims 47
swamp soldiers 117

Syria 72
Szafranski, Richard 236, 244

T-62 199
T-72 200
tabun 163, 167
Taliban 173
tank 13, 114, 140–141, 157–161, 165, 170, 185, 187, 199, 200, 203–204, 206–207, 234, 240, 278
Taylor, Charles 174, 178, 181
technological supremacy 7, 10
terror 108, 262, 271, 282
Thayer Mahan, Alfred 118, 124
Thessaloniki 37, 193, 196
Third Reich 158, 163, 165
third world 249
Thomas, Georg 168
Tiefenrüstung 158, 166
Tiger 165
Tiger II 165
Tilford, Earl H. 237, 242, 244
Tirpitz, Alfred von 85–86, 94, 96–97
Tito, Josip Broz 182, 184–185, 187, 189, 191–196
Tito-Stalin split 189
Total National Defense 182, 194–195
traction trebuchet 9, 30, 38, 41
TRADOC 229, 240, 242, 244
Travers, T.H.E. 140, 148, 151, 176, 274, 276
Treuga Dei 46
Trotha, Trutz von 16, 70
Tsushima 103
Tuck, Christopher 244
Turkey 119, 206
Tyrol 75

um schara 51
United Kingdom 139, 142, 197–198
United Kingdom's Ministry of Defence 267
United Nations 260
U.S. Air Force Research Lab 268
U.S. Army 11, 78, 137, 199–202, 216, 220, 223–225, 229–230, 237, 240–244, 264, 269
U.S. Congress 288, 290
U.S. Department of Defense 264
U.S. Strategic Bombing Survey 137
Urals 155, 162, 164
utopia 8, 98, 99

V2 153, 164, 167
V-22 Osprey 217, 224, 227
Valier, Max 163
Vandals 34
vanguard 101–103, 107
Vegetius 27, 34, 40, 42
Verdun 7, 78, 117, 124–125
Versailles Treaty 156
Vertov, Tsiga 121
Vienna 75–76
Vietnam 81, 83–84, 172, 175, 178, 180, 200, 206, 210–213, 220, 221, 228–229, 233, 239, 240, 244, 266, 282, 288, 294
Vietnam War 81, 83, 175, 178, 200, 206, 210, 212–213, 220, 228–229, 239, 282, 288
violence 3, 5, 7, 31, 57, 61–64, 99, 104, 139, 144, 204, 213, 248, 250, 254, 262, 265, 272, 280
Viollet-le-Duc, Eugène 48
Virginia 76, 223, 225, 240, 244
von Habsburg, Rudolf 72
von Hohenberg, Rudolf 73
Vukmanović-Tempo, Svetozar 187, 194, 196

Walter XXI 165
Walzer, Michael 146–147, 152, 282, 284, 291
War Cabinet 146
Warden, John A. III 235, 242
Warsaw Pact 182, 189, 197, 201, 228–231, 239, 241
Wehrmacht 10, 117, 157–158, 162–164, 166, 168, 170, 177, 180

Weimar Republic 117
Western Front 12, 15, 78, 143, 156
White, Lynn 44
Whites 100
Widukind von Schwalenberg 72
Wiggins, Kenneth 84
Wilhelm II 27, 85–86, 89, 90, 94–97
Wilhelmshaven 87
Wills, J. Elder 128
Wilson, Woodrow 176, 180
wonder weapon 34, 40, 224
Wood, Kingsley 145
Woodmansee, John W., Jr. 233, 241, 244
world policy 86, 88, 90
World Trade Center 173
World War I 1, 3, 12, 15, 77, 98–99, 107, 148, 111, 113–115, 119, 122–125, 151, 153–155, 159, 163
World War II 26, 28, 87, 99, 165, 167, 171, 198, 199–200, 210, 215–216, 218–219, 221, 240, 244, 287, 290, 293
World War III 204
World War Zero 3, 12

XM-1 200–202, 204

Yates, Walter H. 234, 241, 244
Ypres 4, 77
Yugoslavia 11, 79, 182–196

zeppelin 270, 278
Zweig, Stefan 117